Marcin Górnikiewicz / Radosław Bielawski (eds.)

Influence of Russian Activities

Middle-East Europe, the Visegrad Group Countries and Ukraine

With 72 figures

V&R unipress

Bibliographic information published by the Deutsche Nationalbibliothek
The Deutsche Nationalbibliothek lists this publication in the Deutsche Nationalbibliografie;
detailed bibliographic data are available online: https://dnb.de.

© 2023 by Brill | V&R unipress, Robert-Bosch-Breite 10, 37079 Göttingen, Germany,
an imprint of the Brill-Group
(Koninklijke Brill NV, Leiden, The Netherlands; Brill USA Inc., Boston MA, USA; Brill Asia Pte Ltd,
Singapore; Brill Deutschland GmbH, Paderborn, Germany; Brill Österreich GmbH, Vienna, Austria)
Koninklijke Brill NV incorporates the imprints Brill, Brill Nijhoff, Brill Hotei, Brill Schöningh,
Brill Fink, Brill mentis, Vandenhoeck & Ruprecht, Böhlau, V&R unipress and Wageningen Academic.
All rights reserved. No part of this work may be reproduced or utilized in any form or by any means,
electronic or mechanical, including photocopying, recording, or any information storage and
retrieval system, without prior written permission from the publisher.

Printed and bound by CPI books GmbH, Birkstraße 10, 25917 Leck, Germany
Printed in the EU.

Vandenhoeck & Ruprecht Verlage | www.vandenhoeck-ruprecht-verlage.com

ISBN 978-3-8471-1406-2

Contents

Foreword 15

Part I: Poland

Section I: Poland's geopolitical and geostrategic position in the regional Kremlin's game in Europe

Patrycja Wróbel-Bryczek
Chapter 1: The geopolitical situation of Poland in relation to the foreign
policy of the Russian Federation 23

Tadeusz Szczurek
Chapter 2: Geostrategic situation of Poland in relation to the foreign
policy of the Russian Federation 31

Wawrzyniec Kowalski
Chapter 3: Summary and conclusions: Geopolitical and geostrategic
positioning of Poland in relation to the foreign policy of the Russian
Federation in the third decade of the 21st century 37

Section II: Kremlin's "hard power" and "soft power" towards Poland in the first and second decades of the 21st century

Marian Cieślarczyk
Chapter 4: The Kremlin's tough influence on the Polish decision-making
process 45

Marian Cieślarczyk
Chapter 5: Russian "soft power" methodology in influencing the Polish
decision-making process 61

Marcin Górnikiewicz / Tadeusz Szczurek / Marzena Walkowiak
Chapter 6: Summary and conclusions: The perspective of soft and hard impact on the Polish decision-making process in the third decade of the 21st century 75

Section III: The scope of Moscow's informative impact on the Polish decision-making process

Katarzyna Świerszcz
Chapter 7: Qualitative measurement of the level of operability of Russia's policy towards Poland 79

Katarzyna Świerszcz
Chapter 8: Qualitative methods of measuring the effectiveness of Russian influence in Poland in the area of disinformation 89

Katarzyna Świerszcz
Chapter 9: Summary and conclusions: Forecast for the development of the methodology of the Kremlin's information impact on the situation in Poland 97

Section IV: Modeling the Russian impact on Polish foreign and internal policy

Piotr Zaskórski
Chapter 10: Modeling the processes of assessing Russia's influence on Poland 103

Marcin Górnikiewicz
Chapter 11: Quantitative and qualitative cultural foresight of the Russian decision-making process in relation to Poland 117

Marcin Górnikiewicz / Tadeusz Szczurek / Marzena Walkowiak
Chapter 12: Summary and conclusions: Foresight of the Russian influence on Poland in the era of political and economic changes in the third decade of the 21st century 127

Part II: The Czech Republic (Czechia)

Section I: The Czech Republic in the geopolitical and geostrategic vision of Moscow in Europe

Andrzej Jacuch
Chapter 13: The geopolitical situation of the Czech Republic from the Russian perspective 133

Andrzej Jacuch
Chapter 14: The geostrategic position of the Czech Republic and Moscow's disinformation activity 139

Marcin Górnikiewicz / Andrzej Jacuch
Chapter 15: Summary and conclusions: The geopolitical and geostrategic situation of the Czech Republic viewed by the Kremlin: the current state and perspectives for Prague's foreign policy perceived by decision-makers in Moscow 149

Section II: Mechanics of the Russian soft and hard interactions with regard to the Czech Republic

Justyna Stochaj
Chapter 16: The effectiveness assessment of the Russian "hard power" in the Czech Republic 153

Justyna Stochaj
Chapter 17: Russian "soft power" in relation to the national security of the Czech Republic 161

Justyna Stochaj
Chapter 18: Summary and conclusions: Prospects for the current state and the development of the Russian influence on the Czech Republic in the 21st century 171

Section III: Measuring the effectiveness of the Russian impact on the Czech internal and foreign policy

Marcin Górnikiewicz / Tadeusz Szczurek / Marzena Walkowiak
Chapter 19: The effectiveness measurement of the quantitative methods of Russian influence in the Czech Republic 177

Małgorzata Jaroszyńska
Chapter 20: The effectiveness measurement of the qualitative methods of
Russian influence in the Czech Republic 187

Marcin Górnikiewicz / Małgorzata Jaroszyńska
Chapter 21: Summary and conclusions: The perspective of the
development direction of Moscow's foreign policy towards the Czech
Republic 195

Section IV: Foresight of the influence of the Russian impact on the Russian-Czech relations in the area of regional security

Paulina Owczarek
Chapter 22: The use of qualitative foresight methods in the assessment of
relations between Russia and the Czech Republic 199

Paulina Owczarek
Chapter 23: Application of quantitative foresight methods in the
assessment of economic relations between the Russian Federation and the
Czech Republic 205

Paulina Owczarek
Chapter 24: Summary and conclusions: The development foresight of the
mutual Czech-Russian relations in the third decade of the 21st
century 213

Part III: Slovakia

Section I: Moscow's geopolitics and geostrategy in view of Slovakia in the second and third decade of the 21st century

Mieczysław Pawlisiak
Chapter 25: Slovakia in the Kremlin's geopolitics in the second decade of
the 21st century 221

Mieczysław Pawlisiak
Chapter 26: Geostrategic perception of Slovakia in the Kremlin's vision of
foreign policy in the second half of the 21st century 229

Mieczysław Pawlisiak / Marcin Górnikiewicz
Chapter 27: Summary and conclusions: The Russian view on the
geopolitical and geostrategic position of Slovakia in the European balance
of power 237

Section II: Slovakia in the Russian impact zone: the Kremlin's "hard power" and "soft power"

Mieczysław Pawlisiak
Chapter 28: The methodology of the Russian "hard power" towards Slovakia 241

Mieczysław Pawlisiak
Chapter 29: The methodology of Russia's soft influence on Slovakia . . . 249

Mieczysław Pawlisiak / Marcin Górnikiewicz
Chapter 30: Summary and conclusions: The perspective of the Kremlin's hard and soft interactions on the Slovak decision-making process 257

Section III: The assessment of the Russian influence potential on the Slovak decision-making process

Tomasz R. Waśniewski
Chapter 31: The use of quantitative methods in the assessment effectiveness of the Russian influence on Slovakia 261

Tomasz R. Waśniewski
Chapter 32: The use of qualitative methods in the assessment effectiveness of the Russian influence on Slovakia 267

Tomasz R. Waśniewski / Marcin Górnikiewicz
Chapter 33: Summary and conclusions: The perspective of the development of the Russian influence on the Slovakian internal and external policy 273

Section IV: The forecast of the evolution of the Russian-Slovak relations in the context of the Slovak armed forces transformation

Anna Pęzioł / Anna Borucka
Chapter 34: The assessment of the changes in the armed forces in terms of selected factors 277

Anna Borucka / Anna Pęzioł
Chapter 35: Mathematical model for the assessment of national defense expenditure of the Slovak Republic in relation to the Russian Federation 285

Anna Borucka / Anna Pęzioł
Chapter 36: Summary and conclusions: The forecast of potential forms of military and non-military influence of Moscow towards Slovakia 295

Part IV: Hungary

Section I: Geopolitical and geostrategic conditions of Russian activity towards Hungary in the 21st century

Sławomir Byłeń
Chapter 37: The Russian vision of geopolitical order in Central and Eastern Europe in relation to Hungary 301

Sławomir Byłeń
Chapter 38: The geostrategic position of Hungary in the Kremlin's foreign vital influence 315

Sławomir Byłeń / Marcin Górnikiewicz / Radosław Bielawski
Chapter 39: Summary and conclusions: Hungary's geopolitical and geostrategic position as a key element of Russian influence in Central and Eastern Europe 327

Section II: Russian activity in relation to Hungary: The mechanism of using "hard power" and "soft power"

Sławomir Byłeń
Chapter 40: Russian "hard power" towards Hungary: The current state of play and its effects 331

Sławomir Byłeń
Chapter 41: Russian "soft power" as an example of rapprochement between Moscow and Budapest 339

Sławomir Byłeń / Marcin Górnikiewicz / Radosław Bielawski
Chapter 42: Summary and conclusions: The Russian mechanism of influencing the policy of Budapest with the system of "hard power" and "soft power" 353

Section III: The Russian potential and the Hungarian potential: interaction and implications for regional safety

Małgorzata Grzelak
Chapter 43: The effectiveness measurement of the quantitative methods of the Russian impact in Hungary 359

Małgorzata Grzelak
Chapter 44: The effectiveness measurement of the qualitative methods of the Russian impact in Hungary 367

Małgorzata Grzelak
Chapter 45: Summary and conclusions: Implications resulting from the Russian potential to influence the Hungarian decision-making process 375

Section IV: The forecast of the evolution in the Russian-Hungarian interaction in the 3rd decade of the 21st century

Oliver Balogh / Jerzy Zalewski
Chapter 46: Qualitative methods of Hungary's national strategy forecasting 379

Oliver Balogh / Adam Kołodziejczyk
Chapter 47: Quantitative methods of Hungary's internal and external policy forecasting 385

Oliver Balogh / Adam Kołodziejczyk / Marcin Górnikiewicz / Radosław Bielawski
Chapter 48: Summary and conclusions: The forecast of potential implications for regional security resulting from the development of mutual Russian-Hungarian relations 391

Part V: Ukraine

Section I: Geopolitical and geostrategic implications of the Russian policy with regard to Ukraine

Jan Figurski / Jerzy Niepsuj
Chapter 49: The geopolitical situation of Ukraine conditioned by the foreign policy of the Russian Federation 399

Jan Figurski / Jerzy Niepsuj
Chapter 50: The geostrategic position of Ukraine in the strategic and operational plans of the Russian Federation 405

Jan Figurski / Jerzy Niepsuj
Chapter 51: Summary and Conclusions: The Russian perspective on Ukraine's geopolitical and geostrategic position in Eastern Europe 421

Section II: The Russian mechanism of interaction on the Ukrainian decision-making process with the use of the methodology of hard and soft impact

Arkadiusz Jóźwiak
Chapter 52: The methodology of Russian hard impact in Ukraine 429

Arkadiusz Jóźwiak
Chapter 53: The methodology of Russian soft impact in Ukraine 435

Arkadiusz Jóźwiak / Marcin Górnikiewicz / Radosław Bielawski
Chapter 54: Summary and conclusions: Russian interactions of "hard power" and "soft power" as the elements of the mechanics of Russian influence on Ukraine 441

Section III: The assessment of the effectiveness of the Russian impact on Ukraine's internal and foreign policy with the use of the measurement of the Russian impact potential

Paweł Ślaski
Chapter 55: The effectiveness measurement of the quantitative methods of Russia's influence in Ukraine 445

Paweł Ślaski
Chapter 56: The effectiveness assessment of the Russian influence on the Ukrainian decision-making process with the use of qualitative methods 455

Paweł Ślaski
Chapter 57: Summary and conclusions: Determinants and implications of the Russian influence on Ukraine 467

Section IV: The forecast of the development of the situation in Ukraine: The Russian-Ukrainian relations in the third decade of the 21st century

Magdalena Rykała / Jarosław Zelkowski
Chapter 58: The situation in Ukraine in the 2nd and 3rd decade of the 21st Century: Qualitative Forecasting Methods 471

Magdalena Rykała / Jarosław Zelkowski
Chapter 59: The situation in Ukraine in the 2nd and 3rd decade of the 21st century: Quantitative Forecasting Methods 487

Jarosław Zelkowski / Magdalena Rykała / Marcin Górnikiewicz /
Radosław Bielawski
Chapter 60: Summary and conclusions: The forecast of the Russian
Influence on Ukraine in the third decade of the 21st century 495

Summary and final conclusions 497

Foreword

Dear Readers,

There are many books on the market dedicated to international security future predictions. Their authors usually represent a selected field or discipline of knowledge, or even a specific school such as American or Copenhagen in security sciences. On the other hand, there are no positions in which the authors would use the methodology of research in various fields and disciplines. This would allow not only to compare the obtained results, but also to confront and jointly develop the final conclusions. The more authors representing different schools and research methodologies, the greater opportunity for an objective and therefore verifiable result. I believe that the last aspect related to the credibility of the proposed vision of the future is the most important when any prediction is made. Ultimately, only predictions with a high level of verifiability count. For this to be possible, the objective should be achieved. This was the thought of the authors of this book. Striving to confront many different methods, techniques and research tools. Research work of representatives of various fields and disciplines carried out independently one from another. Only to summarize the obtained results and check where they are different and where they coincide, and to determine why this happened. This publication is a record of such research. However, it is surprising that there were not so many differences, and all authors, regardless of the represented fields and disciplines, and the used research methodology, came to similar conclusions. However, it is worrying that these conclusions are not very optimistic. On the other hand, the enormous and internally diverse research potential involved in work on this publication leads us to an assumption that the obtained results are not only as objective as possible, but yet it also very worrying.

The question which needs to be answered is the following one: How will mutual relations and impacts in the area of regional security evolve between the Russian Federation and the countries of Central and Eastern Europe in the 21st century?

Nearly thirty people representing various fields and scientific disciplines were involved in the work, thus contributing to a diverse research methodology which they used in the development of the undertaken issues. Ergo, the work uses methods, techniques and research tools in the field of security sciences, strategic sciences, political sciences, international relations, economic sciences and management sciences. Both qualitative, quantitative and mixed methods were applied.

The work also uses qualitative and quantitative forecasting methods, including an innovative method of cultural forecasting based on the quantitative evaluation of subconscious cultural codes that determine the international decision-making process, when formulating final conclusions for each chapter. As a result here it is the work in which representatives of various fields and disciplines, applying a variety of research methodology corresponding to the sciences they represent, developed individual chapters that fit into the top-down work structure. The most surprising thing is that despite such a great variety of methods, techniques and research tools used, and the making of individual parts of this book by individual authors independently, all of them ultimately came to very similar conclusions. The results of their research work are presented partially in conclusions to individual parts and as a whole at the end of this book.

With respect to the aforementioned structure of the work, it was not a coincidence or the authors' loose deliberation on the future shape of the next scientific item, but a graphic expression of a top-down research process focused on the raised issues. The process is divided into stages, and each part of this book focuses on the study of a specific country: Poland, the Czech Republic, Slovakia, Hungary and Ukraine. Each part, however, consists of four sections dedicated to the following: the geopolitical and geostrategic situation of the analyzed country in terms of the relationship with the Russian Federation; Russia's influence through measures within the scope of "hard power" and "soft power"; measuring the size of the Russian influence potential using selected quantitative and qualitative methods and using prognostic methods (also qualitative and quantitative) to try to construct a forecast/strategic foresight for the development of bilateral relations between the researched country and the Russian Federation as well as the implications of these interactions on the level of regional security and, as a result, the shape of the geopolitical and geostrategic situation in Central, Eastern and Eastern Europe. Each part consists of three chapters, the first two are related to the characteristics of the current state, whereas the third chapter is a summary and contains conclusions of a prognostic nature. As a result, the partial results obtained in this way made it possible to formulate final conclusions for individual countries and a comprehensive view of the regional security using the prism of the directions of development of mutual relations between the Russian Federation and the researched countries in the future.

The applied process of creating the analysis and the forecast prepared on its basis are the result of the teamwork established within the Laboratory of Security Forecasts and Analyzes operating within the Department of Security, Logistics and Management of the Military University of Technology with its seat in Warsaw. The future will show whether the applied innovative process of conducting this type of research will bring results in the form of verifiable and confirmable forecasts in the area of international security. It is worth adding that the adopted time perspective for the formulated forecasts concerned the subsequent decades of the 21st century. Apart from the direction of the development of the situation, the mutual attitude of the surveyed societies in the situation of:

a) Maintaining a strong position of the EU supported by the US in Central and Eastern Europe b) Weakening of the position of the EU and the withdrawal of the US from Central and Eastern Europe, leaving the Russian Federation free in terms of geopolitical and geostrategic activity.

The authors involved in the work on this subject come from both civilian expert and scientific backgrounds, as well as professional active and former officers with significant knowledge and experience in creating analytical and forecasting studies. This special combination of scientific knowledge, extensive and varied scientific and research workshop and practical experience gained from many years of service along with the use of unique and proprietary forecasting methods, resulted in a very detailed and multi-directional analysis, and a forecast of the development of the situation based on hard quantitative and qualitative data. It is worth mentioning that the final content of the forecast contained in the ending was a big surprise for the authors who, while working on individual elements of this book, did not know about the research studies carried out by other authors. The obtained convergence of the results, as well as their pessimistic tone, may prompt a deep reflection on the future shape of the geopolitical and geostrategic situation in the studied part of Europe.

Finally, it is worth emphasizing that this publication is the first published scientific book, which offsets not only the efforts of scientists and experts working within the Laboratory of Security Forecasts and Analyzes, but it also displays substantive guidance of the entire scientific staff of the Department of Security, Logistics and Management. Acting as the initiator, founder and manager of this laboratory, I would like to express my sincere thanks to all my colleagues involved in this project.

Fruitful reading.

Please note: The research in this book covers the period 2020–2021, before the conflict in Ukraine started in February 2022.

Part I: Poland

Part 1: Poland

Section I:
Poland's geopolitical and geostrategic position in the regional Kremlin's game in Europe

Patrycja Wróbel-Bryczek

Chapter 1: The geopolitical situation of Poland in relation to the foreign policy of the Russian Federation

Contrary to the optimism of Francis Fukuyama, the fall of the Berlin Wall and the collapse of the Soviet Union did not bring an end to the conflicts between the great political systems, and the peaceful end of history he predicted and the triumph of the liberal democracy model did not take place (Fukuyama 1992). Moreover, the turn of the second and third decades of the 21st century is characterized by a unique dynamics of events and decisions, which indicate that we are dealing with the process of reconstruction of the geopolitical system, which applies in particular to Eurasia. An arrangement in which the role of the United States of America (USA) as the main decision-maker and creator of the present international order is questioned, primarily by the People's Republic of China (PRC), but also by countries such as India, Turkey, Iran and the Franco-German alliance (Fra-Ger), and the Russian Federation (FR), which are increasingly creating an independent regional policy.

The aim of this chapter is a synthetic analysis of the current conditions and an assessment of the geopolitical situation of Poland in this new system, taking into account the contemporary foreign policy of the Russian Federation in the Central European region.

At the beginning, it is necessary to specify the current (type of view) of "geopolitics" in which this analysis was conducted. This is necessary, because this concept has been constantly evolving since its first use at the turn of the 19th and 20th centuries by the political scientist, Johan Rudolf Kjellén. However, although the terminological workshop of the contemporary geopolitics is very rich, the essence of the concept remains unchanged, defining it as: a way of shaping reality by the leadership elite of societies related to the resources of their territories. Adjusting the strategies and methods of operation of political entities to the geopolitical situation is aimed at securing their own development (raw materials, communication routes) and preventing the taking over of resources by other entities, which would give them the opportunity to gain an advantage.

However, this work does not refer to the description of the reality of all the eminent authors of geopolitical theory, such as: Friedrich Ratzel, Alfred Mahan,

Karl Haushofer or Carl Schmitt, because the aim is to draw conclusions about the geopolitical situation of Poland in the context of the foreign policy of the Russian Federation, and not to conduct considerations on the very concept of geopolitics. Therefore, the work refers primarily to the achievements of the British geographer Halford John Mackinder. He treated Eurasia as a "world island" on which the fate of the whole world depends, and regarded Eastern Europe as its critical region, stating: *"Whoever rules over Eastern Europe rules over the Central Area; whoever controls the Central Area controls the World Island; whoever rules the World Island rules the world"* (Mackinder 1942). When analysing the activity of the largest powers in this region, this statement seems no less valid today than when it was formulated. The more so because in a globalized world, connected by international supply chains, both communication and transport of goods across the Central European lowland are cheaper and more effective than through the Alps or the Carpathians. All key players know this, as well as the fact that the fastest logistics for large armies with heavy equipment is possible on flat and relatively dry terrain, and in the temperate Central European lowlands, food can be produced with ease. This is why, for hundreds of years, the territory of Poland, Belarus and Ukraine has been of key geopolitical importance in the region and in the world, especially for their closest neighbours.

The Russian Federation is the country with the largest area in the world and one of the world's largest military powers (Ayupova, Kussainov et al. 2020). Therefore, from the perspective of the Russian Federation, the issue of Central and Eastern Europe is not its only challenge. It can even be said that it is definitely less important than taking the right position on the two largest political and economic forces: USA and the PRC. However, it should not be forgotten that, in Moscow's opinion, border security can only be ensured if an appropriate sphere of influence over the neighbouring countries is maintained (Brzeziński 1998, Berls Jr. 2021). Therefore, from the point of view of the Russian Federation, the collapse of the USSR and the loss of the surrounding satellite countries, once grouped within the Warsaw Pact, are treated as a threat to the security of the homeland. The more so as many of the former allies in the West are now potential enemies, both on the economic and military levels (belonging to the European Union and NATO).

That is why the Russian Federation shows clear ambitions to fight for its interests in Central and Eastern Europe, putting itself as the main heir of the Union of Soviet Socialist Republics (USSR). If we look at the policy of the Russian Federation from this perspective, we can clearly see that it does not want to and cannot remain a neutral country. The more so as the major world powers, i.e. the US and the PRC, are seeking to take a form of control over Russia or to disintegrate it.

The USA and its allies almost succeeded once, during the presidency of the pro-Western Boris Yeltsin, when the country was on the verge of economic collapse (Buchs 1999). China is also a real threat, as it focuses on the policy of small steps (Wang 2020) and chooses actions counted over decades. Such as, for example, the Chinese settlement in Siberia, which, combined with the depopulation of the eastern territories and demographic problems of the Russian Federation, may lead to the loss of control over the eastern territory in an almost "peaceful" manner (Bordachev 2018).

Taking into account the current situation, however, we can suspect that the temporary threat from the West, and above all from the USA, is more important. That is why the leaders of the Russian Federation preferred to decide on a temporary alliance with the PRC (Sidorova 2019). Also because the rapidly developing China is an excellent outlet for Russian energy resources, as well as advanced military technology, which are two strategic export goods of the Russian Federation (Apokin, Belousov et al. 2015). An excellent project that links this alliance is also the New Silk Road (NSR), forced by the PRC, which has designed and implemented lines running through the territory of the Russian Federation (Sevastianov 2016). Its creation will bring economic profits for both parties.

Of course, apart from the benefits, cooperation with China also poses a certain threat to Russia. It results, among others, from the dependence on Chinese products, which may lead to the collapse of Russian producers, and the risk of taking over Russian companies by Chinese capital. On the other hand, it may be an opportunity to modernize the light industry, and carrying NSR through the territory of the Russian Federation will allow Russia to some extent control the flow of goods between Asia and Europe (Mladenovic and Ponomareva 2018).

Moreover, the development of NSR also affects US interests, which are based on the control of trade through sea communication routes (Bartosiak 2019). It is not in favour of the USA to transfer the goods transport to the land, as they currently have the strongest navy and military bases located at communication junctions in the world ratings (Bartosiak 2019). The USA does not support NSR also because it may lead to the creation of a new system of economic and political alliances in Eurasia, which will accelerate the collapse of the already shaken global domination of the United States (Brzeziński 1998).

This may mean that in the countries through which the NSR lines are to run, there are plans to intensify the activity of American troops and intelligence. It is worth looking at the Middle East (mainly Iran, Iraq, Syria, and Turkey), the Balkan countries, where Romania has retained a leading role, as well as the Central European countries, where Poland is the economic and military leader. An example of this activity may be the decision of November 2016, on the basis of which the sale of the land of the former military unit near Łódź was suspended in order to block the construction of an intermodal terminal for trains to and from the Chinese Chengdu (Czubiński 2017).

An alternative solution for NSR may also be the concept of joining a group of countries in the region into a federation between the Baltic Sea, the Black Sea and the Mediterranean Sea, promoted by part of the current political class in Poland, which in the literature is called the Intermarium or the Three Seas Initiative (Cieplucha 2014).

The intermarium would enable the control of north-south transport from Europe to Asia. But from the point of view of Poland and other smaller countries in the region, the main advantage of this project is not the control of the flow of goods (which the USA would rather care for), but the creation of a political entity independent of the main regional forces of Ger-Fra and the Russian Federation. This concept crosses the interests of Poland and the USA against numerous Russian-German economic initiatives, with the flagship energy project "Nord Stream 2" at the fore (Gotz 2019). However, the implementation of the political intermarium project is uncertain, as the alliance of Central European states with the US-Israeli tandem is not a stable structure. And the US escape from Afghanistan, withdrawal from Syria in 2019 and withdrawal of support for the Kurdish community fighting for their state (Mouritzen 2020), lower America's rating as a reliable ally. One should also not forget about negotiating the countries of Central and Eastern Europe with the PRC under the alternative "16+1" variant[1], which may reverse the existing alliances.

Apart from hindering the implementation of Chinese plans in Europe, the Intermarium also poses a challenge for the Russian Federation, as it may block free trade within the NSR and hinder the transport of raw materials from the Russian Federation to Western Europe. Such a political existence also means the risk of losing influence in small Central European states, which will prevent the policy of surrounding oneself with a cordon of dependent states, which constitute the so-called "crush zone" (Brzeziński 1998).

Poland is a country with over 1000 years of history. Due to its unique location between the Baltic Sea and the Carpathians, it witnessed many historical events, wars and battles that changed the history of the entire continent. Part of this turbulent history is the struggle with Russia, which, despite its common Slavic roots, has always differed from Poland in many civilizational aspects. Starting from religion (Catholicism in Poland and Orthodoxy in Russia) to the type of state organization (in Poland, the model of the western state, and in Russia, a mixed model with many features of the Mongolian legacy).

No wonder then that from the end of the 14th century, when Poland joined the Union with Lithuania, a period of intense competition and repeated wars began,

---

1 http://beltandroadcenter.org/2017/11/07/east-central-europe-on-the-new-silk-road.

which intensified especially in the 16th, 17th and 18th centuries (including the territory of Ukraine). Despite many successes and victories (the Republic won Moscow in passing for 2 years), ultimately due to weaknesses in war and a series of errors caused by the weakness of the noble democracy with the misunderstood "freedom of the nobility", the Commonwealth in 1795 disappeared from the map of the world for 123 years, and its territory was divided among themselves by Austria, Prussia and the Russian Empire.

Several national uprisings in the 19th century ended in failure each time, which significantly weakened Poles under the partitions. Poles had a chance to regain independence only as a result of World War I, when the invaders stood on opposite sides of the front. This enabled, after many hardships and fights, the creation of a fully independent state, when on November 11, 1918, the Regency Council of the Kingdom of Poland handed over the superior military authorities and the supreme command of the Polish Army to Joseph Pilsudski. This date is still celebrated today as a symbolic date of independence.

This event, however, did not end efforts to maintain Polish statehood, because Russia at the same time transformed itself under the pressure of the Bolshevik revolution, which its ideologues, and in particular Vladimir Lenin, wanted to spill over the rest of Europe. The Polish-Bolshevik clashes took place at the turn of 1918/1919, when the Bolsheviks began military operations, at the beginning secretly cooperating with the Germans. Ultimately, however, the war was resolved in favour of Poland, thanks to the victory known as the "miracle of the Vistula" (Bartnicki 2007), considered one of the most important battles in modern world history, because it stopped the communist revolution from taking over the countries of Western Europe (Emelyanova 2017).

Unfortunately, the peace did not last long, because already on August 23, 1939, the two then military powers of the Third German Reich and the USSR concluded the secret "Ribbentrop-Molotov" pact (Konrad 2002), which, according to its secret protocol, planned the conquest or decree of independence of sovereign states: Poland, Lithuania, Latvia, Estonia, Finland and Romania through the USSR and the Third German Reich. Currently, the participation of the USSR in triggering World War II and the attack on the above-mentioned independent states is the axis of disputes in the historical policy of Poland and Russia, because Russia denies the role of the USSR in triggering World War II (Konrad 2002).

Ultimately, World War II ended with the defeat of the Third Reich, with the participation of Poland, which lost the most of the population of all the countries participating in the war (over 6 million victims, constituting about 22.2% of the total population). Such a sacrifice, however, did not allow Poles to regain independence, because the world powers, during the Yalta conference in February 1945, gave Poland over to the sphere of influence of the USSR. In practice, the leaders of the USA and Great Britain gave permission to destroy the Polish armed underground by force, above all the Home Army and the National Armed Forces (Parsadanowa 2010). The President of the USA (F.D. Roosevelt) also pledged that the United States would not support the temporary Polish authorities that would be hostile to the USSR.

That is why Poles consider the decisions of the Yalta conference as consent to the informal occupation of the USSR, which lasted until 1989. The first years after the war were particularly gloomy, when, according to Prof. Jan Żaryn, only in the initial period 20,000 soldiers of the Polish Army died, and over 250,000 people were imprisoned or held in labour camps (Żaryn 2012). Fights between the USSR and the Polish resistance continued for almost 10 years, until the mid-1950s.

Despite the repression and propaganda during the times of the Polish People's Republic, Polish intellectual elites still could not come to terms with the loss of independence. This was reflected in the creation of secret societies, and later legal organizations, the largest of which was NSZZ Solidarność (Kozłowski 2017). The active protests and actions of Solidarność in the 1980s and the activities of the Polish Pope John Paul II contributed to the fall of communism in Poland, and indirectly also to the acceleration of the collapse of the USSR, which in the circles of Russian power is considered "the greatest geopolitical catastrophe of the 20th century and a real drama for Russians" (Putin 2005).

From the beginning of the 21st century, Poland became an active member of the Euro-Atlantic community (NATO, EU), and Russia chose a course of confrontation with Western Europe. Currently, Poland does not pursue an active eastern policy, becoming a hostage of short-term goals in the country's domestic policy (Nowakowski, Kluczkowski et al. 2019). As a result, Poland is a spectator rather than a player in a new geopolitical hand in the region, dependent on its allies. This can be deduced from the inconsistent foreign policy, where, on the one hand, the president of the Russian Federation is not invited to the anniversary celebrations of the outbreak of World War II and the relations with Moscow around the Smolensk catastrophe, in which among others, the President of the Republic of Poland died. On the other hand, there is intensive trade in raw materials or support for Russia's return to the Council of Europe.

This state of affairs may result from the strong ties between the Polish and German economies. This is because Germany is betting on good and intensive trade relations with the Russian Federation. In recent years (2015–2020), however, a deterioration in economic relations between PL-FR has been observed, which is caused, firstly, by the tightening of Poland's relations with the US, and secondly, by the economic difficulties caused by the COVID-19 pandemic, which weakened export trends to the market outside the community.

Summing up, the current geopolitical situation in Poland can be considered difficult. First of all, due to the lower level of stability and predictability in the international sphere, as well as the strategic location of this country on the border of cultures, religions and antagonistic alliances (NATO-Russia; Union-Russia). Taking into account the historical events and the concluded alliances, it is also highly unlikely that the difficulties in Polish-Russian relations will be overcome. Therefore, it seems that the new balance of power in the region of Central and Eastern Europe will be determined by who of the US-PRC pair turns out to be stronger, and whether the US declarations regarding the protection of allies and readiness for further talks on the Intermarium project are true.

References

Apokin, A., D. Belousov, V. Salnikov and I. Frolov (2015). "Long-term Socioeconomic Challenges for Russia and Demand for New Technology." Foresight and Sti Governance 9(4): 6–17.
Ayupova, Z. K., D. U. Kussainov, M. T. Beisenbayeva and W. Nagan (2020). "Central Asian Region at the Focus of Geopolitical Interests." Bulletin of the National Academy of Sciences of the Republic of Kazakhstan(1): 192–198.
Bartnicki, k. R. (2007). "Zwycięstwo w Bitwie Warszawskiej jako Dar Bożej Opatrzności." Warszawskie Studia Teologiczne (XX/1/2007): 205–218.
Bartosiak, J. (2019). Rzeczpospolita między lądem a morzem. Warszawa, Zona Zero.
Berls Jr., R. E. (2021). Strengthening Russia's Influence in International Affairs, Part II: Russia and Its Neighbors: A Sphere of Influence or a Declining Relationship? PhD.
Bordachev, T. (2018). "Greater Eurasia and Russian Foreign Policy Priorities." Asian Politics & Policy 10(4): 597–613.
Brzeziński, Z. (1998). Wielka szachownica. Główne cele polityki amerykańskiej. Warszawa, Bertelsmann Media Sp. z o.o.
Buchs, T. D. (1999). "Financial crisis in the Russian Federation – Are the Russians learning to tango?" Economics of Transition 7(3): 687–715.
Cieplucha, P. (2014). "Prometeizm i koncepcja międzymorza w praktyce polityczno-prawnej oraz dyplomacji IIRP." Studia Prawno-ekonomiczne XCIII: 39–55.
Czubiński, R. (2017). "Łódź: Przetarg na Pryncypalną wstrzymany. Co z chińskim terminalem?", from https://www.rynek-kolejowy.pl/mobile/lodz-przetarg-na-pryncypalna-wstrzymany-co-z-chinskim-terminalem-79739.html.
Emelyanova, E. N. (2017). "Concept of Nation State Building in Decisions of II Congress of Comintern." Nauchnyi Dialog(4): 145–158.
Fukuyama, F. (1992). The end of history and the last man. New York; Toronto; New York, Free Press ; Maxwell Macmillan Canada ; Maxwell Macmillan International.
Gotz, R. (2019). "Nord Stream 2 The politicised pipeline." Osteuropa 69(1–2): 23–+.
Konrad, M. (2002). Polska 1939 roku wobec paktu Ribbentrop-Mołotow. Problem zbliżenia niemiecko-sowieckiego w polityce zagranicznej II Rzeczypospolitej, Polski Instytut Spraw Międzynarodowych.
Kozłowski, T. (2017). Anatomia rewolucji. Narodziny ruchu społecznego Solidarność w 1980 roku., Instytut Pamięci Narodowej.

Mackinder, J. H. (1942). Democratic Ideals and Reality. London National Defense University Press Washington.

Mladenovic, M. B. and J. G. Ponomareva (2018). "Russian-Chinese Relations reffering to the 'One Belt, One Road' Initiative." New Silk Road: European Perspectives – Security Challenges/Risks within the Initiative 16+1: 143–153.

Mouritzen, H. (2020). "'Remember Iraq!' Learning theory and the 2013 non-decision on air strikes against Syria." International Politics.

Nowakowski, J. M., J. Kluczkowski, B. Luft and A. Magdziak-Miszewska (2019). Polityka wschodnia Polski. Warszawa.

Parsadanowa, W. S. (2010). Polityka i jej skutki. Białe plamy – Czarne plamy. Sprawy trudne w relacjach polsko-rosyjskich (1918–2008). A. W. T. Adam D. Rotfeld. Warszawa.

Sevastianov, S. V. (2016). "China's Integration Projects in Asia-Pacific and Eurasia." Mirovaya Ekonomika I Mezhdunarodnye Otnosheniya 60(4): 5–12.

Sidorova, N. P. (2019). "Russian foreign policy: From 'new thinking' to multidirectional strategy." Rudn Journal of Russian History 18(4): 985–1001.

Wang, X. (2020). "Openness, growth convergence and China's development prospects." China Economic Journal 13(1): 82–108.

Żaryn, J. (2012). Żołnierze wyklęci: dziedzctwo, które zobowiązuje. A. Ambroziak, Nasz Dziennik.

Tadeusz Szczurek

Chapter 2: Geostrategic situation of Poland in relation to the foreign policy of the Russian Federation

From a geostrategic point of view, Poland – covering a territory with an area of nearly 314 thousand km2 and having a spatial shape similar to a circle – is a country with favorable conditions for management and defense when waging a war. The population of Poland is nearly 39 million, which is the eighth place among NATO countries. In a crisis situation, the ability of the society to mobilize to counter the threat may be important. In this case, an important factor characterizing Polish society is the almost homogenious ethnic structure, as 97.6% of the population are Poles. These conditions fit well in the implementation of the elementary goal of the state's geostrategy, i.e. securing external borders and *ensuring security by enabling he economic and political consolidation of the core area, on which the state's cohesion and political steering depends* (Bartosiak, 2018, p. 45). The military effort and involvement of Polish diplomacy in improving state security determine the membership of the Republic of Poland in the European Union and NATO. This is also how Poland is perceived by the Russian Federation, whose foreign policy takes into account a number of conditions, including the issues of historical spheres of influence in the area of the former Warsaw Pact, dissolved on July 1, 1991.

When confronting the geostrategic position of Poland with the foreign policy of the Russian Federation, it is worth paying attention to the specific approach of Russia to security policy, different from Western countries. (Yakovlev 2015). Analyzing the source materials – in search of the term *state security system* – it is difficult to find an unequivocal definition of this expression in the Russian terminology. Instead, we encounter the term *military system of the state*, defined as *all state and military management entities, of the Armed Forces of the Russian Federation, other troops (uniformed services), military units and formations, special formations created for the duration of the war (hereinafter – the armed forces, other troops and services), which constitute their foundation and carry out their activities using military warfare, as well as the national defense and industrial complex, whose joint activities are aimed at the armed defense of the Russian Federation and preparation for it* (Military Doctrine of the Russian

Federation, 2014). The Military Doctrine of the Russian Federation provides the use of precision weapons as part of the implementation of strategic force deterrence. The right to use nuclear weapons is also reserved. This occurs in the case of a possible response to the use of nuclear weapons and other weapons of mass destruction against the Russian Federation and / or its allies, as well as in the case of aggression using conventional weapons if the existence of the state is threatened. In such cases, the decision to use nuclear weapons is made by the president of the Russian Federation (military doctrine of the Russian Federation, 2014). In general, the basic Russian documents concerning broadly understood security, the use of the notion of *a state war system*, unlike to the solutions functioning in most democratic countries, where the term *defense system* is used.

As part of the military system of the Russian Federation, apart from the armed forces, there are: state and military management bodies/entities, military and special units and formations specially created for the time of war, as well as the national defense and industrial complex. Essential powers with regard to security policy are reserved to the federal authorities. They are responsible for the right to coordinate the state security policy, including issues of supervision over arms production and the defense industry. The President of the Russian Federation plays the most important role in the security system (Ilyin and Morev 2019). The role of the president's advisory body is performed by the Security Council. The tasks of the Council include developing proposals and solutions regarding the functioning of the Russian security system, strategic objectives, and determining the state of current threats as well as issuing opinions on applications for the introduction of emergency states. The legislature has little competence in the area of security. The State Duma determines federal expenses and approves the state's defense budget. The role of the Council of the Russian Federation is, on the other hand, to approve the decisions of the Duma concerning the plans for financing security and the federal law created by the lower house, presidential decrees concerning the involvement of the armed forces or other military formations to perform state security tasks and their non-statutory tasks, the introduction of states of emergency and the use of the armed forces outside Russia (Федеральный закон, 1996).

The armed forces of the Russian Federation have priority over other services. They are a pillar of the state's military system in relation to the tasks of external and internal policy. The tasks of the armed forces have been defined in detail in three positions of the functioning of the state: in a period of peace, in a state of immediate threat of aggression and in a state of war. The most important tasks of the armed forces during the peace period are: protection of sovereignty, integrity and territorial integrity of the state, strategic nuclear and conventional deterrence, the warning of war threats, ensuring readiness to repel an attack from the air and space, defense of citizens who remain outside the borders, implementation of the mission to maintain (restore) international peace, preventing terrorist activities, securing national interests in the Arctic and in the world's waters. The most important tasks of the Armed Forces in the period of imminent threat of aggression are: reducing the level of threat, increasing the level of readiness, including nuclear deterrence, territorial defense and the implementation of international obligations of the state in the field of collective defense, repelling or preventing, in accordance with the norms of international law, an armed attack on other country that made such a request. In turn, the most important tasks during the war are: repelling aggression, defeating an aggressor, forcing the aggressor to stop hostile actions in accordance with the interests of the state. In addition to defining general tasks, particular types of armed forces and troops are entrusted with specific tasks or a division of tasks, such as possible pre-emptive and retaliatory strikes for the components of the nuclear triad (land and sea components, respectively) and ensuring the safety of *navigation*, protection of the economic zone and combating illegal production and exploitation for the Northern Fleet (Analysis of the new strategy of the National Bank, 2016, pp. 4–5).

The currently implemented main directions of changes in the armed forces are: Departure from the legacy of the former Soviet Union, i.e. the multi-million army, based on the universal mobilization of the manpower and the organization of Equipment and Weapons Bases.

Preparation of pro-Western, well-armed and modernly equipped, flexibly reacting and functioning military units. Introducing a new command system, separating command and planning functions from administration, so that nuclear deterrence and air-space defense tasks can be carried out more effectively.

As part of the land forces, focus on light, and therefore mobile forces capable of rapid and effective response to any theater of operations.

High concentration of units, from a brigade upwards, with the forces and means of reconnaissance and electronic warfare, as well as organic or cooperating units and subunits of special forces, which imply that these units are suitable for the implementation of tasks under the so-called hybrid war (Depczyński, 2016, pp. 8–9). By implementing these changes, the number of personnel was reduced, as part of compulsory service, in favor of the contract service, better training and morale of soldiers, inter alia by increasing the level of social security (Depczyński, 2015, pp. 155–157).

Taking into account a possible military operation against other countries, including the Republic of Poland, it is reflected in the expansion of Russia's military potential (Blank, 1999). The threat to Poland results mainly from the large of military potential of Kaliningrad District, in relation to the needs and the area. Within the Western Military District of Kaliningrad, naval forces, coastal defense forces, air forces, and air and space defense forces are deployed. The most important air unit is the Naval Aviation Base of the Baltic Fleet, including the first fighter squadron – equipped with Su-27 planes – responsible for the air defense of the area. In turn, the third squadron of bomber aviation owns Su-24M attack machines. Other machines are Mi-24 and Mi-8 combat helicopters, Ka-27PŁ anti-submarine helicopters and An-26 transport planes. Anti-aircraft weapons are primarily S-300 systems and the latest S-400 Triumf anti-aircraft and anti-missile systems. There is also an independent anti-aircraft missile regiment stationed in Kaliningrad, equipped with 9K331 Tor-M1 anti-aircraft missile vehicles, providing anti-aircraft cover to land subunits (https://pulaski.pl/). A major threat to the military security system of neighboring countries, including Poland, may be posed by deployed missile forces equipped with Toczka and Iskander missiles. The latter are among the most modern missiles in their class and therefore are of particular concern (Kaliningrad Fortress, 2019).

When focusing on the Kaliningrad District, one must not forget about all of Russia's military power, in particular its nuclear potential. Within the Armed Forces of the Russian Federation, there is the so-called nuclear triad, consisting of the following components: sea, land and air (Kristensen and McKinzie 2015). Apart from it, the generation of new structures of the armed forces deserves attention. Conclusions from documents such as the National Security Strategy of the Russian Federation or the Military Doctrine, as well as conclusions from the armed conflicts of the last 10 years, in particular Georgia (2008) and Ukraine (2013–2020), suggest the emergence of a conventional triad. Its elements will be:
– light (mobile) forces;
– the forces of information impact (operations in cyberspace, information operations, radio-electronic warfare);
– heavy forces (Michalski and Modrzejewski, 2015, pp. 33–34).

The use of the latter is a last resort, and their activities will mainly focus on deterrence. It should be noted that the currently implemented third stage, related to the modernization of equipment, faces budget difficulties related to the economic crisis, in particular EU and US economic sanctions as a consequence of Russia's actions in Ukraine, as well as reduced state budget revenues related to the persistently low oil prices; this will probably reduce the assumed degree of modernization, but the program should not be abandoned (Horska and Moroz et al., 2016). The practice of the recent Russian military operations has shaped the methodology of operation of the Armed Forces of the Russian Federation according to the following phases: 1. 1st phase, military operations: Russia provides arms and soldiers (mercenaries) as well as military advisory assistance; 2. Second phase, after the end of operations: Russia offers to send its own peacekeeping forces without the participation of the international component; 3. Third phase, "freezing" the conflict: Russia uses, inter alia, its military presence guaranteeing the status quo – relative stability, which makes it impossible to finally resolve a given conflict; "Frozen" conflicts with a simultaneous military presence ensure a constant influence on the situation; 4. 4th phase, 'unfreezing' conflicts: in the event of unfavorable political developments, Russian 'citizens' are militarily 'defended'. It is worth noting that the consequence of Russia's effective policy is the fact that Russian troops are stationed on the territories of ten countries, protecting: strategic facilities (Belarus); communication routes (Abkhazia and South Ossetia); the border with Turkey and Iran (Armenia, Turkmenistan); the border with Afghanistan (Tajikistan), the border with China (Kyrgyzstan and Uzbekistan); oil installations (Azerbaijan); Baikonur cosmodrome (Kazakhstan). Such a policy of the Russian Federation must cause concern for its closest neighbors.

In foreign policy and in the concepts of conducting military operations by the Russian Federation, there is a departure from the pursuit of linear clashes of mass armed forces in favor of well-trained, modernly equipped and highly mobile, i.e. light, military units performing their tasks under the so-called hybrid and asymmetric activities (Szczurek, 2014, pp. 11–23). As part of the so-called *hybrid war*, there are two phases: the hidden phase, carried out by non-military means, and the operational-tactical phase, carried out with the use of armed forces: 1. 1st phase of the so-called hybrid war ("crawling conflict") is realized in the form of an impact in the political, economic, social and information spheres on the defense systems of a potential enemy and society; 2. 2nd phase of operational and tactical activities of the so-called hybrid war (the open use of military force takes place in the case of failure to achieve the objectives of the operation in the previous phase); characterized by rapid actions of light units in selected directions, from site to site, and a clear division of competences in the area of operations; the maneuver performer moves units along the *approach routes* and maneuver corridors, from object to object, carrying out tasks in the focal points; the superior protects the wings in the form of reconnaissance activities, isolation, forbidding a maneuver, destructive actions in relation to the defender's defensive systems as air and artillery strikes.

The foreign policy of the Russian Federation towards this part of Europe, which until the beginning of the 1990s was under the influence of the Soviet Union, should be considered with regard to many aspects. A spectacular example is Russia's specific approach to the so-called "Peace operations" carried out by the armed forces of Russia in the territories of the former Soviet Union. As part of peace-keeping and crisis response operations, Russian actions differ far from those generally accepted in the international environment and endorsed by the United Nations. While UN peacekeeping operations are carried out only after the end of the conflict and after obtaining the Security Council or, exceptionally, the UN General Assembly, Russian troops do not respect these principles, engaging in an ongoing conflict and not maintaining neutrality (Legucka, 2015, p. 37). Such a policy confirms Russia's great-power ambitions and forces the countries of the region, including Poland, to protect themselves against hybrid actions (Wiśniewski, 2016, p. 229).

References

(2014) Doktryna wojenna Federacji Rosyjskiej 2014 (tłumaczenie robocze).
(2016) Analiza nowej Strategii Bezpieczeństwa Narodowego Rosji, Bydgoszcz: Centrum Doktryn i Szkolenia Sił Zbrojnych.
(2019) Twierdza Kaliningrad coraz bliżej Moskwy, Warszawa: Raport Ośrodka Studiów Wschodnich.
Bartosiak J. (2018). Rzeczpospolita. Między lądem a morzem. O wojnie i pokoju, Warszawa.
Blank, S. (1999). "Proliferation and counterproliferation in Russian strategy." Korean Journal of Defense Analysis 11(2): pp. 149–189.
Depczyński M., (2016). Pretorianie kremla. Wojska powietrznodesantowe Federacji Rosyjskiej, Warszawa: Bellona.
Depczyński M., (2015). Rosyjskie siły zbrojne. Od Milutina do Putina. Warszawa: Bellona.
https://pulaski.pl/rosyjskie-zdolnosci-w-zakresie-srodkow-izolowania-pola-walki-a2ad-w nioski-dla-nato/ (dostęp: 18.01.2020 r).
Horska, E., S. Moroz and J. Galova (2016). "The EU – Ukraine – Russia Crisis Triangle: Evidence of Local and Global Consequences for International Trade." Global Perspectives on Trade Integration and Economies in Transition: pp. 105–125.
Ilyin, V. A. and M. V. Morev (2019). "The 2018–2019 Regional Election: Voters' Trust in the Authorities Continues to Decline." Economic and Social Changes-Facts Trends Forecast 12(5): pp. 9–24.
Kristensen, H. M. and M. G. McKinzie (2015). "Nuclear arsenals: Current developments, trends and capabilities." International Review of the Red Cross 97(899): pp. 563–599.
Legucka A., (2015). Polityka Federacji Rosyjskiej i Unii Europejskiej wobec konfliktów zbrojnych we "wspólnym sąsiedztwie", praca naukowo-badawcza, Warszawa: Akademia Obrony Narodowej.
Michalski W. and Modrzejewski Z., (2015). Doktryny wojenne innych państw, Warszawa: Akademia Obrony Narodowej.
Szczurek T., (2014). Asymetria w środowisku bezpieczeństwa (in:) Szczurek T. (eds.) Asymetryczne zagrożenia bezpieczeństwa narodowego, Warszawa: Wojskowa Akademia Techniczna.
Wiśniewski J., (2016). Charakter zagrożenia militarnego w świetle doświadczeń wynikających z kryzysu Ukraina–Rosja (in:) Więcek W. and Elak L. (eds.) Teoria i praktyka taktyki w XXI wieku, Warszawa: Akademia Obrony Narodowej.
Yakovlev, V. N. (2015). Legal Foundations of Russia' Military Security. Mirovaya Ekonomika I Mezhdunarodnye Otnosheniya(3): pp. 56–63.
Федеральный закон об обороне от 31 мая 1996 года N 61 – Ф. Раздел II Статья 5 oraz Закон Российской Федерации "О безопасности", от 5 марта 1992 г. No. 2446 – I Статья 16.

Wawrzyniec Kowalski

Chapter 3: Summary and conclusions: Geopolitical and geostrategic positioning of Poland in relation to the foreign policy of the Russian Federation in the third decade of the 21st century

The purpose of this text is to summarize the viewpoints of researchers both in terms of the geopolitical and geostrategic situation of Poland in relation to the foreign policy of the Russian Federation. The author focused mainly on highlighting the key factors shaping the conditions of the special geopolitical and geostrategic position of Poland. The considerations deliberately omit to refer to the previously indicated conceptual issues related to defining the goals of both the geostrategy of the state (Szczurek, 2020) and geopolitics (Bryczek-Wróbel, 2020). The implications of Russia's influence on Poland, both in the geopolitical and geostrategic dimensions, cannot be considered separately, as they are a derivative of the actions of the Russian Federation aimed at strengthening its long-term influence on Western European states, and therefore must be considered as a whole.

Already at the outset, it is necessary to note the implications of Poland's geographical basis, related to the vicinity of the Russian Federation, clearly outlined in the previous sections. One might risk saying that the vicinity of the Russian Federation seems to be the most important factor influencing Poland's security for centuries. The consequences of the geographical location of the Russian Federation are emphasized by researchers, among others Nikolas Gvosdev, according to whom the collapse of the Soviet Union on the one hand and the geographical realities on the other meant that contemporary Russian political elite is characterized by the desire to rebuild Russia's superpower position. According to N. Gvosdev: "There are certain overarching Russian foreign policy goals that guide how the Kremlin sets and defines its agenda for different regions of the world. Whether governed by tsars, commissars or presidents, any Russian leader – and Vladimir Putin is no exception – must deal with the twin challenges posed by Russia's geographic position: extensive and vulnerable land borders coupled with choke points that, in hostile hands, cut Russia off from engagement with the larger world. The traditional Russian approach to these two problems was to push the borders of Russian influence outward to secure the vulnerable core heartland and take control of the various nodes connecting

Russia to the rest of the world" (Gvosdev, 2019). In turn, Agata Włodkowska-Bagan stresses that "At the turn of the 1980s and 1990s, Poland and Russia found themselves in a new geopolitical situation. For Russia, the geopolitical changes were particularly painful. The Federation fell from the rank of a superpower to the group of regional powers with ambitions to regain its lost status" (Włodkowska-Bagan, 2011). There is also no doubt that the turning points influencing today's perception of Poland by Moscow are the effects of the collapse of the Soviet Union and the dissolution of the Warsaw Pact, and, what is equally important, Poland's membership in the North Atlantic Treaty Organization. Although such a statement may seem a truism, it should not be forgotten that in the Russian narrative there are present repeatedly expressed accusations in which one can see the demonstrated threat with the presence of, among others, American military installations in Poland (defence24.pl).

In the geostrategic aspect, the arguments raised by Tadeusz Szczurek, pointing to the exceptional role of the president's office in the Russian security system, should be emphasized. The effectiveness of the security system of the Russian Federation is also influenced by a system of power closer to authoritarianism than to democracy, which results in the effectiveness and stability of Russian foreign policy. It should be mentioned that an emanation of the aforementioned stability is, inter alia, the constancy of the power camp, see Russia's Minister of Foreign Affairs Sergey Lavrov, who has been in office since 2004. It should also be noted that a specific measure of the significant influence of the President of the Russian Federation on the sphere of security and defense of the state is establishing on April 5, 2016, by decree of the President of the Russian Federation, the National Guard of the Russian Federation (prawo.gov.ru). Among researchers, the importance of this fact is emphasized, among others, by Grzegorz Rosłan, according to whom the direct subordination of the Rosgvardiya's structures to the head of state proves the progressing militarization of the state (Roslan 2017). One should also recall T. Szczurek's statement regarding the special role of the Armed Forces among other services (Szczurek, 2020).

Referring to the previously indicated geostrategic conditions, it seems that the particular importance among the above mentioned, has military potential at the disposal of the Armed Forces of the Russian Federation, with particular emphasis on the so-called A2 / AD anti-access systems (S400, S300, Bał, Bastion), located in the Kaliningrad District. This peculiar "unsinkable aircraft carrier" is a tool enabling the projection of military force in the Baltic region. In the doctrine, a similar view to the T. Szczurek's one, is expressed, among others, by Raimundas Lopata. "Kaliningrad has become the heart of Russia's A2 / AD 'bubble', raising new challenges for the security of the Scandinavian countries, Finland, the Baltic states and Poland, ergo Western Europe. Kaliningrad has turned into a diminishing factor in terms of Belarus' geopolitical role. The consistent re-militarisation of Kaliningrad affects the regional states and transatlantic relations alike. Moscow's goal is for the Kaliningrad factor to be of strategic importance in the balance of power dialogue with the West, and the US in particular" (Lopata, 2018). Moreover, the dislocation of the most modern Iskander-M and Kalibr missile systems proves the military potential of the Russian Federation located in the Kaliningrad Oblast.

A reference should also be made to the entire group of threats indicated by Tadeusz Szczurek, resulting from Russia's increasingly frequent use of asymmetric methods. As the author of this text previously pointed out, the greatest challenge related to the use of hybrid activities results from the fact that it is often difficult for a state that is subjected to hybrid activities, to classify them correctly. The author also points out that the concept of hybrid war can be considered in many aspects – it applies to both land operations, sea operations, as well as in the air space (Kowalski).

On the geopolitical level, Patrycja Bryczek-Wróbel emphasizes that Central and Eastern Europe is not, from Russia's point of view, a key area for strengthening its international position. At present, the rivalry with the United States and the difficult cooperation with China are of key importance for the Russian Federation. The latter, in the long-term perspective of decades, may result in China's tendency to subjugate Siberia. The author concludes at the same time that a specific alliance of 'dragon and bear' is based on economic premises – especially the export of natural resources, vide the Power of Siberia gas pipeline, the construction of the Belt and Road Initiative, as well as the military ones, an example of which is the delivery of advanced S400 Triumf Systems to China by the Russian Federation in 2018 (indiatimes.com). There are, however, voices (Allison, 2018) that the alliance between Moscow and Beijing is extremely pragmatic and will be unstable in the long run.

Another reference should also be made to the so-called political conception of Intermarum by P. Bryczek – Wróbel. The idea, which the guiding principle is to institutionalize cooperation between the countries of the region, while at the same time securing the countries of Central and Eastern Europe against Russia (Frenkel, 2017).

Underlining the difficult mutual relations between Poland and Russia, Patrycja Bryczek-Wróbel draws attention to a specific dualism of Polish-Russian relations, on the one hand marked by political conditions, and on the other – by economic pragmatism. It should be added that some Polish entrepreneurs are still trying to establish themselves on the absorbent Russian market.

The conducted summary requires some nuance. It should be noted that the geopolitical and geostrategic conditions of relations between Warsaw and Moscow are influenced not only by direct relations between the two countries, but also by indirect impacts. The author has in mind the strong economic relations between the Federal Republic of Germany and Russia, which were mentioned earlier (Bryczek-Wróbel). Relations, both in the geopolitical and geostrategic aspects, are influenced by international organizations that are peculiar collective security systems, especially the United Nations and the North Atlantic Treaty Organization (Kowalski 2019). It should be remembered that the presence of Russia among the permanent members of the Security Council with veto rights significantly increases the ability of the Russian Federation to influence the international security system, e.g. by blocking resolutions of the Security Council. Also presence in the Security Council: "grants Russia recognition as a great power through permanent membership and veto power on the Security Council" (RAND 2017). It should also be remembered that in the coming years the revision of the content of the UN Charter seems doubtful. The difficult relations between the Russian Federation and the states of Europe and the United States necessarily go beyond the framework of the United Nations. Christian Nünlist and Oliver Thränert express the view according to which: "Putin appears to have made a conscious decision to renounce cooperation with the West permanently. The West, for its part, must prepare for a long-term political confrontation with Russia, a nuclear power with a veto on the UN Security Council" (Nünlist, Thränert, 2015). A similar view that: "(...) that Russia's relationship with Europe and the United States has undergone an irreversible change and will not come back to the pre-2014 status quo (...)", following Sergey Lavrov, Mikhail Troitskiy (Troitskiy, 2016) The view expressed by Robert Foks should be recalled, according to which in the hierarchy of Russia's national interests, the implementation of vital interests of the state is at the forefront – these belong to the highest category. Contra-punctually, the interests of citizens and society are included by R. Foks in the lowest category (Foks, 2007). In the light of the above, it should be remembered that the challenges generated by Russian foreign policy are of an extremely serious nature.

Summarizing the views expressed by researchers indicated in the previous sections, some conclusions can be made.

The considerations presented by Tadeusz Szczurek and Patrycja Bryczek-Wróbel justify the findings that the foreign policy of the Russian Federation in the geostrategic and geopolitical plane is characterized by both pragmatism focused on the implementation of economic goals (Bryczek-Wróbel) and a comprehensive and methodical expansion of the military potential enabling a potential impact implemented by the Armed Forces (Szczurek).

The growing unpredictability of our times indicated by the researchers, the exemplification of which may be the apparent withdrawal of American armed forces from eastern Syria, or the long-term 'freezing' of the conflict in eastern Ukraine stems from the United States' aspirations to counter the growing role of the mighty China which no longer hides its global aspirations. These aspirations are expressed not only in the construction of the Belt and Road Initiative but also in the so-called project The String of Pearls (Kwieciński, 2014). Allied credibility is a specific price to this endeavor. It should not be forgotten that the key element of the security of the Republic of Poland after 1997 is the famous Article 5 of the North Atlantic Treaty. Opinions that appear define NATO and article 5 of the Treaty as "the core of 'hard security' policy" (Bieńczyk-Missala, 2016).

The uncertainty of Polish-Russian relations, understood both in the geostrategic and geopolitical perspective, is also influenced by the increasingly worrying inflation of the international law system, with the coexistence of many countries to set standards for new challenges to international security. In particular, it should be remembered that there are no legal regulations at the international level that would allow for effective counteracting the use of hybrid activities by some countries, i.e. below the threshold of war.

From the authors' views it can be concluded that the foreign policy of the Russian Federation will not only have an extremely significant impact on the situation of the Republic of Poland, both in geostrategic and geopolitical terms, but will also be a factor significantly influencing the shape of European security in the coming years. This will result from the raw material dependence of the economies of European countries on Russian oil and natural gas. We should expect further intensification of Russia's actions aimed at increasing the volume of exported raw materials and expanding the transmission networks, vide Nord Stream 2, South Stream.

Finally, the indicated great-power ambitions of Russia, combined with the growing military potential of the Russian armed forces and the conviction of a significant part of the Russian political elites that the weak political leadership in the 1990s almost led to the collapse of the state, mean that in the coming years the relations Warsaw-Moscow will still be difficult.

References

Allison G. (2018), China and Russia: A Strategic Alliance in the Making, [online] https://nationalinterest.org/feature/china-and-russia-strategic-alliance-making-38727.
Bieńczyk-Missala A. (2016), Poland's foreign and security policy: main directions, *Revista UNISCI/UNISCI Journal*, vol. 40, p. 106. doi.org/10.5209/rev_RUNI.2016.n40.51808.
Bryczek-Wróbel P. (2020), Geopolitical situation of Poland in relation to the foreign policy of the Russian Federation, in: Górnikiewicz M. Bielawski R. (eds.) Influence of Russian activities in the Visegard Group countries and Austria, vol. 1.
defence24.pl, Rakiety Tomahawk w Redzikowie? Rosjanie oskarżają, https://www.defence 24.pl/rakiety-tomahawk-w-redzikowie-rosjanie-oskarzajaeconomictimes.indiatimes.c om, China successfully tests Russia's S-400 missile air defence system, https://economic

times.indiatimes.com/news/defence/china-successfully-tests-russias-s-400-missile-air-defence-system/articleshow/67267551.cms.

Frenkel M., Ruchome piaski Międzymorza, *Liberte*, t. 27.

Foks R. (2007), Rola "bezpieczeństwa politycznego" w systemie bezpieczeństwa narodowego Federacji Rosyjskiej a "nowy rosyjski autorytaryzm", *Rocznik Bezpieczeństwa*, vol. 9, p. 135.

Gvosdev N. (2019), Russian Strategic Goals in the Middle East, *Russia's Policy in Syria and the Middle East: Determination, Delight, and Disappointment*, Institute for European, Russian and Eurasian Studies, Central Asia Program, Paper no. 212, January 2019, p. 4.

Kowalski, W. (2019), "Środowisko potencjału obronnego Polski – porównanie stosunków międzynarodowych. Aspekt prawa międzynarodowego", Stańczyk, K. (eds.) Potencjał obronny Rzeczypospolitej Polskiej.

Kowalski W., (2020) The legal aspects of hybrid air warfare.

Kwieciński R. (2014), Chiński "sznur pereł". Niektóre aspekty strategii ChRL na początku XXI wieku, In: Wardęga J. (eds.) Współczesne Chiny w kontekście stosunków międzynarodowych. Seria: Chińskie drogi, p. 39.

Lopata R. (2018), Kaliningrad in the European Security Architecture after the Annexation of Crimea, *Lithuanian Annual Strategic Review*, vol. 16, p. 303. DOI: 10.2478/lasr-2018-0011.

Nünlist Ch., Thränert O. (2015), Putin's Russia and European Security, CSS Analyses in Security Policy, No. 172.

Presidential Decree No. 159 (2016), О внесении изменения в состав Совета Безопасности Российской Федерации, утвержденный Указом Президента Российской Федерации от 25 мая 2012 г. N 715, available at: http://publication.pravo.gov.ru/Document/View/0001201604050053 [accessed 7 April 2020].

Radin A., Reach C. (2017), Russian views of the international order, RAND Corporation, Santa Monica, p. 36.

Rosłan G. (2017), Rola gwardii narodowej Federacji Rosyjskiej w systemie bezpieczeństwa Rosji, *Modern management review*, vol. 24 (3/2017).

Szczurek T. (2020), Geostrategic situation of Poland in relation to the foreign policy of the Russian Federation, in: Górnikiewicz M. Bielawski R. (eds.) Influence of Russian activities in the Visegard Group countries and Austria, vol. 1.

Troitskiy M. (2016), Russia and the West in the European Security Architecture: Clash of Interests or a Security Dilemma? In: OSCE Yearbook 2015, DOI: 10.5771/9783845273655-67, p. 67.

Włodkowska-Bagan A. 2011, Konfliktowość w stosunkach polsko-rosyjskich In: Bieleń S., Skrzypek A. (eds.), Geopolityka w stosunkach polsko-rosyjskich, p. 1.

Section II:
Kremlin's "hard power" and "soft power" towards Poland in the first and second decades of the 21st century

Marian Cieślarczyk

Chapter 4: The Kremlin's tough influence on the Polish decision-making process

In the life of physical and legal entities, in its various spheres and areas, there is an important – although not always noticed and appreciated notion – called relations. However, it is not sufficiently noticed and appreciated. It is much more common in sociology than, for example, in political science and other scientific disciplines. Perhaps from this, among other reasons, relations between scientific disciplines and fields of knowledge have not been of particular interest to scientists and practitioners. It is not a constructive phenomenon. However, the growing awareness that without inter-, multi- and transdisciplinary research it will be increasingly difficult to describe, explain, predict and solve the swelling problems of the "modern world" – including pandemics. It somehow necessitates the use of a transdisciplinary research perspective[1]. Within its framework a cultural perspective was also applied. The results of such a research approach have been presented in two subsequent subsections of this monograph. What

---

1 *Interdisciplinarity*, as it is traditionally understood, is treated as *a quality of the mind of a scientist* who can navigate within several disciplines and creatively synthesize their achievements. However, it is not easy, and a significant part of the difficulties may result from both formal and structural conditions, as well as being associated with the mental and psychological barriers of researchers. *Interdisciplinarity is nowadays* understood as *a feature of teams* of academics gathering to solve a specific scientific problem, but respecting in principle the distinctiveness of their disciplines. In this context, the problems of boundaries in science are interesting (especially the problem of the "border area" of disciplines), where new sub-disciplines of knowledge originate, including the increasingly recognizable phenomenon of *security culture*. Interdisciplinarity and interdisciplinary research mainly concern crossroads spheres. Let's put it in a simple way, it can be said that interdisciplinary research is associated with *"fusion"*, *multidisciplinary research has features in common with "bonding"*, *multidisciplinary research resembles "distillation"*, *and transdisciplinary research* is commonly associated with "loose stacking" recalling playing with *Lego blocks*. In addition to *knowledge, intuition and imagination* are also useful, as well as a *holistic and systemic perception of reality* and the related *ways of thinking and acting* (Zeidler-Janiszewska, 2016, pp. 9–29; Domańska, 2013, pp. 55–56, Bremer) , 2016, pp. 20–21). In theoretical considerations it seems relatively simple. It is more difficult to apply these recommendations in research practice, as the author could find out when he was the director of the Transdisciplinary Center for Security Problems named after Prof. Bogdański at the University of Natural Sciences and Humanities in Siedlce.

these two sections have in common is the model shown in (Figure 1). In addition to the sphere of *mental, conscious and spiritual culture* (sphere A /), towards which the "soft" interactions of one subject towards another one are usually addressed, this model also takes into account the sphere of *material culture* (C /), in which "hard" interactions are more common. Between them there is the sphere B /, i.e. *organizational culture*, to which, in the twenty first century, more and more importance is attached both in the life of people, institutions and organizations, but also states, communities or alliances, such as the EU or NATO. Therefore, the attention of cooperating entities is addressed towards this sphere. Unfortunately, the sphere B /, that is *organizational culture*, is more and more often exposed to destructive influences undertaken by those entities which, due to the nature of factors in the areas A / and B /, have big problems in establishing constructive relations with other entities and developing cooperation with them. This observation concerns internal relations, but also the relations between the subjects of international life. It is obvious that this phenomenon makes it difficult to obtain the synergy effect and development in the internal and international dimension. This, in turn, contributes to the generation of the potential of negative social emotions addressed against internal or external "enemies".

It can be assumed with high probability that the primary cause of the problems signaled above is the *deficit of trust* (Sztompka, 2007) of some "entities" in relation to others operating in the closer and more distant environment. An additional "ballast" is then also *the deficit of thinking in terms of the common good*. Speaking of trust, it should be mentioned that it is not about a boundless and thoughtless type of trust, but rather about its nature, which can be called *wise*. The essence of *wise trust* is easier to understand by analyzing the way of functioning car traffic on public roads. In this understanding, we take into account the driver's trust in himself/herself (in his/her competences), but also in other users of the common communication space. Trust to a car is also important. It is worth considering these relations in the dynamics of their functioning. It is connected with a more or less realistic assessment of one's abilities in relations with other entities. This in turn largely depends on the way of thinking about oneself and the environment, and in it, about other physical and legal entities. It is one of the important mechanisms of shaping – approaches and attitudes, but also *related behaviors, actions and cooperation* in relations with other entities. It is worth emphasizing once again that the positive or negative effects of actions and cooperation between entities are significantly influenced by the already mentioned way of thinking[2], which is an important element of the

---

[2] It is called by psychologists the "cognitive style" (Klimow 1969; Bruner 1978; Nosal 1979; Matczak 1982; Haman 1985), and by sociologists "technology of the intellect" (eg Marody 1987), although they are not identical.

Figure 1. The main spheres of "soft" and "hard" destructive interactions and the relations between them – an ideal model. Source: own study on the basis of: M.Cieślarczyk, Culture of security and defense, Siedlce 2006, pp. 196–200.

safety culture[3]. And the ways of thinking of a subject are related to its ways of perceiving the environment. It can be a "daltonic" way of perceiving reality and thinking about it only in terms of "black and white", without taking into account various types of "gray" and a whole range of other "colors", or vice versa. Related to this first, the bipolar type of "intellect technology", is a similar, bipolar way of functioning of the emotional sphere of such a "subject". In simplified terms, it can be defined as: "I love-hate", "a friend-enemy", etc. It has an impact on the

---

[3] In a great simplification, it can be assumed that the security culture of an entity is understood as its way of thinking about security and feeling security, as well as the related ways of achieving security (Cieślarczyk, 2006, p. 210).

evaluation process carried out by such a subject, but also on its decisions, behaviors and actions.

In a situation where both sides make attempts to establish and maintain cooperation, then with too large differences in their "cognitive styles", it does not have to be successful. It is particularly difficult when potential partners "work at different wavelengths" (Sedlak, 1980), and the relations between them are disrupted either by random situations or by deliberate or accidental adverse effects of other entities. Then, it is needed not only a considerable credit of mutual, wise trust and understanding, but also time and patience. Unfortunately, the "bipolar" nature of the security culture of physical and legal entities does not go hand in hand with patience and perseverance. When these conditions are not met, then the "other party" is blamed for the lack of cooperation effects, and after some time it goes to destructive interactions. In such a situation, mental activity and practical activities are subordinated to the category of "struggle". Even if there are attempts to take action in terms of "games", it usually follows the "zero-one" convention, serving mainly destructive purposes. Over time, this phenomenon can take the form of a long, debilitating struggle conducted with the use of "hard" and "soft" methods. It is also worth noting that in the 21st century, destructive influences are often addressed towards the presented sphere B /, and in it, against the elements of organizational culture. *The method of creating and managing* chaos is often used by organized crime groups.

At this point, let us dwell on "hard" interactions, not forgetting, however, that they are only one of the elements of the "impact system" (Crozier and Friedberg, 1982). Therefore, it is worth considering them in connection with the others. Understanding the essence of interactions of such a perceived "system" requires the adoption of a research perspective adequate to the needs. In our case it was – generally speaking – a transdisciplinary perspective, in which the dominant role was played by the cultural research perspective.

Taking into account the adopted subject of research, i. e. "methods of hard and soft influence of Russia on Poland", as well as the aim of the research, which was "general characteristics of the most important of these methods together with an attempt to explain the ways of their functioning and the achieved results", the following problem questions were formulated for the purposes of this task:
1. What methods of "hard" and "soft" influence of Russia on Poland are found in scientific literature in various disciplines of knowledge?
2. What conclusions from these analyzes may be helpful for Poland, the EU and NATO and then could they be used for educational purposes and further research?

The subject and objectives of the research outlined in this way as well as problem questions required the use of several research perspectives. Generally speaking, a transdisciplinary approach was applied, in which – as already mentioned – the dominant role was played by the cultural research perspective. Because of its application it was possible to develop a universal research tool.

The basic tool used in the process of recognizing the forms of Russia's influence on Poland, but also in relation to other EU and NATO countries, was the theoretical model presented in the figure above (Figure 1). Its general outline was developed over a dozen years ago during some work related to learning about the phenomenon of security culture. In the following years, this model was developed and enriched. Moreover, during the development of this and the next subsection, it was enriched with another element, marked in blue.

Before we attempt to use this model as a research tool, useful for searching, systematizing and processing information necessary to answer problem questions, it is worth making a few introductory remarks. The preliminary analysis of the literature on the subject showed that the amount of information on the topic of our interest resembles "the sea", and perhaps even the "ocean". This did not facilitate the attempts to answer the problem questions formulated above. The presented model acted as a kind of "sieve" useful in searching and "catching" the necessary information sets and processing them in such a way as to obtain an answer to research problems. How was this model created?

Let us start by saying that the starting point for its development was the adoption of a cultural research perspective. Its usefulness in the modern, increasingly complex world seems to be difficult to overestimate. We began with the analysis of almost two hundred definitions of culture found in contemporary scientific literature, in order to obtain the "instant" form after several stages of work. How did we come to this? In the first stage, approximately one hundred and fifty were left for further analysis in a screening-synthesizing manner from the aforementioned number of almost two hundred definitions of "culture". Subsequent analyzes of these definitions and the search for a "common denominator" among them, made it possible to limit the amount to a dozen or so. Then, it was easier to notice that the collected this way elements of the "puzzles" form three sets. They delineated the three spheres of the broadly understood culture, visible in the central part.

What was the usefulness of this model in the implementation of this research task? It has already been mentioned that the overabundance of information on the issues raised at the first stage of the analysis resembled a "bush" in which it was not difficult to "get lost"[4]. It cannot be ruled out that this is a favorable

---

[4] An additional difficulty was that the same facts were interpreted differently by individual authors in the same country (Zięba 2011; Stolarczyk 2016, Menkiszak 2019; Darczewska 2018), and in some publications there were even contradictory theses of the same author on the same page (Minkina, 2017, p. 77). Such a situation could be convenient for those entities that make a

situation for those "entities" that carry out "fights" and information "wars", which will be discussed in more detail in the next subsection. In this situation, the presented model resembled a specific type of a compass; on the other hand, a kind of three-part "network" facilitating the search and systematization of "caught" collections of information and knowledge. It was especially useful at the stage of describing the facts, processes and phenomena of interest to us. For this purpose, three interconnected parts of this "network" were useful, namely the spheres A /, B / and C /. The remaining elements of this model were used in the second stage of cognition, i. e. in the process of explaining facts and phenomena.

As already mentioned, the term "relations" was used many times in the text. It is so important, that its specification in the footnote to this subsection[5] turned out to be especially useful in analyzes of the "soft" impact of Russia on Poland, but also of the "hard" one. Over the centuries, people have used various ways of "building" relationships with the environment and influencing them in order to ensure the conditions for survival and development. Centuries ago, the basic way of influencing the environment was one that, according to modern terminology, can be classified as "hard". Generally speaking, it was about "making the earth subordinate to mankind." However, over time, this constructive message began to be applied not only to the natural environment, but also to the social one. Plundering, conquering and subjugating the weaker groups by the stronger ones, somehow instinctively appeared at that time. With time, there were wars. After a time, the scope of used tools and methods of interaction, as well as the types of effects obtained as a result, expanded. It was dealt with "so well" that in the second half of the 20th century the world "held its breath" when it stood on the brink of extinction. This happened, among others in connection with the Cuban crisis. ‚Fortunately, wisdom[6] and thinking in terms of the common good pre-

---

great effort by introducing information confusion in their "fights" and information "wars". Sometimes it may even seem convenient for Russia.

5 When writing about relations, we take into account not only bilateral relations between states and societies, in this case Russia and Poland, and the position (process) of shaping relations between these entities, but also their impact on relations with other states and societies, also operating within the EU and NATO. In these analyzes, it is worth taking into account another type of relationship – between destructive and constructive interactions, as well as between aggressive and defensive interactions. By making further details of the impact categories, their type, which is classified as "defensive", can in turn be related to real or imaginary threats. The latter, i. e. imaginary (abstract) threats, may have different conditions. They may be the result of historical experiences and the deep trauma associated with them, causing a number of other negative effects that are culturally passed on to next generations. They can also be triggered on purpose, for example by state institutions or some lobby for the purposes of a "game" with the own society or with external entities.

6 By "wisdom" we mean the ability to use knowledge and other resources for worthy purposes. To find out what is the position of the category of wisdom among other values of modern Man,

vailed over "sick ambitions" and national egoisms. Time will show what conclusions will be drawn by homo sapiens after the COVID-19 pandemic.

It is worth noting that at a certain stage of civilization development, in addition to destructive influences, there were also those that took into account the already mentioned category of "common good", understood not only in the national dimension, but also in relation to the wider community, such as the EU. States and societies participating in such communities have become more clearly aware of the importance of democracy for the Community, in its understanding not only within countries, but also in relations between states. It would be hard to say that this way of thinking is already common at the end of the second decade of the 21st century, as is the transparency of decisions made by the EU[7] leadership and related decisions, actions and interactions, or their deficit. More about this in the next section.

Meanwhile, let us stop at the "hard" interactions in Russia's relations with Poland, but also with other EU and NATO countries. Even a cursory analysis of the available materials shows that this issue could be devoted to a separate monograph. Therefore, in the following considerations, we will pay more attention to methodological reflections useful in the scientific understanding of the discussed issues than to substantive ones. Therefore, the substantive materials used in this part of the monograph will be treated as a specific background useful for searching for ways to conduct in-depth research on these strictly scientific issues. As already mentioned in the available literature, often the same facts are interpreted completely differently by individual authors in the same country. Sometimes even the same author formulates contradictory theses in different places of the same publication, some examples of which are given in footnote 8. These and similar examples indicate the need to use the already mentioned transdisciplinary perspective in research, including the historical-political-science and economic perspective.

Over the centuries, Russian-Polish relations resembled a sinusoid, but with a continuing negative trend for Poland. Looking at the problem more broadly, it can be assumed that it would be difficult to indicate a period when Russian-Polish relations brought positive results for both countries and societies. The Russians blamed and so far they have been blaming the Poles for it. Although in the long history of the "neighborhood" there was a case that the Polish army reached Moscow[8] on July 4, 1610 after the victory of the Battle of Kluszyn,

---

it is enough to analyze the so-called syllabuses in various countries and their universities. The picture is not very optimistic.

7 The fact that this is not an "invented" problem can be proved by the entries in (Biała Księga, 2017, p.17), I quote: "... the decision-making process is still not well understood ...".

8 By the way, it is worth noting that the vast majority of Polish youth do not know this fact, and even if they hear about it, they do not pay much attention to it.

however it did not "stay there" for too long. The brave inhabitants of the Russian capital coped with this problem relatively quickly. Today, the date of that event is celebrated as the National Day of Russia. Similarly, in Poland, the anniversary of the Battle of Warsaw, which took place in August 1920, is celebrated every year. It was probably one of the most important battles that would determine the future of Europe. On the outskirts of the capital of the Polish state, which existed only two years after 123 years of partitions, the Polish army – supported by ordinary and equally unusual citizens and volunteers from several European countries – stopped the "liberating" Red Army. It carried on its banners and bayonets "brotherly, internationalist aid" to the countries of Central and Western Europe.

For this heroic effort in 1920, several thousand Polish officers paid for it with their lives, who in 1939 were deceitfully taken into the Russian captivity. After several months, they were murdered with a shot to the back of the head and buried in deep ditches in the area of Katyn, Kozielsk, Kharkiv and Miednoye. Together with them, thousands of representatives of the Polish intelligentsia, administration, police and border guards found their "eternal rest" there. This massacre, unknown in human history, was also committed insidiously by the NKVD, executing a total of more than 20,000 victims with German weapons and ammunition. And after the "liberation" of Poland by the Red Army in 1945, for several decades Polish society was told that this cruel murder had been perpetrated by the Germans.

Over the centuries, several generations of Poles have paid with their lives or in deportations to Siberia for their attempts to shake off the yoke of Russian slavery. Uprisings in 1794, 1830 and 1863 brought the greatest number of victims. The insurgents were supported by citizens from various European countries and not only that, Polish emigrants fleeing from tsarist persecution also found refuge in Western Europe and the United States. This was still the case in the 1980s. However, the European public opinion was not always aware of what was happening in Poland during the time of the partitions. Used then by the tsarist authorities, the methods of conducting disinformation are described in an interesting way by the world-famous historian N. Davies.

Thus, when Polish uprisings were repeated despite the reforms introduced by the so-called "liberal tsars", the opinion of the West tended to lose patience and believe in the Russian stereotype of an ungrateful and anarchist Pole. In fact, the whole thing was much deeper than that. (...) Indeed, Russian history is full of cases where the most enlightened and seemingly progressive constitutional declarations coincided with the darkest periods of despotism. According to Moscow's way of thinking, any loosening of the formal structures of the autocracy inevitably required a tightening of supervision and control by the responsible authorities. By the same token, the persecution of the most tyrannical politics can usually be masked by announcing a program of radical liberation and at the same time devoid of any legal force (Davies, 2005, p. 587). The author further wrote: "The most important state institution was the Russian army. It was the iron capital of the autocratic government and continuously influenced the lives of all the inhabitants of the empire" (p. 590). It is obvious that it was often directed against its own citizens. The Russian army was supported by the police in this mission. I quote N. Dawies: "The power of the police encompassed all spheres of life, and the only limitation was the energy resources and ingenuity of its countless agents. With the elapse of time, the tsarist police learned to invent problems themselves, which then they had to solve". (Davies, 2005, p. 592). Observing life in contemporary Russia, it is not difficult to notice that many of the methods used by the police and secret services of tsarist Russia show a timeless character. In the area of "liberated" after 1945 Poland, it was visible for many years after World War II. During this period, many Polish patriots lost their lives in a cruel and deceitful way, or were imprisoned for many years. It often happened to them because they had the courage to oppose the lie about the Katyn massacre.

The Polish economy, rebuilt with the great effort of society after the Second World War under the political, ideological and economic "loving care" of the "big brother", could not fully develop its potential. Not only because the then "Polish authorities" were banned from using the aid offered by the United States at the time. Poland's economic backwardness was related both to isolating the country from the most developed societies, and to insidious economic exploitation. It had an impact on the standard of living of Poles and the pace of the country's development. As in the tsarist times, this situation was explained with the "laziness of Poles", while the "market" of the Soviet Union absorbed – like the proverbial sponge – many Polish intellectual, raw materials and food resources. In the Soviet society, there was a conviction that its poverty was connected with the need to "maintain" Poland. And the protests of Polish workers who wanted to shake off the yoke of "brotherly protection" were bloodily suppressed (e.g. Poznań 1956, Gdańsk 1970, and many others). It is also not always remembered that in the Lublin region, Polish railway men blocked the export of food to the Olympics in Moscow in 1980, while in the country, the citizens were humiliatingly rationed out the meat "with food coupons". Also, the ships built in Polish shipyards intended for the USSR had to have a Polish "contribution" in foreign exchange, despite the lack of these funds to meet the basic needs of citizens. It is obvious that similar situations were not met with enthusiasm by the employees of the shipyards and the local authorities of the time. This created an atmosphere conducive to the establishment of the Independent Self-Governing Trade Union "Solidarity", which at one time gathered around 10 million Poles. It was unacceptable to the then USSR authorities.

The fact that this impressive act of solidarity of Polish society did not end with a "sea of blood" was determined by a combination of several favorable factors. They included: firstly, the heroic and wise attitude of Poles[9]; second – the support of the Pope John Paul II; thirdly – the decisive position of the then President of the United States and the Leaders of many European countries, as well as their material assistance. It should not also be forgotten that the vast majority of Polish Army officers would support Solidarity in the event of a possible entry of Soviet troops into Poland[10]. It cannot be ruled out that it influenced the course of martial law introduced in Poland on December 13, 1981. During the martial law period, there were many high-ranking "advisers" (supervisors) from the Soviet Union in Poland. Both during the martial law and after its end in 1983, the patience of Polish society, rarely seen in history before, became apparent. It resulted in general elections in 1989, which marked the beginning of democratic changes, not only in one country.

Another important turning point in Poland-Russia relations was the "disintegration" of the Soviet Union and the withdrawal of the Soviet troops from Poland. The accession of Poland to NATO on March 12, 1999 and to the EU on May 1, 2004 was a kind of "seal" of democratic changes in Poland and the country's entry onto the path of safe development.

Since then, Russia has identified Poland with the West. As a result, any "traps" set by the former "big brother" were easier to see and avoid by joint efforts. According to some journalists, one of such pitfalls was the "Idea of Greater Europe". M. Menkiszak wrote that it was present in the programmatic speeches of Russian leaders from the mid-1990s. According to this author, however, it did not appear in a vacuum. In its content, it contained clear parallels to the earlier concept of a "common European home" in the politics of the USSR (Menkiszak, 2013, p. 8). Although in the first decade of the 21st century, Russia's disintegrative and insidious influence was addressed to various European countries, including Poland, but their results were not as onerous and dangerous as they used to be. This difference was felt especially by Poles, Hungarians and Czechs, who had previously experienced "brotherly help". After Poland joined the EU and NATO, the common "shield" played its role to a large extent. Therefore, when writing about the "hard" influence of Russia on Poland, this problem should be seen in the context of the Community and the Alliance.

---

9 This was most clearly visible in connection with the martyrdom of Father Jerzy Popiełuszko, when Poles behaved very prudently, although there was a fear of emotional reactions and the consequences related to them, even of an international dimension. The behavior of the Poles was different from the one during the previous uprisings.

10 The results of the research conducted on this subject in 1981 by the Institute of Social Research of WAP.

As the analyzes of the Center for Eastern Studies in Poland show, from the beginning of W. Putin's third term (2012), Russia pursued a policy of "soft revisionism". It consisted in contesting and weakening the post-Cold War liberal international order while taking advantage of its economic benefits. However, during the third term (2012–2018), Moscow's revisionism became more aggressive. According to the analysts of the Center for Eastern Studies, the Kremlin used military force at that time and unleashed a cyber-information war against the West and its partners.

Russia has also intensified its attempts to push through economic and political integration in the post-Soviet area and has tightened cooperation with non-Western countries, especially China. At the same time, it returned as an active player to the Middle East and increased its presence in other regions, rebuilding its image as a superpower in Russian society (Putin for the fourth time, 2018, p. 5).

The process of Russia's integration with the world economy observed during the first two terms of President Putin has been reversed. Russia's aggressive foreign policy and the stiffening of the Russian negotiating position on the principles of cooperation with the West have led to, inter alia, the suspension of talks with the EU on a new Partnership and Cooperation Agreement, or the suspension of the OECD accession process. Despite joining the World Trade Organization in 2012, Russia has also intensified its protectionist policy. And since 2014, this country's isolation has deepened as a result of Western sanctions, as well as Russian counter-sanctions and the import substitution program (Putin for the fourth time, 2018, p. 25).

According to experts, an important element of the Russian strategy in the two most likely scenarios will be actions aimed at "breaking" the political synchronization of the policy of Western countries towards Russia, and generally at creating and increasing tensions between Washington and its European allies. It will consist in searching for a partial normalization of relations with individual countries, especially with the use of the prospects of economic cooperation (Putin for the fourth time, 2018, p. 42). This does not mean the lack of other types of interactions, as discussed in more detail later in this article.

According to the analysts of the Center for Eastern Studies, during Vladimir Putin's third presidential term (2012–2018), the increase in Russia's military potential has become a priority of the state's policy, not only in the security dimension, but also in the economic and social dimension. Compared to the previous period, Russia's foreign policy was characterized by greater assertiveness, sometimes turning into open aggression. Implemented armament programs (the so-called State Armament Programs, Russian: GPW), starting with the adopted in 2011 GPW-2020 (program for 2011–2020) and under the GPW-2027 (for 2018–2027) started at the beginning of 2018, are treated as a driving force for economic development (through the development or acquisition from the outside and implementation of modern technologies – also in the civil sector – and the creation of new, highly qualified engineering and production workers). Restrictions on the increase in Russian military spending (observed after 2014) are mainly declarative in nature, without slowing down the process of modernizing the Russian Armed Forces or changing the direction of transformations that the Russian army is undergoing. In general, it can be said that in this period, in the vicinity of Poland and the EU, we are dealing with the use of military force (aggression against Ukraine and military intervention in Syria), territorial conquests (the annexation of Crimea was the first territorial conquest by Russia since the 1940s), an attempt to influence the domestic politics of other countries using, sometimes irregular, armed formations (Ukraine), and the tools of "information warfare" (propaganda and manipulation campaigns in the media controlled by Russia, trolling in social media, cyber-attacks), and financial or media support for anti-system or pro-Russian political forces (Putin for the fourth time, 2018, pp. 32–33).

It is disturbing that on the fundamental – from the Russian point of view – western strategic direction, the Armed Forces of the Russian Federation have achieved a level of relative balance with the local NATO potential, as well as the possibility of working out an operational advantage in a selected part of the European theater of military operations. Such a situation became possible thanks to the intensive expansion of the grouping in the western strategic direction, which has been ongoing since 2015. In all types of troops and services, the increase in potential was achieved mainly through extensive technical modernization, but in the case of the Land Forces and partly the Airborne Forces, the formation of new and expansion of existing units played the most important role. It points out that the Western Military District has the majority of the newly formed tactical unions in recent years, and the unions formed in other military districts are also located in the western strategic direction (in the Rostov Oblast within the Southern Military District) or just beyond the Urals as part of the second wave strategic for the western direction (within the Central Military District). However, no new tactical relationship was formed in the Russian Far East. The Armed Forces of the Russian Federation in the western strategic direction (taking into account the delegated elements from outside the Western Military District, including potential of second-line units from the Central Military District) own 6 divisions and 30 general military brigades, as well as a significant number of support and security units, among which 17 artillery and missile brigades should be considered important from the point of view of the offensive capabilities of the Russian army (most of the latter have already been rearmed with Iskander systems, the rearming of the others should be completed in 2018). It is also worth noting the high concentration of the Russian army with engineering and sapper units (with increasing capabilities in the field of construction and organization of crossings) and transport and radio-electronic warfare units (the Kaliningrad Oblast and the Western Oblasts of Belarus belong to the regions of the world's most concentrated means of radio-electronic warfare) (Putin , 2018, p. 67).

A manifestation of Russia's increasing aggressiveness is also shown on the repeated cyber-attacks[11] (including those on critical infrastructures), massive propaganda campaigns or local attempts to destabilize the political situation (as in Germany or Montenegro), collectively known as "hybrid actions" (Meniszak, 2019, pp. 53). -55).

Due to the limited volume of this material, it is difficult to cite more examples of aggressive, "hard" influence of Russia on Poland and other countries of the Commonwealth and the Alliance. The breakdown of these structures, or at least their clear weakening, is an important strategic goal of Russia, also carried out through soft interactions, but also on the sphere of organization of states and societies, which will be discussed in more detail in the next subsection.

An insightful analyst of Russia's destructive influence on other countries, including Poland, Joanna Darczewska claims that most of the techniques of confronting the Russian Federation with the external environment are indirect, difficult to grasp. Their goal is to implement strategic interests and strengthen Russia's international position, and to "disarm" the enemy. The point is to bring about a situation in which internal actors pursue the goals of the Russian Federation's foreign policy. By using weak resistance and difficulties in identifying the threat, Russia destabilizes the situation in the attacked countries, exerts a destructive influence on their administrative and decision-making structures, undermines the social and economic foundations, as well as the cultural basis (ideology, value system, political culture, rule of law). These are arguments indicating that we are dealing with a simultaneous external and internal, national and transnational threat, which cannot be answered symmetrically. According to J. Darczewska, the destructive actions of Russia are carried out by state and non-state entities in a secret and open, legal and illegal manner. They constitute a continuous process, consisting in the integrated activity of the state on many fronts and using various channels (diplomatic, political, economic, military, social, media), subordinated to the long-term strategy of supporting the Kremlin's policy (Darczewska, 2018, p. 61).

There are many facts indicating that Russia does not rule out the use of military forces in pursuing its imperial policy. This was convincingly described by F. Mogherini, saying: "The armed operations in Donetsk, Luhansk and Mariupol accompanying the capture of Crimea prove that Russia is ready for an

---

11 Poland experienced such an attack shortly after President L. Kaczyński's speech at Weesterplatte on September 1, 2009.

armed conflict and changes to the existing borders. When analyzing Russia's previous behavior in South Ossetia, Abkhazia and Transnistria, the conclusion is drawn that Russian expansion has consistency and logic. As a result of the actions in Ukraine, the West became convinced that it would be difficult to establish partner relations with Russia and that it would remain a serious challenge for many years to come" (Mogherini, 2014).

The analysis of Russia's influence on Poland and other EU and NATO countries through the prism of a very extensive[12] scientific literature from several disciplines and fields of knowledge allows for the formulation of the following hypothesis: with high probability, it can be assumed that Russia uses the assumptions of the chaos theory in its destructive influence. Although it has not yet achieved great effects in this area, some of them are already noticeable.

Using the metaphor called "Rubik's cube" we can use it as follows. If you compare the efforts of the vast majority of countries and societies to a reasonably sensible arranging of this "cube", the actions of the Russian Federation may resemble its decomposition. This metaphor may prove useful in finding a way to more effectively counter Russia's destructive influence. Assuming the optics outlined above, we can imagine a theoretical model in the shape of a cube with a structure resembling a "Rubik's cube". In addition to six large analysis areas, it is possible to distinguish a dozen more, intersecting analysis fields, and at least several dozen more on them, smaller fields, which are marked on the actual Rubik's cube with several colors. Describing these "fields" and "plots" of the destructive impacts carried out by Russia may be the subject of interesting and useful scientific research. In such a transdisciplinary and culturally diverse approach, the project should be carried out by international research teams, consisting of representatives of several disciplines and fields of knowledge, also representing the exact sciences. Taking into account the technical capabilities of modern computers, it can be assumed that the knowledge gathered by these teams may have cognitive and practical value, also in terms of predicting the destructive influence of Russia and counteracting them more effectively than before.

In an extremely optimistic version, it can be found that the knowledge obtained in this way could be useful for "building a new civilization" in the post-coronavirus world, possibly also involving Russia. This knowledge should be particularly useful in identifying the symptoms of major crises, including international ones, earlier than before, and in minimizing their effects more effectively. On the other hand, the wider use of knowledge about the "security culture" in the didactic process will make it easier to understand the importance

---

12 Perhaps too extensive for one man, which did not have to favor the quality and depth of the analyzes.

of the category of "common good" for ensuring the existence, survival and development for future generations, including sustainable development[13].

References

(2017) Biała Księga w sprawie przyszłości Europy, Bruksela.
(2018) Putin po raz czwarty. Stan i perspektywy Rosji (2018–2024), Raport OSW.
Bremer J., (2016) Nauka o zrównoważeniu – w poszukiwaniu transdyscyplinarnej metodologii, Zagadnienia naukoznawstwa, 1 (207), ss. 20–21.
Cieślarczyk M., (2006) Kultura bezpieczeństwa i obronności, Siedlce.
Crozier M., Friedberg E., (1982) Człowiek i system. Ograniczenia działania zbiorowego, Warszawa.
Darczewska J., (2018) Środki aktywne jako rosyjska agresja hybrydowa w retrospekcji. Wybrane problemy, Przegląd Bezpieczeństwa Wewnętrznego, 18.
Domańska I. (2013), Antropologia literatury – projekt interdyscyplinarny czy transdyscyplinarny?, "Przegląd Kulturoznawczy", nr 1, ss. 55–56.
Menkiszak M., (2013) Wielka Europa. Putinowska wizja (dez)integracji europejskiej, Prace OSW, Nr 46.
Menkiszak M., (2019) Strategiczna kontynuacja, taktyczna zmiana, Polityka bezpieczeństwa europejskiego Rosji, Punkt Widzenia, nr 10.
Minkina M., (2017) Rosja-Zachód. Walka o wpływy, Warszawa 2017.
Mogherini F., (2014) Russia is no longer the EU's strategic partner, EurActiv, http://www.euractiv.com/section/global-europe/news/mogherini-russia-is-no-longer-the-eu-s-strategic-partner/.
Sedlak W., (1980) Homo electronicus, Warszawa.
Sztompka P. (2007), Zaufanie. Fundament społeczeństwa, Warszaw.
Zeidler-Janiszewska A. (2016), Visual Culture Studies czy antropologicznie zorientowana Bildwissenschaft? O kierunkach zwrotu ikonicznego w naukach o kulturze, "Teksty Drugie", nr 4, ss. 9–29.

---

13 These seem to be important implications of the survival of the "new" (after the coronavirus pandemic) civilization, favoring "winning" the race against time in the implementation of the most important joint Homo Sapiens mission in the coming decades, which is "the colonization of space". Without it, not only the sustainable development of our civilization will be endangered, but also its survival. Perhaps the adoption of such "optics" will be conducive to shaping a different way of thinking about relations between the subjects of international life, including also the thinking about relations between Russia and Poland, and vice versa. In such a situation, the categories of relationships and influences, all too often used today in a destructive sense, may one day be perceived as dangerous "games in a large sandbox" in which "the bigger takes the toys from the smaller".

Marian Cieślarczyk

Chapter 5: Russian "soft power" methodology in influencing the Polish decision-making process

Several factors influenced the formula of the article adopted by the author. On the one hand, the volume is limited and the development time is relatively short. On the other hand, the "ethereal" and multifaceted nature of the problems undertaken, the "roots" of which often go back many centuries. Individual and collective approaches, attitudes and behaviors arising from these "roots" (see Figure 1, p. 47) are also the cause of internal and international problems, the sources of which may be difficult to recognize. Then, describing and explaining them only in terms of a conflict of interest may be impoverished or even burdened with a significant error of subjectivism. These two groups of conditions could have contributed to the fact that the author of the article – which is supposed to be scientific in nature – tried to avoid the formula of one of the "exciting products" found on the publishing markets in different countries (Абрамс; Kux, 1985; Darczewska, 2018). There was a concern that an article containing an "ordinary" description of the types and methods/ways of Russia's "soft" influence on Poland could itself, by accident, become a tool of some "soft" influence. The above considerations contributed to the fact that the study was tailored as a theoretical-methodological draft based not only on media facts. It attempts to outline a research perspective that may turn out to be useful in the future to better learn and better understand this difficult, multi-layered and multi-faceted problem.

It would be naive to assume that, together with other publications in which similar issues, the current formula of the chapter may significantly contribute to the more effective emergence out of the "vicious circle" of inability to solve many global problems by countries and societies.

This also applies to the ability to deal with the destructive influences of Russia. It cannot be ignored that many problems are related to conflicts of interest that are difficult to reconcile. Unfortunately, too often they result from more or less important needs, often extremely selfish, sometimes awakened in a slightly strange way. This is a hazardous situation in terms of its far-reaching consequences. It is worth emphasizing that this statement does not only apply to "the great of this world."

In passing, another reflection of a more general nature comes to mind at this point. If the coronavirus pandemic does not "force" to try to change the current ways of thinking[1] and individual and collective behavior in many countries, and neither weakens the tendency to "artificially" stimulate individual and collective needs and fuel demand for "strange" types of services, it will be difficult to expect to reduce the amount of unresolved problems and tensions. It can also be dangerous for the future of civilization, taking into account, for example, the degree of concentration of the modern world with means of mass destruction and the nature of high-risk societies (Beck, 2002; Global Risk Society, 2012).

Due to the above-mentioned conditions, an attempt to answer a few problem questions will have a short, synthetic form. Thus, the article will contain more hypotheses than conclusions based on hard data and their in-depth analysis.

Based on the aforementioned assumptions, for the purposes of this part of the monograph, the following problem questions were formulated:
- What kind of knowledge and what research approaches may be useful in describing, explaining and predicting the processes and phenomena related to the "soft" interaction of entities of international life, including Russia, on Poland?
- Which theoretical models as a kind of "research tools" may be useful for a better understanding of the phenomenon of "soft" influence of Russia on Poland?
- Do these models and their use in scientific research enable the formulation of conclusions useful in teaching and research, but also in the practice of improving relations between states and societies?

Based on the elements of the above-mentioned types and areas of knowledge and the relationships between them, several theoretical models have been developed. Some of these models have already been used in empirical research. For the purposes of this article, they acted as useful "tools" in the analysis of available materials, necessary to obtain answers to the research problems formulated above. Although this subchapter mainly deals with "soft" actions, the "hard" interactions and the third type of interactions which could be placed between the two above-mentioned, were also taken into account – somewhat in the background. The tools thus designed were then used to analyze selected literature items describing the types and methods of 'soft' and 'hard' interactions used by Russia in relation to Poland. The aforementioned third type of interactions, let us

---

[1] It is one of the basic elements of the security culture, the deficit of which was particularly clearly revealed, also in the most developed countries, during the COVID-19 pandemic.

call them "cultural and organizational", appeared in the area of analysis. This was the starting point for the development of a multilayer (spherical) model, marked with the symbol 3x3C.

In all the considerations, the category of relations played an important role. It is worth emphasizing that the author did not only mean bilateral relations between states and societies, in this case Russia and Poland, and the condition (process) of relations between these entities. The analyzes as a whole also focused on the influence of bilateral relations on the way they are perceived by other subjects of international life. The analyzes also took into account an extended classification of various types of interactions and the related conditions of relations and relations between two entities. It is about constructive and / or destructive interactions. And under the "destructive" category, a distinction has been made between aggressive (expansive) and defensive. By making further details of the category of "defensive interactions", they were analyzed through the prism of real or subjective (Frei, 1997) or imaginary threats, and the disproportions existing between them. The latter, that is imaginary ("unreal") threats, should be considered through the prism of their determinants. They can be the result of traumatic historical experiences of a society, causing many dysfunctional distortions of consciousness and the related organizational and practical implications, culturally making them over from generation to generation. Imaginary (unreal) threats can also be caused intentionally for the needs of a "game" played by an entity with its own society, or / and by external entities. These can be state institutions or other organizations in the country or abroad, representing the interests of a lobby, a concern or other significant "player" in the international arena. Taking these details into account in the study of relations, interactions and connections between physical and legal entities in the domestic and international dimension may be useful in examining such problems as are discussed in this article.

In the modern, globalized world, it is even more difficult – as has already been mentioned – to scientifically describe the ways and types of "soft" interactions carried out by these players. It is especially difficult when these interactions are assumed to be destructive. They are then masked and hidden in various ways. Therefore, it may be surprising that some of the ways of such interactions, their models[2], seem to be intentionally exposed by sharing them on social media. This

---

2 Black – coordinated by the intelligence services, which are aimed at: gaining influence agents and instrumentalizing unaware people to achieve Russia's goals, assassination and terrorism, fabricating evidence (false documents, fakes), sham groups to carry out acts of provocation, e.g. the devastation of monuments and memorial sites, quasi-military actions: diversion and covert limited use of violence, inspiring demonstrations and riots, bribing, corrupting and blackmailing politicians, creating fake accounts and bot networks to conduct cyber-attacks, propaganda 2.0 and organized cyber protests. Gray – coordinated by the Kremlin, including:

may give rise to reasonable assumptions that it is a method of "soft" interactions, in its assumption functioning similarly to the "threat" of the owned nuclear potential. In the "scientific discussions" of the late 1980s, this type of argument appeared frequently. Although such and similar examples cannot be 100% treated as "hard" facts testifying to the "soft" interactions carried out by the then USSR, and later by Russia, their intensification in a certain dimension of space-time should lead to asking questions and related hypotheses. The search for answers to such and similar assumptions does not have to end with full and immediate success in the implementation of tasks similar to those undertaken in this article. This does not mean, however, that such attempts and emerging hypotheses should not be continued.

The models presented below may be useful for this purpose, especially those of them, the usefulness of which – as already mentioned – has been demonstrated in empirical studies. Therefore, they can be called theoretical and empirical models. We will come back to them later in the article. In the meantime, let us dwell on the methods of analyzing Russia's influence on Poland. At the beginning, we will try to use the historical perspective to search for facts, processes and phenomena in the area of our interest in the "world of history". Then we will use two types of models. One is strictly theoretical. It is called the "3x3C model" and is presented in Figure 1 on p. 47. The two subsequent models, which are a detail of the first, are theoretical-empirical in nature. Let's start, however, with an attempt to show the possibility of using historical knowledge to better understand the problems we are interested in. In his monumental work (Davies, 2001), the world-wide famous historian N. Davies wrote: In the eyes of many Western observers, the misfortunes caused by Poland's incorporation into the Russian Empire are often essentially institutional in nature. Since the Russian autocracy was in contrast to Polish traditions, it was imagined that a few modifications to the government structure – a few concessions to local autonomy, a few gestures towards democratization – would somehow heal the ailments of Poles. Hence, when Polish uprisings were repeated despite the reforms introduced by the so-called "liberal

---

instrumentalizing and inspiring various social groups, including extreme parties and organizations, activities through the Russian NGO sector and controlled international organizations, instrumentalization of Russian foundations and associations, e.g. Russkij Mir, the Russian Historical Society, establishing pro-Russian portals and their financial support, establishing troll factories and organizing pro-Kremlin networks, carrying out social attacks, trolling. White – Kremlin-coordinated activities, such as: propaganda campaigns carried out through multimedia state news agencies (TV RT, Radio Sputnik, RIA Novosti), undertakings implemented through the branches of Rossodrużestwo, RONIKs (Russian science and culture centers) at the Russian Federation embassies, other executive and legislative bodies (e.g. the Commission for the Defense of the Sovereignty of the Russian Federation at the Federation Council), organizing scientific and cultural events (conferences, exhibitions, memory rallies, scholarships and language courses).

tsars", the opinion of the West tended to lose patience and believe in the Russian stereotype of an ungrateful, incorrect and anarchist Pole. Although a lot of time has passed since that period, many examples from recent years and months may indicate that in Russia's influence on Poland and other developed countries, this method is still used ("Polish anti-Semitism", "blaming Poland for the outbreak of World War II"), Etc.). Fortunately, when perceived by other countries and societies, it often has the opposite effect to the intended result. This can be proved both by the speech of the German President, which clearly contrasts with the statements of W. Putin, and also by the echoes of these statements in the world media. This may indicate that this method of action used by Russia "for centuries" does not bring the expected results, and often has counterproductive effects. Nevertheless, in the statements of many Russian theorists there is a view that they appreciate long-term "soft" interactions. Simplifying their statements, it can be boiled down to the statement that "When throwing mud on someone you have to be patient. Sometime it might stick." Or another example. When "green men" appeared in the vicinity of Lugansk, the Russian president said: "Such uniforms can be bought in any store." Also, other, significantly different words uttered by the representatives of the highest Russian authorities systematically reducing their credibility. When other states and societies begin to distance themselves from Russia, it is publicized by its propaganda mouthpieces as a manifestation of hostile attitudes and intentions by the West towards that country. This is how the aforementioned spiral aggravates and leads to tensions and hazardous behaviours.

But let's get back to the historical facts. Another example, taken from the work of N. Davies, shows the influence of the tsarist authorities on the sphere of Poles' consciousness. The author wrote, Within an autocratic empire of 150 million men, which increasingly had to deal with the suppression of unrest in the very heart of Russian soil, 15 million Poles could not count on finding an obedience to their own interests consisting in the transfer of some powers of the central government to lower-level bodies. Their resistance was to be suppressed not with bullets and whips, but through spiritual restrictions, official ostracism and "inner exile." It was largely a psychological war, not a physical one. The longest confrontations took place not in the tumult of barricades, but in the silence of private human consciences. According to many historians, not only in that period but also long afterwards, the vast majority of Russian society was also subjected to similar influences. Its characteristic sensitivity was successively blunted, and the negative emotions emerging in this society were directed towards the "West", including Poland. They were blamed for "all the failures and misfortunes" of that nation. Every Russian who dared to show sympathy for the Polish language or Polish customs ran the risk of trouble. For example, a certain Colonel Krupski, who after the fall of the January Uprising served as a commandant in a Polish town, was demoted by the military authorities for this very reason. There was an accusation against him that "he publicly spoke Polish and danced a polonaise" (a Polish national dance – translator's footnote). Similar harassments were experienced by part of the Russian administration, stimulated – like many groups of that society – by the "culture of fear". This was one of the important factors that made it not well organized and operated efficiently. To quote N. Davies: If the hellish machine of the Russian government ever worked as intended, the future of Poles, as well as of all other minorities, would undoubtedly appear completely hopeless. (…). Life was bearable thanks to the combination of ineffectiveness in action with the changeability of whim and the remnants of the Christian mindset. Especially at the lower levels, the bureaucracy was deliciously corrupt. According to this historian, the situation under the partitions in other parts of Poland was different. I quote: Of course, the moment finally came when the attempts to incorporate the former Polish provinces into Russia failed gloriously. Political integration did not lead to social assimilation. On the contrary, it resulted in the increasing polarization of society. Unlike the situation before 1871 in Austria or Prussia, where a good citizen could reconcile his own Polish patriotism with loyalty to the Habsburgs or Hohenzollerns, in Russia people were forced to choose between conflicting loyalties. It cannot be ruled out that the Russian administration's "zero-one" way of thinking contributed to such behavior. It would be hard to say that it passed into the "annals of history". The above reflection is a good transition to further considerations, taking into account the psychosocial, cultural and praxeological aspects of the analyzed issues. For this purpose, knowledge in the field of security sciences will also be used, especially in one of its sub-disciplines, which is security culture.

Even a cursory analysis of the various types of interactions used by Russia in relation to Poland allows us to notice that although various types and forms of activity were undertaken (Ильясов, 2016), it would be difficult to clearly divide them into "soft" and "hard". Both in theory and in practice, these are more and more often "combined" activities[3], used mainly for destructive purposes. This attention can be related not only to Russia's relations with Poland. This general

---

[3] It seems that not only in theory can they be treated as a preliminary phase to the activities known as hybrid wars. They include: propaganda influencing various target audiences in the country of the aggressor and the countries under attack, creating and inspiring separatist and collaborative groups in the countries being the target of aggression, initiating riots and mass protest actions, subversive and terrorist operations carried out jointly by the aggressor and insurgents, covert support for separatists – with weapons, intelligence, financial resources, as well as activities of irregular formations, actions aimed at destabilizing and weakening the economy of the attacked country, diplomatic and information support for ongoing special projects (Ильясов, 2016).

reflection, also based on historical experience, was an inspiration for the development of the theoretical model, marked with the symbol 3x3C.

We treat the presented model as a system of action (Crozier and Friedberg, 1982). It consists of several basic and several detailed elements. The basic elements of this system are: 1. physical and legal entities, with their approaches, attitudes, behaviors, actions and interactions; 2. three spheres of the broadly understood culture (A /, B / and C /) in which physical and legal entities are "immersed"; this in turn influences their attitudes, behavior, actions and cooperation, and even approaches; 3. environment (closer and further), with other entities inside, 4. internal and external relations.

Sphere A / corresponds to the mental, conscious and spiritual culture. It is at this level that the "soft" impacts from other entities, in this case Russia, are most often targeted. It is done by vectors visible in the upper part of the drawing. The ways of perception and reception of the environment by physical and legal entities on both sides play then an important role. It shapes and perpetuates attitudes and perpetuates or weakens stereotypes.

The second pair of vectors shown in the lower part of the figure are directed towards the third sphere, marked with the symbol C /, that is, material culture. For centuries, Russia has used the "carrot and stick" method in this area. This concerned not only other state entities or conquered and "subdued" societies, but also Russian society. Experience shows that this was often counterproductive. For example – "turning off the tap" of gas supplied from Russia to Poland led Poland to look for another supplier. Meanwhile, Russia's freezing the supply of spare parts for military equipment initially resulted in a very dangerous phenomenon of "technical cannibalism", that is, parts were moved from one piece of equipment to another. Later, a new supplier was contracted not only for spare parts, but also for new types of equipment, including military one. In such a situation, Russia took a "soft" influence, which aggravated the already tense relations between the two countries and societies. As part of the "soft" influence, not only was Poland blamed for it, but traditionally "the West". In this way, self-reinforcing "vicious circles" of tense relations and relations between Russia and the "West", including Poland, were created.

Both historical experience and current observations indicate the need to include in the analyzes of bilateral relations between states, also the case of Russia and Poland, one more sphere of influence – organizational or rather disorganizational. It is marked with the symbol B /. As the two previous spheres (A / and C /) were analyzed in the cultural convention, in the B / sphere we will focus our attention on organizational culture. It is worth noting here that these three spheres in total, as elements of the action system, constitute the phenomenon of security culture. The research conducted so far shows that organizational culture (element B /) systematically connects the other two spheres, i.e. A / and C /. The degree of this coherence is directly proportional to the level of organizational culture and the quality of its "bloodstream", i. e. the level of information culture and information security culture, as well as the legal culture. They are "rooted" in the organizational culture, and by penetrating and connecting systemically all three spheres of the operating system, they serve its coherence and effectiveness, including defense. Perhaps the awareness of this fact means that destructive actions undertaken by various entities are increasingly directed towards zone B /. The tools of these destructive attacks are various forms of informational interactions targeted directly to this zone or through the A / zone[4].

Analyzing the model presented in the dynamics as a "system of action", it can be noticed that the destructiveness of information interactions may spread to the entire system, causing many dysfunctional effects in particular spheres. In the A sphere, it may be the disorientation of the society, caused not only by a low level of information culture and susceptibility to fake news, but also a deficit of knowledge and wisdom and other values important in the 21st century. In the B / sphere, it may result in a low level of legal culture of citizens and the dysfunction of legal provisions as well as reduced efficiency of the functioning of organizational structures. And in the B / sphere, it may hinder the creation and use of modern technologies and civilization backwardness. Then, it can be observed reduced efficiency, effectiveness, economy and operating ability of physical and legal entities, and as a result – difficulties in achieving the synergy effect. Theoretically, it can be assumed that combined destructive activities, directed simultaneously at all three spheres of the "system", may, after some time, lead to its structural decomposition. This remark may refer to a single physical or legal entity, but also to a community or alliance, such as the EU or NATO.

At this point, let us emphasize once again that organizational culture (in the B sphere) performs an integrating and regulating function in relation to the other two spheres (A / and C /). Maintaining a relative balance (harmony) between these three spheres of the broadly understood culture favors the development of entities, including sustainable development. The experience of recent years shows that "corrective" impacts in individual countries do not bring the expected results when they are directed only at the A / sphere. The matter becomes even more difficult when destructive influences appear in this area, which un-

---

4 According to many analysts in Russia, there is a real subordination of the largest media to the state, but above all it was created an extensive disinformation and propaganda machine in order to be used consistently and skillfully to achieve political goals. This happens not only to the Russian society, but also to the external environment. These are also not ad hoc and improvised actions, but complementary undertakings in other dimensions and part of Russia's general strategy, in accordance with the assumption that victory in the information confrontation will translate into the implementation of strategic and political goals (Giles, 2016, pp. 17–21).

fortunately is not an abstract threat. Without significant progress in this area, our civilization is not "doomed" to survive.

As already mentioned, the term "security culture" appeared in scientific publications after the tragic Chernobyl disaster. After a dozen of years, it has been largely covered with "dust of oblivion", but the experiences related to the COVID-19 pandemic will probably contribute to its "dusting" and development. Let us recall some models of security culture at this point. They have not only theoretical and heuristic value, but also empirical and practically useful. The point is that in nationwide empirical research, the research tools developed on the basis of these models and the empirical data collected because of them made it possible to establish the relationship between the level of citizens' safety culture and the quality of the crisis management system functioning in the local dimension. And the knowledge in this field used in the didactic process brought tangible results among students. The research conducted so far shows that the best results can be achieved by starting work with children at a younger school age. Taking into account the limited framework of this subchapter, the following sections will only outline two models of safety culture: ideal and extremely dysfunctional. The mainstream of life runs somewhere between them.

The "axis" of this wheel is the value system, and its "bearing" internalized by the subject of the norm, that is – to simplify – the ways of achieving values. Such a shape of the safety culture model favors the approach of entities and their mutual support, thanks to which the synergy effect[5] is obtained. It is also supported by an appropriate level of information and communication culture of entities. The information and communication culture also serve as a 'vaccine' against the 'post-truth virus', which is also used by Russia in its fights and information wars. As experts claim, the current countermeasures in this area are not effective[6],

---

5 It is worth remembering that "soft" destructive interactions aim at, inter alia, hindering the achievement of this effect by slowing down the development of the attacked entities, knowing that development is a condition for their security in a strategic dimension.
6 "(…) Unfortunately these are reactionary and secondary actions, and often ineffective. The pattern is that Russia dictates its actions to us, it can steer the flow of information, and we only respond. It is largely a Sisyphean job. Above all, we need new measures that will have a positive impact on society and build its resilience. The concept of social resilience first appeared at NATO level, but it is also used nowadays at the European Union level. Unfortunately, this has not yet been included in any strategies at the national level. Meanwhile, building social resilience is a process that is spread over the years and should be systemic in nature. Of course, media education and awareness-raising are needed, but that is not enough. It is also about digital education. New generations obtain information completely differently." (…) "What the European Commission does before the elections to the European Parliament confirms that these are reactionary solutions, not strategic ones. This action was taken too late. Disinformation campaigns were planned much earlier, so some attitudes are already formed. Information bombs a few days before the elections can only strengthen certain messages, but will not consolidate them as well as long-term actions. It could take years. Unfortunately, these

which is largely affected by the differences between the nature of the website security culture.

What is the security culture[7], and the information and communication culture in it, one can see particularly clearly during the COVID-19 pandemic. Its importance, not only in functional but also moral terms, will be easier to analyze "coldly" in retrospect, as "facke nevsy" appearing in this difficult period for everyone.

The considerations so far and their effects allow – according to the author – to provide a generally positive answer to the problem questions posed at the beginning. The article attempts to show that the current state of knowledge in various scientific disciplines and the transdisciplinary way of using it allow the development of theoretical and empirical models. They can be used to describe, explain and predict various types of Russian influence on Poland, but also on other countries of the Community or the Alliance.

The knowledge obtained in this way may be useful in didactic practice and in further empirical research. This also applies to historical knowledge. The article uses as an example the historical facts provided by N. Davies, which were then interpreted through the prism of knowledge in the field of security culture. It made it possible to notice, inter alia, that the accounts of a well-known historian, showing the "zero-one" way of thinking and acting in the Russian administration at the end of the 19th century, did not completely pass into the "annals of history". This is confirmed by many examples from various spheres of life and security of people in this country, but also by the analysis of the relations between former and modern Russia and other countries and societies, including Poland.

This fact can be interpreted in various ways. It may be perceived by some entities as an "opportunity", related to, for example, the reduced effectiveness of

---

reactionary and delayed actions are politically very convenient, because they show that something is being done. Meanwhile, these are mainly appearances of action. The cooperation with large Internet platforms is ineffective, mainly because it is voluntary. It should be remembered that Facebook, Twitter or Google are commercial entities that earn from the exchange of information. They are reluctant to share anti-disinformation data, as these platforms are mainly used today to disseminate disinformation to third parties. We must realize that we need to act in the long term here and create information resilience in society, regardless of the source. After all, in different countries different entities use the same methods as Russia. However, this requires political will" (Information warfare fronts in Poland: who and how wants to influence us, M. Kowalska's interview for Forsal.pl on 5 May 2019).

7 In the simplest sense, "security culture is understood as a universal type of psychosocial and praxeological competence. Sometimes it is assumed that it is a system ("package") of competences, useful to natural and legal entities in various situations, especially in crisis situations. This "package" consists of: a / knowledge and way of thinking about security, b / way of feeling security and threats, c / way / ways of reacting to objectively or subjectively emerging threats or perceived security deficit, d / with a view of own or other entities security, e / in the closer and further dimension of space-time".

Russia's destructive influence on other states and societies. However, on the other hand, this situation can be interpreted as a threat. Because in a strategic perspective, for example in the implementation/completion of the historic mission of "colonizing space" by Homo Sapiens, it may be treated as a dysfunctional factor, making it difficult for potential partners to cooperate constructively in the completion of this mission. The peculiar bridges of cooperation with Russia in this area, which had been built for decades, despite the destructive forms of competition on other grounds, carried out then and nowadays, have not been completely broken. There is also hope. However, the line between hope and naivety can be very thin.

Perhaps at this point it is worth sharing one more reflection resulting from the importance of the culture of security[8] in the lives of states and nations, and in building relations among them. The security culture of Polish and German societies differed significantly in the past (Malinowski, 2003), and they probably differ today, though to a lesser extent. Nevertheless, the ability of both societies to "leave the luggage aside" of difficult historical experiences brings many useful achievements, not only in the bilateral dimension. Therefore, it can be assumed that, despite temporary "turbulences", the current level of security culture and the laboriously built relations between the two countries and societies within the EU may be a good prognosis for the future.

There are many examples showing that the persistent removal by states and societies the conscious "luggage" of various tragic events, including those from the period of wars and partitions, as well as parallel cooperation on visible levels, can bring many positive effects over time. Although the national egoisms which had been consolidating over the centuries in the world did not favor so far the wider dissemination of thinking in terms of the common good, in the third decade of the twenty-first century they facing a "fire test" of the COVID-19 pandemic. There are many examples that in such a situation the importance of the security culture of physical and legal entities is difficult to overestimate, as are the timeless messages of the Rome Club Reports. Although the memory of these Reports has been somewhat covered with the "dust of oblivion" in the globalized and "busy" (Tokarczuk, 2019) world of the 21st century, their practical significance can be more easily perceived when the content of these Reports is analyzed through the prism of the models presented in this part of the monograph. Then it is also easier to notice that the devastating "zero-sum games" conducted by some countries were not and are not rare. It can be optimistic saying that their scope is likely to change with the disappearance of the coronavirus. Time will tell if this will be a sustained trend, as will the expansion of

---

8 Let us remind you that the term "security culture" appeared in scientific publications after the Chernobyl disaster, tragic in its far-reaching consequences also for many European societies.

thinking in terms of the common good or a return to the "good old days" before the pandemic.

According to the author, the phenomenon of security culture hides the potential of hitherto unused practical possibilities. However, it cannot be ruled out that this type of knowledge inspired some theorists in Russia to create models of destructive interactions, which may be indicated by the analysis of the content previously cited in the footnotes of the publication. It can be optimistically assumed that the process of improving the culture of security of citizens in various countries, undertaken in the coming years, will contribute to a civilization turning point (Sadłowska-Wrzesińska, 2018), without which it would be difficult to think optimistically about the future of our civilization. This remark also applies, and perhaps above all, to the importance of an information security culture. It can become an effective "vaccine" against the "post-truth virus" used so far most often for destructive purposes, also within the so-called Russia's "soft" influence on Poland and other countries in the world. Many examples from Europe and overseas show that we are not dealing with this problem yet.

Taking into account the foregoing teaching and research experience, it seems legitimate to say that the security culture of citizens can be diagnosed and improved. Particularly good results in this respect are achieved when this process begins at an earlier school age, and the organization of education at all levels takes into account the assumptions of the Montesori theory (Łukaniuk-Quintanilla, 1998).

References

(2012) *Społeczeństwo światowego ryzyka*, Warszawa.
Beck U., (2002). *Społeczeństwo ryzyka. W drodze do innej nowoczesności*, Warszawa.
Crozier M., Friedberg E., (1982) *Człowiek i system. Ograniczenia działania zbiorowego*, Warszawa.
Darczewska J., (2018). Środki aktywne jako rosyjska agresja hybrydowa w retrospekcji. Wybrane problemy, in: *Przegląd bezpieczeństwa wewnętrznego*, 18.
Davies N. (2001), *Boże igrzysko*, Kraków.
Frei D., (1997) *Sichercheit. Grundfragen der Weltpolityk*. Stuttgart: Verlag W.Kohlhamer.
Fronty wojny informacyjnej w Polsce: kto i jak chce na nas wpływać, wywiad M.Kowalskiej dla Forsal.pl 5.05.2019.
Giles K., (2016) *Handbook of Russian information warfare*, Rome.
Kux D., (1985). *Soviet Active Measures and Disinformation: Overview and Assessment*, "Parameters, Journal of the US Army War College".
Łukaniuk-Quintanilla A., (1998) *Szkoła Marii Montessori – historia i współczesność*. Oficyna Wydawnicza ESPERO.

Malinowski K., 2003 (eds.). *Kultura bezpieczeństwa narodowego w Polsce i w Niemczech*, Poznań.

Sadłowska-Wrzesińska S., (2018) *Kultura bezpieczeństwa pracy. Rozwój w warunkach przesilenia cywilizacyjnego*, Warszawa.

Tokarczuk O., (2019) *Bieguni*, Warszawa.

Абрамс С., *Больше, чем пропаганда: активные советские мероприятия в путинской России*, http://connections-qj.org/ru/article/bolshe-chem-propaganda-aktivnye-sovet skiemeropriyatiya-v putinskoy-rossii.

Ильясов Ф.Н., (2016) *Словарь социальных исследований*, http://www.jsr.su/dic/dictiona ry.html.

Marcin Górnikiewicz / Tadeusz Szczurek / Marzena Walkowiak

Chapter 6: Summary and conclusions: The perspective of soft and hard impact on the Polish decision-making process in the third decade of the 21st century

In 2020, the tough potential of the Kremlin's influence to be used against Poland, shrunk to para-military, mainly propaganda-related. Contrary to appearances, this influence could turn out to be quite effective, especially in combination with a parallel and multidimensional information operation aimed at causing targeted or chaotic mass social phenomena.

Due to the increasingly limited ability to use energy and political mechanisms, the Kremlin could use those mechanisms that it has been carefully developing for several decades, i.e. the so-called "social control" combined with classic intelligence activities based on the use of resources such as spy network and its influence located in political and journalistic circles. Parallel operations of a para-military nature could be carried out, the appropriate publicity of which would be guaranteed by the information mechanisms launched in the meantime. The aim would be to induce a social attitude that could influence the decisions made by political decision-makers who would be additionally motivated by the spy network operating in their direct or indirect information space.

An example of such activities was the information operation conducted around the so-called The "Suwałki Gap", reinforced with military exercises on a very wide scale, then compared to the largest maneuvers from the USSR period. The necessity to incur enormous costs just to show the scale of its own military potential seemed unjustified, unless there were real preparations for an armed operation with the use of unidentified troops, as was the case with Ukraine. Russia would therefore be able to carry out such activities in the future, which could possibly be supported by subversive and sabotage operations aimed, to some extent, at authenticating the parallel media messages and causing social phenomena influencing the decision-making process. However, in the current situation activated by the coronavirus pandemic, it is not expected to open new areas of costly para-military and information operations, also due to the need to maintain the activities already underway in the east of Ukraine and the Middle East.

Section III:
The scope of Moscow's informative impact on the Polish decision-making process

Katarzyna Świerszcz

Chapter 7: Qualitative measurement of the level of operability of Russia's policy towards Poland

It is difficult to undertake an attempt to analyze and evaluate the effectiveness of the impact of Russian policy towards the Polish state in the dimension of information warfare used by Russia in various aspects of our country's life without understanding the essence of Russian thinking about its own state as a superpower. The geographic location of the Russian state and its surroundings, which determine the manner of shaping and making real political processes as well as the related goals and interests of that state together with the deliberate influence and attempts to shape the policy of neighboring countries. This is confirmed by the meaningful words of A. Durgin, who said: "If Russia is not great, it will not be at all. Greatness – our great-Russian vocation. If not – let there be nothing better. Without Russia, the history of the world is unimaginable. Better let the world end" (https://geopolityka.net). The tool and way for implementing Russian ambitions is nowadays, in the age of information and computerization, in the age of cyberspace, not so much a military war as, above all, a non-invasive war, such as information warfare, and more specifically disinformation. It supports Russian activities both in the offensive and defensive dimensions, aimed at the internal and external environment of the state and other countries. This war is particularly evident in the Russian attempt to influence on various levels of social, political, economic, cultural, energy resources and many other fields in relation to European countries, and in particular to the Polish state, thus posing a threat to its national security.

The analysis of the studies of the literature of experts and practitioners dealing – both from the theoretical and practical side – with the development of strategies for effective influence within the framework of non-military combat activities, highlights the special role of information warfare in it. For example, the Russian strategist Col. E. Messner believes that the most important element of this struggle is the unification of his own nation, while gaining supporters among the society of the enemy nation and the internal destruction that is applied to it. By talking about the ways of achieving this goal, the Russian strategist shows the important role that information warfare plays in this task. Well, it is, according to him, the so-called psychological processing at all levels of social strata. One of its many elements is undermining the trust and respect for the state authorities of your country, undermining faith in its strength and defense. This is achieved by activities consisting in proper intelligence reconnaissance, focused both on political topics, which include surveillance of political circles and recognition of social moods, as well as on economic and military issues. The detailed identification of the critical infrastructure is also important, which includes: the state's ICT systems, transport system, energy supply system, energy resources and fuels, food and water supply systems, health care system and many others relevant for the proper functioning of the state and society in it. The role of information warfare, therefore, comes down to developing subversive activities and sabotage (Месснер, 2005, p. 211; Hoskins, 2018, p. 255; Blank, 2013, pp. 31–44).

Its effectiveness is due to the fact that it is based on a network structure that is not formally related to any social groups and organizations. The basis of its operation is the strategy of unguided resistance, i.e. resistance without the main center of management. Groups (circles) involved consciously and / or unconsciously, such as: secondary politicians, radical political and social groups, national and ethnic minorities, various non-governmental organizations, trade unions, entrepreneurs and their associations, industry organizations, discriminated social groups, or finally charity groups – they have autonomy of action. These actions undertaken by the circles are aimed at creating, in the national and international perception, the impression of chaos and the lack of control of its sources (Месснер, 2005, p. 225; Tomasiewicz, 2009, p. 169; Razuvaev, 2007, pp. 78) -88; Herd, 2000, pp. 64–72). This concept of an action strategy used by Russia assumes a dispersed attack, which is undertaken simultaneously on many levels of the organization of social and political life of a given state as an opponent. Moreover, this strategy ignores the established and binding legal order: both national and international, and therefore operates in an asymmetric manner. It should be emphasized that the actions that Russia directs towards achieving specific political, military and economic results, are extremely difficult to detect. This difficulty is due to the fact that the planned events are not linked to the main Russian strategic goal, and to prove Russia to be their inspirer. The methods of information warfare developed today and still being improved have enabled Russia to change its sophisticated policy into a kind of constantly changing and complex theater of operations. This is confirmed by the fact that the Russian government has skillfully sponsored various and even opposing circles, i.e. from extreme right to extreme left; from extremely nationalist to extremely liberal already (Sykulski, 2018, p. 45; Wilk 2017; Świerszcz, 2019a, p. 286). The purpose of this procedure is to create a political game mechanism that facilitates the camouflage of actions and disinformation. It takes a special form of narrative, i.e. a subjective world-view interpretation, occurring depending on the need, in various suitably coordinated configurations, which is addressed to specific environments, both domestic and foreign. These narratives serve to build in the minds of their recipients a specific message that is in line with Russia's political and economic goals.

Let us therefore take a look at some of the activities of the Russian information war directed against Poland in the last days of the 21st century. Their main content is primarily to build a message about the destabilization of the Polish state and its isolation on the international arena. An expression of the narrative created in this way is, for example, creating a negative image of Poland and its society, especially towards the state of Russia as a Russo phobic country – in the minds of the Polish, Russian and other external countries. Meanwhile, as shown by independent studies by two opinion-forming institutes: CBOS (Center for Public Opinion Research) and IBRiS (Institute for Market and Social Research), the attitude of Polish society towards Russia is becoming more and more positive each year (in 2015 – it amounted to 22%; in 2016 – it was 20%; in 2017 – it was 31%) (Attitude towards other nations. Research communiqué, 2017; Azhar, 2015; Świerszcz 2019b, pp. 528–550), despite existing concerns about the security threat from Russia. Thus, the Russian narrative about the Russophobia of Polish society is not confirmed in Polish reality. Another telling example of Russia's influence on Poland through the use of sophisticated information warfare is building a sense of threat to Russia and its society from Poland and its allies; building a sense of threat to Poland itself and its society; and finally inspiring and maintaining antagonisms between Poland and its neighbors and allies, which in turn lead to conflicts and, in consequence, to its isolation on the international arena (Kowalska, 2017; Górnikiewicz, 2018, p. 119). An example of Russia's influence on Poland was the appropriately applied Russian narrative to the decision of the Polish Sejm taken in June 2017 to amend the law prohibiting the promotion of communism or any other system in the Polish state. This amendment declared the removal of monuments of the Soviet soldiers, located outside cemeteries and other places of rest and signs not being monuments but treated as symbols of the communist system in Poland. This decision – as could be expected – met with a great opposition from Russia, which, wishing to take advantage of the convenient situation to pursue its own interests in Poland, immediately launched an anti-Polish information campaign. Its main content was to show Poland as a country that was destroying monuments and cemeteries of the Soviet soldiers who were its liberators; as a Nazi and totalitarian country; rewriting the history of World War II, undermining the participation of the Red Army soldiers in the liberation of its territory from fascism during World War II; and finally as a country where the public does not support the actions of the Polish authorities regarding the introduction of legal changes (Комментарий Департамента информации). It should be noted that the proclaimed Russian disinformation warfare, both

Russian media and propaganda centers were involved, as well as the Russian Ministry of Foreign Affairs and its diplomatic missions around the world, the Ministry of National Defense and social networking sites. In order to strengthen the propaganda and disinformation message, various types of scientific and cultural events have been rganized in Poland and in Russia, duplicating and strengthening official messages. The main goal of these activities is to create a negative image of Poland in the Russian society and in the international environment, as well as to create pressure from international public opinion against Poland, and consequently to influence the decision of the Polish authorities on the above issue (Mironow, no date; Польша объявила войну советским, no date).

The strengthening of Russia's attempts to influence Poland through the use of information warfare (disinformation) is also Russia's suggestion of Poland's co-responsibility for the beginning of World War II. This campaign is particularly active every year: in August – on the anniversary of the Molotov-Ribbentrop Pact, in September – on the anniversary of Nazi Germany's attack on Poland, on September 1, 1939, at the outbreak of World War II, and on September 17, 1939 at the Soviet Union's aggression against Poland. The sophisticated narrative used by Russia shows Poland as a member in an alliance with Hitler, preparing an attack on the Soviet Union. Moreover, in this disinformation, Russia presents itself as a victim of history which Poland, according to Russian manipulations, wants to blame for historical events – reduces the role of the Soviet Union in the events of World War II and cultivates the myth of the great patriotic war started in 1941. Thus, it is trying to effectively its own interpretation of the history of those times and minimize awareness and reliable knowledge about it among the Russian society. The purpose of the information campaign (disinformation) used by Russia in such a way is primarily to build a negative image of Poland both in the Russian community and in the international community. It is also undermining the position of the Polish state in the international arena; suggesting deeply entrenched sympathies of Poles towards Nazi Germany; creating an image of Nazism, allegedly reviving in Poland. This narrative fits in the broader context of the historical policy of contemporary Russia, the main goal of which is to impose on the external audience a Russian false interpretation of history (Wóycicki, Kowalska and Lelonek, 2017, p. 12; Czajko a, Откуда растут ноги; Szyłkowska, 2019, p. 71).

Another example of an attempt of Russia's influence through information warfare against Poland is the message presenting our country and its society in terms of a nationalist, chauvinist state that promotes racism, fascism and Nazism. This negative narrative is used by Russia especially in the context of the refugee crisis in the European Union and Ukrainian immigration to Poland in large numbers, for economic purposes and the desire to study Ukrainian youth at

Polish universities. The main goal of this narrative is to build a negative image of Poland as a country with a negative attitude towards the community of other countries and a threat to them. At the same time, this narrative is intended to cause conflicts on both social and political grounds between Poland and other European Union countries, as well as Ukraine (Trukhanchyev; Kwasniewski; Hryhorova; Czajko b).

When talking about an attempt of the influence of Russia's policy on the Polish state by the negative shaping the image of Poland in the arena of international relations, including relations with its closest neighbour, Ukraine, one more important fact should be noted. Well, reinforcing this negative propaganda and disinformation narrative waged by Russia in the information warfare against Poland is the spreading of false information about Poland's alleged territorial claims against Ukraine. Such an attitude of Russia should not surprise us, if only because Poland has long supported Ukrainian aspirations and its ambitions to be a member of the European Union community, which is inconvenient for Russia's policy and contrary to its interests (Ryabov; Bodakowski; Wojnarowska-Szpucha, 2018, p. 82; Paulukiewicz). Therefore, with this in mind, Russia by applying information warfare against Poland is also trying to influence it in terms of its relations with the European Union. To this end, it tries to weaken the existing structures of the EU community by supporting anti-EU communication in the Polish media; using ideological and even religious issues to build negative messages about the activities of the European Parliament; emphasizing the moral and civilization decline of Western countries; using the narrative about post-colonization and the abuse of Poland by rich Western countries, as well as the immigration and refugees from Africa and the Middle East that threaten Poland because of the open borders of the European Union (This is not immigration, it is colonization of Europe; Wóycicki, Kowalska and Lelonek, 2017, p. 12; Ojala, 2016, pp. 297–313; Bebber, 2017, pp. 394–403; Świerszcz 2020).

Another significant factor is Russia's attempt to influence Poland in terms of shaping its relations with NATO. Russia is particularly opposed to the stationing of NATO troops in Poland, their constantly growing number of bases on our territory, as well as the developing cooperation between Poland and the USA in the field of modernization of military equipment, such as the purchase of 32 American fifth-generation F-35 Lightning II fighters. Russia describes these actions in its disinformation message as an offensive plan by NATO, including Poland and the United States, addressed to Russia, which directly threatens its security. On this basis, Russia considers its undertakings to conduct a confrontational policy towards the West and towards Poland justified. Their expression is the constant confrontation already made in the dimension of information warfare (the Russians are expanding their military bases; Ishchenko; Mitkow, 2018, p. 114).

The energy sector is also a critical area of Russia's attempt to influence Poland. Russian activities conducted in this area are aimed at destabilizing the decision-making processes undertaken by Poland, as well as preventing its effective implementation. The potential goal of Russian actions in the information warfare in this area are three projects that are important for Poland's energy security. These are: the construction of offshore wind farms in the southern part of the Baltic Sea under the "Baltica" project, the construction of the first nuclear power plant in the north of Poland and the implementation of the Baltic Pipe gas pipeline. Russia's destructive actions may include not only the physical destruction or failure of these facilities, but also the use of political measures on the international arena to prevent or block the implementation, or delay planned and already partially completed investments. One of them is, for example, a Polish investment concerning the establishment of a new strategic gas supply corridor on the European market. The Baltic Pipe plays a special role here, as it is to strengthen the diversification of supplies and integrate the markets in the Central European region. The investment involves the construction of a gas pipeline at the bottom of the Baltic Sea, which in 2022 will allow the transmission of gas directly to Poland and Denmark from the deposits of the Norwegian Continental Shelf. It should be emphasized that the Baltic Pipe capacity is to be 9–10 billion cubic metres per year. This fact creates a great opportunity for Poland to be independent of the current supplies from the east, particularly when this project has received both political and financial support from the European Union. At this point it should also be noted that the upcoming termination of the Yamal contract prompts Poland to undertake new strategic activities. They are expressed in the need to build new relations with other countries, enabling a more favorable purchase of blue fuel after 2022. According to the Polskie Górnictwo Naftowe i Gazownictwo (PGNiG SA) Report, it is also planned to expand a cooperation with existing LNG (liquefied natural gas) suppliers and contract with new partners from North America, Australia and Africa (Annual Report, 2019). There is also the cooperation under the Three Seas Initiative, concerning the idea of the so-called Brama Północna (the Northern Gate), which assumes the integration of the Norwegian corridor with the Danish transport infrastructure and the Baltic Pipe gas pipeline to Poland, the increase of the regasification capacity of the Świnoujście terminal to 7.5 billion m3 with an additional possibility of increasing its capacity by another 2.5 billion m3 after 2020, and also the construction of a floating terminal in Gdańsk Bay (Nowak, 2019, p. 313; Świerszcz, 2019c, p. 904). These and many other measures taken by the Polish government to become independent of Russia's energy supplies, and thus to strengthen the country's energy security, are the field of systematic Russian actions trying to destabilize the above plans. An expression of destabilizing actions is, for example, the construction by Russia of the third and fourth lines to the existing Nord Stream gas pipeline connecting Russia and Germany since 2012, along the bottom of the Baltic Sea, with a total capacity of 55 billion m3, which intentionally omits Poland and Ukraine. These activities are a significant blow to European solidarity and prevent the implementation of the vision of the international North-South gas corridor. For Poland and other Baltic states, the Russian implementation of Nord Stream 2 is a long-range and destructive activity (Mogla; Nowak, 2019, p. 313; May, 2018).

References

(2017) Stosunek do innych narodów. Komunikat z badań nr 21/2017, Centrum Badania Opinii Społecznej, in: http://www.cbos.pl/SPISKOM.POL/2017/K_021_17.PDF, dostęp: 16.03.2020.

(2019) Raport Roczny 2019, Warszawa: Polskie Górnictwo Naftowe i Gazownictwo SA.

Azhar U. and Shaheen G., (2015). "Brandishing the Cybered Bear: Information War and the Russia-Ukraine Conflict", Military Cyber Affairs, Vol. 1, Iss. 1, Article 7. DOI: http://dx.doi.org/10.5038/2378-0789.1.1.1001.

Bebber R.J., (2017). "Treating Information as a Strategic Resource to Win the 'Information War'", Orbis, vol. 61, no 3, pp. 394–403. DOI: 10.1016/j.orbis.2017.05.007.

Blank S., (2013). Russian Information Warfare as Domestic Counterinsurgency, American Foreign Policy Interests, 35:1, pp. 31–44, DOI: 10.1080/10803920.2013.757946.

Bodakowski J., Panika na Ukrainie: Nie jest wykluczone, że Polska będzie chciała zająć Lwów. Czy zgadniecie, co ich tak przeraziło?, in: Wolnosc24.pl, http://wolnosc24.pl/2017/07/11/panika-na-ukrainie-nie-jest-wykluczone-ze-polska-bedzie-chciala-zajac-lwow-czy-zgadniecie-co-ich-takprzerazilo/http:/wolnosc24.pl/2017/07/11/panika-na-ukrainie-nie-jest-wykluczone-ze-polska-bedzie-chciala-zajac-lwow-czy-zgadniecie-co-ich-tak-przera-zilo/, dostęp: 18.03.2020.

Czajko I.a, Dlaczego Polacy nie chcą przyjmować migrantów?, Sputnik Polska, https://pl.sputniknews.com/opinie/201706235732890-sputnik-polska-ukraina-migracja/; dostęp: 18.03.2020.

Czajko I.b, Władze Polski nie chcą zauważać zagrożenia ze strony ukraińskich neobanderowców, Sputnik Polska, https://pl.sputniknews.com/opinie/201703295142815-sputnik-polska-irina-czajko-ukraina-neobanderyzm/, dostęp: 18.03.2020.

Górnikiewicz M., (2018). Prognozowanie kulturowe zagrożeń bezpieczeństwa narodowego i międzynarodowego, Warszawa: WAT.

Herd G.P., (2000). The "counter-terrorist operation" in Chechnya: "Information warfare" aspects, The Journal of Slavic Military Studies, 13:4, pp. 64–72, DOI: 10.1080/13518040008430460.

Hoskins A. and Shchelin P., (2018). Information war in the Russian media ecology: the case of the Panama Papers, Continuum, 32:2, p. 255, DOI: 10.1080/10304312.2017.1418295.

Hryhorova D., Польша ставит на национализм, Vesti.ru, https://www.vesti.ru/doc.html?id=2930661, dostęp: 18.03.2020.

https://geopolityka.net/jan-majka-duginiada-cz-3/, dostęp: 15.03.2020.

Ishchenko S., Дивизия США уже рассматривает Калининград в прицелы, Svpressa.ru, https://svpressa.ru/war21/article/183432/, dostęp: 20.03.2020.

Kowalska M. and Lelonek A., (2017). FORECAST: Primary goals of Russian propaganda in Poland for 2017, Center for Propaganda and Disinformation Analysis Foun- dation, https://capd.pl/en/forecasts/177-forecast-primary-goals-of-russian-propaganda-in-po land-for-2017, dostęp: 16.03.2020.

Kwaśniewski A., Czy opozycja w Polsce to faszyzująco – ksenofobiczna banda, Sputnik Polska, https://pl.sputniknews.com/blogs/201707315990172-sputnik-blog-czy-opozycj a-w-polsce-to-faszyzujaco-ksenofobiczna-banda/.

Maj J., (2018) Nowe aspekty sztuki wojennej XXI wieku, Poznań: FNCE.

Mironow W., Сейм за снос: польский парламент проголосовал за уничтожение советских памятников, RT, w: https://russian.rt.com/world/article/402333-polskii-pa rlament-snos, dostęp: 16.03.2020.

Mitkow, S., (2018). Proces identyfikowalności a bezpieczeństwo wyrobów obronnych w łańcuchu dostaw, Gospodarka Materiałowa & Logistyka 11.

Molga T., Trump sprzeda Polsce najdroższy gaz w historii. I będziemy zadowoleni, bo wstajemy z kolan i zrobimy na złość Rosji, http://natemat.pl/211863,trump-opchnie-pol sce-najdrozszy-gaz-w-historii-i-jeszcze-bedziemy-zadowoleni, dostęp: 18.03.2020.

Nowak T., (2019). Czynniki energetyczne w wojnie hybrydowej na Ukrainie – wyzwania dla Polski, in: Perspektywy zagrożeń dla bezpieczeństwa międzynarodowego kreowanych przez Federację Rosyjską, eds. Banasik M. and Rogozińska A., Warszawa: Difin.

Ojala M., Pantti M., (2016). Jarkko Kangas, "Professional Role Enactment Amidst In- formation WarfareWar correspondents tweeting on the Ukraine conflict", Journalism Vol. 19, issue: 3, pp. 297–313.

Paulukiewicz A., Imigranci z Ukrainy. To zagrożenie dla bezpieczeństwa Polski!, Wol- nosc24.pl, http://wolnosc24.pl/2017/04/07/imigranci-z-ukrainy-to-zagrozenie-dla-bez pieczenstwa-polski-ostrzega-autor-portalu-kresy-czy-podzielacie-te-obawy-nasza-son da/, dostęp: 18.03.2020.

Razuvaev V.E., (2007). Legal Issues Involved in Fighting Spam as a Means of Waging an Information War, Russian Politics & Law, 45:2, pp. 78–88, DOI: 10.2753/RUP1061-1940450207.

Rosjanie rozbudowują bazy wojskowe w Kaliningradzie. "Robią to, by sprawdzić reakcję NATO", https://wyborcza.pl/7,75399,24061877,rosjanie-rozbudowuja-bazy-wojskowe-w-kalinigradzie-robia-to.html, dostęp: 20.03.2020.

Ryabov M., "Во Львове каждый камень кричит по-польски" – претензии поляков на Галичину становятся все настойчивей, Politnavigator. net, http://www.politnavigato r.net/vo-lvove-kazhdyjj-kamen-krichit-po-polski-pretenzii-polyakov-na-galichinu-sta novyatsya-vse-nastojjchivejj.html, dostęp: 18.03.2020.

Sykulski L., (2018). Geopolityka a bezpieczeństwo Polski, Warszawa: Zona Zero.

Szyłkowska M, (2019). Potencjał obronny Polski. Poziom strategiczny. Potencjał in- formacyjny, in: Potencjał obronny Rzeczypospolitej Polskiej, Warszawa: PWN.

Świerszcz K., (2019a) Contemporary Civilization Challenges in the Light of the Security Challenges of European Countries on the Example of Poland, in: Proceedings of the 34th International Business Information Management Association Conference (IBIMA), eds. Soliman K.S., Madrid, Spain, 13–14 November.

Świerszcz K., (2019b) Potencjał kulturowy i społeczny, w: Potencjał obronny Rzeczypospolitej Polskiej, eds. Stańczyk K, Warszawa: PWN.

Świerszcz K., (2019c). Podmiotowo-aksjologiczny paradygmat kształtowania strategii bezpieczeństwa i obronności państwa w czasach współczesnych, in: Nauki społeczne w dobie innowacji, eds. Krysiński S, Wikarczyk A. and Żylińska J., Warszawa: EuroPrawo.

Świerszcz K., (2020). Contemporary Civilization Challenges in The Light of The Security Challenges of European Countries on The Example of Poland, Journal of EU Research in Business https://ibimapublishing.com/articles/JEURB/2020/146710/ Vol. 2020, Article ID 146710, 11 pages, ISSN: 2165–9990; IBIMA Publishing; DOI: 10.5171/2020.146710.

To nie jest imigracja to jest już kolonizacja Europy, Globalne-Archiwum.pl, http://globalne-archiwum.pl/to-nie-jest-imigracja-to-jest-juz-kolonizacja-europy/, dostęp: 20.03.2020.

Tomasiewicz J., (2009). Strategia oporu niekierowanego w wojnie asymetrycznej, Przegląd Geopolityczny, t. 1.

Trukhanchyev V., Польша готовит Украину к роли добычи: мнение, Eadaily.com, in: https://eadaily.com/ru/news/2017/07/12/polsha-gotovit-ukrainu-k-roli-dobychi-mnenie, dostęp: 18.03.2020.

Wilk A., Ćwiczenia Zapad-2017 – wojna (na razie) informacyjna, OSW, https://www.osw.waw.pl/pl/ publikacje/komentarze-osw/2017-09-04/cwiczenia-zapad-2017-wojna-na-razie-informacyjna.

Wojnarowska-Szpucha S., (2018). Migracje ludności zagrożeniem bezpieczeństwa społecznego w Polsce, eds: Trejnis Z., Kościelecki L., Wyzwania i zagrożenia bezpieczeństwa i obronności RP w XXI wieku w wymiarze społecznym i technologiczno-środowiskowym, Warszawa: Oficyna Wydawnicza ASPRA-JR.

Wóycicki K., Kowalska M and Lelonek A., (2017). Rosyjska wojna dezinformacyjna przeciwko Polsce, Warszawa: Fundacja im. Kazimierza Pułaskiego.

Комментарий Департамента информации и печати МИД России в связи с принятием Сеймом Польши поправок к закоо запрете пропаганды коммунизма или иного тоталитарного строя, The Ministry of Foreign Affairs of the Russian Federation, http://www.mid.ru/ ru/foreign_policy/news/-/asset_publisher/cKNonkJE02Bw/content/id/2795682, dostęp: 16.03.2020.

Месснер Е., (2005). Хочешь мира, победи мятежевойну! Творческое наследие Е. Э. Месснера, Русский путь, Военный университет русский путь, Москва.

Откуда растут ноги у угрозы территориальной целостности Украины, Rian.com.ua, http://rian.com.ua/columnist/20170813/1026701058.html, dostęp: 18.03.2020.

Польша объявила войну советским памятникам, Svpressa.ru, http://svpressa.ru/world/news/175230/?rss=1, dostęp: 16.03.2020.

Katarzyna Świerszcz

Chapter 8: Qualitative methods of measuring the effectiveness of Russian influence in Poland in the area of disinformation

In an attempt to measure and evaluate the effectiveness of Russian influence in Poland in terms of the information warfare, it is first of all necessary to take into account the essence of Russian mindset about its own country, its power, or even superpower, in terms of "thinking over limits". In other words – taking into account the will to bolster and expand the territory of its own country. This category is an extremely important factor for understanding the way of thinking that is permeated with the constant ambitions and related imperial concepts of the decision-making elites of Russia, that are approved in the whole country. It is the geographical location of the Russian state and its surroundings that have a decisive influence on the way of shaping and making real political processes and the related goals and interests of that state, as well as the deliberate influence and attempts to shape the policy of neighbouring countries. This is confirmed by the expressive words of the Russian philosopher M. Bierdiajew, who stated that: "In the concept of a Russian man there is no narrowness of a European man who concentrates his energy on a small space of his soul, there is no such caution, the rationality of time and space, and the intensity of culture" (Sykulski, 2019, p. 24). A. Dugin also speaks about Russia in a similar vein, who, proclaiming the concept of Greater Europe, led by Russia and Germany, states: "As for Europe directly, in contrast to other plans to create something <greater> in the old-fashioned imperialist approach – let it be a Great Middle East Project or a pan-nationalist plan of Greater Russia or Greater China – we suggest substanlizing a multipolar approach, a balanced and open vision of Greater Europe, as a new concept for the future development of our civilization in its strategic, social, cultural, economic and geopolitical dimensions" (Dugin; Bielawski and Grenda, 2019, p. 17). Elsewhere, A. Durgin writes: "If Russia is not great, it will not be at all. Greatness – our great-Russian vocation. If not – let there be nothing else. Without Russia, the history of the world is unimaginable. May the world end" (https://geopolityka.net, Szyłkowska, 2019, p. 71).

It is worth noting that the basis of the age-old imperial ambitions of the Russian state, which, as A Durgin states, is "a great Russian vocation", has its roots in the Turanian civilization, deprived of, among others, ethics and nationality – for which the reason of existence are constant wars and conquests, and the word and the law related to it have no value (Konieczny, 1999, p. 55; Domalewska and Bielawski, 2019, p. 3268). The tool and method for the implementation of these ambitions is nowadays – in the era of information networks and computerization, in the era of cyberspace – not so much a military war, but above all a non-invasive war, such as information warfare, and more specifically disinformation. It supports Russian activities both in the offensive and defensive dimensions, aimed at the internal and external environment of the state and other countries. This war is particularly visible – in the attempt of Russian influence – on various levels of social, political, industrial, economic, cultural, energy and many other lives, in relation to European countries, and in particular to the Polish state, thus posing a threat for its national security.

This chapter of the monograph aims to show the essence of information warfare (disinformation), the mode of its conduct, as well as its significant role in the attempt to influence the life of the Polish state, in the actions of Russia's policy strategy.

Interacting with the mass media for information and disinformation purposes is one of the oldest ways of Russian action strategy, both in the military and non-military dimension. This is confirmed by the documents of the Security Strategy of the Russian Federation, of September 9, 2000 and of December 31, 2015 (National Security Strategy of the Russian Federation, 2015), which emphasize the growing importance of information and entities involved in its collection, creation and dissemination and controlling in shaping national interests, public relations and relations between states. Information warfare is an action aimed at helping to accomplish the above tasks.

The concept of Information Warfare has not yet been clearly defined. In the Polish literature on this subject, referring to P. Sienkiewicz, information warfare is defined as a variety of offensive and defensive actions. Undertaking these movements allows to reach an information advantage over an opponent and achieve the intended military (political) goal (Świerszcz, 2016, p. 249). The essence of these actions is: first, destruction of the enemy's information resources and the information systems used by him; secondly, ensuring the security of own information resources and the use of these information systems (Sienkiewicz and Świeboda, 2009, p. 90; Świercz, 2019, p. 533; Sienkiewicz, 2017, p. 254). In the American literature on the subject, the Federation of American Scientists defines information warfare as "actions undertaken to achieve information advantage by influencing the opponent's information, information processes based on processing information, information systems and computer networks at the same time protecting own information, processes based on processing information, information and computer networks". In the analysis of Russian literature, the concept of information warfare is understood as: "intense confrontation in the information space, aimed at gaining information, psychological and ideological advantage, causing damage to information systems, processes and resources, critical structures and communication (information and technical, network-centric and cyberwar), weakening political and social systems and massive psychological impact on the army and society" (Sykulski, 2019, p. 83). Colonel S. Komow defines information warfare as a variety of activities aimed at informational support, information counteraction and information protection of own resources carried out according to a uniform plan, in order to reach and keep communication leverage over the other party (Wojnowski, 2015, p. 17). In turn, an anonymous officer of the Military Academy of the General Staff of the Armed Forces of the Russian Federation defines the concept of information warfare as one of the forms of conflict resolution between the parties, the aim of which is to achieve and maintain an information advantage over the opponent. In his opinion, this goal can be achieved by means of information-technical as well as information- psychological measures by influencing the decision-making centers of a given state, its command and control system, population and information resources (Aleksandrowicz, 2016, p. 162). It is also worth paying attention at the understanding of information warfare by W. Cymbał as an analyst of the Ministry of Defense of the Russian Federation, who examines this concept in two dimensions: a narrow and a broad one. In a narrow dimension, information warfare is a form of military operations aimed at gaining an information advantage over the enemy in the field of disseminating, using and processing information and implementing effective decisions that allow to gain an advantage on the battlefield (Aleksandrowicz, 2016, p. 162; Zalewski, 2011, pp. 402–418). In a broad sense, information warfare means a variety of actions that are used by a given state against the civilian population of another state or a group of states in times of peace. These activities are aimed at achieving an impact on social awareness through science, art, culture, the education system, administration and many others, as well as gaining control over the information resources of other countries, sabotaging the development of information technologies in countries considered hostile. The goal is also to neutralize the opponent's communication systems and information networks, or to develop and implement systems that guarantee the security of own information resources (Aleksandrowicz, 2016, p. 162; Świerszcz, 2019a, p. 901). In a very meaningful way, information warfare is defined by A. Manojła, for whom it is an extreme method of confrontation between states, with the use of various modes of information influence, aimed at achieving their strategic goals. The basic form of information warfare are secret information and psychological operations, aimed at, on the one hand, causing clashes in the opponent's systems and information resources, and, on the other hand, at making a psychological, broad manipulation of the consciousness of the entire, given society, and in the further natural consequence of destabilizing the state and the nation. These operations especially attempt to gain an influence on the level of consciousness of a given society, and within it, of an individual, their perception concept about the world – by influencing their consciousness, will and emotions. These activities are especially recommended to be carried out during times exceptional for a given nation, such as: elections, referenda, crisis situations, periods of turmoil or political tensions. In the information warfare understood in this way, the subject of the attack is primarily the information infrastructure and key, decision-making entities responsible for managing activities in the area of politics, economy, science and the armed forces of a given country. The interpretation of the understanding of information warfare is complemented by the reflections of S. Modiestow, who in the information warfare based on information-psychological activities, places particular emphasis on the need to weaken the social structures of a given state, the morals of society, impose its own information matrix on it, and lower the morals of political elites. In military structures, he emphasizes the need to weaken command systems and information circulation, weaken defense capabilities, combat readiness, undermine the authority of both the civilian leadership and the military command and lower its morale (Aleksandrowicz, 2016, p. 138; May, 2003, p. 72) ; Byszof, 2019, p. 286). Information warfare is understood in a similar vein by W. Lefewr, for whom it is an effective tool allowing for the management of the human mind by deeply transforming the mass consciousness of the civilian population and, consequently, changing the moral and psychological state of the nation by using specific techniques and methods of manipulating emotions, perception and awareness of the armed forces, elites and social groups in a given country (the enemy).

The various concepts of the information warfare presented above clearly show that while Western concepts treat this notion in terms of means and methods of action (warfare), Russian ones treat it as a separate category, constituting a completely new kind of war in the 21st century. It should also be noted that the Russian theory of information warfare, having its origin in the Soviet times, using techniques of social manipulation with the use of propaganda and disinformation, is currently being supplemented and reinforced by Russian geopolitical doctrines or ideologies that show the Russian state at the center of the world, at the same time pointing to strategic aim – the need to restore its former role as a world power (Aleksandrowicz, 2016, p. 160; JakeBebber, 2017, p. 398; HeintzePierre, 2015, p. 221; Richards, 2014a, p. 114; Górnikiewicz, 2013, p. 44).

In the area of information warfare, Russia applies a number of its own methods. The most frequently used include: the method of pressure force exerted as a demonstration of military power, creating military alliances, using a political or economic threat, supporting internal forces opposing the government, and many others. Another method is creation and conveying false information about a given situation, use disinformation, provoke the opponent to escalate conflicts and move them to areas that are not a subject of destabilization, forcing them to undertake time-consuming and energy-consuming repressive actions that involve the opponent's strength and resources. A way often used by Russia is also influencing the enemy's decision-making process, for example by publishing a deliberately distorted doctrine of conducting operations, gaining influence over the state's management and control systems, as well as people who perform important political functions, neutralizing the opponent's strategy and its operational thinking, causing its confusion. Another Russian method is to influence the opponent's decision-making time, for example by using unforeseen hostilities; provoking to make irrational or hasty decisions that cause reactions inadequate to the situation. One cannot forget about the distraction method, which consists in taking actions that create the impression of a real or fictitious threat to the opponent, or the method of overloading consisting in transmitting a large amount of contradictory information to the opponent, that results in overloading information systems, creating information noise, and then as a consequence, making a confusion and increased uncertainty in taking a decision. Commonly used by Russia is also the method of paralysis, which leads to arousing fear in the opponent caused by the belief that its political, economic and military interests and many other sensitive areas are at risk. The approach of exhaustion forces the opponent to undertake a large number of unnecessary, time-consuming, energy-consuming and costly actions, whereas the method of staging, which in turn creates a fictitious threat to the opponent, simultaneously allowing the discovery of this fraud, in order to weaken its vigilance, is also worth noting. Russia applies disintegration methods by forcing the opponent to take actions that are contrary to the interests of the alliance in which it is embedded e. g. by creating internal social conflicts, thus leading to internal destabilization and reducing the political, economic and military potential of an enemy. A method of calming down the enemy, which is commonly used by Russia in information warfare, consists in creating in the opponent's consciousness the neutrality or friendly attitude of the future aggressor in order to weaken its vigilance and abandon the plans to strengthen its own military potential, or even reduce spending on the defense and security of its country. The opposite to that is the intimidation approach, often used in the information warfare, that provides false information about the military superiority of the aggressor. A commonly used method is also provocation stimulating the opponent to take actions beneficial for the aggressor. This method is supplemented by the suggestion method understood as creating and transmitting informational stereotypes to the consciousness of the opposing country's society, which include legal, moral and ideological incentives, that in turn are to result beneficial actions of individual social groups in this opposing country in favor of the aggressor. Finally, the way of pressure expressed in discrediting the opponent in the forum of public opinion by revealing compromising information. It should be emphasized here that this sort of information is often false, but also sometimes it happens to be true (Aleksandrowicz, 2016, p. 166; Greathouse, 2014, p. 132; Rõigas, 2018, p. 59; May, 2018, p. 23; Gawlik-Kobylińska, 2018, p. 149; Richards, 2014b, p. 128).

One of the sophisticated methods in the Russian information warfare in the area of political subversion is the fragmentation of a society, which allows for much easier and more effective control (manipulation) of the majority of public opinion through a disciplined, well-organized and determined social minority, imposing the skillfully desired way of thinking on the social majority. This action allows to get the effect of the so-called "crowd" or "collective wisdom", in which the recipient of the imposed information accepts it irrationally, identifying it with the "majority". It must be underlined that this method is based on the fabrication of information, meaning the combination of false and partially true messages. Its base is the polarization of concepts, judgments and opinions; a bipolarity of an image of reality: positive or negative and the maintenance of fear. Such activity uses the concepts of national pride, honor, debt of gratitude in a sophisticated way, and the will to increase the importance of a given person, group, society, nation or state (Greathouse, 2014, p. 144; Górnikiewicz, 2018, p. 53; Razuvaev, 2007, pp. 78–88; Świerszcz, 2020).

Research shows that the effectiveness of Russian information warfare results from its in-depth analysis of the history and broadly understood culture of a given country as the object of its planned influence. This analysis allows to precisely define the national character of a given country: its relatively permanent features, behavior repeated over the centuries, the model of education and upbringing in a given society, acquired patterns of behavior and many others. On their basis, the Russian secret services develop effective strategies for influencing and controlling the state's social perception. L. Sykulski notes that Russia's information warfare activities may be a part of a classic military operation, or even a classic war. It can also be a part of irregular operations that combine classic military operations with irregular operations involving also civilians, or it can be an independent element of state policy, aimed at achieving specific political and economic goals, without the use of direct military force (Sykulski, 2014, p. 88; Baltrusaits, 2017, p. 32; Świerszcz, 2019b, p. 286; Becker, 2016, p. 181).

References

(2015) Strategia bezpieczeństwa narodowego Federacji Rosyjskiej z dnia 31 grudnia 2015 roku, https://poland.mid.ru/web/polska_pl/koncepcja-polityki-zagranicznej-federacji-rosyjskiej/-/asset_publisher/x9WG6FhjehkG/content/strategia-bezpieczenstwa-narodowego-federacji-rosyjskiej?inheritRedirect=false, dostęp: 16.03.2020.

Aleksandrowicz T, (2016). Podstawy walki informacyjnej, Bezpieczeństwo dziś i jutro, Warszawa.

Aleksandrowicz T., (2014). Terroryzm w służbie geopolityki, Przegląd Bezpieczeństwa Wewnętrznego, nr 11(6).

Baltrusaits D.F., (2017). Cyber War: Do We Have the Right Mindset? in: (eds.) Carayannis E., Campbell D., Efthymiopoulos M., Handbook of Cyber-Development, Cyber-Democracy, and Cyber-Defense. Champor: Springer.

Becker W.B., (2016). The Librarian's Information War, Behavioral & Social Sciences Librarian, 35:4, DOI: 10.1080/01639269.2016.1284525.

Bielawski R. and Grenda B., (2019). Wybrane zagadnienia cyberbezpieczeństwa narodowego, Wrocław: Exante.

Byszof N., (2019). Rosyjska wojna hybrydowa, in: Perspektywy zagrożeń dla bezpieczeństwa międzynarodowego kreowanych przez Federację Rosyjską, eds. Banasik M. and Rogozińska A., Warszawa: Difin.

Domalewska D. and Bielawski R., (2019). Social bots as vehicles of spreading disinformation. Implications for state security, in: Soliman K.S., Proceedings of the 34th International Business Information Management Association Conference (IBIMA), 13–14 November 2019, Madrid, Spain. Vision 2025: Education Excellence and Management of Innovations through Sustainable Economic Competitive Advantage, Madryt.

Dugin A., The Greater Europe Project, http://www.4pt.su/en/content/greater-europe-project, dostęp: 15.03.2020.

Federation of American Scientists, Information Warfare, http://fas.org/spp/military/docops/defense/jwsp/jw04i.htm, dostęp: 16.03.2020.

Gawlik-Kobylińska M., (2018) The Four-Dimensional Instructional Design Approach in the Perspective of Human-Computer Interactions, in: Frontiers in Artificial Intelligence and Applications (eds) Petkov N., Strisciuglio N. and Travieso-González C.). IOS Press, Amsterdam, Berlin, Washington DC.

Górnikiewicz M., (2013). Antropologia kulturowa w prognozowaniu zagrożeń militarnych i niemilitarnych – kontekst historyczny, in: Zeszyty Naukowe, Bezpieczeństwo, Świat – Region – Polska, nr 1 (3).

Górnikiewicz M., (2018). Prognozowanie kulturowe zagrożeń bezpieczeństwa narodowego i międzynarodowego, Warszawa: WAT.

Greathouse C.B., (2014). Cyber War and Strategic Thought: Do the Classic Theorists Still Matter?. in: (eds.) Kremer J.F. and Müller B., Cyberspace and International Relations. Springer, Berlin: Heidelberg.

HeintzePierre Thielbörger H., (2015) From Cold War to Cyber War: The Evolution of the International Law of Peace and Armed Conflict over the last 25 Years, Springer International Publishing AG.

https://geopolityka.net/jan-majka-duginiada-cz-3/, dostęp: 15.03.2020.

JakeBebber R., (2017). Treating Information as a Strategic Resource to Win the "Information War", Orbis, Volume 61, Issue 3, 2017, https://doi.org/10.1016/j.orbis.2017.05.007.

Koneczny F., (1999). O cywilizacji łacińskiej, Gliwice: ONION.

Maj J., (2003). Dowodzenie Siłami Zbrojnymi (aspekt narodowy i sojuszniczy), Warszawa: AON.

Maj J., (2018). Nowe aspekty sztuki wojennej XXI wieku, Poznań: FNCE.

Razuvaev V.E., (2007). Legal Issues Involved in Fighting Spam as a Means of Waging an Information War, Russian Politics & Law, 45:2, pp. 78–88, DOI: 10.2753/RUP1061-1940450207.

Richards J., (2014a). A New Cold War? Russia, China, the US and Cyber War. in: Cyber-War: The Anatomy of the global Security Threat. London: Palgrave Pivot.

Richards J., (2014b). Has Cyber War Happened?. in: Cyber-War: The Anatomy of the global Security Threat. London: Palgrave Pivot.

Rõigas H., (2018). Cyber War in Perspective: Lessons from the Conflict in Ukraine. in: (eds) Cusumano E., Corbe M., A Civil-Military Response to Hybrid Threats. Palgrave Macmillan, Cham.

Sienkiewicz P. and Świeboda H., (2009). Sieci teleinformatyczne jako instrument państwa – zjawisko walki informacyjnej, eds. Madej M., Terlikowski M., Bezpieczeństwo teleinformatyczne państwa, Warszawa: PISM.

Sienkiewicz P., (2017) Wyzwania i zagrożenia bezpiecznego rozwoju społeczeństwa informacyjnego, Ekonomiczne Problemy Usług nr 1 (126), t. 2.

Sykulski L., (2019). Rosyjska geopolityka a wojna informacyjna, Warszawa: PWN.

Szyłkowska M., (2019). Potencjał obronny Polski. Poziom strategiczny. Potencjał informacyjny, in: Potencjał obronny Rzeczypospolitej Polskiej, Warszawa: PWN.

Świerszcz K., (2016). Dynamika jakościowo nowych uwarunkowań w konceptualizacji bezpieczeństwa narodowego: dokumenty prawno-polityczne, in: Obronność państwa. Strategie oraz systemy bezpieczeństwa i obronności, eds. Trejnis Z. and Marciniak M., Toruń: Adam Marszałek.

Świerszcz K., (2019a) Podmiotowo-aksjologiczny paradygmat kształtowania strategii bezpieczeństwa i obronności państwa w czasach współczesnych, in: Nauki społeczne w dobie innowacji (eds.) Krysiński S., Wikarczyk A. and Żylińska J., Warszawa: EuroPrawo.

Świerszcz K., (2019b). Contemporary Civilization Challenges in the Light of the Security Challenges of European Countries on the Example of Poland, in: Proceedings of the 34th International Business Information Management Association Conference (IBIMA), eds. Soliman K.S., Madrid, Spain, 13–14 November.

Świerszcz K., (2020). Contemporary Civilization Challenges in The Light of The Security Challenges of European Countries on The Example of Poland, Journal of EU Research in Business https://ibimapublishing.com/articles/JEURB/2020/146710/ Vol. 2020 (2020), Article ID 146710, 11 pages, ISSN: 2165-9990; IBIMA Publishing; DOI: 10.5171/2020.146710.

Wojnowski M., (2015) Zarządzanie refleksyjne jako paradygmat rosyjskich operacji informacyjno-psychologicznych w XXI wieku, Przegląd Bezpieczeństwa Wewnętrznego, nr 12(7).

Zalewski J. (2011), Wokół nowej tożsamości Sił Zbrojnych Federacji Rosyjskiej, in: Bezpieczeństwo obszaru poradzieckiego, Warszawa: Difin.

Katarzyna Świerszcz

Chapter 9: Summary and conclusions: Forecast for the development of the methodology of the Kremlin's information impact on the situation in Poland

Living in a qualitatively new reality, in which information plays a vital role, as well as building and maintaining the independence and security of the state in it, is a growing challenge for all of us. It is the greatest impact of information warfare on a given state (states), whose society and the entire nation become a victim of its psychological and media manipulation, a victim of intellectual and moral manipulation or ideological subversion. Poland, as well as other Western countries, grew out of the Latin (Christian) civilization, which is based on the values of the so-called "Quincunx", i. e. a set of five categories of human existence: good, truth, health, prosperity and beauty – which, according to F. Koneczny, constitute the criterion for assessing civilization[1]. But it seems to lack developed ways of defense and self-defense against information warfare used by Russia. Thus, the question arises: What mechanisms should be used and who should equip society (nation) with them? When looking for an answer to this question, one can say – following the wisdom of life and the rich experience of the nation – that, as D. Koźmierczuk rightly notices, education for the country's security and defense becomes an important key in this area. It should help in acquiring appropriate knowledge, shaping skills, attitudes and value systems that allow for building and protecting state security and peace in the world. The values and attitudes that are universally recognized as universal and necessary for the development and harmonious functioning of each society are particularly important. They are, in addition to those of the "Quincunx": freedom, responsibility, dignity, honesty and self-determination. In a situation where the society, and especially the young generation in it, is fed with disinformation, manipulation and propaganda, sees or experi-

---

1 According to F. Koneczny, good – is related to the sphere of morality; truth – is the domain of natural (knowledge) and supernatural (faith) knowledge; health – is an expression of a human being relationship to its own body; prosperity – is a field that covers economic life; beauty – is an area related to the sphere of human sensitivity. There is a hierarchy in the Quincunx – the spiritual factor has primacy. The center of the geometric structure of the Quincunx is the category of Good (Koneczny, 999; Piotrowski, 2003, p. 41; Świerszcz, 2020; Świerszcz, 2016, p. 250; Zamojski, 2019, p. 18).

ences human rights violations, bloody terrorist attacks, economic and political exploitation and oppression, or discrimination, instilling the values of truth, good, beauty, prosperity, freedom and health, and on their basis, shaping the attitudes of coexistence, tolerance, negotiation skills and resisting all forms of discrimination, is a serious challenge and a difficult task today.

Taking into account the threats of manipulation, disinformation, soft power, demoralisation and indoctrination described above, which can be defined as a cognitive weapon, managing the mind and psyche of a person (society) – the abilities that will help to counteract them are cognitive abilities, such as: the ability of insightful cause-and-effect thinking, perceptiveness, inference, processing information given in verbal, non-verbal and numerical form, spatial orientation, memory and concentration. As it can be seen, not only is information important now, but also, and perhaps most importantly, the ability to select it and analyze it integrally. The messages allow not only to describe and interpret information, but they also provide with the possibility of forecasting, determining current and future consequences. In other words, the messages allow you to anticipate outcomes and future actions.

Particularly noteworthy in its implementation is the Information Security Doctrine of the Republic of Poland (Project 2015), which defines a number of operational tasks for the public, private, civic and trans-sectoral segments, aimed at supporting and protecting the civilian population. These include the concept of operational tasks in the field of information security of the Republic of Poland. As regards the tasks of the public sector at the national level, they are:
- ensuring the functioning of a coherent system of monitoring and distribution of information in the civil and military dimension;
- supporting activities aimed at strengthening the national identity;
- conducting social campaigns to positively influence the image of Poland;
- activities in the field of social communication building the brand of the Republic of Poland; – using the potential of public diplomacy;
- preventing, as part of counterintelligence activities, the activation of selected social groups by a foreign state in order to pursue interests contrary to the interests of the Republic of Poland;
- creating a social capacity to recognize and neutralize disinformation;
- activation of social capital;
- implementation of counter-information mechanisms as well as education and raising awareness of citizens at the national level, among others through media;
- planning the use and production of means of influencing the information environment. In terms of the tasks of the public sector at the international level, they are:

- covering the Polish minority in the region with universal access to all Polish electronic media (radio and TV);
- creating strong competition for the Russian media as the main transmitter of information (propaganda) for this population group;
- cooperation with the countries of the region in broadcasting radio and television programs in Belarus; – reaching the Polish minority in other countries with Polish information programs (radio and television);
- providing this minority with educational programs (history and contemporary politics);
- constant monitoring of the propaganda message directed at Poland and content discrediting Polish foreign policy;
- analysis allowing to identify the sources of the message and, as far as possible, to eliminate sources of disinformation.

As regards the tasks of the private sector, they are:
- cooperation with the public sector in counteracting threats to the information environment; – engagement private commercial broadcasters in the implementation of information tasks towards Polish minority e.g. in Lithuania, scheduled by the public media (a system of incentives and tax reliefs);
- participation in information exchange mechanisms, training and application of the principles of good practice; activity and information reliability towards bodies responsible for supervising the functioning of strategic organizations and companies of the state.

As regards the tasks of the civic sector, they are:
- citizens' involvement and participation in civic projects and movements aimed at enhancing information security;
- self-organization of civil society through self-education, raising awareness on threats and supporting civic capacity to counteract them (e.g. the so-called "good trolls"); – conscious consumption of information content, content analysis (identification of propaganda and disinformation attacks).

In terms of trans-sectoral tasks, they are:
- cooperation of the state sector (services, army, administration at all levels) with the media for a better protection of the state's interests in the information sphere;
- counteracting propaganda and crisis response with the use of social potential;
- proper creation of social attitudes in favor of national security.

The ability to defend against manipulation, indoctrination and propaganda today requires from each of us a mature awareness of our identity and personality learned through upbringing (paideia) and lifelong education, as well as up-to-date and reliable knowledge on the social processes, which are mainly acquired from the mass media (Kaźmierczak, 2017, p. 127).

References

Doktryna Bezpieczeństwa Informacyjnego RP, https://www.bbn.gov.pl/ftp/dok/01/Pro- jek t_Doktryny_Bezpieczenstwa_Informacyjnego_RP.pdf, dostęp: 22.03.2020.

Kaźmierczak D., (2017). Walka informacyjna we współczesnych konfliktach i jej społeczne konsekwencje, Studia de Securitate et Educatione Civili 7, DOI 10.24917/20820917.7.7.

Koneczny F., (1999). O cywilizacji łacińskiej, Gliwice: ONION.

Piotrowski R., (2003) Problem filozoficzny ładu społecznego a porównawcza nauka o cywilizacjach, Warszawa: Dialog.

Świerszcz K., (2016). Dynamika jakościowo nowych uwarunkowań w konceptualizacji bezpieczeństwa narodowego: dokumenty prawno-polityczne, in: Obronność państwa. Strategie oraz systemy bezpieczeństwa i obronności, (eds.) Trejnis Z. and Marciniak M., Toruń: Adam Marszałek.

Świerszcz K., (2020). Contemporary Civilization Challenges in The Light of The Security Challenges of European Countries on The Example of Poland, Journal of EU Research in Business https://ibimapublishing.com/articles/JEURB/2020/146710/ Vol. 2020 (2020), Article ID 146710, 11 pages, ISSN: 2165-9990; IBIMA Publishing; DOI: 10.5171/2020.146710.

Zamojski A., (2019) Federacja Rosyjska – współczesna egzemplifikacja cywilizacji turańskiej, w: Polityka Federacji Rosyjskiej i jej konsekwencje dla bezpieczeństwa międzynarodowego, (eds.) Banasik M., Warszawa: Difin.

Section IV:
Modeling the Russian impact on Polish foreign and internal policy

Piotr Zaskórski

Chapter 10: Modeling the processes of assessing Russia's influence on Poland

The perception of Russia in the context of its impact on Poland's security has many threads and is determined not only by the present day, but also by historical events. Hence, the search for sources of risk of lowering the value of the international security system in which Poland's national security is located (Jagusiak, 2015) seems to be a systemic activity. There are mechanisms to counteract such influences through the growth of Poland's economic potential and its diplomatic support for the systemic reforms implemented in the country. On the other hand, the maintenance and attempts to raise the international prestige of Poland and Poles are visible. This is particularly important because it overlaps with the fact that Poland was the first entity of European security to undertake the construction of a democratic civil society in the Soviet bloc. Thus, relations with entities in the East and the loosening of post-Soviet dependencies were changing rapidly. These phenomena left a permanent mark on Polish-Russian relations (www.tvn24.pl, 2020). All this can be considered in the context of sources and possibilities of materializing threats (ISO 31000, 2018; Liderman, 2007) for the national security system of the Republic of Poland. It is therefore worth making an attempt to quantify these threats and refer to quantitative methods and models that systematize these threats and create a certain matrix of their coincidence, taking into account their vulnerability within the Polish national security system.

An attempt to use quantitative and valuable methods to assess the level of Russia's influence on the politics and situation of Poland in Europe and in the world requires the determination of risk factors and the related level of security as a logical supplement to the estimated risk level. In a descriptive way, it can be assumed that both the level of risk and the level of security require quantification of threats, their potential effects (Zaskórski, 2011, p. 90) when the risk materializes itself, and the possibility of counteracting the risk by determining the opportunities and susceptibility (resilience) to specific threats.

The rhomboidal model (Figure 1) is an intuitive method of evaluating the level of risk identified as the area of a diamond stretched in a coordinate system with four opposite directions. The risk level (case (1)) is then described on the coordinates of the problem complexity of a given threat (X1) and the quantified threat level (X2), e.g. according to the ranking method described below (RFD) and the technology used by the opponent (Y1) and the propagation rate of the effects (Y2). The higher the value of these attributes (longer diagonals of the diamond), the greater its field as an image of the risk level.

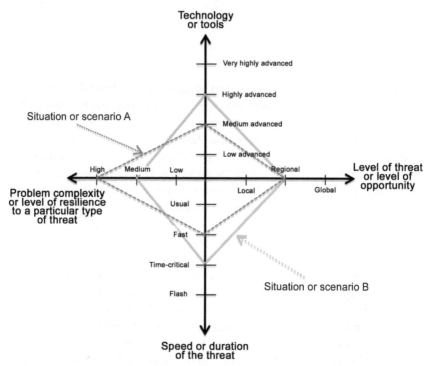

Figure 1. The rhomboidal model in estimating the risk of threats and the level of security (Zaskórski et al., 2015, p. 291)

In the case (2), when the coordinates describe, respectively, the level of resilience to the threat (X1) and the level of opportunities for effective counteracting (X2) and the level of advancement of tools or technology (Y1) and the time of effective counteraction (Y2) – the diamond field will represent the level of estimated safety in a given risk area. This can mean: risk level: VaR = (X1 + X2) (Y1 + Y2) / 2 (case 1) or security level: PB = (X1 + X2) (Y1 + Y2) / 2 (case 2).

The RFD model (Table 1) is a simplified emanation of the so-called QFD method (Quality Function Deployment (Zaskórski, 2012, p. 115) and is based on the identification of risk factors in a compressed system with the possibility of detailing risk factors in a given group of threats. The lines of the coincidence matrix can illustrate the effect of materialization of a given threat (or individual factors) and then the risk level can be estimated or it can be interpreted as an opportunity to counteract the risk and then the determined value can be the evaluated level of security in a given hazard class (da Veiga et al., 2020, pp. 2–20).

Table 1. The matrix of the coincidence of threats and effects (or opportunities of counteracting)

Examples of determinants of the risk of violating the security of Poland by Russia	THREATS	MILITARY	ECONOMIC	INFORMATION-INTELLIGENCE	CYBERSPACE	SOCIAL	IMAGE	PROPAGANDA	TECHNOLOGICAL	ECOLOGICAL	OTHER
EFFECTS	or OPPORTUNITIES										
EFFECTIVE SELF-DEFENCE		O	▽	O	●	O	●	●	▽		O
CONTINUOUS MONITORING OF A SITUATION		O		▽	●	O	O	●	O		
COUNTERACTING WITH OWN FORCES		▽	●	▽			▽		▽		▽
PARTIAL LOSS OF OWN POTENTIAL		●			▽		●	▽			▽
BIG LOSS OF OWN POTENTIAL		▽					▽		●		
INVOLVING THE POTENTIAL OF NEIGHBOURING ALLY STATES		▽			O		▽		O		
INVOLVING THE EU POTENTIAL		▽					O		O		
USING THE NATO'S POTENTIAL		▽	O	O	O	▽	O		▽	▽	▽
CUMULATIVE POINT VALUE OF THE RISK OR SECURITY INDICATOR (when taking into account the opportunities of effective counteraction)		15	6	6	10	4	15	8	12	2	7
RANK OF RISK or SECURITY LEVEL		I	VI	VI	III	???	I	IV	II	VII	V

The Pareto-Lorentz model (Zaskórski et al., 2015, p. 221) is based on the so-called the 80-20 rule, or ABC, according to which in every phenomenon, also in the process of quantification of risk factors, 20% of factors determine 80 effects caused by a given class of threats. This means that each threat has its rank according to the specific level of effect it can cause. The higher the impact on risk, the more important this factor is (lower number on the axis of independent variables). The level of risk and threats becomes a saturated curve that increases slower and slower. In this way, you can conduct a fairly precise analysis of risk factors and eliminate those that slightly affect the level of risk. The ranking process is a simple selection and impact evaluation algorithm.

The use of quantitative methods must be preceded by the identification of sources of potential threats. In the case of relations with Russia, many factors should be taken into account, including historical reluctance resulting from the conflicting roles and interests of the two countries in the context of disputes and feuds in the chain: Russia – the USSR – Russian Federation – Republic of Poland. One should also take into account the fact that currently Poland is the EU member state that is most exposed to the effects of Russia's aggressive foreign policy due to the fact that it borders with the Russian enclave. Another important factor here is the threat that the Kaliningrad Oblast, due to its strategic location, is one of the most militarized regions in Europe. From a systemic perspective, sources of risk should be sought in many areas, not only military, but also economic and social. The more important ones include the lack of acceptance of Russia for the policy of establishing the cooperation with NATO pursued by Poland since 1990 and its long-term active participation in this pact, actually in direct contact on the eastern flank, and moreover:

1. Russia's incomplete settlement of the crimes committed during the Second World War, including, above all, the murder of Polish officers in Katyn and further denying the facts. The investigation into the Katyn massacre was formally closed by the Supreme Military Prosecutor's Office of the Russian Federation in 2005, but without presenting any charges, it is a strong blow to mutual relations, especially without qualifying this event as an act of genocide.
2. Lack of strong support from the EU and the USA for corrective actions against Poland by Russia in the context of the USSR's predatory policy, despite the declaration on friendship and good-neighborly cooperation between the Republic of Poland and Russia (then the Russian Soviet Federative Socialist Republic – RSFSR) signed on October 10, 1990 in Moscow.
3. Remnants of various contacts and interests from the period of stationing combat units in the territory of the Republic of Poland until September 1993, including the issue of the lack of financial settlement, i.e. "Zero option"; Russia has been consistently implementing a policy related to the so-called The Falin-Kwiciński doctrine, which states that after the collapse of the Soviet Union, the withdrawing Red Army is replaced by energy networks, mainly gas and oil connections.
4. Periodic breakdown of economic cooperation and lack of recognition by both parties of the interdependence of interests; The fragility of bilateral relations and economic relations between Poland and Russia, which focus

mainly on trade and energy raw materials, despite the agreement on settling mutual indebtedness and the agreement on economic cooperation, which can be considered as an opportunity in Polish-Russian relations. Nevertheless, Poland's limited acceptance of a long-term agreement on natural gas supplies and the measures taken to diversify supplies may create a new area of threats and reluctance from Russia. It should also be noted here that the USA and Russia have started a competition (Zapałowski, 2015) in the global energy markets, which is additionally revealed by the crisis related to the coronavirus, and Poland is one of the places where Washington and Moscow highlight this contradiction of interests. Moreover, Russia is reluctant to transport American LNG to Europe, which results in a large amount of disinformation and manipulation regarding these supplies and violating the interests of Poland in many other areas (even a propaganda campaign that blamed Poland for the period of the Second World War).

5. Russia's negative actions towards EU unity, an example of which is the Russian-German agreement on the construction of the Nord Stream gas pipeline and the blocking of the Polish voice of opposition. This area also includes Russia's economic sanctions to limit the import of agricultural products and food from the EU (www.cprdip.pl). The sanctions, which were quite unpleasant for Poland as one of the victims of this action, caused the loss of the Russian sales market and that loss was calculated not only to economic losses, but also to more dangerous political consequences in Poland through pressure from Polish producers on the political elite (an attempt to influence the local government elections in November 2014, presidential elections in May 2015 and parliamentary elections in October 2015).

6. No recognition for the Poland's posture after the interventions and acts of deprivation of independence by the Russian Federation directed against such countries as Chechnya and Ukraine, including the annexation of Crimea. Continuous remembering of the so-called "Eastern Partnership", which was supposed to increase the EU's involvement in democratic changes in Armenia, Azerbaijan, Belarus, Georgia, Moldova and Ukraine, as it was treated by Russia as "partnership against Russia".

7. Using the framework agreement on technical and military cooperation, including the supply of post-Soviet spare parts for Polish armaments for destructive activities to Polish needs. Unfulfilled demands of the Russian Federation regarding compensation for damages that it would incur in this respect due to Poland's accession to NATO and the EU.

8. Overactivity of the Russian intelligence, both in previous years and also today, as well as symmetrical reactions in bilateral relations, e.g. the immediate expulsion of Russian diplomats on the charges of espionage for Russia. An additional problem is certain historical conditions, which should

also be taken into account as a source of the risk of too strong and selective influence on Poland. It is the result of, among others, the document entitled "The Report on the activities of Military Information Services officers and employees", in which the MIS officers are indicated as agents of Russian influence in Poland. Of particular importance is fostering distrust in political circles and the possibility of blackmailing its representatives and influencing the shaping of public opinion (influence on journalists). In addition, it is also worth taking into account the threats resulting from economic and business impacts.

9. The problem of the aircraft crash of April 10, 2010 under Smolensk, which remains unresolved to date, maintains difficult relations between Russia and Poland in this area, despite various gestures and even the proclamation by Russia of April 12, 2010 as the day of national mourning in Russia. The final reports of the Russian and Polish commissions differ from each other, and in 2011 the Russian Interstate Aviation Committee shifted the blame for the tragedy to Poland. The results of Polish research and findings are still not recognized. In addition, the issue of returning the wreckage of a government plane to Poland is still alive.

10. Models, instruments and tools of information policy related to the extensive use of Internet portals, large-scale TV stations and other electronic media (e.g. the so-called troll factories), which, together with the institutes and foundations financed by the Russian government, are to disseminate content, profiling among recipients, an image of reality in various places around the world, adequate to the goals of the Russian state's policy. Their task is to propagate expansive content in an appropriate form, including sowing confusion, destabilizing the social and political situation in various countries, and inciting conflicts between neighbors (e.g. by emphasizing historical disputes). Poland, Central Europe and the Western Balkans are priority areas for Russia in this regard. The methods and means of action are used to build a broadly understood infrastructure enabling to exert an influence on key political processes in the region with the assumption of taking control over these countries and often, for example, blocking NATO enlargement to the Balkan states and weakening the influence of Western countries.

11. Stoking disputes between national minorities, such as Polish in Lithuania and Ukraine, Ukrainian in Poland, or Hungarian in Ukraine and Slovakia. Russia's intelligence expansion in recent years has been correlated with the resurgence and intensification of hostile attitudes in relations between different countries in the context of disputes over the past or the status and situation of national minorities.

12. A very significant threat to the security of Poland in the long term is the growing business ties of Russian companies with entities from Central Eu-

rope and the Balkans in many areas of the economy, In practice, this may mean the possibility of interference in the affairs and policy of a given state by Putin's Russia, represented by both state-owned and private companies (large corporations), which are fully controlled by Russia's security apparatus. The threats to the activities of Russian criminal groups operating in Europe should be viewed in a similar way.

13. In 2001, President Vladimir Putin outlined a new foreign policy towards the West with an emphasis on cooperation with NATO and supported the anti-terrorist coalition.
14. The Prime Minister of Russia, Vladimir Putin, wrote a letter to the Polish in 2009, in which he was telling about cooperation and reconciliation as well as he declared his willingness to settle accounts with the past. He also announced that he would undertake research on illuminating difficult events in the history of both nations and declassify the archives of both countries. Moreover, contacts between the chiefs of staff of the armed forces of Poland and Russia were resumed, and military cross-border cooperation was restored.
15. In 2010, the documents on the Katyn case were declassified and published, and moreover, the Russian president provided the Polish side with 67 volumes of documents on the Katyn massacre. On November 26 of that year, the Russian Duma adopted a unique, historic resolution "On the Katyn tragedy and its victims", recognizing the Katyn massacre quite spectacularly as a crime of the Stalinist regime, which, however, has limited legal consequences.
16. Thanks to the achievements of the so-called shale revolution – the US may displace Russia from its role as an exporter of raw materials, depriving it of this important lever of pressure also on Poland, which is an important antidote to the implementation of the above-mentioned Falin-Kwiciński Doctrine.
17. Polish opportunity and strength lies in the lack of a significant Russian minority in Poland. The main tool of influence, for example in Estonia and Latvia, is a very large Russian minority or strongly pro-Russian population groups in eastern Ukraine or Belarus. They constitute the intelligence recruiting base, as well as the base for building political groups financed and led by Russia.
18. Polish opportunity and strength in effectively counteracting the negative influence of Russia in our country are not so strong cultural or religious ties, such as in Serbia, Macedonia, Montenegro or Bulgaria. Also, the strength of sentiments to the Soviet times, even in post-communist circles, is not as significant as in the case of the Czech Republic or Slovakia.

19. Poland cannot directly threaten Russia and its global interests, but it can introduce quite troublesome disturbances, for example, Poland leads the countries that seek new American bases, and American soldiers are already stationed in large numbers close to the Polish borders. Russia then has to monitor the situation on an ongoing basis and change the deployment of forces in Belarus accordingly, and then relations with this country are periodically disrupted and require some tribute. In the face of such events, a constant threat of their escalation arises, and the absence of Poland in such an anti-Russian group would mean that only the Baltic countries and Romania would remain there, which significantly weakens the potential (Sułek, 2018) and the ability to counteract even local interests of Russia.

Each event, both positive and negative, implies specific outcomes, including losses or vulnerabilities (or an appropriate level of resilience), respectively. The existing relations with Russia and its attempts to influence Poland have resulted in various outcomes. The more important ones include:

Russia's economic sanctions in 2014 changed the structure of Polish food exports (Table 2).

Table 2. Selected effects of threats in the economic sphere (www.cprdip.pl, 2020)

Index	2013	2014	2015	2016	Remarks
Total food exports	20,4	21,9	23,6	24,1	The export of food products accounts for around 7.1% of total exports
Bilion euro	1,25	0,88	0,398	0,372	Visible decline in value
Export to Russia	-	30	55	5,1	Russia, as a recipient of food products from Poland, declined from 15th to 18th place in 2016
% Decrease in exports to Russia Increase in % of exports to the EU	-	7.1	7,7	1.1	It is also important that Polish exports outside the EU and the CIS countries increased in 2015 by 13% to EUR 3.1 billion, which is positive

These figures illustrate that the Russian sanctions have activated the Polish side to penetrate the global market and have become an opportunity to go beyond the Russian market and to deny that Polish food producers can become independent of the Russian market. One should bear in mind the losses incurred by some producers who were highly dependent on Russian customers. The restrictions resulted in serious losses in the local dimension, but led to the diversification of sales markets, which is an important component of Poland's security resulting from a lower susceptibility to this class of disturbances controlled by Russia.

1. Prospective plans to build a fuel hub in Świnoujście and to resell LNG imported from the USA, Qatar or Norway to its neighbors, which until recently has been completely dependent on imports from Russia;
2. The United States may become a key partner in the implementation of the Polish nuclear project, which would also be an element of the diversification of solutions across the EU as opposed to the Russian technology on which Hungarian and Belarusian investments are based. The USA wants to compete with Russia also in the field of the so-called civil atom. Washington has already unblocked its nuclear industry for foreign investment and reached agreements with, for example, Poland and Saudi Arabia;
3. Poland may aspire to become the leader of the Central European States agreement, i.e. The Three Seas Initiative (Bartosiak, 2018), the foundation of which is a common gas market, open to LNG supplies, among others, from the USA;
4. Due to Russia's consistent activity in Latvia and Estonia, pro-Russian parties have been able to develop their activities over the past few years, and have gained a significant position and real influence on political processes and access to sensitive data in the field of defense and security. This type of tool gives Russia the opportunity to influence the internal situation and relations with its neighbors, especially in conditions of a real conflict, e.g. Ukraine (Racz, 2015);
5. Russia's expansive activities may be transferred, based on a certain pattern, from other areas of Europe (the Balkans, Ukraine) to Poland and the EU, which may result in a number of threats to our security and strategic interests. This may result from activities aimed at provoking and escalating internal conflicts and conflicts with our neighbors, weakening the allied relations and the hitherto good position in the EU. The conflict in eastern Ukraine, an attempt to change Poland's attitude towards this conflict combined with promises of benefits (e.g. the so-called "partition" of Ukraine, the restoration of Lviv) and interference in its internal affairs as well as the expansion of military infrastructure at our borders are the result of the anticipation of political and military instability in the immediate vicinity of Poland and the Baltic states;
6. Russia's aggressive intelligence offensive in our region may manifest itself in placing Russian agents in such places where they may have easier access to strategic information about NATO. A manifestation of such actions was the case of Herman Simm, the head of one of the agencies responsible for the cooperation with NATO, and the subsequent arrests of officers from the Estonian army and security services, suspects and convicts for the cooperation with Russian intelligence. This may also apply to Poland, which confirms the seriousness of the situation and the legitimacy of forecasting

(Zacharias et al., 2008, pp. 89–118) an increase in the risk of such attitudes and their consequences;
7. Russia's long-term investments in the construction of energy infrastructure have made both Poland and Europe dependent on the supply of its energy resources. In addition, a strong intelligence offensive (Zalewski, 2016) and setting, in decision-making, expert and opinion-forming circles of European countries people, striving for the interests of Russia in the field of energy, brought tangible results and establishment of a fairly coherent lobby of companies, groups and countries blocking rational initiatives in being autonomous from supplies from Russia. It is worth mentioning here that the implementation of diversification projects is hindered by the reduced solidarity of some traditional partners (e.g. Hungary), that are strengthening the dependence on Russia;
8. The dissemination of Russian attitudes and values in Poland is a multifaceted process, but its effects, due to historical conditions, are not significant. Poles are characterized by quite strong resistance to Russian propaganda (for example, "Radio Sputnik" has only 0.01% of recipients in Poland). Besides, in the broader media space, virtually no one refers to its "factual materials". Each system of action, including the system of mutual relations between Poland and Russia (www.polskieradio.pl, 2020), triggers specific vulnerabilities to certain threats, but also mobilizes its resistance to relevant threats and crisis situations (Crandall, Parnell and Spillan, 2014), and sometimes it also exposes some of them as burdened with too much risk. These are rational behaviors. Hence, Poland sees some opportunities to limit its vulnerability to the deliberate and destructive influence of Russia. The most important events in this area include:
9. In March 2020 in Kiev, the authorities of the energy and environmental protection sector of Ukraine confirmed the conclusion of an agreement with the Americans on LNG supplies from the USA to Ukraine, which will be carried out by Poland;
10. Poland as an important ally of the USA in Europe, being a relatively large country belonging to NATO and the EU, lying in a critical place, may be an excellent location for communication and energy centers as well as transmission routes;
11. The USA can offer Poland and its partners raw materials that are competitively priced in relation to those from Russia, fixed in monopolistic practice, so that the Polish paid more for Russian gas than the Germans. These intentions fit well with the Polish plans and many countries in the region that want to limit the influence of the policy of the Russian monopoly-supplier, and thus also the creator of the political order in Europe and in the world;

12. Germany's passivity in the face of Russia's behavior in the field of energy economy directs Poland's actions towards American assistance and support. This has already been backed by some consequences, as the Russian economy suffered losses as a result of the American shale revolution, which brought large amounts of oil and gas to the market. Additionally, the construction of Nord Stream 2 was blocked;
13. The United States intends to use its oil potential to a large extent, which may prove its high susceptibility to the implementation of such a proposal, which was particularly evident during the visit of the US Secretary of State Mike Pompeo in Minsk, who confirmed that America was ready to meet 100% of Belarusian demand for oil;
14. Countries such as Poland can protect themselves against the influence of Russia and have measurable results including the American supplies, which is both an opportunity and susceptibility to such actions in a view of the strategic goal of intensifying activities aimed at diversification and limiting Russia's influence on Polish affairs in various contexts.
15. An important aspect of reducing Poland's susceptibility to Russian influence is counteracting Russia's intelligence offensive throughout Europe, the scope and effectiveness of which has become apparent as a result of recent actions by the secret services of the USA, the Netherlands and Great Britain. This exhibition covers only one area where Russia is at war with the West, and its aim is to acquire a strategic advantage over the Euro-Atlantic political space. From the Russian point of view, this has a strong impact on the continuity and survival as well as maintenance of President Putin's regime in the country;
16. Anti-American and anti-EU and more generally anti-Western feelings and sentiments, which are a historical implication of the Cold War period, may be a specific vulnerability to Russia's influence. These inconsistencies are especially topical in the nationalist and more broadly right-wing, but also anti-system, pacifist and anti-capitalist circles that reside in every European country;
17. The forward-looking assessment of Russia's vulnerability to influence in Poland tends to be optimistic, and its efforts to bring the countries of Central Europe and the Balkans into its orbit of influence so far can be considered rather ineffective. Russia does not have a positive potential that is technologically and economically attractive, which would confirm the competitiveness of its offer for the countries and societies of our region. The fact that Russia's actions are dominated by instruments of a forceful nature, aimed rather at causing phenomena generating a state of political instability and enforcing economic dependence. All this causes a general deterioration of social relations and living conditions of the population. Therefore, irre-

spective of business ties and various pro-Russian sympathies and resentments, Polish society is convinced that the benefits of being a member of the EU have multiple advantages over the benefits of stronger ties with Russia;
18. Poland should perceive Russian militarism and neo-imperialism as a real threat that may reach beyond the perspective of a mid-term conflict. The probability of this happening is determined by the needs of the present Russian authorities to mobilize support for the regime and thus to distract the population from internal socio-economic problems. Hence, Poland should be prepared primarily for a "subversive war", but without excluding the possibility of a real conflict.

The current state of relations between Poland and Russia – despite periodic fluctuations – seems to be relatively stable. Russia uses relations with Poland as an element of its deterrent tactic in its sometimes aggressive propaganda. Poland probably expects an objective assessment of historical events and difficulties (www.abw.gov.pl, 2020). It all depends on the young generation, which, however, has a weaker historical memory. Young Russians often know from their media that Poland is an anti-Russian country in Europe, and much less is said about Poland in the Russian media than it was in the previous decade.

Russia's actions are still dangerous, and the experience of both Georgia and Chechnya, and now Ukraine, shows that the arsenal of ways of conducting aggressive politics is changing without ruling out solutions using the hybrid warfare model (Hybrid warfare, 2015). Continuous monitoring of threats, analysis and risk assessments with particular emphasis on quantitative-valued models stimulates the completeness, comprehensiveness and consistency of these assessments, even if a specific measure is only a rough estimate. This enables the use of methods of comparative analysis of various scenarios of a crisis situation development, shaping situational awareness (Endsley, 2015, pp. 101–111) and choosing a relatively optimal variant of action.

References

(2015) Hybrid warfare. Challenge and Responce, "The Military Balance", nr 115.
Bartosiak J., (2018). Rzeczpospolita między lądem a morzem. O wojnie i pokoju, Warszawa: Zona Zero.
Crandall W.R., Parnell J.A., Spillan J.E., (2014). Crisis Management: Leading in the New Strategy Landscape, SAGE Publications, Thousand Oaks.
da Veiga A., Astakhova L.V., Botha A., Herselman M., (2020). Defining organisational information security culture – Perspectives from academia and industry. Computers & Security, 92.

Endsley M.R., (2015). Final reflections: Situation awareness models and measures. Journal of Cognitive Engineering and Decision Making, 9(1).

ISO 31000:2018, Risk management – Guidelines, International Organization for Standardization, Geneva.

Jagusiak B. (eds.), (2015). Współczesne Wyzwania Bezpieczeństwa Polski, Warszawa: Wojskowa Akademia Techniczna.

Liderman K., (2007). Initial identification of the concept of "natural disaster" and hazard characteristics with a particular focus on information security, Research Project No. PBZ-MNiSW-DBO 01/1/2007, Warsaw: Military University of Technology.

Racz A., (2015). Russia's Hybrid War in Ukraine. Breaking the Enemy's Ability to Resist., FIIA Report 43, Helsinki: The Finnish Institute of International Affairs.

Sułek M., (2018). Potęga Państw 2018 i międzynarodowy układ sił w procesie zmian – raport potęgometryczny, Warszawa: Aspra.

www.abw.gov.pl, dostęp 2020-05-01.

www.polskieradio.pl, dostęp 2020-05-01.

www.tvn24.pl, dostęp 2020-04-30.

Zacharias G.L., Macmillan J., Van Hemel S.B. (eds.), (2008). Behavioral modeling and simulation: From individuals to societies. Committee on Organizational Modeling from Individuals to Societies, Washington: The National Academy Press.

Zalewski J, (2016). Intoksykacja psychologiczno-informacyjna głównym elementem wojny informacyjnej prowadzonej przez Federację Rosyjską, "Studia Bezpieczeństwa Narodowego", nr. 9 2016, Warszawa.

Zapałowski A., (2015). Bezpieczeństwo Polski w geopolitycznej grze Zachodu z Rosją, Warszawa: Europejskie Centrum Analiz Geopolitycznych.

Zaskórski P. (eds.), (2011). Managing an organization under the risk of loss of information continuity, Warsaw: Military University of Technology.

Zaskórski P. et al., (2015). Zarządzanie projektami w ujęciu sytemowym, Warsaw: Military University of Technology.

Zaskórski P., (2012). Asymetria informacyjna w zarządzaniu procesami, Warsaw: Military University of Technology.

Marcin Górnikiewicz

Chapter 11: Quantitative and qualitative cultural foresight of the Russian decision-making process in relation to Poland

Cultural foresight is a quantitative and qualitative prognostic technique. The use of it requires raw qualitative data showing the perceptual and decision-making patterns of the studied society. With such data obtained in the course of research questionnaire (e.g. a diagnostic survey technique), it is possible to start transferring the collected information into quantitative data. Then, by completing the prognostic tool called Cultural Codes Matrix (CCM), belonging to this technique, with this data, one can develop foresights of the decision-making process of the studied society. Then, by comparing the past decision-making process with the established values of the cultural codes as quantitative data, the values are verified. If any discrepancies in the established values, and the values resulting from the decision-making process carried out in the past are observed, it is possible to make a correction by specifying the appropriate values of cultural codes. This in turn allows to develop verifiable foresights about the future decision-making process of the studied society (Górnikiewicz, 2018, pp. 17–52).

The study used data collected and processed for the ICC when developing the cultural foresight technique in 2018. The values of the Russian cultural codes established at that time remain valid, which was examined and verified again by the author during the research conducted both in 2019 and at the beginning of 2020[1]. It is worth mentioning that the values of cultural codes using the shortest possible time perspective are valid for at least one generation, and research conducted over the past hundred years shows that the values of cultural codes usually undergo marginal changes over at least a few generations (Hofstede and

---

[1] Research conducted by the Laboratory of Security Forecasts and Analyzes of the Security and Defense Institute of the Department of Security, Logistics and Management of the Military University of Technology for the ongoing analysis of the Russian decision-making process in connection with the development of the situation in Eastern Europe, with particular emphasis on Russian-Belarusian and Russian-Ukrainian relations. In the light of research, in 2019, an increase in the risk of Russian intervention in relation to the eastern-southern areas of Ukraine was found, which was upheld in the foresight prepared at the beginning of 2020 in connection with the development of COVID-19.

Fink, 2007; Hofstede and McCrae, 2004). Today, we are dealing with an exceptional situation caused by the development of the global information society and intensive mutual communication between the representatives of the young generation coming from many culturally diverse societies, which in turn may lead to a gradual averaging f these values for young people active in the virtual space (Szczurek, 2019, pp. 47–94). Then, the process of changing the value of cultural codes, which previously could have lasted several hundred years, may now take several dozen years, i. e. a period corresponding to the life activity of one generation. It should also be taken into account that in the case of representatives of political decision-making elites, they come from a specific generation, and moreover, they will have an impact on political decisions for at least two or three decades. Therefore, research done in 2018 should still be valid in 2020. To be sure, as mentioned earlier, an additional test was performed to verify the values of the cultural codes established at that time, which proved that these values did not change.

A study conducted in 2018 clearly shows that the values of cultural codes influenced X% of decisions made by Russians in the area of international security. Only X% of decisions resulted not from subconscious cultural codes, but from subconscious individual codes, which in a given situation influenced the decisions of significant international relevance. Thus, the CCM for the cultural codes of the Russians and the Foresight Tool are presented below, along with the possible content of decisions in specific situations. The situations were developed on the basis of content published in the mass media and concerning the Russian perspective towards Poland – from the most probable to the least probable in the current balance of power in Central and Central-Eastern Europe. This allowed for the identification of the four most popular scenarios for the further development of the international situation:
- Poland remains in NATO and the EU (Table 1)
- Poland leaves the EU, but remains allied with the US (Table 2)
- Poland remains in the EU, but loosens its alliance with the US (Table 3)
- Poland leaves the EU and loosens its alliance with the US (Table 4)

Each of the identified scenarios was devoted to a separate study to determine its level of probability. The results of the study are presented in the graphical form in the ICC table (Matrix of Cultural Codes), in which the descriptive parts dedicated to the correlation between the forecasted situation and the value are described in the table below after adding the used marking AD and the ordinal number. This solution made it possible to clearly present the research results in the table without extending all windows too much. Thus, the ICC contains only a foresight of the development of the analyzed situation, using the values of cultural codes determining the Russian perspective and the decision-making process.

Table 1. Description of the impact of average values on the decision-making process of Russia in relation to Poland in a situation when Poland remains in the structures of NATO and the EU

	WR/NR	SM/KO	RW/ST	DT/KT	SL/KM	WN/NN	WS/NS
The Russians	WR	KO	RW	DT	SL	WN	NS
Poland remains in NATO and in the UE	AD. 1	AD. 2	AD. 3	AD. 4	AD. 5	AD. 6	AD. 7
Description of the influence of average values on the decision	The Russians will limit themselves to informational and possibly economic activities aimed at Poland, while currently, due to the economic crisis caused by the COVID-19 pandemic and involvement in two serious conflicts, Moscow will limit itself in the next two years to increasing information activities aimed at dividing Polish society as well as differentiating Polish decision-making circles and the EU circles, and, if possible, the American ones.						

AD. 1 – Poland is perceived by the Russians as a part of the American and EU sphere of influence, while the European Union is treated as an incoherent union of internally divided states, and therefore it is much more important for the Russians to consider Poland mainly as an element of the American sphere of influence, where membership of NATO is only a confirmation as well as a formal, legal and organizational obstruction to official actions aimed at Poland. From the Moscow perspective, the actions taken against Poland will be automatically interpreted in Washington as an attack against American interests.

AD. 2 – Through a group of allied states, the Russians pursue to establish international organizations and achieve their goals. They prefer to act jointly with other countries than to pursue their interests alone. In carrying out actions against Poland, Moscow would seek any international support, even if it was fictitious, to support its actions.

AD. 3 – The Russians are prone to rivalry, and thus to initiate conflicts and resolve disputes by force. The Russians, knowing that they are much stronger, will seek to resolve international problems as quickly and forcefully as possible. In the case of Poland, the conflict could mean a clash with the much stronger United States, supported by the European Union.

AD. 4 – The Russians are willing to plan for the long term, at least for several or several dozen years. Unfortunately, the impact of the Selectivity value discussed below means that long-term plans that require consideration of many factors often fail despite the misconception that everything has been carefully identified and planned. This means that actions aimed at Poland can also be planned with such a distant perspective, but at the same time with a high degree of probability they will not take into account many factors, which may contribute to their premature start or failure.

AD. 5 – The Russians perceive the international reality only through the prism of their own regional interests, so when planning actions against Poland, they may not take into account many circumstances related to far-reaching and global consequences, if such could occur. They would be prepared to act on the belief that they had carefully identified and tested the consequences of such actions beforehand, but in reality they might find that they did not take into account some factors. A similar situation took place during the conflict in Ukraine, where an increase in patriotic attitudes and a broad, social grassroots movement aimed at the aggressor was not foreseen, which effectively not only limited the territorial range of separatist actions, but also made it impossible to carry out many previously planned subversive and sabotage operations in other cities in the east of the country.

AD. 6 – The Russians are reluctant to get involved in situations where the outcome is judged uncertain. In other words, they are not willing to take risks. At the same time, the influence of Selectivity means that they can miscalculate their chances and judge them as very high when in fact they will not. Then Moscow may become involved in a situation in which, if properly calculated, it would never find itself. In the case of Poland, the recognition of this country as a part of the American and EU sphere of influence means that the Russians' calculations would indicate a high risk of failure if open military actions were taken. Thus, the Russians are likely to use measures that would not lead to an allied intervention that would greatly complicate Moscow's situation in the region.

AD 7. – The Russians are not able to comprehensively use all available opportunities and resources, an example of which is still only a slightly modernized mining industry, not to mention the limited exploitation and processing of many other raw materials. An example of a society with a High Self-organization is the Japanese, who were able to turn their island homeland into an economic and technological empire, despite the lack of at least a fraction of the initial resources at the disposal of Russia. In the case of Poland, this means that the Russians will not be able to fully use the potential arising from the special relations they maintain with the Visegrad and Weimar countries, and the international context of the Belt and Road Initiative.

Table 2. Description of the impact of average values on Russia's decision-making process in relation to Poland in a situation when Poland leaves the EU structures, but remains in the alliance with the US

	WR/NR	SM/KO	RW/ST	DT/KT	SL/KM	WN/NN	WS/NS
Russians	WR	KO	RW	DT	SL	WN	NS
Poland leaves the UE but remains in the Alliance with the USA	AD. 8	AD. 9	AD. 10	AD. 11	AD. 12	AD. 13	AD. 14
Description of the influence of average values on the decision		The Russians will limit themselves to informational and possibly economic activities aimed at Poland, while currently, due to the economic crisis caused by the COVID-19 pandemic and involvement in two serious conflicts, Moscow will limit itself in the next two years to increasing information activities aimed at dividing Polish society as well as differentiating Polish decision-making circles and the EU circles, and, if possible, the American ones.					

AD. 8 – From the Russians' perspective, remaining Poland in a strong alliance with Washington will be interpreted as remaining Poland in the American sphere of influence.

AD. 9 – Poland will be perceived as an allied state with Washington, pursuing common interests with the US in this region of the world.

AD. 10 – Russia may compete with Washington by further driving a wedge between Poland and Brussels and using this strategy to weaken the American position in Europe, which could lead to the political and economic isolation of Poland, which has left the EU structures. Then, on the one hand, Poland will be even more closely tied to American interests, but on the other, Moscow will achieve the opportunity to establish better cooperation with the European Union, which will allow it to further break the EU's unity by pursuing its particular interests with individual member states. The ideal for Moscow would then be an alliance between Russia and the European Union aimed at the American sphere of influence in Europe.

AD. 11 – Russia will pursue its goals even in the long term, assuming, on the one hand, ever closer cooperation with the weakened EU, further undermining any cooperation between Brussels and Washington, and the continuation of breaking the internal cohesion of the European Union. The goal would be a confrontation between the European Union and the United States, or bringing about the breakup of the European Union. Actions aimed at Poland then would only be derivatives of this strategy.

AD. 12 – Perceiving the realization of own interests only through the prism of regional conditions will negatively affect the implementation of the above-described strategy by not taking into account the impact of global factors conditioned by the volatility of the situation in other parts of the world and the events that occur in the entire world, and having a large impact on the international and national security of individual countries, e.g. progressing climate changes, an increase in the activity of previously unknown viruses and bacteria, powerful changes in the mentality of young generations of most countries, subsequent economic crises resulting from the transition of the world economy from industrial to post-industrial- informational, including the development of works on AI which is becoming more and more common in every aspect of life.

AD. 13 – Seeking to confront the European Union with the United States or to break up the Union by information and social means, rather than striving for a direct clash with one of the two powers. Most likely, Russia will not take into account China's growing international activity in these plans, which may decide on the future of this country at the right moment, which will then neutralise all plans. In this situation, Poland will be treated in Moscow as an element of the game between Russia, the United States, and the successively weakened European Union.

AD. 14 – The inability to comprehensively use the available resources will make China more and more colonize the eastern fringes of the Russian empire, moving closer to the center. This process, spread over decades, will make the Russians realize in such a situation, but it will be too late. Against this background, Moscow will not be able to take full advantage of the opportunities arising from the initiated US-European conflict.

Table 3. Description of the impact of average values on Russia's decision-making process in relation to Poland in a situation when Poland remains in the EU structures and loosens its alliance with the US

	WR/NR	SM/KO	RW/ST	DT/KT	SL/KM	WN/NN	WS/NS
Russians	WR	KO	RW	DT	SL	WN	NS
Poland remains in the EU but loosens the alliance with the US	AD. 15	AD. 16	AD. 17	AD. 18	AD. 19	AD. 20	AD. 21

Table 3 *(Continued)*

	WR/ NR	SM/ KO	RW/ ST	DT/ KT	SL/ KM	WN/ NN	WS/ NS
Description of the influence of average values on the decision	Russia will begin to take increasingly harsh information, social, intelligence, economic and, ultimately, para-military actions, the original goal of which will be to take control of Warsaw's sovereign decision-making process in order to weaken the European Union, and then, after reaching this goal, a complete and formal takeover of a control over the Polish decision-making process within the appropriate formula of international cooperation.						

AD. 15 – The European Union is treated in Moscow as an alliance of loosely connected states without a clearly defined command center, and therefore as an international organization that can be a subject to various influences both on the Union as a whole and on individual states. As a result, Poland will then begin to be treated as a country towards which Moscow can resume decisive and sharper actions than before. Therefore, one can expect an increase in intelligence and propaganda activity, as well as the impact of economic and political means. Russia will strive to gradually take control of the political decision-making process in Poland, while using Poland as an element of weakening the structure of the European Union. At the same time, it will make efforts to prevent Poland from re-establishing any cooperation with Washington, which would be the greatest threat to Russia's plans.

AD. 16 – Russia will then strive to create various forms of international cooperation with Poland by signing various treaties and agreements to prepare the ground for participation in joint international organizations under the more or less official leadership of Russia.

AD. 17 – Decision-makers in Moscow will assume that Poland has been largely isolated and will be ready to take decisive economic, political, information and social measures if necessary. In this situation, it is also possible to resort to paramilitary measures in extreme cases, which Russia has already tested to a limited extent in relation to Georgia, and then to Crimea and Ukraine.

AD. 18 – In long-term plans, Poland should remain formally free from Russian influence as long as the formula of destructive influence on the cohesion of the European Union is exhausted. When this formula is exhausted, the process of closer integration of Poland with Russia will begin within the framework of the previously adopted international formula.

AD. 19 – Due to selectivity, the Russians will not take into account Chinese influence, and Beijing may have its own plans for Poland in the context of the global geopolitical game. An example of this is Beijing's desire to involve Poland in the Belt and Road Initiative, and there will be no place in this plan for a too strong Russian position. Factors that the Russians did not foresee will probably emerge, which will destroy their overly long-term plans.

AD. 20 – The Russians, aware of the lack of a decisive, especially military response from the weaker European Union, will not have any concerns about taking strong and decisive measures against Poland.

AD. 21 – The lack of the possibility to comprehensively use all available opportunities, on a properly distant stage of implementation of plans – strategic and targeted at Poland, will probably make the Chinese emerge. A sudden return to the game by Washington cannot be ruled out either.

Table 4. Description of the impact of average values on Russia's decision-making process in relation to Poland in a situation when Poland leaves the EU structures and loosens its alliance with the US

	WR/NR	SM/KO	RW/ST	DT/KT	SL/KM	WN/NN	WS/NS
Russians	WR	KO	RW	DT	SL	WN	NS
Poland leaves the EU and loosens the alliance with the US	AD. 22	AD. 23	AD. 24	AD. 25	AD. 26	AD. 27	AD. 28
Description of the influence of average values on the decision	The Russians will strive to take control over Poland as quickly as possible, taking into account the possibility of using all available means, including military ones, and ignoring possible consequences, e. g. – like any sanctions.						

AD. 22 – Poland remaining outside all international structures will be considered weak and the so-called no-man's land, which Russia will want to develop as soon as possible. Among other things, to prevent Poland from being taken over by another power or any bloc of states. Apart from the EU structures, Poland will also lose its importance as an element potentially useful in destabilizing the EU structures, and therefore even more ready to be taken over directly.

AD. 23 – Russia will strive to achieve even an apparent international legitimacy for the actions taken by harnessing the support of a part of the international opinion or by establishing a coalition of states for this purpose.

AD. 24 – In this case, the Russians will be ready to use all forces and means to seize the control of Poland as quickly as possible, including classical military means. Of course, they will use political, informational, social, economic and para-military measures first. The most convenient scenario for the Kremlin would be one in which Warsaw and Moscow conclude cooperation aimed at subordinating Poland to Russian interests. If this option did not come true or would require too long, creating the risk of Poland re-entering the American or European orbit, the Russians will quickly move to decisive actions, not paying attention to the consequences of any sanctions, being aware that such an opportunity may not be repeated.

AD. 25 and 26 – Russia in its plans will meticulously take into account possible counter-actions taken by Brussels or Washington, but it will almost certainly not take into account Chinese actions in the full spectrum, or ever more, perhaps, other countries with emerging powers such as India or Brazil. It may therefore happen that the Russian detailed plan to take control of Poland at a later stage will not be implemented as a result of the actions of other emerging powers, more aware of playing their own national interests on a global, rather than regional, dimension. It is also possible that the price for taking over the center of Europe will be the loss of Russia's eastern borders to China.

AD. 27 – Awareness of the opportunity ahead, coupled with impunity, will make the Russians ready for a great deal just to regain real control over Poland.

AD. 28 – Failure to fully take into account its own possibilities resulting from the new international situation, as well as the interests of other countries on a global scale, will make Russia's plans either fail or Moscow will have to pay a high price for their implementation. The only option favorable for Russia would be to carry out its plans as quickly as possible, almost surprising all other powers potentially interested in participating in the newly created international situation.

References

Górnikiewicz M., (2018). Prognozowanie kulturowe zagrożeń bezpieczeństwa narodowego i międzynarodowego, Warszawa: Wojskowa Akademia Techniczna.

Hofstede G. and Fink G., (2007). Culture: organisations, personalities and nations. Gerhard Fink interviews Geert Hofstede. *European Journal of International Management*, 1, pp. 14–22.

Hofstede G. and Mccrae, R. R., (2004). Personality and culture revisited: Linking traits and dimensions of culture. *Cross-Cultural Research*, 38, pp. 52–88.

Szczurek T., (2019). Wyzwania dla bezpieczeństwa – niepewna przyszłość, między zagrożeniami a szansami, Warszawa: Wojskowa Akademia Techniczna.

Marcin Górnikiewicz / Tadeusz Szczurek / Marzena Walkowiak

Chapter 12: Summary and conclusions: Foresight of the Russian influence on Poland in the era of political and economic changes in the third decade of the 21st century

As a result of the applied quantitative and qualitative methods and the review of the presented variants of the development of the situation, the first of the described scenario of the cultural foresight method seems to be the most probable. Such conclusions were combined with the fact that the Polish authorities adopted an eminently Euro-Atlantic orientation in terms of maintaining the political and military alliance and strengthening their position in NATO structures, as well as the awareness of the political and economic benefits resulting from participation in the structures of the European Union. Washington also cares about the presence of one of its most faithful allies in the European community due to the possibility of cooperation with Warsaw on the occasion of pursuing various interests important from the point of view of both capitals. In conclusion, the Polish authorities intend to remain in alliance with Washington and the European Union, regardless of the media overtone created for the purposes of domestic policy. For this reason, Russian actions aimed at Poland will still be limited to political, information, social, intelligence and, to a very narrow extent, economic measures. The Polish authorities are also aware of the seriousness of the situation, which was most clearly demonstrated by the crisis in Ukraine, which also means that they will not be interested in any loosening of relations with Washington. On the other hand, changes taking place on a global scale, such as the transition of some societies from the level of late industrialism to the level of early post-industrialism, climate changes and the emergence of new viruses and bacteria will intensify the economic and financial crisis, motivating young generations of many countries, mentally prepared for the revolution, for taking various actions. The approach to regulating the world economy will probably also completely change, which will be, on the one hand, a consequence and, on the other hand, another driving force for faster and faster changes. The growing strength of social movements may lead to significant changes in Russia itself, but also in other political systems with still immature democratic standards, which in turn may lead to a destabilisation of the whole region.

Chapter 12. Summary and conclusions: thought of the Russian influence on Poland in the era of political and economic changes in the third decade of the 21st century

Part II: The Czech Republic (Czechia)

Section I:
The Czech Republic in the geopolitical and geostrategic vision of Moscow in Europe

Andrzej Jacuch

Chapter 13: The geopolitical situation of the Czech Republic from the Russian perspective

The aim of this chapter is to define, analyze and evaluate the geopolitical situation of the Czech Republic in relation to Russia's actions. It takes into account the geopolitical conditions of the Czech Republic, also in the historical context; the position of the Czech Republic within wider European security; general nature of Czech-Russian relations; the idea of Russian foreign policy in relation to the Czech Republic and the Czech political forces supporting Russian actions. The main assumption adopted by many authors used in this publication is that the Czech Republic is a key country for the activities of both Russian intelligence services and disinformation aimed at political destabilization, increasing economic influence, undermining the sovereignty of the Czech Republic and the role of the European Union.

According to Cohen (Cohen, 2015, p. 16) geopolitics is defined as "the analysis of the interactions between geographic location and prospects on the one hand, and political processes on the other. Political processes include forces that operate at the international level and those on the national stage that influence international behavior. Both the geographic setting and political processes are dynamic, and each one influences and is influenced by the other. Geopolitics addresses the consequences of this interaction." Geopolitics studies the movements and strength of power in geographic space, either for military operations or strategic control in peacetime (Spykman, 1942).

Kučerová (Kučerová, 2015) using qualitative research focusing on contextual relations in the region of Central Europe in a historical perspective, justifies the hypothesis that the countries of the region, including the Czech Republic, are an object of geopolitical interests, not their actual subject.

The Czech Republic is a landlocked country in Central Europe with a population of 10.65 million (2019) in the area of 78.866 km2. The Czech Republic has a natural border in the form of mountain ridges in the west and north and borders with allied countries in the east and south. The Czech Republic borders Austria, Germany, Poland and Slovakia. The capital city is Prague. The historical regions of the Czech Republic are the Bohemia to the west, Moravia to the east and Czech Silesia to the northeast. These regions coincide with the basins of the main rivers of the country, the Elbe and Vltava for Bohemia, the Moravia for Moravia and the Oder River for Czech Silesia. The location of the Czech Republic and the relatively flat landscape have historically contributed to the prosperity of the region, placing it at the center of some of the oldest trade routes in Europe (Stratfor).

In the period from the 11th to the 19th century, the Czech Kingdom was an essential part of the Roman Empire. It went through a golden age during the reign of the Czech king and Roman emperor Charles IV. In the institutional field, Charles IV was the author of the Golden Bull, an imperial constitutional law that was in force from 1356 until the collapse of the Holy Roman Empire. During the reign of Charles IV, Central Europe, thanks to its capital, Prague, which had a population of around 40,000, became the geopolitical center of the medieval European world. However, later religious disputes, the papal schism (1378–1417), the growing influence of religious reformers, and the Hussite requirements leading to the war in the Czech Kingdom did not favor regional development. A brief renaissance of the region took place under King George of Podebrady (1420–1471), who was a man of great diplomatic talents (Kučerová, 2015).

World War I fundamentally changed the political map of Europe, especially for the Central European region. Nation states arose in Central Europe. Slavic states in Central Europe created a buffer zone preventing the absorption of this region by the Germans and Russians. And given the revolution in Russia that plunged the Russians into chaos, poverty and totalitarianism, there was a threat, according to Mackinder, that the people of Eastern Europe might then lean more towards the German concept of order. In such a case, a more democratic society like Czechoslovakia could serve as an example against the autocracy of Germans and Russians, which is their common feature (Kučerová 2015, pp. 178–179).

In Czechoslovakia, representatives of the future independent state spoke at the Paris Conference (1919–1920) of two equivalent languages – Czech and German. However, the Czechoslovak idea eventually pushed other nationalities out of mainstream politics. During this period, six to ten languages[1] were spoken in Czechoslovakia. It was not a homogeneous or unified ethno-linguistic space, but one that led to geopolitical games. Interwar Czechoslovakia was an attractive destination for refugees. During the Bolshevik Revolution, there was an influx of immigrants from Russia who easily obtained asylum in Czechoslovakia, similar to the German exiles in the late 1930s. The 1918–1919 military conflict between Hungary on the one hand and Czechoslovakia and Romania on the other, which

---

1 Namely Czech, German, Slovak, Hungarian, Polish, Ruthenian, Ukrainian, Yiddish, Romani, Romanian – obviously a central European melting pot in practice, because one language functioned as an umbrella in every region.

took place in Upper Hungary and Russia and concerned the newly established Czechoslovakia and Transylvania, to which Romania referred, was essentially a continuation of World War I. As a result of the treaty of Trianon, 3,425,000 ethnic Hungarians remained outside the country. In fact, the event has had political repercussions to nowadays (Kučerová, 2015).

During World War II, the territories then known as Czechoslovakia were occupied by the Nazis, and later fell into the Soviet sphere of influence. The process of communization of Central and Eastern Europe led to the formation of the Soviet bloc, but under different conditions, depending mainly on previous historical experiences. Most of the actors involved were countries with undemocratic development, with the exception of Czechoslovakia, which was considered a truly democratic and relatively tolerant country (Kučerová, 2015). The fall of the Iron Curtain allowed the countries of Central Europe to rebuild after more than forty years of deliberately disrupted traditional economic relations, subject to political liberalization. In 1993, Czechoslovakia peacefully divided itself into the independent states of the Czech Republic and Slovakia. In 1999, the Czech Republic joined NATO, and in 2004, the European Union. Today, the Czech Republic is a dynamic, export-driven economy with low unemployment. However, its deep connection with the German economy is both an advantage and a threat, as the Czech economy is subject to fluctuations in the economic health of its main trading partner (Stratfor).

As a small Central European country, the Czech Republic is trying to balance its membership of the European Union with the protection of its national sovereignty. So far, the Czech Republic has not joined the euro area. The Czechs deepen their ties with their neighbors from Central Europe through the Visegrad Group, which includes Hungary, Poland and Slovakia (Stratfor).

The Russian Federation, with imperial thinking about Russia and the concept that the countries of Central Europe are in the Russian sphere of influence, seeks to undermine the sovereignty of Central European countries, including the Czech Republic.

A Russian geopolitician whose views influenced the Kremlin's contemporary foreign policy, Alexander Dugin considers the Axis countries, that is, Germany and Italy, to be Central Europe. He does not consider the Czech Republic, Slovakia, Poland and Hungary as the countries of Central Europe, but as the East, and since the 1930s the area under the direct influence of the USSR as a geopolitical entity (Kučerová, 2015). In the 1930s, these Central European states were still fully sovereign players in international relations and tried to engage in international cooperation in accordance with their wishes, but sixty years later, Dugin attributes them to the East, seeing them as part of the East (Kučerová, 2015). Twenty years after the fall of the Iron Curtain, Russia is surprised that the countries of Central Europe really want to break away from the Russian sphere of influence. Contemporary Russian policy, including the one presented in the pro-government media, talks about the need to rebuild and strengthen Russian influence in the region, especially in the Czech Republic.

Czech-Russian trade, like in other countries of the Visegrad Group, has been growing despite EU sanctions since 2017. In 2018, it amounted to approximately USD 9.8 billion, and was the highest since 2014 (USD 11.7 billion). Despite its increase, the Czech Ministry of Agriculture accuses Russia of sabotaging the development of economic relations.

Energy security is a key topic in Czech-Russian relations. The Czech Republic is dependent on Russia, and the Russian energy giant Rosatom is the sole supplier of fuel for the Temelin nuclear power plant. The Czech energy sector is of interest to Russian business, especially Gazprom, and is an area of particularly intense activity by Russian information services.

The Czech Republic is in favor of projects reducing the negative effects of its energy dependence on Russia. Nevertheless, the Czech Ministry of Industry and Trade has supported the construction of the Nord Stream 2 gas pipeline. The Czech Republic counts on strengthening its position as a transit country for Russian gas, which thanks to the Gazelle gas pipeline (extension of the Nord Stream gas pipeline), as well as the planned EUGAL gas pipeline in larger quantities it would go to the Czech Republic, and then to Austria and Slovakia, for example. Therefore, despite the dependence on Russian gas imports, the Czech authorities have made little efforts to diversify the sources of this raw material. In addition, Russia's Rosatom has a chance to expand units at the Dukovany nuclear power plant. According to the presented schedule for the implementation of this investment in November this year, the contractor is to be selected in 2022.

There are politicians of significant influence in the Czech Republic who sympathize with the actions of the Russian Federation. This is President Miloš Zeman, most of the representatives of the Communist Party of Bohemia and Moravia, several representatives of the Czech Social Democratic Party and some representatives of the extreme right.

President Zeman is used by the Kremlin to disrupt Czech society from within. He undermines the membership of the Czech Republic in NATO and the EU, denies the organized military presence of Russia in Ukraine, and calls for the lifting of sanctions against the Russian Federation. Russian state media present him as a European ally of Vladimir Putin, a critic of the Russian opposition and a fighter against the United States (Janda and Víchová, 2017). The Czech Information Security Service (BIS) warns in its annual report against the infiltration of Russian capital related to the shadow economy into the Czech environment and the strengthening of the Kremlin's political influence in the Czech Republic (Janda, 2017). Due to the convenient central geographic location of the Czech Republic, they have always been a convenient theater for Russia's dynamic activities and covert operations. According to a report by the Czech Information Security Service (BIS), Russian intelligence officers often operate under the diplomatic cover of the Russian embassy, which has more employees than embassies of other countries (Annual Report, 2016). There has been a Soviet espionage base since 1969 in Prague, which never left the country and never revived its contacts after the Velvet Revolution. These former Soviet agents are now active in organized crime circles and are trying to influence politics and increase the Czech dependence on Russia (Janda and Kundra, 2016).

Andrzej Jacuch

Chapter 14: The geostrategic position of the Czech Republic and Moscow's disinformation activity

The aim of this chapter is to define, analyze and evaluate the geostrategic situation of the Czech Republic in relation to the activities of the Russian Federation (FR). It takes into account the foreign policy strategies of the Russian Federation towards the Czech Republic. It was assumed that in the current geostrategic situation, a full-scale war is unlikely. The main hypothesis is that the Russian Federation treats the Czech Republic as a key country for espionage and disinformation activities and as a zone of economic influence. On the other hand, the influence of the Russian Federation is mainly of propaganda, disinformation and economic character. The content of this chapter deals with the issues of the methodology of Russia's influence on the Czech society and the Czech political elite.

Geostrategy is the geographical direction of the state's foreign policy. More specifically, geostrategy describes where the state focuses its efforts by anticipating military power and guiding diplomatic action. Geostrategy describes this direction of the state's foreign policy and does not apply to motivational and decision-making processes. Thus, the geostrategy of the state does not have to be motivated by geographical or geopolitical factors. The state may project power over a given location for ideological reasons, interest groups or simply the whim of its leader (Grygiel, 2006).

The strategy of the Russian Federation (FR) aims to transform the European security order and its principles of upholding it. The central element is mainly the militarization of the Kaliningrad Oblast and Crimea, and the destabilization of Ukraine. A full-scale war with European countries remains an unlikely scenario. Compared to the West, the Russian Federation has less economic or conventional military capabilities. Therefore, it attaches the highest importance to both nuclear deterrence and asymmetric methods and instruments, i.e. means of maintaining strategic parity with the West. Dmitry Trenin, director of the Carnegie Moscow Center, says that "since February 2014, the Russian Federation has been acting de facto in the war mode, and the leader of the war is RF President Vladimir Putin" (Suchankin and Czakiris, 2017).

In Russian military doctrines, information warfare is considered a key element of modern military operations and assigned the task of developing Russian capabilities in this area (Darczewska, 2015). In 2013, the Chief of the General Staff of the Russian Armed Forces, General Valerij V. Gerasimov, wrote: "The role of non-military means of achieving political and strategic goals has increased, and in many cases has exceeded the effectiveness of military force". He proposed using disinformation to achieve Russian political goals. According to Gerasymov's doctrine, the Arab Spring and the South Ossetian War showed that non-military methods of conflict – including information warfare – are more effective than the power of conventional weapons. Russia sees "non-linear" actions consisting of military and non-military elements combined in an integrated, comprehensive strategy as the future of hostilities (Герасимов, 2013). According to Gerasymov's doctrine, non-military methods of conflict – including information warfare – are more effective than the power of conventional weapons.

Russian strategists have developed an approach – "information confrontation" (informacionnoje protivoborstvo) (Шушков, 2015) – where Russian propaganda is feasible in both war and peace, reflecting its "lasting" nature.

In the current geostrategic situation, Russia is exerting an influence on the Czech Republic using non-military means, mainly through the actions of secret services, disinformation and propaganda, as well as exploiting the country economically.

Russian espionage and disinformation activities are visible in every country where the Russian Federation sees the potential to pursue its own interests. Its diversity and scale prove the interest in the Czech Republic from the Russian Federation. It is very intense in the Czech Republic and has a negative impact on bilateral relations.

Disinformation and propaganda activities gained particular importance with the transfer of information communication to the web, including social media, which allowed them to freely transfer and share them. As shown by numerous examples in the Czech Republic, for the purposes of disinformation campaigns, hackers are employed, who, by hacking into local news portals and placing prepared information there, try to negatively influence local communities, and thus build aversion and prejudice against neighboring nations (Gliwa and Olech, 2020). The Czech Republic found itself on the front lines of the Russian disinformation war. The Russian Federation uses a well-developed network of influence in the Czech Republic and is increasingly effective in its campaign (Morozov, 2020).

The Russian services finance institutions that create deceptive messages on the Internet, aimed at destabilizing the political situation. Deceptive messages gain credibility thanks to mass sharing on social media – they are usually sent out by Facebook, Twitter or Reddit users. The message prepared in this way reaches up to several million recipients and is sometimes picked up by the mass media, which at the same time makes it credible. The disinformation is fueled by politicians who cite untrue news about their opponents.

This is confirmed, inter alia, by BIS (*Bezpečnostní informační služba – Security Information Service), special intelligence service of the Czech Republic, responsible inter alia, for counterintelligence and internal security of the country*) report for 2018, which lists, inter alia, attempts to influence the decision-making processes in the Czech Republic, spreading disinformation and pro-Russian propaganda, as well as attacks by Russian hackers, e. g. on the Czech Ministry of Foreign Affairs (data theft). The legitimacy of the warnings by the Czech services is demonstrated, among others, by disrupting the network of Russian hackers, linked to the Federal Security Service and financed by the Russian state (Prague Monitor, 2019).

According to BIS, the Russians are extremely active in the Czech Republic, spreading false information about the EU, NATO, the war in Syria, Donbas, the migration crisis and, recently, the COVID-19 pandemic. The goals of Russian propaganda are:
- sowing doubts among Czechs that democracy is the best system of exercising power; – strengthening the negative image of the European Union and NATO;
- influencing internal social moods;
- discouraging the public from participating in various democratic processes, including influencing the results of local, parliamentary and presidential elections; – the attitude of society towards the authorities and public institutions in order to escalate conflicts among citizens, and also by distorting the perception of other nations and immigrants.

As early as 2015, BIS stated that Russian information operations in the Czech Republic focus on: "weakening the power of influence of the Czech media (hidden infiltration of Czech media and the Internet, mass production of Russian propaganda and state-controlled disinformation); strengthening the information resistance of Russian recipients (prefabricated disinformation from Czech sources for Russian recipients); influencing the perception and thinking of the Czech public, weakening the will of the public to resist or confront (information and disinformation overload of the audience, relativization of truth and objectivity, promotion of the motto "everyone is lying"); creating or promoting inter-industry and inter-political tensions in the Czech Republic (setting up puppet organizations, hidden and open support of populist or extremist actors); disrupting the cohesion and readiness of NATO and the EU (attempts to disrupt Polish-Czech relations, disinformation and disturbing rumors slandering the US and NATO, disinformation posing a virtual threat of war with Russia); damaging Ukraine's reputation and isolating the country in the international arena (involving Czech citizens and organizations in influential operations clandestinely carried out in or against Ukraine by Russia). The above actions pose a threat to the Czech Republic, the EU and NATO not only in connection with the conflicts in Ukraine and Syria. The infrastructure designed to achieve these goals will not disappear with the end of both conflicts. At any time, it can be used to destabilize or manipulate Czech society or the political environment, if Russia wants to do so" (Výroční, 2015).

In October 2019, the BIS and the National Headquarters for Counteracting Organized Crime reported the detection and disruption of a network in the Czech Republic that had been set up by the Federal Security Service, a Russian intelligence operation (Czech, 2019).

The official channels of anti-Western coverage are Russia Today TV and Sputnik News. The strategy of information activities of the Russian Federation is often to drop a lot of very abstract information into the information space, which constitute a "smoke screen" for a real disinformation target. The information stream is being released into the media space for the sole purpose of disguising the true purpose of disinformation through a simple psychological mechanism. Within the stream of abstract and seemingly false information, the recipient will be able to accept as true what, unlike the improbable one, seems logical and true. At the same time, this will be the goal of the disinformation campaign (Gliwa and Olech, 2020).

Official Russian quasi-media project in the Czech language – the website Sputnik interacts with disinformation along with many entities that directly or indirectly serve the interests of the Russian Federation. Information prepared and disseminated by Sputnik is transferred to varying degrees by other portals, which can be described as "satellites". Using these networks, this information reaches a wider audience. These portals publish content based on facts, but they change their meaning or sense and add a negative narrative to it, which is a denial of journalistic reliability. It happens that these portals create news based on subjective opinions or unverified sources. Often, using simple and non-journalistic language and through populist slogans, they achieve the support of more radical and shocking recipients (Gliwa and Olech, 2020).

There are around 40 Czech-language websites with no known links to the Russian government that repeatedly publish false reports and spread manipulative narratives, often motivated by praise for Russia or economic interests. Most of these disinformation and manipulation websites are largely opaque, revealing the names of authors, financial resources, or owners. A similar situation occurs in the case of social media campaigns, which more often focus not only on supporting Russia, but also on arousing social emotions. Many of these sites don't even produce their own content, but only translate foreign, very low-quality articles. The number of applications per week is very high and is strengthened by sharing them on social networks, especially on Facebook.

One of the most radical is the Protoproudi (Upstream) website. As Gazeta Wyborcza writes for the Czech think-tank European Values, Russian propaganda is most active in the subject of Islam, immigration and terror, trying to spread fear among Europeans and divide the European Union. In one of the publicly available reports, BIS writes that this is an easy task, as both opponents and supporters of accepting refugees in the Czech Republic very often use "demagogic arguments and half-truths" (Kokot, 2016).

Disinformation disseminated on Czech-language websites and social networks often comes from foreign servers, mainly from official Kremlin channels or English-language conspiracy websites such as Global Research or Southfront.

In the Czech Republic, articles spread on pro-Russian websites claiming that NATO intends to attack Russia from Eastern Europe without the consent of the authorities. (MacFarquhar, 2016).

In December 2016, the Russian news site Lenta.ru falsely reported that Ukraine had offered to accept migrants from the Middle East "in exchange for visa-free travel to the EU", a fabricated story that was quickly translated and picked up by the Czech news site Nová republika ("Beware of non-governmental organizations", 2016). This example of Russian-language information spreading to a Czech-language news website testifies to the global scale of disinformation campaigns at a time when borders are not a barrier against information operations carried out by state entities with recognized or contested international statutes (Helmus, Bodine-Baron et al., 2018).

According to the Warsaw Institute, two of the most widely read pieces of disinformation of 2017 come from the well-known Aeronet website, which does not provide any information about its structures. The first reported an alleged radioactive cloud over Europe from "a strange explosion at a French nuclear power plant," accusing European governments of keeping it a secret and advising Czech citizens to buy iodine tablets and dosimeters. In fact, the slightly increased level of radioactive iodine in the air probably came from a different source, more to the east, and was in no way dangerous to human health, unlike the iodine tablets humans are supposed to digest. The second example illustrates very well the typical response of disinformation websites to any natural disaster or terrorist attack. Following the recent tragic chemical attacks in Syria, Aeronet reported that there is evidence that the attacks in Idlib were carried out by White Helmets and the CIA.

On a global scale, Russia used information activities to influence the election results. As indicated by the report "Hostile Social Manipulation Present Realities and Emerging Trends", in 2017 the parliamentary elections in the Czech Republic ended with a successful result for the Kremlin (Gliwa and Olech, 2020).

The Czech President Miloš Zeman plays a key role in the Czech disinformation scene, supporting Russian interests. Although he considers the Russian annexation of Crimea to be unlawful, in a speech to the Parliamentary Assembly of the Council of Europe in October 2017, he suggested that Russia should pay compensation to Ukraine for the occupation of the peninsula. In addition, President Zeman maintains in a friendly personal relationship with President Vladimir Putin, including official visits to Russia. On the initiative of the presidents of both countries, an annual Czech-Russian Discussion Forum was launched in 2018, gathering e.g. academic circles. The president of the Czech Republic is trying to counteract the actions of critics of Russia's policy. There are many people in his environment who are or have been associated with Russian business.

The president repeats the disinformation and narratives originating in the Internet pro-Russian centers (for example, he repeated the untruth about the alleged act on the Ukrainian language (Hendrychová, 2014). These websites also give him support when he needs it. President Zeman's statements and opinions are regularly repeated by disinformation centers. He is portrayed as the only person in the Czech Republic who actually cares about his citizens. There are also other politicians who help to spread disinformation either intentionally or because of their ignorance. Across the political spectrum there are people who usually share articles from these websites on their social networks, and sometimes they trust reports that are not factual (Víchová, 2016).

The coalition government of the centrist ANO and the Czech Social Democratic Party (ČSSD) does not present a coherent policy towards Russia. The prime minister and leader of ANO, Andrej Babiš, is in favor of dialogue with Russia, and perceives the EU sanctions as a negative factor for the Czech economy. Until now restrained in criticizing Russia's actions towards Ukraine, however, he condemned the annexation of Crimea during his visit to Kiev. The chairman of the lower house of the Czech parliament, Radek Vondráček, is considered to be the most favorable cooperation with Russia in ANO. He criticizes Russia's international isolation and in October 2017, during the visit, he met, among others, with politicians covered by EU sanctions. On the other hand, the Minister of Foreign Affairs, Tomáš Petříček (ČSSD), supported the expulsion of three Russian diplomats in a gesture of solidarity with Great Britain after the poisoning of Sergei and Julia Skripal in March 2018. Petříček's actions, however, are not identical to the party's line, whose program objective is to keep the "good, strategic relations with Russia". The Communist Party of Bohemia and Moravia is considered a clearly pro-Russian party on the Czech political scene, to which the minority government of ANO-ČSSD owes a vote of confidence.

As polls show, there is a very high level of Euro-skepticism in the Czech Republic. However, sympathies towards Russia remain. The current president is generally opposed sanctions against Russia. The Czech society is, to some extent, susceptible to information from the Russian propaganda.

According to the Czech Center for Public Opinion Research (CVVM), the Czechs support for the country's membership in the European Union is falling. In 2019, only two fifths of Czech citizens (37%) expressed satisfaction with the Czech Republic's membership of the European Union, and more than a quarter (26%) were dissatisfied (CVVM, 2019).

The Czech sociological research company STEM reports that 24.5 percent of citizens trust media linked to Russian propaganda, 38 percent. believes in the responsibility of the United States and NATO for the Ukrainian crisis, and 19.6 percent is convinced that there are no Russian armed forces in the Donbass (Kokot, 2016).

According to the 2017 report of the International Republican Institute, as many as 38% of Czech respondents believe that Russia defends European values. According to OECD statistics, 46% of citizens in the Czech Republic believe that the mainstream media attempt to be impartial. The lack of trust of the others, in turn, translates into the need to look for alternative sources of information – websites or social media, which almost become a hotbed of untrue or deliberately falsified content.

According to a 2017 survey by the Slovak think-tank GLOBSEC, the Czechs believe that they should geopolitically stand somewhere between the West and the East and remain as neutral as possible. According to this poll, 30% of Czechs also believe that the best political system would be an autocracy, and 49% do not believe the mainstream media.

The Czech Republic has extensive experience in the fight against Russian disinformation, which is common there in the so-called alternative and social media, as well as conducted by pro-Russian activists. The Center Against Terrorism and Hybrid Threats, part of the Ministry of the Interior, which has been operating since January 2017, contributes to reducing disinformation. Its tasks include the fight against external propaganda, also in the context of possible influence on the course of the elections. The center monitors the internet network and media coverage, corrects false information, reacts to stories of disinformation that pose a threat to internal security, and tracks the most important narratives spread by foreign powers and proposes new legal solutions. The Center also coordinates activities in various ministries in the field of counteracting hostile influence and training and education of civil servants (Janda and Víchová, 2017).

In the non-governmental sector, civil society initiatives monitor Russian activities and block the Russian Federation from spreading its influence in the Czech Republic. The Czech think-tank **Evropské hodnoty** has a Kremlin Observation Program (Kremlin Watch) that monitors disinformation activities in the Czech Republic. The Czech organization **Člověk v tísni** provides teachers with educational materials on disinformation campaigns and organizes workshops and lectures on media literacy. **The Masaryk University** conducts research on techniques of manipulation by websites used for disinformation. Moreover, the Zvolsi.info initiative shows young people how to validate their sources and select objective and credible news, and show manipulation and teach them how to disclose them. Individual journalists conduct research to reveal the origins and connections of people behind disinformation projects in the Czech Republic (Kremlin Influence, 2017).

Czech-Russian political relations are deteriorating despite the pro-Russian activity of President Zeman. They are also influenced by the local government authorities and the BIS counterintelligence, not subject to the government and supervised by the Czech parliament. This complexity makes it difficult for other countries to possibly influence the Czech Republic's decisions in this field.

The disruption of the network of Russian hackers, the removal of the monument of the Soviet Marshal Ivan Koniev in Prague, and the intensification of relations between the Czech Republic and Ukraine and the USA also contributed to the deterioration of political relations.

Apart from the Russian aggression on Ukraine and the sanctions, this was also caused by Babiš's visit to Kiev and gestures of support for Ukraine, intensification of Czech-American relations – including extradition to the US of the Russian hacker Yevgeny Nikulin – as well as Russia's retaliatory actions, including the cancellation of Minister Toman's visit to Kazan. Despite disinformation from Russia, the overall direction of Czech foreign policy remains unchanged. The Czech Ministry of Foreign Affairs constantly supports the integrity of Ukraine (Česká podpora Ukrajině, 2017) and considers it a priority country for cooperation in transformation. The Czech Republic recognizes the so-called people's republics in eastern Ukraine as a gross violation of international law (Prohlášení MZV, 2017).

An expression of the deteriorating bilateral relations were the disputes over monuments commemorating figures associated with the end of World War II in the Czech Republic. The first of them – USSR Marshal Koneev – was removed in September last year by the decision of the Prague district council. The second one is the construction of a monument commemorating the soldiers of the Russian Liberation Army (ROA) collaborating with the Third Reich, who joined with the other side, contributed to the liberation of Prague before the advent of the Red Army. Both initiatives have been criticized by the Russian Ministry of Foreign Affairs.

Despite the deteriorating Czech-Russian political intergovernmental cooperation, and because of the increase in trade and the strengthening on energy integration, bilateral economic relations are developing. The Czech authorities support the construction of the Nord Stream 2 gas pipeline (Ogrodnik, 2019). Czech decision-making centers have repeatedly emphasized that trade is harmed by the EU's policy of sanctions against Russia. The Czech Republic will oppose the maintenance of these restrictions if a significant part of the EU countries is in favor of such a solution. For the Prime Minister Babiš, economic and energy interests are more important than diplomatic relations or historical policy.

References

(2016) Annual Report of the Security Information Service for 2015, Security Information Service (BIS), https://www.bis.cz/vyrocni-zpravaEN890a.html?ArticleID=1104.
(2017) Česká podpora Ukrajině, Velvyslanectví České republiky v Kyjevě, http://www.mzv.cz/kiev/cz/vzajemne_vztahy/ceska_podpora_ukrajine/index.html.
(2017) Vulnerability Index, GLOBSEC Policy Institute, http://www.globsec.org/upload/documents/vulnerability-index/globsec-vulnerability-index.pdf.
(2017). Kremlin Influence Index, Media Sapiens, http://osvita.mediasapiens.ua/content/files/dm_iik_engl_pravka-compressed.pdf.
(2019) CVVM, Public Opinion on the Czech Republic's Membership in the European Union – April 2019, Prague, 2019, https://cvvm.soc.cas.cz/media/com_form2content/documents/c6/a4921/f77/pm190502.pdf.
(2019) Prague Monitor, Czech counterintelligence disrupted Russian hacker spies and Hezbollah network, warns ultra-right targeting of Muslims could contribute to radicalization, http://praguemonitor.com/2019/11/01/czech-counter-intelligence-disrupted-russian-hacker-spies-and-hezbollah-network-warns-ult.
(2020) GLOBAL FIREPOWER, Military Strength Ranking, https://www.globalfirepower.com/countries-listing.asp.
Cohen S.B., (2015). Geopolitics, The Geography of International Relations, Third Edition, Published by Rowman & Littlefield, Maryland.
Darczewska J., (2015). Diabeł tkwi w szczegółach. Wojna informacyjna w świetle Doktryny Wojennej Rosji. Punkt Widzenia OSW, nr 50, Warszawa.
Gliwa S. and Olech A.K., (2020). Relacje polsko-czeskie a rosyjska dezinformacja. Czy destabilizacja stosunków jest możliwa? CyberDefence24.pl, https://www.cyberdefence24.pl/relacje-polsko-czeskie-a-rosyjska-dezinformacja-czy-destabilizacja-stosunkow-jest-mozliwa.
Grygiel J., (2006). Great Powers and Geopolitical Change. Baltimore: The Johns Hopkins University Press.
Helmus, T.C., Bodine-Baron E., Radin A., Magnuson M., Mendelsohn J., Marcellino W., Bega A. and Winkelman Z., (2018). Russian Social Media Influence – Understanding Russian Propaganda in Eastern Europe, RAND CORPORATION, USA, www.rand.org/t/RR2237.
Hendrychová, K., (2014). Český prezident užívá nepravdivá tvrzení podle linie Kremlu, European Values Think-Tank, http://www.evropskehodnoty.cz/cesky-prezident-uziva-nepravdiva-tvrzeni-podle-linie-kremlu/.

Janda J. and Kundra O., (2016). Schéma fungování vlivu Ruské federace v České republice, European Values Think-Tank, http://www.evropskehodnoty.cz/wp-content/uploads/2016/08/SCH%C3%89MA-FUNGOV%C3%81N%C3%8D-VLIVU-RUSK%C3%89-FEDERACE-V-%C4%8CESK%C3%89-REPUBLICE1.pdf.

Janda J. and Víchová V., (2017). The Kremlin's hostile influence in the Czech Republic: The state of play, Warsaw Institute, https://warsawinstitute.org/kremlins-hostile-influence-czech-republic-state-play/.

Janda J., (2017). Policy Shift Overview: How the Czech Republic became one of the European leaders in countering Russian disinformation, European Values Think-Tank, http://www.europeanvalues.net/wp-content/uploads/2017/05/Policy-shift-overview-How-the-Czech-Republic-became-one-of-the-European-leaders-in-countering-Russian-disinformation-1.pdf.

Kokot M., (2016). Czesi powołują rządowy zespół do walki z rosyjską propagandą. "Zagrożenie dezinformacją", Gazeta Wyborcza, https://wyborcza.pl/7,75399,21177810,czesi-powoluja-rzadowy-zespol-do-walki-z-rosyjska-propaganda.html.

Kremlin Watch Report, https://www.kremlinwatch.eu/.

Kučerová Irah, (2015). Geopolitics of Central Europe – A Historical View, Annales Universitatis Apulensis. Series Historica.

MacFarquhar, N., (2016). "A Powerful Russian Weapon: The Spread of False Stories," New York Times, http://www.nytimes.com/2016/08/29/world/europe/russia-sweden-disinformation.html.

Morozov A., (2020). They are Convinced that Russia Should Follow Guerrilla Tactics, https://euvsdisinfo.eu/they-are-convinced-that-russia-should-follow-guerrilla-tactics/?highlight=czech, EUVSDISINFO.

Ogrodnik Ł., (2019) Komplikacje w stosunkach Czech z Rosją, Polski Instytut Spraw Międzynarodowych (PISM), https://www.pism.pl/publikacje/Komplikacje_w_stosunkach_Czech_z_Rosja_.

Prohlášení MZV k tzv. "lidovým republikám", Ministerstvo zahraničních věcí České republiky, 18. 7. 2017, http://www.mzv.cz/jnp/cz/udalosti_a_media/prohlaseni_a_stanoviska/x2017_07_18_prohlaseni_mzv_k_tzv_lidovym_republikam.html.

Spykman N. J., (1942). America's Strategy in World Politics: The United States and the Balance of Power, Harcourt Brace, New York.

Stratfor, https://www.stratfor.com/region/europe/czech-republic.

Víchová V., Kdo sdílí prokremelské weby na facebooku?, European Values Think-Tank, 30. 6. 2016, http://www.evropskehodnoty.cz/wp-content/uploads/2016/07/Kdo-sd%C3%ADl%C3%AD-prokremelsk%C3%A9-weby-na-facebooku4.pdf.

Výroční zpráva Bezpečnostní informační služby za rok 2015, https://www.bis.cz/vyrocni-zprava890a.html?ArticleID=1104.

Герасимов В.В. (2013). Ценность науки в предвидении//Военно-промышленный курьер, № 8(476). 27 февр, http://www.vpk-news.ru/articles/14632.

Шушков Г.М., Сергеев И.В., (2016). Концептуальные основы информационной безопасности Российской Федерации // Актуальные вопросы научной и научно-педагогической деятельности молодых ученых: сборник научных трудов III, Всероссийской заочной научно-практической конференции (23. 11. 2015–30. 12. 2015 г., Москва) / под общ. ред. Е.А. Певцовой; редколл.: Е.А. Куренкова и др. – М.: ИИУ МГОУ.

Marcin Górnikiewicz / Andrzej Jacuch

Chapter 15: Summary and conclusions: The geopolitical and geostrategic situation of the Czech Republic viewed by the Kremlin: the current state and perspectives for Prague's foreign policy perceived by decision-makers in Moscow

Russian geopolitics towards the Czech Republic is largely determined by the location of this relatively small, but economically dynamic country. Since 2011, the priorities and objectives of foreign policy have defined Germany and Poland, the main neighbors of the Czech Republic, as key European partners. The USA and NATO play the role of national guarantors of the Czech Republic's security, while the EU countries are seen as key economic and political partners. Thus, in the eyes of the Kremlin, the Czech Republic may be one of the elements of the buffer zone stretching between Western and Eastern Europe. The above-mentioned economic potential, favorable natural conditions, resources, the level of qualifications of the workforce and over the centuries-old tradition of population migration are also important, which in turn allows for a wide range of possibilities as part of various geopolitical activities initiated in Moscow. After the start of the conflict in Ukraine and Russia's annexation of the Crimean peninsula, the Czech Republic is fully aware of the threats posed by the Kremlin, despite the fact that President Miloš Zeman is working to maintain relations between the two countries, denies the presence of Russian troops in Ukraine and has repeatedly criticized the EU sanctions against Russia. Thus, from a geopolitical point of view, the Czech Republic, like Austria, belongs to the category of neutral / friendly countries that Moscow is trying to use in the great game for primacy in Europe, to which end the path leads through the gradual and deliberate corrosion of the structure of the entire European Union.

However, from a geostrategic point of view, the location of the Czech Republic in a key point of trade routes, in a mountainous environment and with a potential position of a favorable position during a possible armed conflict (not without significance is also the friendly / neutral attitude of the Czechs towards the Russians) increases the importance of this country in the long-term geostrategy of the Kremlin, more than Austria, as it was discussed previously. The Czech Republic was ranked 34th out of 138 countries assessed by the GLOBAL FIREPOWER portal. For comparison, the Russian Federation has a PwrIndx of 0.0681, while the Czech Republic has a PwrIndx of 0.5531, where a score of 0.0000 deemed "excellent".

The Russian Federation has a strong influence on the Czech Republic by using non-military means, which include the activities of secret services, including disinformation and propaganda operations. For example, the Sputnik website is an official Russian quasi-media project in the Czech language. There are also many others that directly or indirectly serve the interests of Russia. In 2017, the Czech government established the Center for Counteracting Terrorism and Hybrid Threats. Its task is primarily to monitor disinformation centers in the Czech Republic, responding to disinformation narratives that pose a threat to internal security; coordinating efforts in different ministries to counter hostile influences, training and educating civil servants. The answer to the disinformation activities and propaganda of the Russian Federation is: presenting reliable information in the free press and transmitting it via social media; informing the public that certain information is fake news and counteracting disinformation.

Relations between the Czech Republic and the Russian Federation are related to the legacy that the Czechs gained from the time of communism and the invasion of Czechoslovakia by the Warsaw Pact troops in 1968. The Czechs are pragmatic in dealing with Moscow, focusing mainly on economic and energy interests. However, Czech policymakers have repeatedly expressed concerns about the state of democracy and the protection of human rights in Russia. Energy security is one of the particularly sensitive topics in contemporary Czech-Russian relations. Especially, the Czech Republic is currently highly dependent on the energy policy of the Kremlin, and the Czech energy sector is of interest to Russian business, especially Gazprom. The latter institution has already been used many times in strictly political and informational activities, often inspired and conducted by Russian secret services.

Due to the complexity and, at the same time, the mutual permeability of the sphere of activity of the services, business and politics, many Czech politicians currently active, openly sympathize with Russia. The Kremlin's key political allies include, for example, President Miloš Zeman himself, and many representatives of the Communist Party of Bohemia and Moravia, as well as representatives of the Czech Social Democratic Party, and even a few supporters from the Czech extreme right.

The Czechs are the most Eurosceptic in the Visegrad region, but NATO still has strong support, with the exception of locating NATO facilities on Czech soil.

Section II:
Mechanics of the Russian soft and hard interactions with regard to the Czech Republic

Justyna Stochaj

Chapter 16: The effectiveness assessment of the Russian "hard power" in the Czech Republic

Actions that are taken by Russia in the Czech Republic under the so-called hard influence exert a great impact on the shape of public opinion and legislative decisions taken by the Czech parliament. Taking into account the various historical conditions related to the common Slavic roots and the Soviet government, you should be aware that the Czechs have been and still are, to some extent, related to Russia. These connections (of a historical nature do not pose a threat). The threats may come from the recently intensified Russian influence in various spheres of Czech life (Smoleňová and Chrzová, 2012, p. 7).

In view of the significant, hard influence of Russia on the Czech Republic, it is currently a very big challenge to ensure the security of the state and the Czech society. Both countries are connected by a network of dependencies. When these relationships result from voluntary actions of the population and cultural interpenetration, they are not identified as threats. On the other hand, when they constitute deliberate and studied actions by the authorities or actions carried out at the request of the authorities, they become dangerous from the point of view of Czech security. Therefore, it was considered that an important problem today is the presentation of the characteristics of the so-called Russia's hard influence on the Czech Republic. To investigate this issue, in particular, the analytical-synthetic research method was used, which allows to assess in which activities, in particular, Russia has a hard impact on the Czech Republic. Moreover, in the course of the research, other theoretical methods were used, such as abstraction, comparison and conclusion

It should be emphasized that Russia's strategic interests are pursued by non-military means and indirect methods, such as:
- disinformation of the political elites, military commanders and the public by manipulating information, fabricating information, falsifying reality (fake news), distracting attention from
- the real actions taken by Russia and their goals (i.e. disinformation activities called in the Russian language "maskirovka");

- intoxication, control and social maneuvering, i.e. intentionally influencing society to achieve specific benefits;
- compromising, corrupting and blackmailing political and military elites;
- stoking internal and international tensions and disputes, supporting separatist tendencies and ethnic and religious conflicts;
- organizing provocations, demonstrations and manifestations (using the "protest potential"); – supporting opposition groups, resistance movements and extremist circles;
- creation of institutions, associations, foundations, organizations, armed paramilitary groups controlled by special services;
- inspiring events that destabilize the internal situation;
- conducting subversive, diversionary, sabotage and terrorist activities in order to evoke a feeling of uncertainty and threat in the society (Bryjka, 2018, p. 169).

As the author of the article points out, F. Bryjka, the common part of all the listed activities carried out by Russia is to cause chaos over which Russia is able to control. Thanks to these activities, it is possible to influence the socio-political situation of individual countries by causing crises, and then proposing solutions through actions favorable to Russia. The presented categories of actions taken by Russia can be classified into two categories: hard and soft.

According to the Cambridge Dictionary, hard interaction can be understood as "the use of a country's military power to persuade other countries to do something, rather than the use of cultural or economic influence" (https://dictionary.cambridge.org/pl/dictionary/english/hard-power). In the presented approach, hard interaction is equated with the use of military force. On the other hand, according to T. Stępniewski, the hard components of strength include mainly two categories: military and economic (Stępniewski, 2017, p. 42).

The author develops the definition of hard influence by formulating categories of activities that can be classified as hard. The hard actions taken by Russia include:
- not withdrawing military units,
- undertaking military actions (often camouflaged with the support of the so-called separatists), – "passport expansion",
- taking over infrastructure,
- energy resource price diversification,
- embargo on crude oil and natural gas,
- trade sanctions (ban on the import of wine, vegetables, meat) (Stępniewski, 2017, p. 44). When analyzing the global situation and actions taken by Russia in the international arena, it was concluded that the following actions should be added to the hard category: – intelligence and espionage,
- disinformation,

- extremist and paramilitary groups,
- organized crime groups,
- influencing the decisions of politicians,
- influencing the blocking of protective and defense activities undertaken by the West, e.g. in
- terms of building an anti-missile shield,
- cyberattacks.

The above-mentioned actions should be classified as hard when they result from the political will of a particular country. Actions taken in the hard category may be conducted in an open or covert manner. It should be underlined that this category, as well as the soft one, includes activities such as: disinformation and influence on politicians and their decisions. The author concluded that these two groups of activities can be contained in both categories of impact, both soft and hard, due to the consequences that a given impact may cause. If, as a result of political influence or disseminated disinformation, typically military actions or actions that make it impossible to implement own defense can take place, then the exerted influence engenders effects strongly and negatively felt by the population. Otherwise, they can be classified as activities with soft effects.

The first category of hard-type activities includes intelligence and espionage activities. The authors of the research paper devoted to Russia, point to the great involvement of the Russian intelligence in the Czech Republic. "The Czech Republic is believed to be a regional hub for Russian intelligence. Czech security experts assess that intelligence personnel represent around one-third of the Embassy staff in addition to those without diplomatic cover" (Smoleňová and Chrzová, 2012, p. 2). The large number of staff employed at the embassy, estimated to be carrying out intelligence tasks, is a proof of the great involvement of the Russian intelligence in the Czech Republic.

The following quote is also evidence of the great involvement of Russian intelligence in the Czech Republic: "The Czech intelligence services have been forced to acknowledge the existence of Russian threats due to the Kremlin's intensive espionage activities on Czech soil. Russian spies are thought to be some of the most active foreign agents operating in the Czech Republic. They also try to cooperate with the Russian community in the country. Some of these agents have had to be expelled from the Czech Republic, although the Czech Foreign Ministry has not escalated the conflict publicly because of possible reciprocations from Moscow" (https://www.kremlinwatch.eu/countries-compared-states/Bohemia/).

Another group of activities undertaken in the field of hard influence exerted by Russia on the Czech Republic includes disinformation activities. "There are forty to fifty platforms that actively spread pro-Russian disinformation and Kremlin-inspired narratives in the Czech Republic, most of them active since

2014. Only the Czech version of the international outlet Sputnik is financed by the Russian government, other media outlets claim no allegiance to Kremlin" (Smoleňová and Chrzová, 2012, p. 2). These activities were classified as hard impact due to the fact that disinformation activities are carried out on a large scale, as evidenced by the large number of portals devoted to providing information in line with the Kremlin's narrative, as well as the financing of their activities. It is true that one portal is officially allocated to finance the activities. In many others, however, an unclear network of financial connections and remittances was observed.

Extremist and paramilitary groups that are emerging and operating in its territory pose a very great threat to the Czech Republic. In particular, Russian or Kremlin-inspired groups. In terms of the growth of paramilitary groups, the Czech Republic is no exception, as this trend has been observed across Europe. "Following the turbulent events since 2014, several countries in Europe have witnessed a growing number of paramilitary groups, voluntary semimilitarized units whose tactics, structures and training simulate those of the regular armies" (Smoleňová and Chrzová, 2012, p. 10).

Among the extremist groups, a group called Order of the Nation deserves special attention, as it clearly receives Russian support. "Traces of support can be seen among extremists and paramilitary groups as well, yet only a few go beyond the ideological support. The only exception is the extremist political movement Řád národa (Order of the Nation) headquartered in a villa that belongs to the Russian Embassy" (Smoleňová and Chrzová, 2012, p. 2). The activities of the Order of the Nation are particularly dangerous due to a widespread ideology that can lead to undesirable actions and negative consequences for the population.

Moreover, the following social movements and paramilitary groups operating in the Czech Republic are among the entities expressing support for the Russian policy and identifying themselves with the actions taken by the Kremlin:
- Czechoslovakian Reservists,
- National Self-Defense,
- Security Corps (Bryjka, 2018, p. 173).

All paramilitary and extremist groups operating in the Czech Republic have their own leaders. They can be especially dangerous when they use social media to influence society. "Among the fiercest supporters of pro-Russian narratives are several extremist groups and individuals with limited impact on the political debate. They are mostly active on social media and online and occasionally organize rallies and protests. One such example is a proRussian activist and former MP, Jiří Vyvadil, who established a Facebook group "Jiří Vyvadil's Friends of Russia in the Czech Republic" with approximately 8,000 members and is a contributor to the disinformation outlet Parlamentní Lista" (Smoleňová and

Chrzová, 2012, p. 9). Spreading the pro-Russian narrative should contribute to the emergence of interest in a given leader. Running a business with the use of social media, e. g. Facebook, is good from the point of view of the Czech Republic as it gives the opportunity to trace all the movements made by the leaders of the organization and its members with decision-making powers. Thanks to this, it is possible to collect evidence proving the specific type of actions taken and, in the event that they are not legal, constitutes the basis for bringing charges.

Among the existing extremist and paramilitary groups, it is very difficult to prove pro-Russian ties, and in particular to indicate the sources of their financing. This problem was described by Smoleňová and Chrzová. "There are also several documented cases of direct Russian financial support for extremist groups or pro-Russian activists. The money travels through various financial gambits, using several intermediaries that are then difficult to track back to its original source. One illustrative case study of Russian financial support for subversive forces in the Central Europe is connected with the name of Alexander Usovsky, a Belarus-born writer and pro-Russian ideologue. According to leaked messages, exposed by Ukrainian hackers Cyber Hunta and Cyber Alliance, Usovsky had throughout 2014 and 2015 received money from people and businesses close to Konstantin Malofeev, a Russian billionaire previously accused of financing insurgents in Donbas and Crimea. Usovsky then channeled the money to several pro-Russian fringe groups in the Visegrad countries to finance subversive efforts and demonstrations" (Smoleňová and Chrzová, 2012, p. 10).

The activity of organized crime groups was also included in the category of hard Russian influence in the Czech Republic. First of all, due to the fact that the leaders of these groups have large financial resources to implement their plans and achieve their goals. In particular, these objectives concern the Czech economy and its privatization what in turns opens the way to exercise influence on it. In addition, the leaders of these organizations often also have specialist expertise, which makes their operations even easier. An exemplary situation of this type was described as follows: "Post-Soviet organized crime appeared in the Czech Republic at the beginning of the 1990s. Organized crime from the former Soviet Union invaded Czech territory, starting gang wars with competing organizations for zones of in‾uence, and building up the kryshas – argot for the 'roofs' – of the racketeering networks. When the dead bodies of famous Russian hat-sellers trading in old Soviet Army uniforms across eastern Europe were found in the tourist area near the Charles Bridge in Prague, the Czech police announced that the assassinations were the result of personal quarrels among the hat-sellers. Nobody thought that the incoming post-Soviet ma fi a would liquidate independent competitors. Shortly afterwards, small, more-or-less independent organized crime groups, as well as envoys of strong post-Soviet criminal syndicates, equipped with unlimited financial resources and excellent professional knowledge, appeared in the Czech Republic, interested in the Czech economy and privatisation process" (Nožina, 2004, p. 444). The main areas of activity of organized crime groups operating in the Czech Republic include: illegal drug trafficking, illegal human trafficking, illegal weapons, explosives and nuclear materials trafficking, counterfeiting, financial crimes and money laundering, illegal trade of arts, theft and smuggling of vehicles, crimes against the environment. (Nožina, 2004, pp. 454–458).

The confirmation of the presence of the Russian diaspora in the Czech Republic, in particular among groups involved in organized and extremist crime, was also emphasized by Mareš and Šmíd (Mareš and Šmíd, 2020).

The hard impact activities also include the impact on Czech politics. The following political parties are among the entities operating in the Czech Republic that openly support Russia or duplicate the Russian narrative:
- Freedom and Direct Democracy,
- National Democracy,
- The Party of Social Justice for Workers,
- Czech Social Democratic Party (Bryjka, 2018, p. 173).

Smoleňová and Chrzová also saw confirmation of the pro-Russian involvement of selected political parties in the Czech Republic. "Among the more disciplined pro-Russian groups are Czech far-right parties, such as National Democracy (ND) or Worker's Social Democratic Party (DSSS). ND is led by Adam B. Bartoš who is known for his xenophobic and anti-Semitic views and has participated in several receptions and events organized by the Russian Embassy in Prague" (Smoleňová and Chrzová, 2012, p. 9).

Support for Russian activities in the Czech Republic is expressed at the highest level. "President Zeman has repeatedly called for the lifting of economic sanctions against Russia and promoted friendly relations and closer economic cooperation. Among his closest allies and supporters are such figures as Martin Nejedlý or Zdeněk Przejek, entrepreneurs with well-established ties to Russian businessmen and diplomats who have consistently lobbied for Russian business interests in the Czech Republic" (Smoleňová and Chrzová, 2012, p. 7).

It is particularly irresponsible to engage in actions that may cause international political disputes, as follows: "Several MPs have traveled to the Donbass and / or Crimea since 2014 on so-called 'observation missions', thus breaching Ukrainian law and causing diplomatic disputes" (Smoleňová and Chrzová, 2012, p. 2).

Of particular importance from the point of view of Russia's hard influence on the Czech Republic, is its influence on blocking the protective and defense activities undertaken by the West. A perfect example was Russia's influence on the US-Czech negotiations conducted in 2002–2011 on the construction of the anti-missile shield. The operations carried out by Russia turned out to be successful. Actions taken by Russia in the Czech Republic will most likely be duplicated in other member states of the North Atlantic Treaty Organization. (Dodge, 2020). The possibility of replicating the model of activities applied in the Czech Republic by Russia in the international arena is particularly important, and in this respect, actions undertaken by Russia should be of particular interest.

In terms of opposition to the construction of the anti-missile shield in the Czech Republic, the Russians managed to exert great pressure on the Czech public opinion. "Recently, Russia successfully rallied public opinion against the construction of a radar base in the Czech Republic that was to have been part of the U.S. missile-defense shield. And it has pressured other European countries, such as Germany, to oppose putting former Soviet republics on a path to NATO membership" (Feifer and Whitmore, 2010, p. 25).

From the point of view of Russia's hard influence on the Czech Republic, information operations, and cyber-attacks carried out by Russian hackers, deserve special attention, especially when more that they are carried out in a repeatable manner. "This is not the first time international authorities have cooperated to catch a hacker like Yevgeniy, as many Russia-sponsored cyberattacks often operate outside of Russia itself while targeting other countries, Frank Cilluffo, the director of the George Washington University Center for Cyber and Homeland Security . "The Czech Republic has been used as a launch pad for such behavior for quite some time, so I think it's pretty significant that they're stepping up their activity here". Mr. Cilluffo tells The Christian Science Monitor." (Weston Williams Staff, 2016)

References

Bryjka F., (2018). Rosyjskie "środki aktywne" w przestrzeni euroatlantyckiej in: Grabińska T., Kuźniar Z. (eds.), Bezpieczeństwo personalne a bezpieczeństwo strukturalne, Wrocław: Akademia Wojsk Lądowych.

Dodge M. (2020), Russia's influence operations in the Czech Republic during the radar debate, Comparative Strategy, DOI: 10.1080/01495933.2020.1718989.

Feifer G., Whitmore B., (2010) The Velvet Surrender, "New Republic", 00286583, 9/23/2010, Tom 241, Numer 15.

Fiszer J., (2016). Zadania i cele polityki zagranicznej Władimira Putina, Myśl Ekonomiczna i Polityczna, Nr 1 (52).

https://dictionary.cambridge.org/pl/dictionary/english/hard-power.

https://www.kremlinwatch.eu/countries-compared-states/czechia/.

Mareš M. and Šmíd T., (2020). The Russian and North Caucasus Diaspora in the Czech Republic: Between Loyalty, Crime and Extremism. In: Holzer J., Mareš M. (eds.) Czech

Security Dilemma. New Security Challenges. Palgrave Macmillan, Cham, https://doi.org/10.1007/978-3-030-20546-1_6.

Menkiszak M., (2019). Strategiczna kontynuacja, taktyczna zmiana. Polityka bezpieczeństwa Europejskiego Rosji, Warszawa: Ośrodek Studiów Wschodnich.

Nožina M., (2004). The Czech Republic: A Crossroads for Organised Crime. in: Fijnaut C., Paoli L. (eds.) Organised Crime in Europe. Studies of Organized Crime, vol 4. Springer, Dordrecht, https://doi.org/10.1007/978-1-4020-2765-9_16.

Quinn P. and Prát S., (2018). Russian Cultural Communities within the Czech Republic: Economics, Perceptions and Integration, "Journal of Identity and Migration Studies", Volume 12, number 1.

Smoleňová I. and Chrzová B. (eds.), (2012). United we stand, divided we fall: the Kremlin's leverage in the visegrad countries, Prague Security Studies Institute.

Stępniewski T., (2017). "Gra sił w kontestowanym sąsiedztwie Unii Europejskiej i Rosji", Studia Europejskie – European Studies Affairs. Nr 4.

Weston Williams Staff (2016), International cooperation helped nab Russian hacker in Czech Republic, Christian Science Monitor, 08827729, 10/19/2016.

Justyna Stochaj

Chapter 17: Russian "soft power" in relation to the national security of the Czech Republic

Russia poses a very big challenge to Czech security policy. Due to the special geopolitical, historical and cultural relations of Czechoslovakia, compared to other European countries, guaranteeing the security of the Czech Republic is a very big challenge (Mareš, Holzer and Šmíd, 2020). The Czech Republic and Russia were already connected by a large network of dependencies in the past. "Due to the Czech Republic's complicated and turbulent past with Russia, the migration of Russian speaking migrants remains a divided social, economic, and political issue well into the present day. However, despite the common negative perception of Eastern migrants, Russian migration has continued to increase dramatically over the past several years. According to the Czech Statistical Office, there are currently around 35,000 Russian foreigners within the Czech Republic, a number which has been steadily increasing from the 1990s onwards. As the third largest national community within the Czech Republic (falling behind only Ukrainians and Vietnamese,) the lifestyles, community demographics, and roll within the labor market all create significant impacts on the greater Czech society" (Quinn and Pràt, 2018, p. 47). It should be emphasized, however, that the main reason for migration from Russia is the so-called pushing factors. "Similar to Ukrainian populations, which comprise the largest non-EU migratory group within the Czech Republic (…), Russia's migratory population is largely driven by the existence of strong push factors. These include unpredictable levels of unemployment, and, according to 2017 OECD report on the country, below average life expectancy, basic sanitation, water quality, and air quality. However, while 'push' factors explain the desire to leave Russia, their existence alone does not provide the explanation for their destination of choice" (Quinn and Pràt, 2018, p. 49). There is a mutual relationship and influence between the migrants and the local community of a country inhabited by migrants. Russian migrants must meet a number of conditions necessary to be able to benefit from the goodness of the Czech social system. For example, they can study for free under certain conditions, one of which is the command of the Czech language. However, it must not be forgotten that after some time migrants become a part of the local community and co-create it. This means that they convey certain behaviors and norms to the Czech community, thus influencing it.

In view of the extensive, soft influence of Russia on the Czech Republic, it is currently a great challenge to ensure the security of the state and the Czech society. There was in the past and there are also great dependencies between both countries in the past. In a situation where they were and are natural consequences resulting from voluntary actions of the population and cultural penetration, they do not pose a threat. On the other hand, when they constitute deliberate actions and a well-thought-out policy of the authorities aimed at exerting an imperceptible influence on the functioning of the state and society, these actions turn out to be dangerous from the point of view of the security of the Czech Republic. The significance of the observed increase in Russia's influence in the Czech Republic is equally important. Therefore, it was considered that an important problem today is how the characteristics of the so-called Russia's soft influence on the Czech Republic is presented. To investigate this issue, in particular, the analytical-synthetic research method was used, which allows to assess in which activities, in particular, such a soft influence of Russia on the Czech Republic can be viewed. Moreover, in the course of the research, other theoretical methods were used, such as abstraction, comparison and inference.

The concept of soft impact is understood differently by Russia and the West. For the West, it means being able to influence others to achieve the anticipated results through attraction rather than coercion or payment. For Moscow, soft power represents Western interventionism as a destabilizing force, it concerns the need to engage in an information campaign, as well as providing state support to promote Russian culture and language, and counteract "soft attacks" on Russia. For Russia, soft power is a tool that can only be ruled by the state (Monaghan, 2016).

The term of the so-called soft impact can also be understood as also known soft power, or "soft" means used to achieve goals, is an extension of the possible ways of influencing and achieving goals by actors in international relations. It is therefore an attempt to show the "other face of strength", i. e. an opposition to the "hard" components of power – military and economic. Soft power also means the ability (e.g. a state) to achieve results by attracting and persuading others (e.g. states) to adopt their goals through persuasion rather than violence and threats. The resources of the state's "soft power" are most often: 1) cultural attractiveness of a given state; 2) political ideas and values (if they occur both inside and outside the state) and 3) foreign policy of the state (when it is perceived by other actors and when it has moral value and social legitimization) (Stępniewski, 2017, p. 42). The use of the so-called soft influence relies primarily on the use of peaceful means to encourage and convince people to be right. As noted in the quotation provided, these measures do not use force.

For comparison, another definition of the so-called soft power was proposed on the basis of the activities of one pro-Russian organization. Actions taken by it are to result in to the elimination of the independence of states. "Russki mir uses a variety of instruments to achieve its goals: from creating centers of influence in neighboring countries, through attempts to limit their sovereignty and control their economic, political, information and religious structures, to influencing their historical policy, as well as cultural and linguistic reality. This is called soft power, which, if effectively applied, may lead to a gradual elimination of state independence" (Wasiuta, 2017, pp. 74–75). Taking into account the presented definition, the importance of the possibility of gradual elimination of the independence of states should be emphasized. The nature of the activities undertaken as a part of soft interaction is very mild and does not allow suspicions to arise in the society as to the activities undertaken by the entity using soft interaction. Hence, a soft interaction can be very dangerous for the society and the state that is influenced.

Many authors emphasize the effectiveness of soft impact, which is a very good tool that allows to "eliminate the opponent with its own hands" (Diec, 2015, p. 84). It should be emphasized that soft power is a voluntary choice made by society. The soft interaction is naturally shaped over a very long time. However, it is not an action that can be introduced by any legal provisions. (Tsygankow, 2018). This may mean taking control over a society without even realizing it. Moreover, it could be considered as a voluntary choice that will be supported. Through the use of soft influence, Russia has adopted an approach to implementing and achieving specific goals.

According to T. Stępniewski, the activities described as soft power undertaken by Russia include: – performing rhetoric of fraternity,
- multilateral institutions that offer benefits to their members,
- investments of strategic importance,
- visa-free travel and open labor market,
- providing protection to authoritarian regimes,
- introducing the model of "sovereign democracy",
- deciding on the image of the world in the media (Stępniewski, 2017, p. 43).

According to W. Putin, the new concept of the country's foreign policy should use modern methods of influencing other states, such as: economic diplomacy and "soft power, i. e. the state's ability to collect allies and obtain influence in the world through the attractiveness of its own culture, ideology and politics" (Fiszer , 2016, p. 182). It is a response to the actions and attitudes of the West which, according to Russia, are the source of the problems. The Russian side emphasizes that the West in particular uses the so-called soft interaction. "Its economic policy is responsible for the global crisis, the security policy implemented through unilateral actions destabilizes the world and provokes Islamic radicalism, and finally – using soft power against other regions manipulates the social consciousness of the masses, imposing on them values alien to their civilizations" (Diec, 2015, p. 184). This narrative explains the Kremlin's use of soft influence on other states as a response to the actions taken by the West. The Czech Republic, as a member of the European Union, was one of the countries that imposed sanctions on Russia in 2014. These sanctions greatly affected the economic relations between the Czech Republic and Russia. As a result of the sanctions imposed, Russia exerted a significant influence on the Czech Republic through: a decline in exports, a decline in investment inflow and a decline in the number of Russian tourists in the Czech Republic. (Coufalova and Zidek, 2017). The consequences of the sanctions imposed on Russia did not have a negative impact only on Russia, but also on the Czech Republic, which in several particularly important areas felt the situation changed for the worse. One example is the impact on Czech tourism. Many tourists from Russia come to the Czech Republic. "Karlovy Vary is a well-known spa town located in the Northwest District of the Czech Republic, and is particularly popular among Russian tourists. On almost every street, shop, and restaurant, translations are offered in Cyrillic as Russian acts as one of the most prevalent languages within the area. Russian tourism in the region is so high that the nearby Karlovy Vary International Airport offers flight only to Moscow and St. Petersburg. As a major cultural and economic center for Russians within the Czech Republic, the trends of this region provide insight into larger patterns of Russian movement within the country" (Quinn and Prát, p. 53). Currently, it is indicated that the city of Karlovy Vary has lost its attractiveness for Russians. On the other hand, other destinations, such as Prague and Bohemia, have retained their significance or recorded only a slight decrease in tourism.

Russia's influence on the Czech Republic can also be observed in the energy sector. By its actions, the Kremlin is trying to make other regions of the world dependent on its own supplies. The supply of raw materials, and more specifically their blocking, gives the possibility of exerting political pressure in the event that the state does not make decisions favorable to Russia. "The Kremlin uses its energy potential to achieve its political tasks, buys strategic objects of a selected country, and takes over the most important political structures of states that are elements of the *Russkiy mir (Russian mir – Russia's Neighborhood Policy)*. In addition, there is extensive propaganda of the benefits of cooperation with Russia. The official organs of the Russkiy mir are not always creating a state of permanent instability within states, calling for the fight against "инородзик" – *foreigners* (i. e. people of other nationalities) on a religious and ethnic basis, or under the pretext of combating terrorism" (Wasiuta, 2017, p. 75).

There is an apparent presence of Russian companies in the Czech energy sector. These activities make it possible to influence the direction in which the energy sector in the Czech Republic should develop. (Jirušek, Kuchyňková and Vlček, 2020).

In terms of energy resources, many countries, including the Czech Republic, are dependent on Russian gas and fuel supplies. Russia has the largest energy reserves in the world and, after Vladimir Putin was elected in 2000, Moscow began an aggressive push into European oil and gas markets. Putin started seizing back the energy assets that the government had privatized in the 1990s, and, before long, some of the most powerful Russian energy players were practically indistinguishable from the state. Putin saw the means to pursue his long-cherished goal of restoring Russia to the ranks of the great powers, which he had outlined in his doctoral thesis. The logic was simple: The more countries depended on Russia for their energy needs, the more leverage Russia would have over them. Moscow initially set its sights close to home, on the Eastern and Central European countries it had once controlled, and where it could still draw on a network of useful connections (Feifer and Whitmore, 2010, p. 22). It should be emphasized that dependence on supplies is supposed to make Russia a great power. Thus, along with the supply of energy resources, it is planned to put pressure on societies and politicians who are to make decisions that favor the Kremlin's narrative.

Russia's actions and intentions are aimed at maintaining Russian leadership in the Czech nuclear energy sector. "The subsidiary of state-owned nuclear agency Rosatom, TVEL, is the sole supplier of nuclear fuel (at least until 2020) for both the Temelín and Dukovany power plants. In line with the State Energy Concept, the new tender for the Dukovany power plant is being prepared and Rosatom is likely to be a serious contender" (Smoleňová and Chrzová, 2012, p. 3).

In the context of the Czech energy sector, it should be noted that from the beginning of its independent foreign policy after 1989, Czechoslovakia, and then the Czech Republic, have sought to diversify its energy mix and energy sources through its actions. These actions were aimed at reducing Russia's influence in terms of energy supplies. The Czech government prevented the Russian side from taking over some strategic industries. (Fawn, 2018). Undertaking activities related to independence from Russian gas and fuel supplies ended in a fiasco. The Czech Republic is largely dependent on Russian supplies of raw materials. Companies such as Gazprom and Lukoil are in the lead. "Between these kinds of shadowy entities and major contracts with companies like Gazprom and Lukoil, the Czech Republic relies on Russia for nearly 80 percent of its natural gas" (Feifer and Whitmore, 2010, p. 24).

Through various activities, the Kremlin is also trying to influence Czech politics. One of the activities undertaken is financing the activities of selected

Czech politicians. "On the right, Klaus's sympathies are assured: He was key to Lukoil's expansion in the country, according to Czech media, meeting in secret with the company's CEO. Schwarzenberg, the foreign minister, is an outspoken critic of Russia, but in the ruling coalition, he is somewhat of an outlier. Russia also has powerful friends on the left. Earlier this year, Respekt, a well-regarded investigative magazine, reported that Lukoil was financing the new left-wing Citizens Rights Party, headed by a popular former prime minister, Miloš Zeman. The party denies the accusations, but admits taking money from Russian-linked lobbyists, such as Miroslav Šlouf, a former communist youth leader and Zeman's longtime chief adviser" (Feifer and Whitmore, 2010, p. 24).

Some other examples of Russia's influence on Czech politics can be found based on the support some Czech political parties have expressed towards the actions of the Russian government. "Examples of the Kremlin's influence can be found across the entire political spectrum. The most consistent supporter of Russia among Czech political parties is, however, the Communist Party of Bohemia and Moravia" (Smoleňová and Chrzová, 2012, p. 2).

Moreover, as a part of the Russian emphasis on Czech policy, one can also emphasize the influence exerted on the Czech government, including former president Klaus. "Jiri Kominek, an analyst with the Jamestown Foundation, says Moscow is putting" unprecedented "lobbying pressure on the Czech government, and Klaus has already endorsed Atomstroy- export, although he has no formal role in the proces" (Feifer and Whitmore, 2010 , p. 25). It was not only former President Klaus who expressed his support for the Russian side. Miloš Zeman, currently in office, is also doing this. "Both are known for their close links to the Russian business community and have repeatedly participated in the annual Rhodes Forum, "Dialogue of Civilizations", organized by the Russian oligarch Vladimir Yakuni" (Smoleňová and Chrzová, 2012, p. 2).

The importance of Russia's influence on Czech politics was also noticed by the authors of the Kremlinwatch website, which indicated the number of seats in the Czech parliament by representatives of political parties identifying themselves with the pro-Kremlin narrative. "In the 2017 Czech legislative elections, the far-right party Freedom and Direct Democracy (SPD) gained 22 seats in the 200-seat Chamber of Deputies. The party, led by Tomio Okamura, is very friendly towards the Kremlin, as illustrated by the fact that 5 of its MPs are members of a Facebook group called "We want out of the EU and NATO – Russia is our true friend"" (https://www.kremlinwatch.eu/countries-compared-states/czechia/).

Moreover, there is a great deal of interest on the part of Russia in establishing its diplomats in the Czech Republic. Their number was estimated to be much greater than that of representatives of other countries. "With fifty-five accredited diplomats (ninety-two including spouses) in 2017, the diplomatic mission of the Russian Federation is disproportionately larger than the diplomatic missions of the Czech Republic's Western allies. Through both overt and covert activities, the Embassy plays a pivotal role in the Kremlin's influence operations" (Smoleňová and Chrzová, 2012, p. 2).

In the Czech Republic, there is also Russian economic and business influence present. It can be observed in particular in the connections between Russian and Czech companies. Tracking the relations between enterprises of both countries is not always possible due to the complicated network of connections. "Despite relatively small, yet not unimportant, bilateral trade and FDI, many of the Kremlin's business operations are likely obscured through an extensive web of foreign subsidiaries. The official data, therefore, hardly captures the full picture of Russian economic influence in the country" (Smoleňová and Chrzová, 2012, p. 3).

The first example of a large business impact is the company Gazprom. Over the past decade, Gazprom and other Russian firms have seeded a number of firms in the Czech Republic, connected via an impenetrable web of shell companies around Europe. BIS concluded in its 2009 annual report, "It is highly likely the complex ownership structure is aimed at camouflaging links to the Russian Federation" (Feifer and Whitmore, 2010, p. 23)

Another example of Russia's influence on Czech companies is Vemex. "(…) that sells Russian natural gas. Since it emerged in 2001, seemingly from nowhere, it has captured around 10 percent of the Czech retail gas market. Its ownership structure is essentially indecipherable. To wit: Vemex is owned by companies based in Switzerland, Germany, and Austria, one of which is Centrex Europe Energy & Gas, which was founded by Gazprom's financing arm and registered in Austria, and, according to the European Commission, owned by two companies, one registered in Cyprus and another controlled by Gazprom's German subsidiary" (Feifer and Whitmore, 2010, p. 23).

There are many non-governmental organizations in the Czech Republic whose owners favor the views of Russia. Their actions are so hazardous that they can have a large social impact based on the fact that they are not related to politics. "Several pro-Russian NGOs, such as the Institute of Slavic Strategic Studies, take part in pan-Slavic congresses which serve as networking opportunities and further integration within the pro-Kremlin informal 'club' of NGOs" (Smoleňová and Chrzová, 2012, p. 2). The mere creation of opportunities for establishing relationships between the citizens of the Czech Republic and Russia is not wrong. The situation is worse when the information provided and the actions taken as a result may contribute to the destruction of the existing order and order in the Czech Republic. The following other examples of non-governmental organizations favoring the Kremlin can be presented: Bohemian-Moravian Pan-Slavic Congress (ČMSS) and the Institute of Slavic Strategic Studies (ISSS). "The ČMSS has been active since 2009 and aims to unite Slavic national minorities in the

Czech Republic. It is headed by Zdeněk Opatřil, who co-owns a tourist agency that organizes trips to Russia and other postSoviet countries. Besides his economic interest in the region, he is known from personal communication for pro-Slavic sympathies and unconcealed support for pro-Russian separatists in Ukraine. In 2015, Opatřil accompanied by Senator Jaroslav Doubrava to occupied Crimea where they met with the Prime Minister of the Republic of Crimea, Sergey Aksyonov (...) The ISSS presents itself as a think tank and was officially registered in 2013. Its Director, Radmila Zemanová-Kopecká, is a frequent participant at antiWestern and pro-Russian rallies and a former member of the SPOZ party that was created to support president Miloš Zeman (no family relation). A journalist by profession, Zemanová publishes articles and commentaries on media platforms often spreading disinformation such as ParlamentníLI (Parliamentary Letters) and SmartNews, or provides interviews to Kremlin-owned Sputnik News" (Smoleňová and Chrzová, 2012, p. 8).

Another example of a non-governmental organization influencing social attitudes is presented by the Youth Time International Movement (YTIM) which is one of the organizations with more visible links to Russia which was launched in 2010 and currently resides in Prague. It is a youth branch of the Rhodes Forum, "Dialogue of Civilisations", which is presented as an "alternative international discussion platform." It was established by Russian oligarch Vladimir Yakunin, until recently a sanctioned, powerful ally of Vladimir Putin that also served as the CEO of Russian Railways until 2016. The YTIM is responsible for organizing events for young people worldwide. Among its flagship programs are roundtable discussions, leadership development initiatives and summer schools. In the Czech Republic, the movement, however, maintains a rather low profile, rarely entering the public debate (Smoleňová and Chrzová, 2012, p. 8). The activity of this type of organization is of particular importance in shaping the attitudes of young people, some of whom may take up very important functions in the state in the future.

The disinformation activities undertaken on various websites and in the media are also important for the Czech Republic. They are one of the most effective methods of action, because false information (fake news), provided that it is credible, allows to directly influence people. It is pointed out that there are several pro-Russian media in the Czech Republic, which aim to reach primarily Russian-speaking audiences. "There are also several Czech-based media in Russian that spread proRussian and anti-Western narratives and manipulative content that primarily target the Russian-speaking community. The most influential among them are Prague Telegraf, Prague Express and Artěk. Artěk was previously subsidized by the Czech Ministry of Culture, but that support was suspended as in 2015 following protests from some members of the Russian minority and Czech historians" (Smoleňová and Chrzová, 2012, p. 11).

In the virtual world, one can also observe the pro-Kremlin narrative and spreading false information. "There are forty to fifty platforms that actively spread pro-Russian disinformation and Kremlin-inspired narratives in the Czech Republic, most of them active since 2014. Only the Czech version of the international outlet Sputnik is financed by the Russian government, other media outlets claim no allegiance to Kremlin" (Smoleňová and Chrzová, 2012, p. 2). Many of the organizations sowing disinformation do not disclose information about their funding or hide their relationship with Russia. This is where the real danger lies. If people who received specific information were able to verify the source of funding for a specific information sender, perhaps they would be aware that it may not be fully true. The special importance of one internet platform, which has a very large impact on the Czech population should be indicated. "Outlet ParlamentníLI (Parliamentary Letters) has become by far the most successful of the disinformation platforms, attracting attention by emotionally-charged articles with catchy titles. Pro-Russian and anti-Western articles prevail within its content. The outlet has strong links and unique access to President Miloš Zeman" (Smoleňová and Chrzová, 2012, p. 2). The described platform operates with great success mainly through the way of posting messages that have an emotional impact on the recipient.

References

Coufalova L. and Zidek L., (2017). The impact of sanctions on Czech economic relations with Russia, in: Cingula M., Przygoda M., Detelj K. (eds.), Economic and social development, Varazdin development & enterpreneurship agency, Varazdin.
Diec J., (2015). Geostrategiczny wybór Rosji u zarania trzeciego tysiąclecia. Tom 1. Doktryna Rosyjskiej polityki zagranicznej. Partnerzy najbliżsi i najdalsi, Wydawnictwo Uniwersytetu Jagiellońskiego.
Fawn R., (2018). Czech Republic in: Ostrowski W., Butler E. (eds.), Understanding Energy Security in Central and Eastern Europe: Russia, Transition and National Interest, Taylor and Francis, DOI: 10.4324/9781315651774.
Feifer G. and Whitmore B., (2010). The Velvet Surrender, "New Republic", 00286583, 9/23/2010, Tom 241, Numer 15.
Fiszer J., (2016). Zadania i cele polityki zagranicznej Władimira Putina, Myśl Ekonomiczna i Polityczna, Nr 1 (52).
Holzer J., Jirušek M. and Kuchyňková P., (2020). Russia as Viewed by the Main Czech Political Actors. in: Holzer J., Mareš M. (eds.) Czech Security Dilemma. New Security Challenges. Palgrave Macmillan, Cham, https://doi.org/10.1007/978-3-030-20546-1_3.
https://www.kremlinwatch.eu/countries-compared-states/czechia/.
Jirušek M., Kuchyňková P. and Vlček T., (2020). Business as Usual or Geopolitical Games? Russian Activities in Energy Sector of the Czech Republic In: Holzer J., Mareš M. (eds.)

Czech Security Dilemma. New Security Challenges. Palgrave Macmillan, Cham, https://doi.org/10.1007/978-3-030-20546-1_5.

Mareš M., Holzer J. and Šmíd T., (2020). The Hybrid Campaign Concept and Contemporary Czech-Russian Relations. in: Holzer J., Mareš M. (eds.) Czech Security Dilemma. New Security Challenges. Palgrave Macmillan, Cham, https://doi.org/10.1007/978-3-030-20546-1_2.

Monaghan A., (2016). The new politics of Russia. Interpreting change, Manchester University Press.

Quinn P. and Prát S., (2018). Russian Cultural Communities within the Czech Republic: Economics, Perceptions and Integration, "Journal of Identity and Migration Studies", Volume 12, number 1.

Smoleňová I. and Chrzová B. (eds.), (2012). United we stand, divided we fall: the Kremlin's leverage in the visegrad countries, Prague Security Studies Institute.

Stępniewski T., (2017). "Gra sił w kontestowanym sąsiedztwie Unii Europejskiej i Rosji", Studia Europejskie – European Studies Affairs, Nr 4.

Tsygankow A. (eds.), (2018). Routledge Handbook of Russian Foreign Policy, Routledge.

Wasiuta O., (2017). "Russki mir" jako narzędzie imperialnej polityki Kremla, Przegląd Geopolityczny, Nr 21.

Justyna Stochaj

Chapter 18: Summary and conclusions: Prospects for the current state and the development of the Russian influence on the Czech Republic in the 21st century

Russia was a constitutive topic of Czech politics and Czech political thought. Russia has been the subject of dichotomous, intellectual and popular reflections (Holzer, Jirušek and Kuchyňková, 2020). Considerations regarding the conducted reflections allowed the Czechs to come to the conclusion that Russia has too much influence on their country. In addition, they resulted in a government document in which a comprehensive analysis of the influence and dependence of other countries on the Czech Republic, including Russia, was conducted. "However, the most fundamental document was the product of the National Security Audit, conducted by the government in 2016, with a chapter devoted to the influence of foreign powers. It includes a SWOT analysis summarizing the strong and weak aspects of the Czech Republic's vulnerability and presents specific recommendations for enhancing resilience, including the establishment of centers for the evaluation of disinformation campaigns within relevant authorities, the creation of a system of education for public officials to make them more resilient towards foreign influence, and active media strategies for important democratic institutions or measures concerning media law" (https://www.kremlinwatch.eu/countries-compared-states/Bohemia/).

The Russian methodology of impact with the use of soft power and hard power, in the case of the Czech Republic, has been focused mainly on the former. This seems fully understandable considering that the Czech Republic belongs to the countries classified as natural / friendly towards the Kremlin's policy in Europe. Thus, the influence of economic (not to mention military and paramilitary) hard power could, in consequence, bring much more losses than benefits. At least in the contemporary realities, in which the Czech Republic is the "starting point" for further actions, often destructive, but aimed at selected EU countries. As a result of the literature review, activities undertaken by Russia as part of a soft impact on the Czech Republic include activities related to financing the activities of Czech politicians and exerting influence on Czech politics – from taking seats in the Czech parliament by political parties associating pro-Russian members, and ending with support openly expressed for the Russian side by the former and present president of the Czech Republic. The second very important activity included in the category of the Russian soft influence on the Czech Republic is building close economic relations, but without using them negatively, and in the direction of gaining favor of the business elite. It takes place mainly through the often hidden financing of the activities of Czech companies by Russians. Closely related to the economic impact is the creation of a network of Russian connections with Czech companies. As with the economic impact, the transactions in progress are difficult to identify, which makes it difficult to demonstrate the network of Russian ties. As part of the soft influence, the creation of the Czech energy dependence on Russia also deserves attention. It takes place mainly through dependence on gas and oil supplies. The energy dependence of the Czechs makes it possible to exert political pressure in situations inconvenient for the Kremlin. Creating a network of non-governmental organizations has been defined as another category of soft-impact activities. It was described as particularly dangerous due to the dissemination of the pro-Kremlin narrative and influencing the Czech society, and above all, on young people, who in the future will set the directions in which the Czech state will follow. The soft-impact activities also include the use of online platforms to spread disinformation. It should be highlighted that their importance is growing significantly, especially considering the possibility of reaching a large number of recipients in a very short time. It must be emphasized that the soft category, as well as the hard category, includes activities such as disinformation and influencing politicians and their decisions. It was recognized that these two groups of activities can fall into both categories of impact, both soft and hard, due to the consequences that a given impact may cause. If, as a result of political influence or disseminated disinformation, typically military actions or actions that make it impossible to implement own defense can take place, then the exerted influence produced effects strongly negatively felt by the population. Otherwise, such an action may be classified as an action with a soft effect.

As a result of a number of the activities described above, there are positive attitudes towards Russians in the Czech society, which may also be partially related to the common Slavic origin (Quinn and Pràt, 2018, p. 47). "However, while some hold pro-Moscow views simply out of conviction, most are influenced by a deliberate Russian strategy advanced by those with close business and personal ties to the Kremlin" (Smoleňová and Chrzová, 2012, p. 2). The Russian-Ukrainian conflict and the consequent annexation of Crimea "led to a further polarization of Central and Eastern European countries, where the situation today is completely different than it was 12 years ago. While Poland perceived this conflict in terms of "hard" security, with an emphasis on military threat, the main challenge for the Czech Republic, Hungary and Slovakia was the future of their economic and energy cooperation with Russia" (Fiszer, 2016, p. 192). The annexation of Crimea and the eastern part of Ukraine's territory makes it worth rethinking the way Russia operates, both in terms of soft and hard influence exerted by this country on other nations. The activities that cannot be clearly classified as "soft" or "hard", and which are carried out by the Kremlin on a very large scale, include activities carried out by the Russian secret services (Baumann, 2020). In fact, as in the years of the Cold War, intensive intelligence activities are conducted without major restrictions, which can be observed on the example of the invariably large number of intelligence employees actively operating under the banner of the Russian embassy in the Czech Republic. Another theatre of action from the pantheons of special actions are all kinds of disinformation operations, the scale of which can be evidenced by a large number of Internet portals using various methods of reaching recipients, in particular, using methods that allow you to have an emotional impact on society.

A separate category of activities, which is much closer to the means used under "hard power", is the activity of all kinds of criminal, paramilitary and extremist groups that permeate the structures of Czech society in many ways. In this case, of course, we are not talking about a broad scale, as in the case of disinformation activity, but about precise actions aimed at specific elements of the economic system or aimed at reaching and binding certain Czech communities. The political sphere, which is another important area in the intelligence activity of many countries, is broadly understood politics, where, within many political parties, you can find active politicians who often represent different views, and their views fit into the Russian narrative (Hellman and Wagnsson, 2017). The results of such actions include public support for the Kremlin's policy by the President of the Czech Republic, selected politicians, or the blocking of US-Czech negotiations on the construction of the anti-missile defense shield, and the fact that the Russians exert a significant influence on Czech public opinion in this regard. In recent years, there have also been many cyber-attacks, which due to their infrastructural nature should be included in the arsenal of hard measures.

Finally, it is worth remembering that the described Russian influence in the Czech Republic is, compared to other countries, very limited and targeted at specific people or environments, so as not to lose the positive reception it has built over the years in the eyes of the majority of the Czech society. Ultimately, this effective interaction through "soft power" contributed to many successes, such as the blocking of the construction of anti-missile shield elements described above. Conducting cyber-attacks is "safe" because it is not possible to directly prove the source of the attack, and at the same time it is a testing ground that the Russian power could not deny itself (Huhtinen and Rantapelkonen, 2016). Therefore, despite the partially destructive nature of this type of activity, it cannot be directly classified as intentionally hostile, because if the Kremlin goes on the offensive, many other elements can be expected, such as the use of personal and economic ties, and the use of criminal and extremist circles in the Czech Republic. Therefore, it can be assumed that cyber-attacks may still occur under controlled conditions and on a limited scale, while intelligence and disinformation activities, as well as strengthening mutual economic relations between the Czech Republic and the Russian Federation, will certainly continue to be intensified.

References

Baumann M., (2020). 'Propaganda Fights' and 'Disinformation Campaigns': the discourse on information warfare in Russia-West relations. *Contemporary Politics,* 26, pp. 288–307.

Fiszer J., (2016). Zadania i cele polityki zagranicznej Władimira Putina, Myśl Ekonomiczna i Polityczna, Nr 1 (52).

https://www.kremlinwatch.eu/countries-compared-states/czechia/.

Hellman M. and Wagnsson C., (2017). How can European states respond to Russian information warfare? An analytical framework. *European Security,* 26, pp. 153–170.

Holzer J., Jirušek M. and Kuchyňková P., (2020). Russia as Viewed by the Main Czech Political Actors. in: Holzer J., Mareš M. (eds.) Czech Security Dilemma. New Security Challenges. Palgrave Macmillan, Cham, https://doi.org/10.1007/978-3-030-20546-1_3.

Huhtinen A.M. and Rantapelkonen J., (2016). Junk Information in Hybrid Warfare: The Rhizomatic Speed of Social Media in the Spamosphere. *Proceedings of the 15th European Conference on Cyber Warfare and Security (Eccws 2016),* pp. 136–144.

Smoleňová I. and Chrzová B. (eds.), (2012). United we stand, divided we fall: the Kremlin's leverage in the visegrad countries, Prague Security Studies Institute.

Quinn P. and Prát S., (2018). Russian Cultural Communities within the Czech Republic: Economics, Perceptions and Integration, "Journal of Identity and Migration Studies", Volume 12, number 1.

Section III:
Measuring the effectiveness of the Russian impact on the Czech internal and foreign policy

Marcin Górnikiewicz / Tadeusz Szczurek / Marzena Walkowiak

Chapter 19: The effectiveness measurement of the quantitative methods of Russian influence in the Czech Republic

In this chapter, the results of quantitative and quantitative-qualitative research have been collected, and then processed using theoretical techniques such as analysis, synthesis and comparison. The adopted research goal was to measure the effectiveness of the Russian influence on the Czech decision-making process with the use of quantitative methods. As a result, the obtained data, that was re-processed using deductive and inductive techniques to present average quantitative data allowing the visualization of the level of effectiveness of the Russian influence on the Czech Republic with a graphical model. The indicator used to assess the potential was the scale of comparison with the potential of other countries in relation to the analyzed economic data, political and social data and military data on the defense potential of the Czech Republic.

The economic data presented in this section is closely related to the crisis caused by the COVID-19 pandemic, which first resulted in a global collapse in demand for oil and natural gas. As a result, the forecasts for the Russian economy indicated a decline in GDP by 4–6% in 2020. According to the International Energy Agency, demand for oil fell in April this year by an average of 25%. An additional stimulus to the decline in prices was the lack of an agreement between Saudi Arabia and Russia, which ultimately led to rivalry between the two mining tycoons of this raw material. The drop in prices triggered by the global epidemic and price war led to a drop in the price of a barrel of Ural oil to $ 29 in March, and then to $ 16.2 in April. The price started to gradually return to the baseline level with the global trend to thaw the economy due to the slowdown in the epidemic development in most countries around the world and concern about the possibility of economic closure in autumn due to the forecasted possibility of its second wave. On May 27, 2020, the price of a barrel of Ural crude oil returned to the level of USD 34.43. It is worth adding that the lowest price drop was recorded on 02/04/2020 at the level of USD 13.37, from a relatively stable and so far highest level on 09/01/2020, USD 65.73 per barrel (https://www.wnp.pl). Revenues from the sale of crude oil constitute nearly 40% of the Russian budget, which means that in terms of planning this budget at the end of last year, after the current increases, it may in an optimistic scenario generate only half of the planned revenues, which will reduce the total budget value by as much as 20% (Słomski, no. date). To sum up, it also means fewer possibilities of economic impact on the countries of the former Eastern Bloc by regulating the scale of exports and imports. These conclusions are confirmed by economic data for the first quarter of 2020, where the stable situation in January and February contributed to a relatively good overall result, but at the same time, as a result of changes in the Russian economy since March, exports decreased by 15%, i.e. to USD 88 billion. In April, in line with the assumptions, GDP fell by nearly 20%, and there was also a significant increase in the number of the unemployed by nearly 100%. The latest data is justified by the dramatic situation in Russian business, where the economic activity index in April reached the level of 31 points (a level below 40 points means a serious economic crisis) (https://pl.tradingeconomics.com).

The question then arises as to how the decision-makers in Moscow plan to fill the budget gap that is emerging at a dramatic pace. First of all, the deficit can be supplemented from the National Welfare Fund (NWF), where in April there were funds worth USD 165 billion, i.e. corresponding to about 11.3% of GDP. Unfortunately, this sum should be reduced by USD 28 billion, which was allocated to the government buy-back of Sberbank shares. Thus, the real figure in April was less than 8% of GDP. The Russian government has at its disposal the Central Bank of Russia's currency and metal reserves worth US $ 567 billion. Thus, Moscow does have the means to cover both this year's deficit and at least next year's deficit. On the other hand, reaching for reserves would be a sign of economic and political desperation. Thus, in government circles, the idea of increasing the sovereign debt by 1.5–2% of GDP appeared, which could be related to the acquisition of shares in the aforementioned Sberbank, which could generate adequate income to cover the increased debt, while keeping most of the reserves intact. Another tool is the sale of securities and loans, which does not encounter any major difficulties in the case of the Russian government, due to the high credibility guaranteed, for example, by the huge resources of raw materials and the potential possibility of selling modern weapons and space technologies. For example, in the first quarter, securities for 0.5 trillion rubles were sold and it is planned to borrow at least 0.6 trillion rubles in the second quarter. Overall, public debt, compared to many other countries, is still relatively small (at 14% of GDP), which is also a strong argument for Russia's credibility as a borrower or issuer of securities (Gurvich, 2020).

In the ranking of countries with which the Czech Republic is related to export and import relations, Russia ranks twelfth in terms of exports with a value of USD 4.98 billion in 2019 (after selected European countries and the United States) and eighth in terms of imports with a value of 4.3 billion USD (after selected European countries and China). In both cases, the highest turnover is recorded with

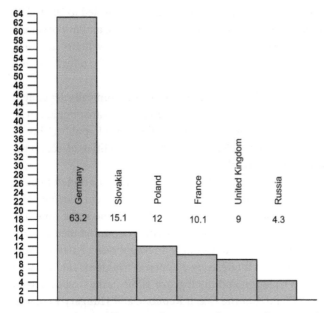

Figure 1. Czech Republic Exports by Country (https://tradingeconomics.com).

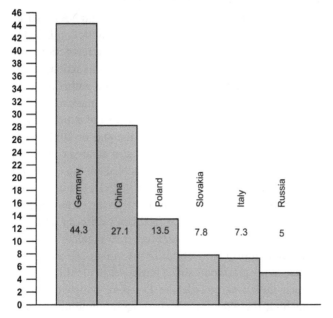

Figure 2. Czech Republic Imports by Country (https://tradingeconomics.com).

Germany – for comparison, exports to Germany in 2019 amounted to USD 63.27 billion, which accounted for 32% of the total value of exports, and imports were USD 44.03 billion, which corresponded to 25% of the total value of imports. Against this background, in 2019, exports to Russia accounted for only 2.2%, and imports for 2.8% of the total value.

This data clearly shows that the Czech Republic is not economically dependent on relations with Russia, and any possible perturbations in this area would not be particularly severe for Prague and the inhabitants of the Czech Republic. Thus, it can be assumed that Russia does not have any real possibilities of economic influence on the political decisions taken in Prague.

After the collapse of the Warsaw Pact, the Czech Republic continued to be of strategic interest to Russian secret services. Prague was an excellent starting point for the entire Central and Eastern and Central Europe. At the same time, the Russians who wanted to conduct information activities (from the media to intelligence) had greater freedom than, for example, in neighboring Poland, where American and Western European interests overlapped to a large extent. It can be assumed that the main information and intelligence effort in the first decade of freedom was placed on Poland, but the Czech Republic and Hungary were also treated in Moscow with due seriousness, sparing no efforts to constantly strengthen and, as far as possible, develop Russian influence.

With the expansion of the borders of the European Union and NATO structures to the former Communist Bloc countries, the Czech Republic continued to leave a lot of freedom to Russian activity, despite the emerging restrictions and adversities. It can be assumed that the special interest in Russian activity in the Czech Republic began after the annexation of Crimea and the outbreak of the conflict in eastern Ukraine. At that time, a lot of information unmasking Russian activity began to appear in the information space, an example of which may be the effects of the national security audit published at the end of 2015, which showed that, like the entire West, the Czech Republic is also an area covered by Russian hybrid activities. In 2017, a special unit was established, the Center for Counter-Terrorism and Counteracting Hybrid Threats (CTHH, Centrum Proti terorismu a hybridním hrozbám) (https://www.mvcr.cz). In the same year, the National Cyber and Information Security Office (NÚKIB, Nádrodní úřad pro kybernetickou a informační bezpečnost) was established to regulate cyber security and protect classified information (https://www.nukib.cz). From the Czechs side, there were also many grassroots social initiatives to identify cases of Russian propaganda. Such initiatives include the Evropské hodeństwo think tank, that initiated launching the Kremlin Watch programme aimed at presenting Russian information activity in public space (https://www.kremlinwatch.eu).

On the other hand, many people involved in political movement, especially among the Czech communists or the somewhat antagonistically populist right-wing circles, with their views and slogans, often fit into the narrative created in Moscow (e. g. Komunistická strana Čech a Moravy, KSČM, the Communist Party of Bohemia and Moravia and the right-wing populist party for Freedom and Direct Democracy – Svoboda a přímá demokracie, SPD, Freedom and Direct Democracy

It is also worth noting the particularly large staff of the Russian embassy in Prague (nearly fifty diplomats and eighty people providing technical support), apart from the consulates in Ostrava, Brno and Karlovy Vary (https://warsawinstitute.org). The first city has become famous for over twenty years for organizing well-known NATO Days with the participation of representatives of most NATO countries and a military equipment show; the second one is home to the only Czech military university. It turns out that in such a small country as the Czech Republic, the Russian Federation maintains a particularly extensive diplomatic structure. In connotation with the existence of a strong pro-Russian political base and intensive information campaigns in the mass media, it can be assumed that Russian information activity runs in two directions: – using the technology of social engineering aimed at shaping social attitudes – using the intelligence facilities to attract people and institutions that can be used in information operations.

The approach presented above finds some confirmation in the reports published and made publicly available every year by the Czech counterintelligence service BIS (Bezpečnostní informační služba, Security Information Service). The authors of the reports indicate the activity of Russia and China as the greatest threats to Czech political sovereignty (https://www.bis.cz). In 2013, an interview with the former head of the Czech military intelligence, Andor Sandor, was published, which pointed to the effectiveness of the Russian methodology of social engineering in shaping public opinion, which resulted in, among others, blocking the installation of a part of the American anti-missile shield not by supporting the attitudes of friendship and alliance with Russia, but by causing dislike of the American foreign policy pursuing its own goal without considering the costs (https://www.rp.pl). This kind of rhetoric found fertile ground, as did the narrative aimed at the Czech Republic's integration with the European Union, which was aimed at limiting Czech sovereignty (https://przegladbaltycki.pl). It is therefore worth taking a closer look at the actual effectiveness of propaganda activities conducted in this way.

Table 1. Most in former Eastern Bloc approve of shift to multiparty and free market systems (https://www.pewresearch.org)

State	Disapprove multiparty system (%)	Disapprove market economy (%)	Approve of change to multiparty system (%)	Approve of change to market economy (%)
Poland	8	8	85	85
East Germany[1]	12	13	85	83
Czech Rep.	11	16	82	76
Hungary	20	72	19	70
Russia	48	51	43	38
Lithuania	19	20	70	69
Ukraine	35	38	51	47
Slovakia	22	23	74	71
Bulgaria	37	36	54	55

The presented research results clearly show that the vast majority of the Czechs support the democratic and free market system in relation to the solutions from the past system associated with the Russian model.

Table 2. Largely positive views about the EU and its impact on member states (https://www.pewresearch.org)

State	They have a favourable view of the EU (%)	Their country's membership in the EU has been a good thing (%)	The economic integration of Europe has strengthened their country's economy (%)
Poland	84	67	71
Lithuania	83	59	62
Bulgaria	77	54	25
Sweden	72	60	51
Slovakia	70	59	58
Germany	69	74	69
Hungary	67	62	65
Netherlands	66	59	60
Spain	66	67	59
Italy	58	50	22
UK	54	48	54

---

1 Respondents in areas corresponding to former German Democratic Republic.

Table 2 *(Continued)*

State	They have a favourable view of the EU (%)	Their country's membership in the EU has been a good thing (%)	The economic integration of Europe has strengthened their country's economy (%)
Greece	53	55	35
Czech Rep.	52	40	51
France	51	54	42
EU Median	67	59	56

The presented results show the attitude of the Czech society towards the functioning of their country within the structures of the European Union, which is important as it presents the real power of the pro-Russian media whose narrative is targeted against integration with the European Union and the alliance with the United States within NATO. A rather disturbing picture emerges, because despite enormous support for democratic and free-market solutions ensuring a decent standard of living, only half of the respondents supported the European integration.

Table 3. Generally, Central and Estern Europeans approve of shift to multiparty system and free market economy (https://www.pewresearch.org)

State	Multiparty system (%)	Market economy (%)
Poland	85	85
East Germany[2]	85	83
Czech Rep.	82	76
Slovakia	74	71
Hungary	72	70
Lithuania	70	69
Bulgaria	54	55
Ukraine	51	47
Russia	43	38

Table 4. Except in Russia, uptick in those saying economics situation is better than under communism (https://www.pewresearch.org)

State	2009 (%)	2019 (%)
Poland	47	74
Czech Rep.	45	61

---

[2] Respondents in areas corresponding to former German Democratic Republic.

Table 4 *(Continued)*

State	2009 (%)	2019 (%)
Lithuania	23	56
Hungary	8	47
Slovakia	29	45
Russia	33	27
Ukraine	12	25
Bulgaria	13	24

Table 5. Many people say EU membership has strengthened their national economies (https://www.pewresearch.org)

State	They have a favourable view of the EU (%)	Their country's membership in the EU has been a good thing (%)	The economic integration of Europe has strengthened their country's economy (%)
Poland	71	17	12
Germany	69	6	26
Hungary	65	18	16
Lithuania	62	18	20
Netherlands	60	1	39
Spain	59	2	39
Slovakia	58	19	24
UK	54	5	41
Czech Rep.	51	25	24
Sweden	51	11	38
France	42	4	54
Greece	35	15	50
Bulgaria	25	27	48
Italy	22	19	58

The presented research results confirm the previous findings. In 2019, Russia sold weapons worth US $ 6.4 billion to the Czech Republic, and it is worth noting that since 2010 the value of exported weapons ranged from US $ 5.3 billion to US $ 8.7 billion depending on the year. Due to the specific nature of special trading, it can be concluded that Russia has been the gaining party in these transactions since 2014, struggling with the need to generate revenues in order to supplement and develop reserves in the event of various crises, including those caused by constantly conducted hostilities. The Czech armed forces intrinsically do not constitute a significant military force in the structures of the North Atlantic

Alliance so far, and therefore decision-makers in Prague could risk a gradual transition from post-Soviet-Russian weapons to the Western one without a fear of a sudden loss of defense capabilities. To sum up, Moscow is mainly interested in maintaining this outlet, so it is the Czech Republic that may exert greater pressure on Moscow in this area than the other way around.

The Czech Republic, on the other hand, has not been selling high-value weapons for years, an example of which can be the total sales for 2018, which amounted to USD 64 million compared to 2010–2017, where the value of weapons sold varied from USD 4 million to USD 150 million depending on the year, while only in 2015 it was the above-mentioned high value and in 2016 amounted USD 148 million. Moreover, the sale of weapons usually did not exceed USD 100 million, which, with the grossly higher turnover in arms imports from Russia, indicates a stronger dependence of Moscow on Prague than Prague on Moscow.

References

Gurvich E. and Suslina A., (2020). Fiscal Policy During the Time of the Pandemic, ECONS, www.econs.online.
https://pl.tradingeconomics.com/russia/manufacturing-pmi.
https://przegladbaltycki.pl/14926,miedzy-polityka-ideologia-i-interpretacja-historii-rosyjskie-media-wobec-europy-srodkowo-wschodniej.html.
https://warsawinstitute.org/pl/czy-czesi-sa-rusofilami/.
https://www.bis.cz/public/site/bis.cz/content/vyrocni-zpravy/en/ar2017en.pdf.
https://www.kremlinwatch.eu/#welcome.
https://www.mvcr.cz/cthh/clanek/centre-against-terrorism-and-hybrid-threats.aspx.
https://www.nukib.cz/en/about-nukib/.
https://www.pewresearch.org/global/2019/10/15/european-public-opinion-three-decades-after-the-fall-of-communism/.
https://www.rp.pl/artykul/1035650-Rosjanie-nie-boja-sie-nikogo.html.
https://www.wnp.pl/nafta/notowania/ceny_ropy/?zakres=12.
Słomski D., Putin ma coraz większy problem. Tania ropa naftowa rozkłada budżet, https://www.money.pl/gospodarka/putin-ma-coraz-wiekszy-problem-tania-ropa-naftowa-rozklada-budzet-6495175806900353a.html, dostęp: 01.04.2020.

Małgorzata Jaroszyńska

Chapter 20: The effectiveness measurement of the qualitative methods of Russian influence in the Czech Republic

Qualitative research in sociology and psychology is associated with qualitative data analysis, while in statistics with the term analysis of qualitative data. The qualitative description is the equivalent to description at a level of characteristics. Thus, it is generated by its attribute i. e. an element that is often abstract and in logical terms is a definition of a concept that, according to information theory, reflects a set of information of the same type about the examined object (Baborski, 1979). Thus, information about objects is considered to be of the same type. In qualitative research, the researcher's awareness of the sense and purposefulness of the research and the final shape of the information obtained from it is extremely important (Crotty, 1998; Mertens, 1998; Lincoln and Guba, 2017; Neuman, 2014). Assuming that, by definition, the researcher is a party to the research, his or her personal experiences are superimposed on the research process, and the interpretation of facts is subjective, so there is no possibility of impartiality.

The perception of the Russian influence on the Czech Republic varies in this country. The views of Czech local authorities influence the views of society and increasingly affect relations with Russia. It is also difficult to talk about the coherent policy of the coalition centrist government (ANO) and the Czech Social Democratic Party (ČSSD) towards Russia, which indirectly influences the perception of Russian influence over the Czech Republic. An example of this is the adoption of different attitudes towards the sanctions imposed on Russia by the EU and the US.

The prime minister and leader of ANO, Andrej Babiš, is a supporter of a dialogue with Russia, and perceives the EU sanctions against that country as a negative factor for the Czech economy. The chairman of the lower house of the Czech parliament, Radek Vondráček, is considered to be the most favorable for the cooperation with Russia in ANO. He criticizes Russia's international isolation. In turn, the Minister of Foreign Affairs, Tomáš Petříček (ČSSD), was a supporter of the expulsion of three Russian diplomats in a gesture of solidarity with the United Kingdom after poisoning Sergei and Julia Skripal in March 2018.

His views, however, are not identical to the party's line, whose program objective is to maintain "good", strategic relations with Russia. The Communist Party of Bohemia and Moravia is an unequivocally pro-Russian party in the Czech Republic. President Miloš Zeman is the greatest advocate of close Czech-Russian relations. He supports Russian interests by opposing EU sanctions imposed on Russia, and by supporting the construction of the Nord Stream 2 gas pipeline.

Trade between Russia and the Czech Republic and the deepening of energy integration between these countries contributes to the development of bilateral economic relations between these countries. Recently, it has been noticeable that due to the devaluation of the ruble, the recession of the Russian economy and economic sanctions imposed on Russia, trade exchange between these countries has slightly weakened. Already in 2015, the Czech security service (Bezpečnostní Informační Služba, BIS) warned in its annual report against the penetration of the Czech economy by Russian capital related to the shadow economy and against the strengthening of the Kremlin's political influence in the Czech Republic.

According to the data as of April 30, 2018, the trade turnover between the Czech Republic and Russia in the period from January to December 2016 amounted to CZK 195,395 million. Compared to the same period of 2017, it increased to CZK 212,861 million. In 2016, exports from the Czech Republic to Russia amounted to CZK 75,210 million, while imports to the Czech Republic amounted to CZK 83,887 million. In 2017, these figures amounted to CZK 82,246 million and CZK 114,849 million, respectively. (Guide to the Czech market, 2018).

In 2015, the Czech Republic recorded a trade deficit with Russia in the amount of EUR 1005 million, while in 2017 the trade deficit with Russia decreased and amounted to EUR 775 million, i. e. the surplus of imports over exports decreased by 32.9% (Foreign trade Czech Republic).

In 2018, the Czech Republic recorded a slowdown in economic growth. According to preliminary data from the Czech Statistical Office, GDP increased by only 2.9%. A year earlier, the economy grew at a rate of 4.4%. The economic growth was mainly driven by internal factors and partly by foreign demand. In 2018, there was an increase in household expenditure (by 3.2%) and capital expenditure (by 10.5%). Exports developed dynamically, reaching the value of EUR 171 billion in 2018 (an increase by 6.2%) (Czech Republic).

Contrary to economic relations, political associations deteriorated significantly. In recent months, this was due to, inter alia, disrupting the network of Russian hackers, removing the monument to the Soviet Marshal Ivan Koniev in Prague, and intensifying the Czech Republic's relations with Ukraine and the US.

The Czech Republic and other countries of Central and Eastern Europe are among the priority goals of Russian disinformation, designed to weaken the ties linking the Czech Republic with the EU and NATO, and in the long term to detach the country from European and Euro-Atlantic ties. The intention is to restore the Kremlin's influence. Russia has no doubt that the implementation of these plans will take time. Therefore, the confusion of Czech society and the undermining of democratic rule is the way to achieve the goal.

Assuming that the actions of the Russian Federation towards the Czech Republic are deliberate and intentional, it is possible to analyze the effectiveness of these actions. It is known that the main instrument for creating conditions enabling the implementation of the foreign policy and geopolitical goals of the Russian Federation are the secret services of this country: officers of the Foreign Intelligence Service (SWR), the Federal Security Service (FSB) and the Main Intelligence Directorate (GRU). These services use "active measures", which include: information and psychological activities, disinformation, "maskirovka (a *military doctrine developed from the start of the twentieth century and it covers a broad range of measures for military deception, from camouflage to denial and deception*-translator's footnote.)", special propaganda, provocations, diversion and sabotage. (Darczewska and Żochowski, 2017).

In order to present the non-military measures and indirect methods of influence of the Russian Federation in more detail, it can be agreed that these are (Wojnowski, 2005): – disinformation of the political elite, military commanders and the public by manipulating information,
- fabrication of information,
- falsifying reality (fake news),
- distracting attention from Russia's real actions and goals,
- intoxication, social oversight and maneuvering, i.e. intentionally influencing society to achieve specific benefits,
- compromising, corrupting and blackmailing political and military elites,
- fueling internal and international tensions and disputes,
- supporting separatist tendencies and ethnic and religious conflicts,
- organizing provocations, demonstrations and manifestations (using the "potential of protest"),
- supporting opposition groups, resistance movements, extremist circles,
- creating institutions, associations, foundations, organizations, armed paramilitary groups controlled by special services,
- inspiring events that destabilize the internal situation,
- subversive, diversionary, sabotage and terrorist activities in order to create a feeling of
- uncertainty and danger in the society.

The Czech Republic, due to its location in the center of Europe, was an area of high activity of the Kremlin's operations. The BIS report (Janda) indicates that it is the Russian services that are most active in this area.

Prague, the capital of the Czech Republic, partly because of its convenient location in the middle of Europe, has always been fertile soil for the Kremlin's active measures and covert operations. According to the BIS Annual Report, in 2015 the Russian services were the most active among the intelligence services in the Czech Republic (Annual Report of the Security Information Service, 2016). This is indicated, for example, by the number of employees of the Embassy of the Russian Federation in the Czech Republic. In 2017, it had 48 diplomatic staff and 81 administrative and technical staff. At the same time, 40 diplomats worked at the US embassy and 25 at the Chinese embassy (Břešťan).

According to Czech counterintelligence, a Soviet espionage base has existed in Prague since 1969. Currently, Russian agents operate in the circles of organized crime, while exerting influence on "big politics" and increasing the dependence of the Czech Republic on Russia (Janda and Kundra)

The entity that directly or indirectly serves Russia's interests are Czech-language websites, which often disseminate disinformation and manipulative content. The official site is Sputnik, the rest of which are about 40, not officially affiliated with the Russian government. Distorted information on the Internet and in social media often comes from foreign servers, from official Kremlin channels or English-language conspiratorial portals, such as Global Research or Southfront.

Disinformation content is provided anonymously on these websites and their funding sources are unknown. As an example of influencing recipients through various types of social networks is running campaigns focused, for example, on supporting Russia or arousing negative emotions towards refugees in Europe.

As in many other countries, online media and social networks are the main source of disinformation in the Czech Republic. These are both sources of disinformation and channels of dissemination. The disinformation is mainly about foreign policy and international affairs. Events in the Czech Republic are becoming more and more distorted. The 2018 elections in the Czech Republic could be an example of it. Milos Zęman's opponent, Jiří Drahoš, was presented as a former collaborator of the StB – the Czech secret police during the communist era, as a supporter of unrestricted immigration (Janda and Vichova, 2018).

The pro-Western national consensus in the Czech Republic is being challenged by some parties and politicians who are becoming supporters of anti-Western ideologies. The Freedom and Direct Democracy Party (SPD), with 22 seats in the parliament, is clearly Eurosceptic and far-right. Another advocate of these views is the Communist Party of Bohemia and Moravia (KSČM). Dissatisfaction with NATO and EU membership and activities is becoming more and more popular in the Czech Republic. This type of social feeling is also used by Russian sympathizers, who are also the major political parties.

The President of the Czech Republic, Miloš Zeman himself and other politicians play a large role in conveying untrue information. An example of this type of information is, for example, the presence of the Bandera followers in Ukraine (Nepoužívejte termín banderovci, kárají vědci Zemana. A nabízejí radu). M. Zeman is considered a pro-Russian creator of the Kremlin's agenda and a propagator of the Kremlin's narrative. He was the propagator of the information that the return of Crimea to Ukraine is impossible. He also claimed that N. Khrushchev made a mistake in handing the peninsula over to Ukraine (Wenerski, 2017). He also expressed his support for Russia by taking part, as the only European leader, in the celebration of the end of World War II in 2015. At that time, the celebrations were boycotted due to Moscow's interference in Ukraine.

The goal of the portals that publish information and opinions about the president is to increase his popularity and make his actions accepted.

It can be predicted that M. Zeman had also a great influence on the emergence of Islamophobic attitudes in society. According to Coda Story, he described himself as a tolerant atheist and in fact he is the country's foremost Islamophobe (CodaStory, 2017).

It was not uncommon for representatives from other political options, perhaps out of their ignorance, to provide information from uncertain sources and not supported by facts. An example of such a message was the information about the radioactive cloud over Europe. The message indicated that the reason for this was the explosion at a nuclear power plant in France. The truth turned out to be different, and mostly proved that the cloud was not a threat (Hoax). In turn, Vojtěch Filip, the leader of the Communist Party described Ukraine as a neo-Nazi state supported by the USA. (Political Capital, 2017).

A complete and comprehensive assessment of the Kremlin's impact on Czech society is possible only on the basis of up-to-date data. This type of information has not been found. Perhaps such studies have not been conducted, but it is also possible that such data is classified. The last research was conducted in 2016 in cooperation with the STEM agency and in 2017 by the Slovak think-tank GLOBSEC. This research made it possible to assess the level of trust in democratic institutions and the media. One can assume that the Czech society believes in disinformation content and trusts the media from which this message comes. However, on the basis of these studies, it is not possible to determine the effectiveness of Russian influence in the case of specific actions carried out by the Russian Federation (The Kremlin's hostile influence in the Czech Republic: the current state of affairs).

References

(2016) Annual Report of the Security Information Service for 2015, Security Information Service (BIS), https://www.bis.cz/vyrocni-zpravaEN890a.html?ArticleID=1104, (dostęp: 26.03.2020).

(2017) Political Capital, The Russian Connections of Far-right and Paramilitary Organizations in the Czech Republic, https://bit.ly/2qVUYM2 9 dostęp: 24.03.2020).

(2018) Przewodnik po rynku czeskim, Warszawa: Polska Agencja Inwestycji i Handlu S.A.

Baborski A., (1979). Teoria języków formalnych a modelowanie systemów dynamicznych, vol. 157, Wrocław: Prace Naukowe Akademii Ekonomicznej we Wrocławiu.

Břešťan R., Ruské velvyslanectví v Praze je stale při síle, Působí na něm nejvíce lidí ze všech ambasád, Info.cz; http://www.info.cz/cesko/ruske-velvyslanectvi-v-praze-je-stale-pri-sile-pusobi-na-nem-nejvice-lidi-ze-vsech-ambasad-11275.html, (dostęp: 26.03.2020).

CodaStory, (2017). The Czech Republic's Phantom Muslim Menace. https://bit.ly/2Ww0GAd (dostęp: 26.03.2020).

Crotty M., (1998). The foundations of social research – meaning and perspective in the research process. Thousand Oaks: Sage Publications.

Darczewska J. and Żochowski P., (2017). Środki Aktywne. Rosyjski towar eksportowy, Punkt Widzenia OSW, nr 64.

Handel zagraniczny Republiki Czeskiej , https://czechrepublic.trade.gov.pl/pl/czechy/gospodarka/252408,handel-zagraniczny-republiki-czeskiej-w-i-polroczu-2017-r-.html [dostęp: 26.03.2020].

Hoax, Radiační mrak nad Evropu z utajené exploze ve francouzské elektrárně, Manipulátoři.cz, http://manipulatori.cz/hoax-radiacni-mrak-nad-evropou-utajene-exploze-ve-francouzske-elektrarne/, (dostęp: 26.03.2020).

Janda J., Ondrej K., Schéma fungování vlivu Ruské federace v České republice, European Values Think-Tank; http://www.evropskehodnoty.cz/wp-content/uploads/2016/08/SCH%C3%89MA-FUNGOV%C3%81N%C3%8D-VLIVU-RUSK%C3%89-FEDERACE-V-%C4%8CESK%C3%89-REPUBLICE1.pdf, (dostęp: 24.03.2020).

Janda J., Policy Shift Overview: How the Czech Republic became one of the European leaders in countering Russian disinformation, European Values Think-Tank; http://www.europeanvalues.net/wp-content/uploads/2017/05/Policy-shift-overview-How-the-Czech-Republic-became-one-of-the-European-leaders-in-countering-Russian-disinformation-1.pdf, (dostęp: 26.03.2020).

Janda J., Vichova V. et al., (2018). "The role of the Kremlin's influence and disinformation in the Czech presidential elections." European Values Think Tank. https://bit.ly/2kYhilz (dostęp: 25.03.2020).

Lincoln Yvonna S. and Guba Egon G., (2000). Paradigmatic controversies, contradictions and emerging confluences. in: Lincoln Yvonna S., Denzin Norman K. (eds.), Handbook of qualitative research, Thousand Oaks: Sage Publications, United States.

Mertens Donna M., (1998). Research methods – integrating diversity with quantitative and qualitative approaches. Thousand Oaks, Calif.: Sage Publications.

Nepoužívejte termín banderovci, kárají vědci Zemana. A nabízejí radu, Lidovky.cz; http://www.lidovky.cz/nepouzivejte-termin-banderovci-karaji-vedci-zemana-nabizeji-radu-p90-/zpravy-svet.aspx?c=A140828_145147_ln_zahranici_msl, (dostęp: 28.03.2020).

Neuman, W. Lawrence, (2014). Social research methods – qualitative and quantitative approaches. Boston: Edinburg Gate, Harlow.

Republika Czeska, www.gov.pl (dostęp: 23.03.2020).

Wenerski Ł., (2017). The Visegrad Countries and "Post-Truth.", https://bit.ly/2C3b1do (dostęp: 23.03.2020).

Wojnowski M., (2005). Koncepcja "wojny nowej generacji" w ujęciu strategów Sztabu Generalnego Sił Zbrojnych Federacji Rosyjskiej, Przegląd Bezpieczeństwa Wewnętrznego, nr 13.

Wrogie oddziaływania Kremla w Republice Czeskiej: obecny stan rzeczy https://warsawinstitute.org/pl/wrogie-oddzialywania-kremla-w-republice-czeskiej-obecny-stan-rzeczy/ (dostęp: 23.03.2020).

Marcin Górnikiewicz / Małgorzata Jaroszyńska

Chapter 21: Summary and conclusions: The perspective of the development direction of Moscow's foreign policy towards the Czech Republic

Manipulating Czech public opinion and its elites is a method of realizing the Kremlin's strategic interests. The low cost, a low risk and potential high benefits of such activities have made manipulation one of the primary tools for influencing Czech society. Activities undertaken in the information space do not fit into the conventional concept of war (Baumann, 2020). One should note, however, that the offensive nature of these actions means that they should be treated as a form of aggression and interference in the internal affairs of other countries. Actions of this type may lead to unrest, protests, riots, regime changes, rebellion, etc. Seeing the threat from Russia, it is important to control the level of Kremlin's influence on Czech society. It is possible by conducting research by research centers. Audit should also be targeted at identifying, analyzing and exposing disinformation by intelligence and counter-intelligence services.

Being aware that active measures have the greatest impact on public opinion, it seems extremely important to strengthen civil society by supporting think-tanks, independent media and non-governmental organizations dealing with the fight against Russian disinformation. Their role should be both analytical and educational.

In the economic and military spheres, no real dependencies have been noted that would enable Moscow to possibly influence Prague's domestic or foreign policy. At the same time, Russian information centers are working to shape anti-EU and anti-American social attitudes among Czechs, referring to strengthening the sense of national independence and the resulting strength, without promoting at all, however, as was the case in Ukraine, pro-Soviet attitudes, which in the Czech Republic, due to a high standard of living, would not meet with the favor of society. The adopted narrative line of strengthening by the national media belonging to people with views consistent with the Russian narrative, provoked a division within the society into a part supporting further European integration and the economic benefits resulting from this integration, and a second part with opposing views, not associating Czech economic growth with presence in the European Union. Such views can be considered a success of

Russia's information campaigns, reflected in the results of the parliamentary elections, which, in turn, is associated with the possibility of influencing the Czech decision-making process.

After analyzing, synthesizing and comparing the collected data, and then subjecting it to the processes of deduction and induction, it can be concluded that the only realm of Moscow's influence on the shape of Czech politics is the information influence carried out mainly through media centers. This action brings tangible results, so the decision-makers in Moscow do not see any real need to incur additional costs related to strengthening economic relations, or even exploiting political influence to achieve greater revenues from both imports to the Czech Republic and profitable sales of Russian weapons to the government in Prague.

References

Baumann M., (2020). 'Propaganda Fights' and 'Disinformation Campaigns': the discourse on information warfare in Russia-West relations. *Contemporary Politics,* 26, pp. 288–307.

Section IV:
**Foresight of the influence of the Russian impact
on the Russian-Czech relations in the area of regional security**

Paulina Owczarek

Chapter 22: The use of qualitative foresight methods in the assessment of relations between Russia and the Czech Republic

The political and economic transformations that began in Russia in the late 1980s made it possible to build a market economy. The adopted key reforms, including privatization, influenced the functioning of enterprises and the share of the state sector in the economy. Moreover, they defined the initial specifics of the Russian economic system, which in the following years, was changing under the influence of important economic and political events, such as the crisis of 1998, which implied an evolution of the corporate sector structure, and changes on the political scene at the turn of the 20th and 21st centuries.

Unlike Russia, the Czech Republic is one of the youngest independent European states, operating since January 1, 1993 and continuing the tradition of Czech statehood, which for centuries had various organizational and systemic forms. One of the main goals of Czech foreign policy since the beginning of the political transformation in 1989 has been European integration, which culminated in joining the European economic and political structures on May 1, 2004 (Filip, 2003, p. 145), (Pacześniak and Perottino, 2017).

The purpose of this chapter is to identify and forecast further development of mutual Russian-Czech relations in the area of economic security. This goal was achieved through a critical analysis of the literature on the subject and the use of qualitative prognostic methods – comparative analysis and SWOT analysis. The conducted analysis made it possible to conclude that out of the qualitative prognostic methods, two of the indicated approaches turned out to be optimally effective due to the nature of information resources and the research methodology adopted by the authors of the used materials.

The analysis of the economic system of the Czech Republic requires the definition of the very concept of the system and the indication of the main evaluation criteria and features enabling its precise description. As T. Kowalik assumes (Kowalik, 2005, p. 15), the economic system is a set of economic entities and other units, functioning according to specific rules, incentives, orders and prohibitions in the field of production, distribution, exchange and consumption of goods and services. A slightly narrower approach is proposed by J.W. Bossak

(Bossak, 2006, p. 19), who recognizes that the economic system is a part of the entire institutional system of the state, constituting an internally coherent set of institutional factors determining the mechanisms and economic activity of society and the achieved results. L. Balcerowicz (Balcerowicz, 1993, pp. 14–15), in turn, distinguishes the possibility of defining the economic system in a broad and a narrow sense. In broad terms, the economic system includes various, relatively permanent determinants of economic activity (material resources and intangible institutions), the economic activity itself and its results. In turn, in a narrow sense, it is a set of permanent intangible determinants of economic activity and its effects, which the Author treats as economic efficiency.

The country's economic system is formed as a result of a complex socio-political process under certain historical conditions. It includes the following elements (Swadźba, 2009, pp. 42–43): – economic order – organization of the economy and its structure (economic system, well-formed and socially regulated order);
- economic factors – resources, human capital, climate;
- economic processes: production and distribution and their results (the amount and growth of national income, employment, foreign trade, income distribution structure).

The analysis and description of a country's economic system requires the definition or measurement of at least most of the following evaluation criteria and elements: – decision coordination mechanism and form of ownership of means of production;
- efficiency of the economy functioning;
- the role of the state in the economy, its activity in the real and regulatory sphere (share in enterprise ownership, the size of the budget in relation to GDP, expenditure structure);
- ownership structure and level of guarantee of property rights;
- the level of development and effectiveness of the financial system (including the capital market, banking system);
- monetary and tax policy;
- functioning of the labor market and the social security system.

The existing conceptualisations of economic systems, despite the different approach, are convergent in its definition. The dominant position assumes that the economic system is a set of institutions that shape the making and implementation of decisions related to the production of income, saving, investment and consumption, and shapes the general situation of the state and its potential.

The characteristics of the Russian Federation and the Czech Republic presented in the table below (Table 1) displays both countries in the following areas: general data, information characterizing government, purchasing power, market, business, trade, sociodemography as well as energy and environment.

Table 1. Comparative analysis of economic potential of the Russian Federation and the Czech Republic (https://countryeconomy.com)

General data	Russia	Czechia
Area	17 075 400 km²	78 866 km²
Population	146 877 088	10 649 800
Inland waterways	0,52%	2%
Political system	Federal state	Parliamentary republic
Membership	Incl. UN, Interpol, ILO, IMO, UNESCO, WHO, commonwealth of the Independent States, WTO, IPU, ISO, OPCW,	Incl. UN, UE, NATO, Schengen zones, The Council of Europe, OECD, Vishegrad Group
Army	1,027 mln troops	31 163 troops
Government		
2018 r.	Russia	Czechia
Annual GDP	$ 1,657,290 M	$ 245,226 M
GDP per capita	$ 11,289	$ 23,113
Debt	241,945	79,642
Debt per capita	1,648 $	7,478 $
Expenditure	$ 540,326.4 M	$ 99,750.1 M
Defence expenditures	$ 65,123.4 M	$ 2,755.4 M
Expenditures per capita	$ 3,681	$ 9,366
Corruption index	28	59
Innovation index	46º	27º
Purchasing power		
2020 r.	Russia	Czechia
Unemployment rate	4.7%	2.0%
Market		
2020 r.	Russia	Czechia
US exchange rate	78.7223	25.3510
YTD stock exchange	-18.25%	-28.15%
Business		
2019 r.	Russia	Czechia

Business activities	31º	35º
Motor vehicles production	1,642,088	1,427,563
Trade		
2018 r.	Russia	Czechia
Export	$ 443,129.0 M	$ 202,260.9 M
Import	$ 248,704.0 M	$ 184,652.3 M
Sociodemography		
2019 r.	Russia	Czechia
Global peace ranking	154º	10º
% immigrants	7.93%	4.81%
% reefugees	7.15%	8.56%
Energy and environment		
2018 r.	Russia	Czechia
Emission of tonnes of CO_2 per capita	12.14	10.44

The collected information is the basis for another comparative analysis and SWOT analysis. SWOT analysis is commonly and mainly used in strategic management of an organization. It is a diagnostic tool and is used at the very beginning of the process of determining strategic plans. The analysis is a means that allows you to compare the strengths and weaknesses of the organization with opportunities and threats. Strengths and weaknesses are internal, inherent in the organization, while opportunities and threats are external, in the environment of individuals (Gawroński, 2010, p. 171).

According to the literature, four categories of factors are defined (Asejczyk-Woroniecka, 2016, pp. 311–321):
- external positive – opportunities;
- external negative – threats;
- internal positive – strengths;
- internal negative – weaknesses.

The analysis of strengths, weaknesses, opportunities and threats made it possible to evaluate the mutual relations and possible impacts of the Russian Federation on the Czech Republic.

Table 2. SWOT analysis of the Czech Republic in the context of relations and interactions of the Russian Federation

Opportunity (positive, external)	Threat (negative, external)
- In terms of GDP (purchasing power parity) the Czech Republics ranks much lower than Russia; - The Czech Republic is a much safer country than Russia in terms of the risk of war and the prevalence of physical crime; - As a NATO member, the Czech Republic receives support in preventing the spread of regional conflicts, and also acts as a guarantor of the external security of the member states; - Membership in the United Nations ensures the development of cooperation between nations and promotion of respect for human rights; - Compared to Russia, the Czech Republic is twice as innovative country as the Russian Federation;	- The area of the Czech Republic is 216 times smaller than that of Russia; - The Czech Armed Forces are relatively new and they were created in 1993; - The Czech Republic is one of the least militarized countries in the world, taking 114th place out of 194 UN members, while Russia is 6th; - As a NATO member, the Czech army participates in ISAF and KFOR missions;
Strong points (positive, internal)	Weak points (negative, internal)
- The percentage of Czech residents living below the poverty line is negligible; - The Czech Republic is a much smaller ecological debtor compared to other developed countries; - Compared to Russia, the unemployment rate is less than half in the Czech Republic, which has been below the average of the developed countries for a long time;	- The Czech Republic still maintains a high rate of corruption-generating phenomena compared to other EU countries; - Compared to Russia, the Czech Republic transfers a negligible proportion of military spending;

The conducted SWOT analysis of the Czech Republic in relation to the Russian Federation indicated that there are areas where the Czechs are doing much better than the Russians, including internal security of the country, state innovation, unemployment, poverty. The effect of this is probably the fact that the Czech Republic took 20th place in the World Happiness Report ranking organized by the United Nations in 2019. Russia, on the other hand, ranks 68, which confirms that the inhabitants of the Czech Republic are much more satisfied with the functioning of their economic system than the Russians (UN Report, 2020).

The economy of the Czech Republic is considered to be one of the most stable of all post-socialist countries. Since the division of Czechoslovakia, the country has implemented a number of economic and structural reforms, a state finance recovery program, and the privatization and restructuring of state-owned enterprises. However, this does not change the fact that in relation to the Russian Federation it is a new, small and very weak country in terms of military potential, which gives the Russian Federation an absolute advantage, belonging to the group of the world's greatest powers.

References

Asejczyk-Woroniecka M., (2016). Zastosowanie analizy SWOT w doskonaleniu zarządzania jednostkami administracji terytorialnej, Finanse, Rynki Finansowe, Ubezpieczenia nr 6 (84), cz. 1, pp. 311–321.

Balcerowicz L., (1993). Systemy gospodarcze. Elementy analizy porównawczej. Warszawa: Szkoła Główna Handlowa.

Bossak J.W., (2006) Systemy gospodarcze a globalna konkurencja. Warszawa: Szkoła Główna Handlowa.

Country comparison Russia vs Czech Republic, https://countryeconomy.com/ (dostęp 26.03.2020).

Filip J., (2003). Ústavní právo České republiky 1. Brno: Masarykova univerzita a Doplněk, 2003, s. 145.

Gawroński, H., (2010). Zarządzanie strategiczne w samorządach lokalnych. Warszawa: Wolters Kluwer.

Kowalik T., (2015). Systemy gospodarcze. Efekty i defekty reform i zmian ustrojowych. Warszawa: Fundacja Innowacja.

Pacześniak A. and Perottino M., (2017). Europejska polityka Czech, ETE Working Paper, Opole (3), Nr 4, http://www.europejczycy.uni.opole.pl/biblioteka/docs/europejczycy_no-3_tom-4.pdf.

Raport ONZ, https://worldhappiness.report/ed/2019/ (dostęp 29.03.2020).

Swadźba S. (eds.), (2009). Systemy gospodarcze. Zagadnienia teoretyczne. Katowice: Akademia Ekonomiczna.

Paulina Owczarek

Chapter 23: Application of quantitative foresight methods in the assessment of economic relations between the Russian Federation and the Czech Republic

Political relations, and thus mutual relations in the area of national security of the Czech Republic and the sphere of influence of the Russian Federation, have been constantly fluctuating for years. For example, the positive development of mutual trade in the early 1990s /was suspended by the financial and banking crisis in Russia in the second half of 1998, and the Czech export fell to just $ 381 million. Between 2003 and 2013, there was a turn, the Czech export to Russia increased tenfold. In light of this development, the growth of the Czech export to the Russian Federation was also reflected in the Czech Republic's strategy for 2012–2020, in which Russia was among the 12 priority markets and accounted for 3.8% of total Czech exports and imports.

Over the past few years, relations between the Czech Republic and the Russian Federation have worsened steadily. At the end of 2019, further diplomatic conflicts broke out. The Information Security Service (BIS) has exposed and broken up a Russian hacker network operating in the Czech Republic. The removal of the monument to the Soviet marshal from Interbrigady Square, which for years had been the subject of much deeper dispute than the historical conflict, further strengthened the anti-Bohemian campaign.

The purpose of the chapter is to assess the current relations shaping the national interests of the Russian Federation and the Czech Republic using quantitative forecasting methods. To achieve the goal, a statistical analysis was used, the results of questionnaire studies and the results obtained with the use of the Delphi method were used in statistical calculations. Necessary to present the essence and specificity of the problem is to present the theoretical aspects of the penetration process and the theory of international influence, as well as to define the relationship between these categories of international impact.

There are many concepts of political influence in the literature on the subject. The notion of impact belongs to the category of intersystem activities and characterizes relations between entities operating on the international arena.

The interaction processes of the system and the environment are described by terms such as power-force-influence. In order to define the concept of influence in detail, then it should be considered in connection with the concept of power. The category of power appears in international relations in the form of institutionalized influence, but it is most often applied to internal relations that are centralized (Pietraś, 2018, pp. 102–103).

The concepts of influence and power are practically equated, and political scientists most often use the concept of power, which means power and strength, and is understood as: the goal of foreign policy, the ability to control the international environment, the ability to force other participants of international relations to behave or act in a specified way or as a synonym for the term influence (Schimmelfennig, 2017, p. 22).

According to K.W. Deutsch, the concepts of power and influence are narrower than power, and they are identical in only one respect, both mean the use of stimuli in interpersonal relationships that trigger certain behaviors (Deutsch, 1966, p. 124).

It is also often possible to find the thesis that power is a qualified form of influence, and two forms of influence are distinguished: overt and potential (Kowalski, Lamentowicz and Winczorek, 1986, pp. 81–120).

The potential influence is at the disposal of a person who, having appropriate resources and a possibility to use them, could, if he/she so wished, cause changes in the behavior of other people desired from his/her own point of view. The difference between power and influence lies in the measures that are at the disposal of the dominant entity; they allow the implementation of coercion against the subordinated entity. Power and influence are two forms of the same phenomenon, in pure form, two poles of the same axis. There is no fundamental qualitative difference between them (Campbell, 2007/2008).

The concept of reducing power to influence was also presented by H. Simon, who uses both terms interchangeably (Burłatki and Gałkin, 1978, pp. 17–27).

R.F. Hopkins and R.W. Mansbach are of the opinion that influence is an active aspect of power (Kostecki, 1988, pp. 110–132).

According to S. Ehrlich, the concept of power is broader than the concept of influence by two elements (Ehrlich, 1974, p. 34):
- who has power takes a key position in the decision-making process and nominally only he or she has the power to make an imperative decision;
- those who have power are equipped with instruments for the implementation of sovereign decisions that force obedience to these decisions.

The side of the political relationship that has influence over the other, tends to cause the existing state of affairs to change or to maintain it by triggering an appropriate political decision in the dependent party. Political influence with a high level of effectiveness can be described as political domination (Johnston, 2001, pp. 487–515; Miarka, 2018, pp. 89–110).

Z.J. Pietraś treats international influence as a substitute for power in domestic relations and analyzes it in terms of action: an acting subject, object, means and methods, and results of action. According to him, influence is the ability of a participant in international relations to persuade other participants to behave in a certain way (Pietraś, 2018, pp. 122–125).

In conclusion, power and influence are two separate phenomena that can occur simultaneously. The main difference between them boils down to the possibility of using stimuli that trigger a specific behavior, their degree of intensity, as well as their effectiveness in achieving the goal. Power requires institutionalization, which ensures its high efficiency, while the effectiveness of influence depends primarily on the strength of pressure and used means, as well as the ability of the subject to be influenced to withstand this pressure.

The Czech Republic has over 10 million inhabitants. On the other hand, data obtained from the Ministry of the Interior indicate that the total number of foreigners living there is estimated at 438,000.

Since 2004, the number of Russians living in the Czech Republic has doubled to 35,000 in 2017, making the Russians the third largest group of foreigners after the Ukrainians and the Vietnamese. The Russians still justify the choice of the Czech Republic with better health care and political reasons (Country comparison, 2020).

The analysis of economic relations between the Czech Republic and the Russian Federation will be carried out taking into account statistics describing the basics of economic cooperation, mutual energy policy and foreign trade.

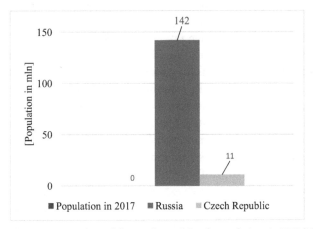

Figure 1. Comparison of the Russian and Czech populations in 2017 (The Prague Security Studies Institute).

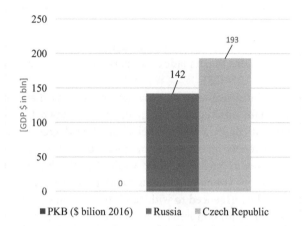

Figure 2. Comparison of Russian and Czech GDP in 2017 (The Prague Security Studies Institute).

Russia's economy is classified as a mixed and constantly developing economy, belongs to one of the world's leaders in terms of economic potential, and is the eighth largest in the world with regard to nominal GDP.

The basis of economic cooperation between countries is reflected, inter alia, in trade (export and import). The volume of Czech trade with the Russian Federation in the late 1990s was historically low, but from the beginning of the new millennium it started to increase significantly (Kratochvıl, Cibulkova and Benes, 2006, pp. 497–511).

The share of the Czech Republic in Russian exports fluctuated strongly in 2010–2016. In 2012, the share of exports dropped from 1.6% to 0.4% as a result of sanctions and the fall in the ruble exchange rate; in 2015 there was also a significant decline, but since 2016 it has been steadily increasing and in 2018 it reached the value of nearly 90 billion crowns (15 billion Polish zlotys). However, it is still only 2% of the total Czech exports of goods and services (Power, no date). In light of this development, the growth of Czech exports to the Russian Federation was also reflected in the Czech Republic's strategy for 2012–2020, in which Russia was among the 12 priority markets.

In 2013, exports of food products to Russia amounted to USD 71 million, while 3 years later in 2016, they decreased by USD 12 million and amounted to USD 59 million. In the same year, almost half of Czech exports to Russia were machinery and equipment. The energy policy is different between countries. The dependence of European Union countries on Russian resources is not the same. Based on statistical data, it is confirmed that small countries are more dependent than large ones. Oil imports from Russia cover over 75% of the demand of seven countries: Bulgaria, the Czech Republic, Finland, Hungary, Lithuania, Poland and Slovakia, while gas imports – 75% of the demand of twelve countries: Austria,

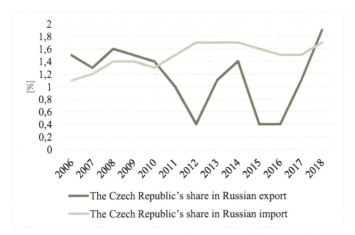

Figure 3. The share of the Czech Republic in Russia's foreign trade (%) (The Prague Security Studies Institute).

Bulgaria, Czech Republic, Finland, Lithuania, Latvia, Poland, Romania, Slovakia, Slovenia and Hungary (Eurostat Statistics Explained, 2020). In the gas markets of some countries in these regions, Gazprom not only acts as a supplier, but also as a distributor and co-owner of gas companies.

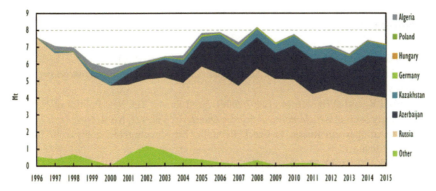

Figure 4. Import of the Czech crude oil (The Prague Security Studies Institute).

In 2015, Russia covered 56% of Czech crude oil imports. The Druzhba pipeline is the main supply channel. Russia's share in oil imports to the Czech Republic is currently declining. Since 2016, most of the oil products imported by the Czech Republic come from the neighborhood, i.e. from Germany (36%), Slovakia (30%), Poland (21%) and Austria (7%) (Country comparison, 2020).

In the case of natural gas, virtually all imports come from Russia, which is one of its largest exporters.

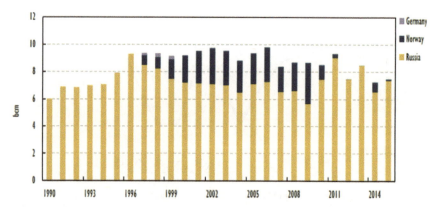

Figure 5. Import of natural gas to the Czech Republic (bilion cubic metres = bcm) (The Prague Security Studies Institute).

The share of nuclear energy in the Czech Republic's total electricity production is also noteworthy, as the electricity demand of which increases annually by an average of 2.3%. In 2016, there were 6 nuclear reactors in operation in the Czech Republic, which accounted for 29% of the country's total electricity production. The Czech Republic receives all its nuclear fuel from Russia.

References

(2016) Czech Statistical Office, https://www.czso.cz (dostęp: 2016).
Burłacki F. and Gałkin A., (1978). Socjologia, polityka, stosunki międzynarodowe, Warszawa.
Campbell K. and O'Hanlon M., (2007/2008). Hard Power: The New Politics of National Security Journal Article *Political Science Quarterly,* Vol. 122, No. 4, New York.
Country comparison Russia vs Czech Republic, https://countryeconomy.com/ (dostęp 26.03.2020 r.).
Deutsch K.W., (1966). The Nerves of Goverment, New York – London.
Ehrlich S., (1974). Władza i interesy. Studium struktury politycznej kapitalizmu, Warszawa.
Eurostat Statistics Explained, https://ec.europa.eu/eurostat/statistics-explained (dostęp 25.03.2020 r.).
Johnston A.I., (2001). Treating international institutions as social environments. International Studies Quarterly 45, pp. 487–515.
Kostecki W., (1988). Polityka zagraniczna. Teoretyczne podstawy badań, Warszawa.
Kowalski J., Lamentowicz W. and Winczorek P., (1986). Teoria państwa i prawa, Warszawa.
Kratochvıl P., Cibulkova P. and Benes V., (2006). Foreign policy, rhetorical action and the idea of otherness: The Czech Republic and Russia, Communist and Post-Communist Studies 39, pp. 497–511.

Miarka A., (2018). International position of the Russian Federation in the second decade of the 21st century – selected aspect, Studia Politicae Universitatis Silesiensis, T. 21, pp. 89–110.

Pietraś M., (2018). Państwo w późnowestfalskim ładzie międzynarodowym, in: *Państwo w czasach zmiany*, (eds.) Pietraś M., Hofman I., Michałowski S., Lublin.

Power A., Audit of EU-Russia Relations, http://www.ecfr.eu/page/-/ECFR-2_A_POWER_AUDIT_OF_EURUSSIA_RELATIONS.pdf (dostęp 20.03.2020 r.).

Schimmelfennig F., (2017). Internationale Politik, Paderborn.

The Prague Security Studies Institute, http://www.pssi.cz/russia-s-influence-activities-in-cee/economic-relations-between-the-visegrad-countries-and-russia (dostęp 26.03.2020 r.).

Paulina Owczarek

Chapter 24: Summary and conclusions: The development foresight of the mutual Czech-Russian relations in the third decade of the 21st century

Assessing and forecasting economic relations as the hard core of the national security of the Czech Republic in relation to the fluctuations in the foreign policy of the Russian Federation is not easy due to the constantly changing conditions shaping the influence and relations of both states. According to a 2019 survey by the Center for Public Opinion Research (CVVM), in Prague a majority of the Czech society believes that the conflict in Ukraine is a threat to Europe (65% of respondents) and a direct challenge to Czech security (55%).

The Czechs, despite the existing strong dependence on energy supplies from Russia, are trying to gradually achieve a higher level of energy independence by diversifying oil supplies (Goldthau and Sitter, 2015). This approach is slowly starting to bring its first results, e.g. in the first half of 2018, the share of Russian oil fell to 55%. Diversification took place as the Czech Republic increased its oil imports from Azerbaijan (which currently accounts for 26% of crude oil imports) and from Kazakhstan (14%). The share of nuclear energy in electricity production in the country is currently 33%, the implemented strategy envisages its increase to 46–5% by 2040 (Eurostat Statistics Explained, 2020).

In 2019, the Czechs also signed a contract for the supply of test fuel assemblies, provided by Westinghouse Electric Sweden. Perhaps this is the beginning of independence from Russia and the launch of a broader cooperation with another supplier of nuclear fuel. The data of the Russian Federal Customs Service also confirms that the revenues from oil exports decreased by 6% in 2019 compared to 2018, and from gas exports – by 15.3% (CSO, 2016).

In March 2020, the Czech Republic announced that it is ready to negotiate with the Russian Federation to unblock mutual relations and is interested in a pragmatic and balanced solution to problematic issues. Due to the fact that the Czech Republic is a country uniquely linked by a network of economic dependencies with Russia, it will be worth moving towards building a friendly environment and safe relations, which may be confirmed for several years now by the growing support for pro-Russian and anti-American policies. It can therefore be proved that, on the one hand, some Czech elites are satisfied with the current situation of deep interdependence largely based on economic relations, but on the other hand, some Czech politicians are striving to gradually and non-aggressively gain more and more independence without taking actions that could provoke the Russians to sudden and disruptive decisions. The stability of the economic development of the Czech Republic is therefore quite high, and at the same time the level of possible dependence on the Russian side seems acceptable when considering possible acts of economic aggression. Summing up, the most convenient area for a possible Russian aggression is the economic system of the Czech Republic, while the economic condition of the smaller state is quite stable and is characterized by a long-term growth perspective, to a limited extent dependent on possible aggressive Moscow's policy. This allows us to believe that the Czech Republic is not only mostly resistant to any economic aggression, but also, through skillfully conducted foreign policy, it will not lead to situations that could spark real crises in relations with its powerful neighbor.

Over the last few years, a very good relationship has been somewhat toned down, leading to a situation which does not threaten proper cooperation in economic cooperation that is profitable for both parties. Although Russia is one of the most important trading partners of the Czech Republic, the Russian market took only twelfth place on the list of priority markets with 3.8% of total Czech exports and imports. Thus, the possible loss of the Russian market would be felt by the Czech economy, but it would certainly not be the cause of a long-term crisis. Decision-makers in Moscow are fully aware of this state of affairs, and therefore would suffer significant economic and political losses by taking negative economic impacts on the Czech Republic. Therefore, such actions would not be in line with the Moscow's strategic interests in the region of Central and Eastern Europe if the long-term international standpoint that Russians are in favour of was used.

Due to the geographic location and membership of the EU and NATO, the possibility of military intervention or a paramilitary hybrid operation is also not very high, and the only area of possible influence may be the area of information warfare conducted with the use of mass and social media (Hellman and Wagnsson, 2017). At the same time, without the possibility of a strong economic impact, autonomous information activities would probably have a limited range, and thus their effectiveness would not be too high. Therefore, no major crisis in Russian-Czech relations is expected in the coming years

References

Goldthau A. and Sitter N., (2015). Soft power with a hard edge: EU policy tools and energy security. *Review of International Political Economy*, 22, pp. 941-965.

Hellman M. and Wagnsson C., (2017). How can European states respond to Russian information warfare? An analytical framework. *European Security*, 26, pp. 153-170.

Part III: Slovakia

Section 1:
Moscow's geopolitics and geostrategy in view of Slovakia in the second and third decade of the 21st century

Mieczysław Pawlisiak

Chapter 25: Slovakia in the Kremlin's geopolitics in the second decade of the 21st century

Slovakia is classified as a small European country. It is located in Central Europe. It has no access to the sea, it is a mountainous country with a moderate climate. It is perceived as a reasonably developed country compared to other European states. It covers an area of 49,036 square kilometers and is inhabited by 5,431,622 citizens (https://www.populationof). These two figures place Slovakia on the 126th and 110th positions, respectively, among all countries in the world. These positions are not very impressive, but Slovakia ranks much higher in economic and political rankings. Despite this, in the classifications of the geopolitical category, it is also included in the group of small countries.

Taking into account the theoretical foundations describing the meaning of the concept of geopolitics and the title of the chapter, it should be assumed that the aim of the study is to present the relationship between the geopolitics of Slovakia in relation to the current geopolitical goals of the Russian Federation. In order to achieve such a goal, it is necessary to try to solve two basic problems. The first is formulated as a question: what is the geopolitical potential of Slovakia and the Russian Federation? The second problem is to define: Can the geopolitical potential of the Russian Federation influence the functioning of Slovakia as an independent state and to what extent? In an attempt to solve the indicated dilemma, theoretical methods such as the analysis of contemporary literature will be used (Dyduch and Skorek, 2020; Fitzová and Matulová, 2020; Kudela et al., 2020; Muchová and Raškovič, 2020; Novakova, 2020; Settey and Gnap, 2020; Wanner, Seier and Pröbstl-Haider, 2020). Besides, the study of other source documents dealing with the broadly understood geopolitics of Slovakia and the Russian Federation, as well as the synthesis and inference, being the final product of previous analyzes, will be taken into account.

To assess today's Slovakia, it is necessary to go back to the times when Slovakia was a part of Czechoslovakia. At that time, Czechoslovakia was considered a medium-sized country. As a result, the citizens of the then Czechoslovakia felt that they were representatives of a medium-sized state and their sense of self-worth was at least good in this respect (Mali 2011, pp. 415–435). After the break-up and the creation of two separate states, they were included in the group of small states. This is due not only to the physical size of the country, but also to the view of politicians who believe that Slovakia is a small country in Central Europe. Slovak geographers (Ivanička 1999, p. 35; Šmihula 2000, p. 57) consider that parameters such as population and territory size indicate that it is appropriate to define Slovakia as a small European state. Not only in theory, but also in practical terms, the size criterion for classifying countries is ambiguous and highly imprecise. Disseminating in the consciousness of a particular society the belief that they live in a large, medium or small state should depend on measurable indicators or measures, and not only be the result of subjective feelings of individual citizens, political leaders or people who are heard in a given environment. An interesting view is that a state can be considered small when it presents itself in the same way, which in turn leads to the fact that it is perceived by its neighbors or its citizens (Drulák 1997, p. 35). It is also noted that the number of small countries, for example in Europe, has been growing recently. These countries, usually having large countries with great demographic, economic and military potential as neighbors, are forced to take actions that allow them to function effectively in these conditions. The general political situation in the world after the end of the so-called the Cold War was a favorable factor for the emergence of small states. The vast majority has been and is beneficial to their development, especially in political and economic terms. The rules of conduct in force in the global economy, such as the free market or competition, have become a specific driving force of development (Drulák 1998, p. 67).

The above-mentioned tendencies and conditions for functioning on a global scale have become favorable from the point of view of the needs and expectations defined by the Slovak society. It is more and more commonly believed that the perception of a country whether it is large, medium or small does not depend solely on the number of people and the size of the territory. It is also important to see other components that make it possible to determine the size of the country. One of them is the factor of state power. It is understood as the capability or ability to influence the behavior of other countries with their actions or attitudes and prompting them to a situation in which it is possible to implement their own plans or goals. Because of a skillful use of its power, even a country classified as small can effectively pursue its political or even economic goals. This is usually done through its actions aimed at larger states, which, apparently, could impose their will on smaller states. It is also possible that a small state, through its actions, can achieve its goals in relation to other larger states, even those located in other regions of the world (Balazs, Faulkner, Schimank 1995, pp. 613–632).

Bearing in mind the aforementioned content, one may be tempted to say that a small country does not have to be weak. It may turn out to be an important, or even a strong, political or economic player in a global perspective in various areas

(Drulák 1997, p. 38). When assessing Slovakia, taking into account the basic parameters such as population and territory size, it turns out that it is the smallest country among all in Central and Eastern Europe. However, it is important to understand that the power of the state depends not only on the above-mentioned parameters, but also such components as, for example, the manner of conducting internal and external policy (Sułek 2011, p. 13). The quality of this policy is a derivative of a number of different factors, such as the real economic potential, location (geographic location), the type and stability of the political system, the existing and internationally perceived state institutions and the way internal society is organized. An example of such an understanding of state power may be an attempt to compare countries with similar demographic potential, such as Bosnia and Herzegovina, Denmark, Finland, Georgia, Croatia, Jordan, Kyrgyzstan, Nicaragua, Papua New Guinea and Turkmenistan with Slovakia. It turns out that Slovakia is one of the strongest in this group in terms of power (Lach 2014, p. 19). This allows us to conclude that the unfavorable geographic parameters mean that Slovakia is classified as a small country, but its position measured by a real power (Sułek 2015, pp. 27–28) means that Slovakia is perceived as a small country but playing a significant role in the international arena.

The geographical location of Slovakia somehow forces us to look at its position in relation to its powerful neighbor, which is undoubtedly the Russian Federation. When attempting to assess the geopolitical situation of the Russian Federation in relation to Slovakia, it is justified to define the parameters by which it should be conducted. These can be, for example, measurable parameters indicating the amount of resources or economic opportunities.

Table 1. Parameters illustrating the geopolitical position of Slovakia in relation to the Russian Federation

No.	Specification /parameter/	Slovakia	Russian Federation	Ratio
1	Area (thou. km^2)	49035	17 075 400	1:348
2	Population	5 445 802	146 877 088	1:270
3	Gross Domestic Product (GDP – bn $)	94,9	1719,9	1:18
4	Gross Domestic Product per capita ($)	17491	11947	1,46:1
5	Export (mld $)	35,0[1]	449, 964[2]	1:13

1 (http://www.tcig-euroregiontatry).
2 (https://eksport.pl).

Table 1 *(Continued)*

No.	Specification /parameter/	Slovakia	Russian Federation	Ratio
6	Production of electrical energy	37000 GWh[3]	1064,1 TWh[4]	1:29
7	Military expenditure (bn $)	1,0	70,0	1:70
8	Natural gas reserves (mld m²)	0,0	38,9 bln m3[5]	-
9	Crude oil reserves	0,0	17,4 mld ton[6]	-

When analyzing and assessing the figures for Slovakia and the Russian Federation, clear conclusions should be drawn. Firstly, Slovakia as a single state is not an economic or military competitor to the Russian Federation. The awareness of this fact is present among Slovak politicians and hence their actions are aimed at strengthening political and military ties with the widely understood West, materialized in the form of the European Union and NATO. These two basic conclusions in a way direct the geopolitics of the Russian Federation towards Slovakia. As a consequence of this situation, various political, economic and, in a sense military, activities aimed at, among others, Slovakia are carried out by the organs of the Russian Federation. It should also be noted that all activities of the Russian Federation have one major strategic goal in the geopolitical area. It is building a land empire. To achieve this goal, it is necessary to neutralize the United States, inter alia, by displacing its military and economic influence from Europe. After this stage is completed, the ultimate goal of the activities of the Russian Federation is to build three geopolitical axes: Moscow – Berlin, Moscow – Tehran and Moscow – Tokyo (Sykulski 2013, p. 353–356).

To achieve the strategic geopolitical goal, the Russian Federation uses the entire range of available instruments subordinated to the state administration, as well as nominally independent or private. All of them are practically under the influence of state authorities. This applies in the first place to the intelligence and security services, diplomacy, the Armed Forces of the Russian Federation, state and private enterprises, as well as other scientific and economic organizations operating in the Russian Federation.

3 (https://www.wnp.pl).
4 (https://www.bp.com).
5 (https://energia).
6 (https://www.pl/naftwnpa).

Taking into account the political, military and, above all, economic conditions, the Russian Federation uses its full potential to achieve its geopolitical goals. We are talking about intelligence, military and diplomatic potential. The Armed Forces of the Russian Federation, state and private enterprises and all scientific and research institutions and even universities, all of them, regardless of formal ownership or subordination, are dependent on the central authority and implement its policy. In turn, the existing global conditions characteristic of the first half of the 21st century mean that the Russian Federation is forced to conduct geopolitics in relation to the European Union and the North Atlantic Alliance / including Slovakia / in a veiled manner. It is based on the fact that all kinds of information policy tools are used, including the internet portals, TV stations and other electronic media. They are co-created and financed by the power structures of the Russian Federation, and their task is to disseminate content that shapes the image of reality in line with the Kremlin's policy goals. The activities of intelligence services, propaganda agencies, diplomatic missions and economic organizations are aimed at creating in some countries an economic and political situation in line with the interests of the Russian Federation. In practice, this can take place, for example, by interfering with the election process. Such a situation, although not fully confirmed, took place during the last presidential election in the United States. In addition, the activities of the above-mentioned services strive to build a business infrastructure operating in accordance with the interests of the Russian Federation. The Security Service of the Russian Federation, in consultation with the intelligence services, also deals with the manipulation and disinformation of public opinion, as well as with intelligence penetration of key opinion-forming centers and the state authority. There are also activities that inspire and escalate social conflicts and tensions in international relations. Each time, the selection of specific measures, methods and areas of influence depends on the specifics of a particular state, with particular emphasis on its role and importance in the implementation of the strategic goals of the Russian Federation. In view of the above, the activities of the Russian Federation in the field of geopolitics aimed at Slovakia are each time adequate to the goal that is to be achieved. As an almost certainty, it should be assumed that some instruments are universal and apply not only to Slovakia, but also to other member states of the European Union and NATO. This may consist in sowing confusion and destabilizing the social and political situation in individual countries. As far as Slovakia is concerned, the heating of long-standing historical disputes between Slovakia and Hungary is symptomatic. It is the historical memory of the Slovaks in relation to the times of the functioning of the Austro-Hungarian Monarchy and the treatment of the Slovak population as people of an inferior category that remains the subject of not fully explained international problems to this day. The activities of the Russian Federation may also involve inspiration and stimulation in the information and political space of topics that polarize European public opinion, which in turn may lead to a crisis in the implementation of the European integration project.

References

Balazs K., Faulkner W., Schimank U., (1995). Transformation of the Research Systems of Post-Communist Central and Eastern Europe: An Introduction, "Social Studies of Science", 25(4), SAGE Publications.
Buček J., Gurňák D., Ištok R., Slavík V., Szöllös J., (2009). A new state in central Europe – the changing political geography, in: Slovak Geography at the Beginning of the 21st Century, eds. Ira, V., Lacika, J., Bratislava: GÚ SAV.
Drulák P., (1997). Co dělat, když jste malý, "Mezinárodní politika", vol. 21, nr. 5 Bratysława.
Dyduch J. and Skorek A., (2020). "Go South! Southern dimension of the V4 states' energy policy strategies – An assessment of viability and prospects", *Energy Policy*, 140, p. 111372. doi: https://doi.org/10.1016/j.enpol.2020.111372.
Fitzová H. and Matulová M., (2020). "Comparison of urban public transport systems in the Czech Republic and Slovakia: Factors underpinning efficiency", *Research in Transportation Economics*, 81, p. 100824. doi: https://doi.org/10.1016/j.retrec.2020.100824.
http://www.tcig-euroregiontatry.eu/aktualnosci,16.html, dostęp 16.03.2020.
https://eksport.pl/2019/03/11/specyfika-rosyjskiego-eksportu/, dostęp 16.03.2020.
https://energia.rp.pl/surowce-i-paliwa/ropa/18355-rosja-ma-niewyobrazalnie-duzo-ropy-gazu-i-diamentow, dostęp 16.03.2020.
https://www.pl/naftwnpa/rosja-ma-ropy-jeszcze-na-33-lata,356422.html, dostęp 16.03.2020.
https://www.bp.com/en/global/corporate/energy-economics/statistical-review-of-world-energy/downloads.htm, dostęp 16.03.2020.
https://www.wnp.pl/energetyka/energetyczne-problemy-slowacji,257543.html, dostęp 16.03.2020.
Ištok R., Plavčanová D. and Wilczyński, P.L., (2016). Sytuacja geopolityczna Słowacji, Przegląd Geopolityczny, 16.
Ivanička K. and Slovensko, (1999). Genius loci, Bratislava: Eurostav.
Jean C., (2003). Geopolityka, Wrocław.
Krejčí O., (2005). Geopolitics of Central European Region. The view from Prague and Bratislava, Praha.
Kudela, P. et al. (2020). "Does daylight saving time save electricity? Evidence from Slovakia", *Energy Policy*, 137, p. 111146. doi: https://doi.org/10.1016/j.enpol.2019.111146.
Łaszczuk A., (2010). Analiza geopolityczna potęgi państw, Geopolityka elementy teorii, wybrane metody i badania eds. Zbigniew Lach, Jan Wendt Częstochowa: Instytut Geopolityki.
Macała J., (2010). Czym jest geopolityka? Spory wokół jej definicji, Geopolityka elementy teorii, wybrane metody i badania eds. Zbigniew Lach, Jan Wendt, Częstochowa: Instytut Geopolityki Częstochowa.

Mali F., (2011). Policy Issues of the International Productivity and Visibility of the Social Sciences in Central and Eastern European Countries, "Sociology and Space", 48(3), Ljubljana.

Moczulski L., (1999). Geopolityka. Potęga w czasie i przestrzeni, Warszawa.

Muchová Z. and Raškovič V., (2020). "Fragmentation of land ownership in Slovakia: Evolution, context, analysis and possible solutions", *Land Use Policy*, 95, p. 104644. doi: https://doi.org/10.1016/j.landusepol.2020.104644.

Novakova L. (2020). "The impact of technology development on the future of the labour market in the Slovak Republic", *Technology in Society*, 62, p. 101256. doi: https://doi.org/10.1016/j.techsoc.2020.101256.

Settey T. and Gnap J., (2020). "Comparison of Price and Emission Levels of Air Passenger Transport and International Bus Transport in the Slovak Republic", *Transportation Research Procedia*, 44, pp. 129–136. doi: https://doi.org/10.1016/j.trpro.2020.02.019.

Šmihula, D., (2000) Priestor pre Slovensko, "Literárny týždenník", vol. 13, nr 5.

Sułek M. and Kobryński R., (2015) Potęga 2015: międzynarodowy układ sił w procesie zmian: raport potęgometryczny, Warszawa: Polskie Towarzystwo Geopolityczne.

Sułek M., (2011). Metodyka analizy geopolitycznej (na przykładzie potęgometrii) "Przegląd Geopolityczny" tom 3, Warszawa: Polskie Towarzystwo Geopolityczne.

Sykulski L., (2013). Integracja polityczna Eurazji we współczesnej rosyjskiej myśli geopolitycznej in P. Eberhardt (eds.), Studia nad geopolityką XX wieku, Warszawa: "Prace Geograficzne" nr 242.

Sykulski L., (2014). Bibliografia geopolityki współczesnej (1989–2009), Częstochowa.

Sykulski L., (2014). Geopolityka. Skrypt dla początkujących, Częstochowa.

Sykulski L., (2019). Rosyjska geopolityka a wojna informacyjna, Warszawa: Wydawnictwo PWN.

Tesař J., (1994). Slovensko v geopolitickom priestore, "Slovenské národné noviny", vol. 4, nr 24, Bratysława.

Wanner A., Seier G. and Pröbstl-Haider U., (2020). "Policies related to sustainable tourism – An assessment and comparison of European policies, frameworks and plans", *Journal of Outdoor Recreation and Tourism*, 29, p. 100275. doi: https://doi.org/10.1016/j.jort.2019.100275.

Żarna K., (2018). Determinanty polityki zagranicznej Republiki Słowackiej, Krakowskie Studia Międzynarodowe współpraca międzynarodowa – uwarunkowania globalne i regionalne numer 4 (XV), Krakow international studies (eds.) Anna Paterek, Kraków.

Mieczysław Pawlisiak

Chapter 26: Geostrategic perception of Slovakia in the Kremlin's vision of foreign policy in the second half of the 21st century

Terminology covering the geostrategic issue (Ediger, 2019; Mustaphi et al., 2019; Smith and Jaleel, 2019) is often associated with geopolitics (Knyazeva, 1999; Kirby, 2001; Kistemann, Dangendorf and Schweikart, 2002; Rakhimov, 2010) and sometimes the correlation between these terms is shown. An example may be the recognition of geostrategy as a sub-discipline of geopolitics (Sykulski 2009, p. 35) or the treatment of geopolitics and geostrategy as two equal subjects in political science (Boczarow-Suliborski 2002, pp. 44–54). Some of the authors who deal with geopolitics and geostrategy even believe that geostrategy is superior to geopolitics (Dybczyński 2013, pp. 77–81). Bearing in mind the content promoted by various authors, it can be concluded that geostrategy is nowadays perceived as wartime geopolitics or as geopolitics perceived through the prism of military potential. This understanding of geostrategy is now widely used, although it should be noted that today's strategy has not only a military dimension, but is ubiquitous in considering economic issues (Ištok, Plavčanová, Wilczyński 2016, pp. 109–119). There are also views that indicate that geostrategy should be viewed as a part of geopolitics that focuses on issues related to competition or rivalry between the two sides in both peace and war. Taking into account the above content, it seems legitimate to assume that geostrategy is primarily concerned with issues directly or indirectly related to military aspects.

The subject of geostrategic analyzes in relation to Slovakia should be the current geopolitical conditions regarding the functioning of the state (Ištok, Plavčanová, 2015, pp. 4–20). These analyzes are necessary to assess the demographic, economic and military potential in relation to other countries, including the Russian Federation. The results of the conducted assessments seem necessary to specify economic strategies, military doctrines and to outline national interests, the fulfillment of which is necessary for the functioning in the conditions of the first half of the 21st century. Therefore, it can be assumed that geostrategy in relation to Slovakia should be the basis for defining assumptions and, consequently, conducting foreign policy, taking into account the geopolitical environment in which the country exists and functions. Slovakia should also remember that the environment is not constant and unchanging and it is necessary to track and respond to changes as they occur. Slovakia is therefore obliged to adopt a geostrategy that takes into account the geopolitical conditions existing in the 21st century.

The aim of this chapter is to present the content that shows the geostrategic situation of Slovakia as one of the members of the North Atlantic Treaty Organization, especially in relations with the Russian Federation. Bearing in mind the objective presented in this way, it seems reasonable to conclude that the research problem is the question: what is the geostrategic situation of Slovakia in relation to the Russian Federation in the first half of the 21st century? To solve such a specific research problem, the method of analyzing all available information related to the current political situation in Slovakia will be mainly used. On this basis, conclusions and outcomes will be presented in a synthetic form, indicating possible directions for the development of the geostrategic situation in Slovakia.

Taking into account the above-mentioned conditions and its own national interest, Slovakia adopted factors that set trends and directions of its own international policy. These factors are nothing more than a system of interrelated and mutually conditioning rationale, the inclusion of which causes a specific, concrete effect, as expected by the Slovak authorities (Čič 2012, pp. 46–55). However, it should be remembered that geostrategy is an extremely complex issue, as it must take into account a number of various factors that affect foreign policy, considering the real international environment. In theoretical studies it can be found that these factors can be classified into two groups. One is causative factors and the other is conditioning. Both contain various environmental variables, the occurrence of which may be a factor favorable or difficult to achieve political and geostrategic goals (Zięba 2004, p. 17).

In theoretical studies, one can also come across the view that an important factor determining the foreign policy of a given country is the perception / understanding / of the international environment by own society, the ruling elite, and attitude towards other countries. These determinants are a derivative of the level of political culture, education, perceived values system, religious beliefs and the views of a society. One should also not forget about the importance of historical experiences, which play a significant role in relation to Slovakia (Łoś 2007, p. 15).

When assessing the geostrategic situation of Slovakia in relation to the Russian Federation, it is impossible to ignore the issues related to the assumptions of the foreign policy implemented by the Russian Federation. Well, official documents say that eleven key (directional) tasks are being carried out as a part of foreign policy (https://poland.mid.ru). By analyzing their content, one can come to the conclusion that the pursued foreign policy still aims at hegemony not only in the area of Central and Eastern Europe, but also in the whole world. Therefore, when perceiving the context of geostrategy, one should also look at the foreign policy of the Russian Federation through the prism of its military, economic or demographic potential.

Slovakia's geostrategic situation with regard to the Russian Federation should be assessed taking into account many different areas. It seems that the following parameters should be used for the assessment:
a) size of the territory (area);
b) number of population;
c) average population;
d) amount of gross domestic product;
e) amount of gross domestic product per capita;
f) national defense expenditure;
g) national defense expenditure per capita;
h) number of the armed forces;
i) number of militaries per 1,000 inhabitants;
j) number of militaries per 100 km2;
k) number of tanks;
l) number of armored personnel carriers;
m) number of artillery pieces (excluding rockets);
n) number of airplanes and helicopters.

Table 1. Geographical and military parameters of Slovakia and Russian Federation (https://data.worldbank.org/)

No.	Specification	Slovakia	Russian Federation
1	Area (km^2)	49 035	17 075 400
2	Population (mln)	5 445 802	146 877 088
3	Average population (number/km^2)	111	8,56
4	The amount of gross domestic product (mld $)	94,9	1719,9
5	The amount of gross domestic product per capita ($)	17491	11 947
6	National defense expenditure (bn $)	1,0	70
7	National defense expenditure per capita ($)	183	476
8	Number of the armed forces (mln)	0,0135	1,454
9	Number of militaries per 1000 inhabitants	2,5	9,9
10	Number of militaries per 100 km^2	27,5	0,11
11	Numer of tanks	30	2200
12	Number of armored personnel carriers	530	6700
13	Artillery systems (excluding rockets)	68	6500
14	Number of aircrafts and helicopters	65	3600

When reviewing the geostrategic situation of Slovakia in comparison with the potential of the Russian Federation, one fundamental conclusion emerges. This is a comparison between the proverbial David and Goliath. The individual figures show the overwhelming advantage of the military potential of the Russian Federation over Slovakia. They clearly show that the potential of Russia is many times greater and is able to dominate a country such as Slovakia. This statement is due, inter alia, to the recent actions of the Russian Federation. This was and is the case in relations between the Russian Federation and Ukraine, as well as in the activities carried out in the Caucasus region. It was in February 2014 that the Russian Federation began military actions against Ukraine. It was then that the takeover and annexation of Crimea took place and the hybrid war began in Donbas. The activities of the Russian Federation concerning geostrategic interest have also been taking place in the South Caucasus region. It is there (Georgia, Armenia, Azerbaijan) that political threats take place in various forms and shapes, and at the same time are combined with offers in the economic and military spheres. This is a deliberate activity with a geostrategic dimension that allows the Russian Federation to exert influence on security in this region. A factor contributing to this activity of the Russian Federation is regional instability, skillfully fueled by various Russian services. Bearing in mind the above, there may be concerns about the geostrategic situation of Slovakia in relation to the current foreign policy of the Russian Federation. In the event of a real threat, it is difficult to imagine a situation in which Slovakia is a real opponent of the Russian Federation. It is enough to make a quantitative comparison of only some military parameters, such as:

a) the Russian Federation possesses 76 times more armed forces than Slovakia;
b) the Russian Federation possesses 73 times more tanks than Slovakia;
c) the Russian Federation possesses 95 times more artillery (without rockets) than Slovakia;
d) The Russian Federation possess 13 times more armored personnel carriers than Slovakia.

The presented figures do not reflect the full situation in terms of comparing the military potential of Slovakia and the Russian Federation. It would be appropriate for the Russian Federation to add elements that Slovakia does not and probably will not have. This includes: 2,038 nuclear warheads, 367 active warhead carriers, 130 tactical missile systems, 57 submarines and 191 surface vessels, including 1 air cruiser, 4 cruisers, 15 destroyers, 4 frigates, and 78 corvettes. Summing up, it can be said with full responsibility that the comparison of the geostrategic potential between Slovakia and the Russian Federation is definitely in favor of the latter state. The people responsible for the security and foreign policy of Slovakia are fully aware of the situation. Therefore, today's authorities, understanding and realistically assessing the potential of Slovakia, strive to locate it in Western and international structures (Żarna, 2015, pp. 67–68). This pursuit did not become a one-off act, but was a process fully supported by the Slovak society. A moment after the break-up of Czechoslovakia and the creation of a new state, which Slovakia was and today is, a goal was defined, which was to set the direction of activity and concerned the confirmation of the belonging of the Slovak nation to the Latin civilization – Western Europe. It was then realized that there might not always be favorable political and economic consequences resulting from such aspirations of the Slovak nation. In the initial phase, the difficulties resulted, among other things, from the maladjustment of the economic structure of the state and the state of social consciousness, which for decades was shaped like a totalitarian system. An important stimulus was the desire for independence, rooted in the minds of Slovaks. When it happened in 1993, it was time to take personal and social responsibility for the new state existence in the not always favorable internal and external conditions. It was especially important as Slovakia was in a less favorable situation when it gained the position of a sovereign state compared to, for example, the Czech Republic. This situation caused certain difficulties, especially economic ones. On the other hand, the positive thing was that after gaining its own statehood, Slovakia was recognized without any problems by all countries in the world, without exception, including countries from the group of the world powers.

Along with the recognition in the international arena, there has been a search for its own national path allowing for development and peaceful coexistence. At the same time, an internal transformation took place, especially in the economic and political area (Bajda, 2018, pp. 122–134). Efforts were made to fully integrate within the European Union and the North Atlantic Pact. In the initial period, internal politics exercised by people at least mentally associated with the totalitarian system were not always conducive to integrating. In the years 1993–1997, there was a discussion at various decision-making levels and in different international organizations on the inclusion of Slovakia into Western structures, especially NATO (Ištok, Plavčanová and Wilczyński, 2016 p. 114). At that time, the Slovak government headed by Vladimir Meciar was convinced that Slovakia, due to its geopolitical importance, had to be brought into the fold of NATO members. The government was convinced that Slovakia was of key importance as a kind of bridge that could connect the West with the East. The megalomania of some politicians was great, and it resulted from a misconception that the assessment of the geopolitical and geostrategic potential of Slovakia could not be based solely on the conviction of its own greatness and power.

It is worth recalling here that the Slovak analyst expressed the conviction that Vladimir Meciar's policy could lead to a situation in which the Czech Republic, Hungary and Poland would become NATO members, and Slovakia, together with

Romania, Bulgaria and Ukraine, would be unable to join the North Atlantic Treaty Organization and they will constitute, in a way, second-class countries in the so-called "New Central Europe" (Duleba, 1997, p. 14). He also envisaged blocking Slovakia in its efforts to join Western structures. Including Slovakia in the group of "inferior" countries would be tantamount to a kind of degradation in the international arena, which society did not agree with. It gave way to its determination during the referendum in March 1997, when the Slovaks unequivocally opted for membership in NATO. This attitude resulted, inter alia, from the fact that Slovakia, as a small country, is not able to ensure its own security in the existing geostrategic conditions. The democratic elections carried out in 1998 led to important changes in domestic politics, which also influenced the international environment. Slovakia's Prime Minister Mikulas Dzurinda, with public support, directed his main efforts to ensure internal stabilization and economic transformation. In international activity, efforts have been focused on bringing Slovakia into the Western structures. The effectiveness of the government's actions led to the admission of Slovakia to the European Union and NATO, which also resulted in joining the Schengen area. All of this happened in 2004. The consequence of these events was that the eastern border of Slovakia also became the external border of the European Union. Slovakia's eastern neighbor is Ukraine, which poses a potential threat due to the conflict in Donbas. It is also not without a significance that the transport routes of energy carriers (gas, oil / from Russia, via Ukraine to the west run through the territory of Slovakia). A consequence of this political, economic, industrial and military situation is the need for the Slovak power elite to pursue an open policy both to the West and to the East. Membership in the European Union and NATO has visibly changed Slovakia's status and its perception on the international arena. As a result, Slovakia increased its importance and improved its position in the international arena. It has become a desirable ally of many highly developed countries in the world. Membership in various international structures allows Slovakia to pursue its own internal and foreign policy, and thus may pursue ambitious goals, especially economic ones.

By making a kind of summary of the content of Slovakia's road from its proclamation to the present day, it can be stated that there were various stages or phases on this road. The first – when Slovakia, in a way, stood out for independence, its geostrategic position in relation to the Russian Federation was not favorable. The differences in potential in all respects spoke in favor of Russia. The situation changed dramatically with the Slovakia's accession to the North Atlantic Treaty and the European Union. As a result, there is a military and economic power behind Slovakia, which results in a relative sense of security, and military parameters no longer play a decisive role in considering Slovakia's geostrategic situation in the context of its relations with the Russian Federation.

Answering the question – what is the geostrategic situation of Slovakia in relation to the Russian Federation in the first half of the 21st century? It can be said that the situation is not comfortable, but taking into account all political, economic and military conditions, one should be inclined to show the way for the future. It should assume as a basis and a guideline that the only reasonable solution in the first half of the 21st century is cooperation and understanding of the goals and interests of each country. In this case, this applies to Slovakia and the Russian Federation. Such a message may be important especially for the societies living on the European continent.

References

Baczwarow M. and Suliborski A., (2002). Kompendium wiedzy o geografii geopolitycznej i geopolityce. Terminologia. Warszawa: Wydawnictwo PWN.
Bajda P., (2018). Małe państwo europejskie na arenie międzynarodowej : polityka zagraniczna Republiki Słowackiej w latach 1993–2016, Warszawa: Wydawnictwo Naukowe Uniwersytetu Kardynała Stefana Wyszyńskiego.
Čič M., (2012) Národ a štát: (v súradniciach národných a štátnych záujmov), (eds.) Martin, Bratysława: Matica Slovensko.
Duleba A., (1997). Geopolitická futurológia pre Slovensko, "Dominofórum", vol. 6, nr. 11. Bratysława.
Dybczyński A., (2013). Geopolityka, Warszawa: Wydawnictwo Poltext.
https://data.worldbank.org/indicator/MS.MIL.TOTAL.P1?locations=RU-SA, dostęp 09.03.2020.
https://poland.mid.ru/web/polska_pl/koncepcja-polityki-zagranicznej-federacji-rosyjskiej/, dostęp 08.03.2020.
Ištok R. and Plavčanová D., (2015). European journal of geopolitics, Geostrategic position of Slovakia, Kraków: Polish Geopolitical Society.
Ištok R., Plavčanová D. and Wilczyński, P.L., (2016). Sytuacja geopolityczna Słowacji, Kraków: Przegląd Geopolityczny.
Kirby A., (2001). "What in the world? Notes on Peter Taylor's Political geography: world economy, state and locality", *Political Geography*, 20(6), pp. 727–744. doi: https://doi.org/10.1016/S0962-6298(01)00029-4.
Kistemann T., Dangendorf F. and Schweikart J., (2002). "New perspectives on the use of Geographical Information Systems (GIS) in environmental health sciences", *International Journal of Hygiene and Environmental Health*, 205(3), pp. 169–181. doi: https://doi.org/10.1078/1438-4639-00145.
Knyazeva H. (1999). "Synergetics and the images of future", *Futures*, 31(3), pp. 281–290. doi: https://doi.org/10.1016/S0016-3287(98)00132-3.
Łoś R., (2007). Polityka zagraniczna Słowacji.
Mustaphi C.J., Courtney et al. (2019). "Guidelines for reporting and archiving 210Pb sediment chronologies to improve fidelity and extend data lifecycle", *Quaternary Geochronology*, 52, pp. 77–87. doi: https://doi.org/10.1016/j.quageo.2019.04.003.

Rakhimov M., (2010). "Internal and external dynamics of regional cooperation in Central Asia", *Journal of Eurasian Studies*, 1(2), pp. 95-101. doi: https://doi.org/10.1016/j.euras.2010.04.002.

Smith H. D. and Jaleel A., (2019). "Marine policy: The first four decades", *Marine Policy*, 108, p. 103652. doi: https://doi.org/10.1016/j.marpol.2019.103652.

Sykulski L., (2009). Geopolityka, Słownik terminologiczny, Warszawa: Wydawnictwo PWN.

Żarna K., (2015). Od Mečiara do Dzurindy: główne kierunki polityki zagranicznej Republiki Słowackiej w latach 1993-2002, Rzeszów: Wydawnictwo Uniwersytetu Rzeszowskiego.

Zięba R., (2004). Uwarunkowania polityki zagranicznej państwa, Zięba R. (eds.) Wstęp do teorii polityki zagranicznej państwa, Toruń.

Mieczysław Pawlisiak / Marcin Górnikiewicz

Chapter 27: Summary and conclusions: The Russian view on the geopolitical and geostrategic position of Slovakia in the European balance of power

In the 21st century, Central Europe and the Western Balkans remain the priority area of geopolitical activities of the Russian Federation. In relation to the adopted geopolitical assumptions, a geostrategy was also developed that includes actual plans of impacts in various directions, which partial elements concern individual countries, and sometimes even selected territories within these countries. The area of influence indicated above is considered to be a kind of strategic foreground of the Russian Federation. As a result, the above-mentioned methods and techniques of influence are used in this region in the long term, as they exert a significant influence on key political processes that determine the geopolitical situation in the entire region. In the long term, they are to allow them to take control of these countries, including Slovakia, and drag them into the sphere of influence of the Russian Federation.

The use of tensions between national minorities and individual ethnic groups has been and still is one of the traditional tools in shaping geopolitics by the Russian Federation. In its geopolitics, Moscow applies various tools, which may also include controlling religious conflicts. This is done by creating specific events taking place on the socio-religious background and skillfully awakening them to a level where they become tools of the so-called social control. It is visible, among others, in Slovakia, where disputes with the Hungarian minority living in this country have been stoked for years. At the same time, the intelligence expansion of the Russian Federation in recent years coincided with the resurgence and intensification of hostile attitudes and behavior of Slovaks towards Hungarians, as well as the deterioration of relations between these countries, although both belong to the Visegrad Group.

It can also be observed that in the countries of Central and Eastern Europe, the sympathies of post-communist circles are artificially stimulated, which is especially the case in the Czech Republic and Slovakia. As a consequence, this results in a high level of support for political forces, as well as for individual politicians who promote a vision of international politics in line with the concept presented by the authorities of the Russian Federation, and take various actions to strengthen political and economic relations with the Russian Federation.

Slovakia, as a small country in terms of territory, population and economic potential, is not a significant opponent in geopolitical activities conducted by the Russian Federation. Decision-makers in Moscow view Slovakia as a convenient element in a wider geopolitical game. In this context, it is extremely important for Slovakia to be a member of a number of international organizations of economic, political and military importance. This situation means that Slovakia itself is not able to create geopolitics solely for its own use. It must take into account its place, role and potential as a member of a larger community. On the other hand, the Russian Federation, as a global market player, is able to create geopolitics in relation to Slovakia by its actions on the international arena, striving to lead to a situation where Slovakia will not be an opponent, but an ally of the Russian Federation.

To sum up, the geopolitics of the Russian Federation, having a detailed image in the strategies of political, military, economic and information influence, embraces Slovakia as an element of the game in Central and East-Central Europe conducted in parallel with other European Union member states and NATO member states. At the moment, Moscow does not have any real means of peacefully destabilizing the geopolitical and geostrategic situation of that country (economic, political), but it can still exert influence through broadly understood information activities (embracing political and diplomatic means), including all activities carried out by secret services. The military variant could only be launched if not only non-military measures failed, but also if Slovakia found itself outside the structures of the allied international organizations which support it. At the same time, such a scenario would only be implemented if the above conditions were met in a situation in which such a demonstration of power beyond the occupation of the country had a much deeper geopolitical goal. For the above reasons, it follows that Slovakia is perceived as a natural-friendly country (similarly to Austria and the Czech Republic) towards Moscow, possible to use to a limited extent in a wider game of influence, and also a country with which it is worth maintaining proper relations. All this makes Slovakia a relatively safe country with no real opponents having a geopolitical interest in disrupting the economy, society or military potential.

Section II:
Slovakia in the Russian impact zone:
the Kremlin's "hard power" and "soft power"

Section II:
Slovakia in the Russian infosphere:
the Kremlin's "soft power" and "sharp power"

Mieczysław Pawlisiak

Chapter 28: The methodology of the Russian "hard power" towards Slovakia

The foreign policy pursued by the Russian Federation in the first half of the 21st century is multifaceted and ambiguous in relation to other entities on the international arena. It can be gentle, and even friendly towards some countries that previously formed the Commonwealth of the Independent States. Pursuing a hard, even brutal policy, for example in relations with Ukraine, can also be noticed. Seeing the ambiguous behavior of the Russian Federation in the international arena, it is advisable to present its relations with one of the smallest countries in Europe – Slovakia in more detail.

The purpose of this chapter is to present the conditions, reasons and methods of the Russian Federation's hard influence on a small European state like Slovakia. For such a goal, it is important to sort out the main – fundamental research problem, the content of which is the question: why is the Russian Federation adopting a tough policy towards Slovakia and what it is going to achieve in this way? Answering this question requires the use of theoretical research methods such as the analysis of the literature on the subject and official documents dealing with the foreign policy of the Russian Federation in the first half of the 21st century. Based on the information obtained in this way, a synthesis will be carried out, ending with final conclusions.

Historical determinants are one of the most important and even fundamental foundations of today's foreign policy of the Russian Federation. The basis of today's foreign policy is the understanding of the national identity and the role that the Russian nation has played from the beginning of its existence, that is, from the seizure of power in Veliky Novgorod by Rurik, the leader of the Vareska team called the Rus people. It took place around 882, when the Varangians subjugated the Slavic and non-Slavic tribes inhabiting Eastern Europe and mastered the water trade route leading through the rivers in the Baltic and Black Sea basins. The city of Kiev became the capital of the state called Kievan Russia (Heller, 2000, pp. 14–15). This country went through various vicissitudes. It was itself the target of an attack or acted as an aggressor. National identity was developing all the time. It seems that the events of the 20th century have left a significant mark on today's foreign policy. This applies to the First and Second World Wars, the October Revolution and, above all, the breakup of the Union of Soviet Socialist Republics. The latter event, in particular, was a shock, as the Russian Federation had to come to terms with being one of at least three real leading powers (the United States, China and the Russian Federation) in the international arena.

In these conditions, it is assumed at least from the theoretical point of view, that the current foreign policy of the Russian Federation is focused on defining several priorities, the fulfillment of which is to ensure the defense of the global interests of the state. These essential interests in the first half of the twenty-first century are three areas, namely strategic and military security, state sovereignty and independent economic development. Such an understanding of the essential interests means that the actions of the entire state are focused on:

a) ensuring the protection of the state and bolstering its homogeneity by maintaining territorial integrity taking into account the specificity resulting from its location on two continents; b) counteracting attempts to upset the political balance on both continents / Europe and Asia /, as uncontrolled activities may contribute to the disturbance of the global balance; c) building a civil society and thus bringing the Russian Federation to a fully democratic country; d) maintaining the zone of political and economic influence in the area of the functioning of the former socialist state camp (Miarka, 2018).

The content of the last of the presented areas of interest of the Russian Federation reveals some cards concerning the conduct of foreign policy towards its closer and more distant neighbors. You can also perceive the political aspect in other areas, because every action perceived by the society in the world contains in its essence the element of politics.

Persons occupying managerial positions in the Russian Federation are of the opinion that in terms of hard influence on other countries, including Slovakia, the greatest positive effects may be brought by the so-called "soft power". It is an action considered as one of the most important and effective elements of foreign policy used by many countries in the world in the 21st century. It makes it possible to achieve the intended goals in those areas where standard diplomatic activities do not bring positive solutions. Such reasoning is not always fully understood in the circles of power in the Russian Federation. It is treated only as a specific supplement to hard strength to carry out specific tasks. An example of this in the European area is the use of real forces and means to support separatism in Moldova, conduct energy blackmail against Ukraine or intensify cyber-attacks in Estonia.

The general exposure to the way in which the foreign policy of the Russian Federation is conducted in the first half of the 21st century indicates general trends that materialize in relation to a particular state or group of states. In official documents concerning the foreign policy of the Russian Federation in Europe, the name of the European Union is first mentioned, including Slovakia. Therefore, measures aimed at the entire Union should be seen as having an equivalent impact on every Member State, such as Slovakia, for example. This is in fact the case, although diplomatic and economic activities differ from country to country. Nevertheless, the starting point in assessing the tough influence of the Russian Federation on Slovakia should be its attitude towards the European Union.

When making an attempt to analyze and evaluate the foreign policy of the Russian Federation towards Slovakia and the entire European Union, it should be realized that it is and probably will be carried out in order to achieve also goals related to internal policy. It turns out that the official and fundamental element of the present foreign policy of the Russian Federation is the confrontation with the broadly understood West, but this policy must be limited and controlled in such a way as to produce a positive internal effect. This is done in such a way that the authorities of the Russian Federation escalate or cause existing disputes and disagreements, at the same time making efforts to prevent them from getting out of hand. The task of these measures is, inter alia, to mobilize society in the face of the threat posed by the West, led by the United States and the European Union. Therefore, it should be stated that an important element of this strategy in the foreign policy of the Russian Federation is to show the strength of the state, and above all its leaders, in the person of Vladimir Putin. On the one hand, the activities carried out are to cause fears among their own society, and then the authorities show a human face while defending the interests of the citizens of the Russian Federation. The consequence of such a sequence of events is the strengthening of trust in the state, which, thanks to the attitudes of society and the position of leaders, is perceived on the international arena as strong and intended to play an important role in world politics (Balcer, 2018).

The European Union, including Slovakia, is one of the main directions of foreign policy pursued by the Russian Federation in the 21st century. A meaningful factor in this approach is the fact that the most important economic partners of the Russian Federation are located in Europe. This primarily applies to the recipients of Russian gas and crude oil. From the point of view of today's European Union, the historical perspective is crucial. It was from the 13th century that Europe was associated as the area that was against Russia at that time in ideological, economic and territorial terms. In addition, Europe has always been associated by Russia as an area that can unite in certain situations, or create a specific community, reaching solutions such as today's European Union, which includes Slovakia. An additional characteristic of the countries in Europe is the pursuit of broad integration, which has an economic dimension – the European Union and a political and military one in the form of the North Atlantic Treaty.

The existence of strong institutions, of which Slovakia is a member, influences the approach of the Russian Federation to foreign policy issues. Choices must be made regarding the impact on individual states, which, through tough politics, may be weakened, strengthened or forced to interact with the Russian Federation (Potulski, 2008, pp. 353-371).

When making an in-depth assessment of the foreign policy of the Russian Federation, which is targeted at Slovakia and other European Union countries, it is not difficult to notice that the power in the Kremlin is primarily driven by pragmatic considerations. It does not exclude the influence of factors related to their own situation and internal policy on the content of foreign policy, as well as the awareness of societies capable of assessing the actions of the Russian Federation on a global scale. Equally important is the influence of the European Union on countries that were previously or still remained in the sphere of interest of the Russian Federation. This applies in particular to activities supporting institutional transformation. The effect of this approach is the desire to ensure rational conditions for the functioning of states. In the longer term, the influence of the European Union is to constitute a pro-development impulse allowing for decisive economic development. This kind of influence of the European Union on the states that gained true independence after the collapse of the Soviet Union took place in the nineties of the last century. It ended with a significant increase in the number of members of the European Union, which today includes Slovakia, among others. The mere increase in the number of Member States did not, however, eliminate Euroscepticism, which takes different faces in different countries. It also depends on the way the new political elites exercise power in the countries of Central and Eastern Europe (Neumayer, 2008, pp. 135-160). Slovakia was admitted as a member of the European Union on May 1, 2004. This process resulted in an unprecedented economic development, as well as other former countries of the so-called Eastern Bloc, which was not very favorably received by the authorities of the Russian Federation.

The changes among the new members of the European Union primarily concerned the creation of a civil society, which should be active and reveal the ability to self-organize. Through this, it is able to define and achieve its goals without any unnecessary impulse from any state institutions. This means that civil society is able to function independently of state institutions. The practical independence of society from the organs of state authority is not the same as competition, especially for certain influences or privileges. It can be said that civil society understood as a community that understands common needs, and at the same time strives to meet these needs, is the proverbial thorn in the side of the people holding power in the Russian Federation. Despite this, the European Union, including Slovakia, continues to promote the so-called "Institutional rehabilitation/sanitation." In practice, this means creating a foundation for systemic changes consisting in the creation of systems in which a single leader plays a smaller role and increases the importance and powers of collegial bodies. Historical experience shows that such a method of exercising power may be more effective in solving problems, especially economic ones, and thus allows to generate economic growth. The effect of such an approach is greater economic freedom, stability of business conditions and reduced susceptibility to corruption.

The presented position of the European Union, and thus of Slovakia, is at present completely unacceptable to the power elites of the Russian Federation (Mali, 2011, pp. 413–435). The current model of the Russian Federation's functioning does not envisage any changes the introduction of which would change the existing status quo. There are two reasons for this approach. Firstly, the empowering of social and political institutions, as well as the reduction of hierarchically complex bureaucracy, diminishes the importance and role of the individual, and, above all, hinders "manual control" and making only the right decisions by people, not always democratically appointed. The second reason is that Western-style changes could lead to economic success in a short time, which would mean that the post-Soviet model is not the best solution. Moreover, such changes would very likely result in relatively quick economic success and positive social transformation in individual countries – this, in turn, would demonstrate the weakness of the Russian model, which is unacceptable from the authorities' point of view.

To conclude the above, one can be sure that the Russian Federation, although it does not present this view aloud, considers the European Union, including Slovakia, its main enemy, as it is a very strong competition in the post-Soviet area. This is especially noticed in relation to the view of Ukraine and its efforts to come closer to the West. It should also be remembered that Slovakia is its western neighbor, which is also treated by the Russian authorities as one of the countries of the former post-Soviet area (Harasymenko, 2016, pp. 125–135).

The quantitative and qualitative development of the European Union and the promotion of the economic model based mainly on the rules of the market economy lead to the actual limitation of the influence of the Russian Federation on European territory. Thus, it can be assumed that in geopolitical terms, the Russian Federation treats the European Union as a political and economic entity that poses a particular threat to its interests. This is due to the fact that the Russian Federation does not have convincing arguments to compete in the so-called soft power area, consisting in the ability to gain allies and gain influence due to the attractiveness of its own political economic system and the presented level of general culture. Such arguments in their arsenal have the countries associated in the European Union. In this situation, the Russian Federation is looking for other arguments to pursue its political goals.

The easiest solution from the point of view of the authorities of the Russian Federation is to use asymmetric instruments – hard power (Campbell and O'Hanlon, 2008, pp. 706–708). Opinions that especially strong military pressure on the countries of Central and Eastern Europe are able to replace the decreasing economic impact capacity are preferred. It is also believed that, in addition to military pressure, it is worth taking advantage of a dominant position and applying economic pressure, using for this purpose the dependence of some countries on raw materials at the disposal of the Russian Federation. There are, however, some restrictions on the use of raw materials to conduct a hard policy towards Slovakia, as the budget of the Russian Federation is largely dependent on revenues from the sale of gas and crude oil.

As a part of the tough influence of the Russian Federation on Slovakia and other European states, there is a tendency to weaken or even completely liquidate European structures (Sykulski, 2013, pp. 354–355). This is now the main goal of foreign policy, which in the language of diplomacy is called a geopolitical game. Its essence and meaning are perceived especially in the second decade of the 21st century, when Great Britain leaves the European Union, and at the same time the crisis of European institutions is observed. The authorities of the Russian Federation, led by its President Vladimir Putin, take advantage of the political turmoil in individual countries, thus seeking to weaken European integration. These activities are carried out on many levels, although sometimes they have negative economic effects for the Russian Federation. Through actions, the fear of the Russian Federation is growing in Europe, which is a fuel for creating, among other things, the need to build small homelands with an emphasis on the word homeland. As a result, the existing strong ties are weakened, which is not only a dream, but the main goal of the political activity of the Russian Federation. The aspirations of Moscow politicians and decision-makers concern the weakening or even abandonment of the soft power policy by the European Union. Such a sequence of events could lead to a situation in which a new European order will take place, in which the Russian Federation will have a significant share, which, using the divided continent and its geopolitical position, will create politics in the countries of the former socialist bloc, including Slovakia.

It should also be noted that at present, no conflict-triggering attitudes are perceived in the real actions of the Russian Federation. The officially proclaimed position even speaks of the willingness to cooperate, however, on the condition of equal treatment. This is difficult to achieve today after the annexation of Crimea and the active participation of the Russian Federation in the conflict in Donbas. When assessing a tough policy towards Slovakia, one should also take into account camouflaged activities that can be conventionally divided into different segments.

The first segment / area / can define a variety of activities aimed at upsetting internal stability in individual countries. It is carried out with the use of various tools, and a typical example may be the support given to radical parties, the intensification of cyber-attacks or the conduct of an information warfare, but conducted at the level of social networks. In this way, the aim is to convince citizens of Slovakia, among others, that their main and only enemy is the European Union, the functioning of which is the source of all problems at the national level. The second segment / area / impacts are the European institutions that the Russian Federation would like to collapse. This would create the conditions for a more effective influence on individual countries, including Slovakia.

Economic entities operating in various countries are a separate object put under pressure by the Russian Federation. By applying various economic stimuli, the Russian Federation leads to a situation where certain economic entities interested in cooperation with the Russian Federation put pressure on their state authorities to accept the attitude and policy of the Russian Federation. This activity becomes quite effective in some circles. Some openly anti-Russian political centers consciously support the implementation of Russian plans. In diplomatic circles, the term "useful Kremlin's idiots" is sometimes used, pointing to people and entire political groups which, by promoting the national interest, contribute to the implementation of the policy of the Russian Federation (Tchaikovsky, 2017, pp. 132).

References

Balcer A., (2017). An alliance of authoritarian regimes? Turkey towards Iran and Russia – conclusions for the European Union. Institute for Advanced Studies "ISZ Analyzes".

Campbell K. and O'Hanlon M., (2007, 2008). Hard Power: The New Politics of National Security Journal Article Political Science Quarterly, Vol. 122, No. 4 New York.

Czajkowski M., (2017). The Current Foreign Policy of the Russian Federation and the European Union – Basic Issues, XIV No. 2, Krakow: Krakow International Studies.

Harasymenko V., (2016). The policy of the Russian Federation towards the post-Soviet area in the light of the realistic paradigm, Przegląd Geograficzny, Warsaw: Institute of Geography and Spatial Development Stanisław Leszczyński.

Heller M., (2000). History of the Russian Empire, Warsaw: KIW Publishing House.

Mali F., (2011). Policy Issues of the International Productivity and Visibility of the Social Sciences in Central and Eastern European Countries, "Sociology and Space", 48 (3), Ljubljana.

Miarka A., (2018). International position of the Russian Federation in the second decade of the 21st century – selected aspects, Studia Politicae Universitatis Silesiensis, T. 21, pp. 89–110.

Neumayer L., (2008). Euroscepticism as a Political Label: the Use of European Union Issues in Political Competitions in the New Member States. European Journal of political science, Wiley-Blackwell.

Potulski J., (2008). Socio-cultural context of the international activity of the Russian Federation, University of Gdańsk.

Sykulski L., (2013). Political integration of Eurasia in contemporary Russian geopolitical thought, in P. Eberhardt (eds.), Studies on the geopolitics of the 20th century, "Przegląd Geograficzne" No. 242, Warsaw.

Włodkowska-Bagan A., (2017). Russia's policy in the post-Soviet area Eastern Humanist Yearbook vol XIV, Radzyń Podlaski: Society for Science and Culture "Libra" international position of the Russian Federation in the second decade of the 21st century – selected aspects International position of the Russian Federation in the second decade of the 21st century – selected aspects.

Mieczysław Pawlisiak

Chapter 29: The methodology of Russia's soft influence on Slovakia

The methodology of soft influence as a part of conducting foreign policy in the 21st century is becoming broader and broader and it is a tool that does not cause armed conflicts, and at the same time leads to the achievement of the assumed goals. It is used by almost all countries, but its scope and effectiveness vary. This is due to the fact that the external policy goals of each country in the world may be different, as well as the potential of using soft influence towards selected countries. The geopolitical and geostrategic conditions in which soft influence in foreign policy is carried out, are also important.

Taking into account the above contents and understanding the position of the Russian Federation in the world and the position taken by Slovakia, it should be assumed that the purpose of this chapter is to indicate which soft methods the Russian Federation influences and can influence on the functioning of a small European state such as Slovakia. With the above goal in mind, it is legitimate to conduct research on three fundamental problems. The first can be formulated as a question: what are the main foreign policy objectives of the Russian Federation aimed at the countries of Central and Eastern Europe? The second problem is related to the answer to the question: are the applied soft methods of influencing the functioning of Slovakia by the Russian Federation effective and bring the intended effect? The third problem can be summarized in a rather perverse question: to what extent does the functioning of the state organs of Slovakia favor soft influence on the part of the Russian Federation?

Solving the presented problems requires the use of specific research methods. Taking into account the subject matter of the research, the analysis of the contents embraced in various theoretical studies will be used, as well as generalizations and inference allowing to conclude the arguments on the subject of the chapter.

The last twentieth century turned out to be the bloodiest period in the history of mankind. It is estimated that about 10 million people died during the First World War. Activities carried out during the Second World War claimed almost 60 million people. In addition to these two great wars, there were several dozen different smaller wars in the 20th century. Between 250,000 and a million people died in each of them. To this, the losses resulting from the violence used during the wars should be added. It is estimated that in the 20th century, almost 190 million people lost their lives as a result of wars (Ferguson 2007, pp. 35–55).

The figures quoted above are commonly known in the power circles of countries classified as economic, political and military tycoons. Additionally, they are aware that the accumulated military potential in the form of nuclear and conventional weapons is capable of destroying life on earth (The Military Balance, 2020). Reality understood in this way forces the rulers to define their goals in foreign policy and, in the longer term, to define how to achieve these goals with the least effort and resources. At the same time, these activities should be conducted in such a way as not to expose other participants in the political game. In official documents, the Russian Federation provides a number of rather detailed foreign policy objectives (https://poland.mid.ru/web). By analyzing their content and referring them to the European area, it can be stated that the objectives of the foreign policy of the Russian Federation towards the countries of the European Union, and thus towards Slovakia, are activities aimed at:

a) maintaining good economic relations, which will allow to maintain and continue the economic development of the Russian Federation on the high level;
b) rebuilding the sphere of influence among the countries of the former communist bloc;
c) ensuring military security on a global scale;
d) ensuring the position of a global power with the ability to influence world politics on economic and military issues.

The objectives of the foreign policy of the Russian Federation, shown in a condensed form, are in real action each time refined and adapted to the object, state or region they are concerned about at a given moment. It is publicly said that the strategic dimension of the Russian Federation's policy in the Euro-Atlantic region is oriented towards shaping peace, security and stability. It is also considered necessary to respect the principles of mutual trust, security and cooperation based on equal rights. From the declarative point of view, the presented content can be seen as an ideal approach to conducting foreign policy. Practice, however, shows completely different behavior. One of the flagship examples is the current conflict in Ukraine and the earlier annexation of Crimea. It can be concluded that this behavior of the Russian Federation towards Ukraine was possible for two reasons. First of all, the earlier ties and relationships that were rooted in the times of the Soviet Union were used. The second factor was the fact that in military and economic terms Ukraine was and is much less powerful than the Russian Federation and did not have time to become a member of European and world military and economic alliances. The Russian Federation, in accordance with its fait accompli policy, seized foreign territory knowing that the winners were not judged.

When attempting to relate such an action by the Russian Federation to any state that is a member of the European Union or the North Atlantic Alliance, it cannot be said that such a situation could not have taken place. Behind each of its members is the NATO Command and the European Union authorities. Thus, the fear, or even the fear of reacting, prevents the Russian Federation from taking reckless military or paramilitary action. However, this does not mean that the authorities of the Russian Federation have resigned from activities that would enable them to achieve their goals.

An example of such a soft influence within the framework of foreign policy is, inter alia, Slovakia (Ištok and Plavčanová, 2015, pp. 4–20). It is true that official documents state that the Russian Federation is focused on supporting an intensive and mutually beneficial dialogue with the EU on basic foreign policy issues, and on further development of practical cooperation in the spheres of foreign and military-political policy (https://www.mid.ru/en/main_en). However, practice shows something completely different. A tool currently used by the Russian Federation, and created even during the Cold War, are anti-American and anti-EU and, generally speaking, anti-Western sentiments. They are especially popular in nationalist and extreme right-wing circles, but also in anti-systemic, pacifist and anti-capitalist circles currently noticed in Slovakia (Balazs and Faulkner; Schimank, 1995, pp. 613–632). This provokes political, diplomatic and economic actions by the Russian Federation aimed at breaking the unity of the European Union and the North Atlantic Alliance. Slovakia is the main bridgehead supporting such activities. It is this country that, in its foreign policy, not only now, but since its inception, perceives the Russian Federation not as a competitor but as an authentic partner. This attitude of the authorities in Bratislava is very positively received in the Kremlin. Therefore, the authorities of the Russian Federation skillfully and in a veiled manner support the present position of Slovakia in the international arena, and on the other hand, through diplomatic and economic activities, they attempt to ensure the favor and even friendliness of the authorities in Slovakia.

The current actions of the Slovak government in agreement with the government of the Russian Federation lead to the continuation of the relaxation and maintenance of good relations with the Russian Federation on various levels of political, economic and military life. The materialisation of such behavior in Slovakia and the Russian Federation took place in June last year, when the Prime Minister of Slovakia, Petr Pellegrini, paid a visit to Moscow at the invitation of the Prime Minister of the Russian Federation. During this visit, Slovakia expressed its readiness to buy gas from the newly built Nord Stream 2 gas pipeline. It seems obvious that it was encouraged to do so by representatives of the authorities of the Russian Federation. The incentive concerned ensuring the continuity of gas supplies and the promised preferential prices. This is a typical soft influence of the Russian Federation on other states (Mali, 2011, pp. 415–435). This is the case in Slovakia. It should also be noted that this action by the Russian Federation has brought another political benefit, namely it is a step towards deepening the split among the members of the Visegrad Group, which is a visible goal of the Kremlin's foreign policy.

The soft influence of the Russian Federation on Slovakia has a significant impact on domestic politics and the functioning of the state in the realities of the 21st century. This is expressed in the fact that relations with the Russian Federation do not constitute a political consensus. The result of this situation is the necessity to practice foreign policy as a resultant of the three parties forming the ruling coalition: the social democratic SMRU-SD, the Slovak National Party SNS and the Hungarian minority group MOST-HÍD. Being aware of this reality in Slovakia, the Russian Federation tries to win over individual supporters through soft influence (Ištok and Plavčanová; Wilczyński, 2016, pp. 109–110). It is estimated that the leader of the Slovak National Party, Andrej Danko, who is also the chairman of the Slovak parliament, is currently presenting the most favorable attitude towards cooperation with the Russian Federation. Due to his function and personal views, he took part in two editions of the International Forum for the Development of Parliamentarism organized by the Russian State Duma. It is symptomatic that he was the only representative of this rank from the European Union. Complementing Andrej Danko's political views was his participation in the celebration of the end of World War II in May 2019. This Slovak party and state activist has loudly questioned the advisability of the economic sanctions imposed on the Russian Federation by the European Union.

Having such a foothold in the power camp in Slovakia, the Russian Federation has an easier task in conducting soft politics, because its Slovak supporters accept Moscow's actions without much hesitation. The stance of President Zuzana Čaputova, who plays mainly representative functions in foreign policy, is an obstacle, which is not very significant for the soft influence of the Russian Federation on Slovakia. She reiterates the criticism of her predecessor, President Andrej Kiska, about the way foreign policy is conducted. The President of Slovakia expressed her dislike of the Russian Federation's policy and activities on the international arena, recognizing the legitimacy of the sanctions imposed on Moscow, adding that the actions of the Russian authorities pose the greatest threat to world security. She also takes the position that the unity of the European Union and NATO is an unquestionable value.

An obstacle to the decisive action of the authorities in Bratislava towards Moscow is the support of the Slovak society for closer cooperation with the

Russian Federation. These sentiments, as well as ethnic conflicts with the Hungarian minority, are the basis for Moscow's soft influence on Slovakia. This is established on the application of the old Roman principle of "divide and rule", according to which disguised actions lead to antagonization of the Slovak society with the Hungarian minority (Herasymenko, 2016, pp. 125–135). This allows for building internal tensions with regard to Slovakia, and at the same time leads to a tightening of relations with the Republic of Hungary. As a result, there is a strain on unity and unanimity among the members of the former Visegrad Triangle and the entire European Union (Leonard and Popescu, 2008, pp. 21–38). In this way, it is easier for the government of the Russian Federation to influence the internal and external policy of Slovakia and some countries of Western Europe. These influences took real dimension and the government of Peter Pellegrini (2018–2020) sought to increase cooperation with the Russian Federation, while remaining a full member of the European Union. Slovakia's real action was to support the votes of Slovak delegates – the restoration of the right to vote in the Parliamentary Assembly of the Council of Europe for the Russian Federation. The official translation was that such an action would facilitate the dialogue with Moscow, although it has not changed its policy towards Ukraine and continues to occupy Crimea. The activities of the Slovak government in line with the needs of the Russian Federation were multifaceted. Another example is the position of the Bratislava authorities that there is a need to involve the authorities of the Russian Federation in solving global problems. In pursuing this policy direction, a representative of the Slovak authorities participated in a meeting with the Russian Minister of Foreign Affairs, Sergey Lavrov, during which the issue of cooperation within the Organization for Security and Cooperation in Europe (OSCE) was discussed, under the Slovak presidency.

It is also true that, in order to maintain the appearance of full membership in the European Union, Slovakia has often emphasized the need to strengthen Slovakia's cooperation within the EU and to bolster its transatlantic ties. At the same time, it is constantly striving to improve relations with the Russian Federation. It was Slovakia that was the only country of the Visegrad Group and one of the eight European Union countries which, in response to the poisoning of Sergei Skripal, did not expel Russian diplomats in a gesture of solidarity with Great Britain. It limited itself to summoning the ambassador from Moscow for consultations in Bratislava and asked the Russian ambassador to Slovakia for explanations. Such behavior is extremely symptomatic, but it also indicates that the soft influence of the Russian Federation on Slovakia is extremely effective.

Another area of pressure and soft influence of the Russian Federation on Slovakia is the economic area. In 2014, there were events that led to a decline in raw material prices and, at the same time, economic sanctions of the European Union against the Russian Federation took place (Firlej, Firlej, Mierzejewski,

2016, pp. 53–59). This state of affairs lasted until 2017, when there was a revival of Russian-Slovak trade. In order to boost contacts and economic turnover, the Russian Federation invited the Prime Minister of Slovakia to the 23rd International Economic Forum, which was held in Saint Petersburg in June 2019. It was then that the President of the Russian Federation, Vladimir Putin, through a personal meeting with the Prime Minister of Slovakia, Peter Pellegrini, showed how to interact diplomatically, in a soft way, on one of the European Union countries.

The soft influence of the Russian Federation on Slovakia continued when Peter Pellegrini was invited to pay an economic visit to Moscow. This resulted in the signing of two energy cooperation agreements. Both related to the supply of nuclear fuel to the Bohunice and Mochovce nuclear power plants for the years 2022–2025 (https://www.cire.pl/), with the possibility of their extension until 2030 (http://alexjones.pl/). Such an action gives the authorities of the Russian Federation a weapon that can be used as a form of soft pressure on Slovakia's foreign policy, for example by controlling prices for nuclear fuels or artificially limiting the possibility of storing waste after producing electricity in a nuclear power plant. It should be presumed that such pressure took place because initially Slovakia wanted to maintain the status of a transit country for Russian gas. As a result, Slovakia's position in the initial period was against the construction of the Nord Stream 2 gas pipeline. However, the position has changed, as previously noted, and the Slovak government is striving to increase gas transmission within the North-South corridor, i.e. from the Nord Stream gas pipeline through Germany and the Czech Republic to Slovakia (https://warsawinstitute.org/). It can be concluded from this that soft arguments in the foreign policy of the Russian Federation in relations with Slovakia bring positive results. This leads to a situation in which the position of Poland is, in a sense, marginalized, at least in the area of gas transmission from the East to Western Europe.

Slovakia's policy, while maintaining the appearances of the unity of the European Union, decided to build a gas interconnector with Poland, which would ultimately supply gas, e.g. from the gas terminal in Świnoujście to Slovakia (https://www.wnp.pl/). An interesting as well as extraordinary move in foreign policy between the Russian Federation and Slovakia is the position of former Slovak Prime Minister Peter Pellegrini (until March 20, 2020) (https://www.msn.com), who in earlier talks with the authorities in Moscow expressed his gas interest from the Russian Turk Stream gas pipeline. This shows the actual position of Slovakia in relations with the Russian Federation.

When attempting to summarize the presented content, one should first refer to answering the questions constituting the problems under study. Well, when analyzing and assessing the content of the articles, websites and other theoretical studies, it can be clearly stated that the goal of the Russian Federation's foreign policy is to rebuild the sphere of influence before the collapse of the Soviet Union. Thus, taking the position of a superpower in the international arena. In order to achieve this goal, the Russian Federation is ready to pursue its policy from the position of force, fait accompli, or to softly influence those countries where it brings certain benefits.

In order to answer the question whether the way in which the Russian Federation conducts soft foreign policy towards Slovakia has brought positive results, there can be only one answer. It is Slovakia, which is susceptible to the influence of the Russian Federation, which is one or perhaps the only staunch ally of the Russian Federation among all the members of the European Union. It was Slovakia, through the soft influence of the Russian federation, that became its ally camouflaged, which at key moments showed compliance and understanding for the Kremlin's foreign policy.

References

(2020). Chapter Three: North America, The Military Balance, 120:1, pp. 28–63, DOI: 10.1080/04597222.2020.1707963.

Balazs K., Faulkner W. and Schimank U., (1995). Transformation of the Research Systems of Post-Communist Central and Eastern Europe: An Introduction, "Social Studies of Science", 25(4), SAGE Publications.

Ferguson N., (2007). The War of the World: Twentieth-Century Conflict and the Descent of the West, Penguin Group.

Firlej K., Firlej Ch. and Mierzejewski M., (2016). Znaczenie sankcji gospodarczych dla bilansu handlu zagranicznego krajów grupy Wyszehradzkiej w obszarze rolnictwa, roczniki naukowe, tom XVIII, zeszyt 3, Poznań: Stowarzyszenie Ekonomistów Rolnictwa i Agrobiznesu.

Fiszer J.M., (2016). Zadania i cele polityki zagranicznej Władimira Putina, Myśl Ekonomiczna i Polityczna, nr 1 (52), Warszawa: Oficyna Wydawnicza Uczelni Łazarskiego.

Herasymenko V., (2016). Polityka Federacji Rosyjskiej wobec obszaru postradzieckiego w świetle paradygmatu realistycznego, Przegląd Geopolityczny, Kraków: Polskie Towarzystwo Geopolityczne.

http://alexjones.pl/aj/aj-swiat/item/148968-slowacja-rozwija-wspolprace-energetyczna-z-rosja.

http://www.mid.ru/brp_4.nsf/0/6D84DDEDEDBF7DA644257B160051BF7F.

https://poland.mid.ru/web/polska_pl/koncepcja-polityki-zagranicznej-federacji-rosyjskiej.

https://warsawinstitute.org/wp-content/uploads/2020/01/New-Gas-Pipeline-Geopolitics-in-Central-and-Eastern-Europe-Warsaw-Institute-report.pdf.

https://www.msn.com/pl-pl/wiadomosci/other/te-zdj%C4%99cia-przejd%C4%85-do-historii-tak-wygl%C4%85da%C5%82a-zmiana-w%C5%82adzy-na-s%C5%82owacji-w-dobie-koronawirusa/ar-BB11wbyO dostęp 23.03.2020.

Interkonektor gazowy między Polską i Słowacją już w budowie, https://www.wnp.pl/gazo wnictwo/interkonektor-gazowy-miedzy-polska-i-slowacja-juz-w-budowie,330768.ht ml.

Ištok R. and Plavčanová D., (2015). European journal of geopolitics, Geostrategic position of Slovakia, Kraków: Polish Geopolitical Society.

Ištok R., Plavčanová D. and Wilczyński P.L., (2016). Sytuacja geopolityczna Słowacji, Kraków: Przegląd Geopolityczny.

Leonard M. and Popescu N., (2008). Rachunek sił w stosunkach Unia Europejska – Rosja, Londyn-Warszawa: Europejska Rada Spraw Zagranicznych oraz Fundacja im. Stefana Batorego.

Mali F., (2011). Policy Issues of the International Productivity and Visibility of the Social Sciences in Central and Eastern European Countries, "Sociology and Space", 48(3).

Rosatom będzie nadal dostarczać paliwo dla elektrowni jądrowych na Słowacji, https://www.cire.pl/item,181698,1,0,0,0,0,0,rosatom-bedzie-nadal-dostarczac-paliwo-dla-elekt rowni-jadrowych-na-slowacji.html.

The Ministry of Foreign Affairs of the Russian Federation, https://www.mid.ru/en/main _en.

Mieczysław Pawlisiak / Marcin Górnikiewicz

Chapter 30: Summary and conclusions: The perspective of the Kremlin's hard and soft interactions on the Slovak decision-making process

Summarizing the content of the two previous chapters, it can be assumed that the Russian Federation, taking advantage of many years of tradition and experience, uses various methods of influence in its foreign policy targeted at European countries, selected according to the specific nature of their addressee and gauging the current conditions in a given place and time. With regard to Slovakia as a small European state, in the opinion of the decision-makers in Moscow, there is no need for direct, hard political, military or economic influence. What is certain, however, is that a hard influence on the European Union may cause an accidental impact on Slovakia as a full member of international structures. It is worth noting that looking much further in the distant time horizon, in the event of the collapse of the European community, the Russian Federation would be able to reactivate its former sphere of influence by extending it to the countries of Central and Eastern Europe, including Slovakia. It follows that the long-term geopolitical goals of the Russian Federation are rooted in a time when the Soviet Union was one of the world's two superpowers.

In the national mental sphere, the Slovaks are mostly neutral or sympathetic towards Russia. Thus, the attitude of the Slovak government with a positive attitude to the policy of the Russian Federation would not be possible without public support. It is this divided society, which still remembers its historical past and adheres to communist traditions, that are the mainstay and foundation of Slovakia's strong ties with the Russian Federation. Proof of such attitudes is, inter alia, the result of the recent elections, when the opposition party OĽANO won the victory (words: Obyčajní Ľudia a nezávislé Osobnosti, pl. Ordinary People and Independent Personalities), and no representative of the Hungarian minority entered the Slovak parliament. It is difficult to predict unequivocally at present what future actions in the area of Slovakia's foreign and internal policy may be, but it seems that in the near future the course for European integration, with simultaneous economic cooperation, in particular with the Russian Federation, will be continued. This approach seems the most sensible both from the point of view of Slovakia's national interest and the present ruling camp. In conclusion, decision-makers in Moscow will also continue a gentle course designed to further strengthen mutual relations, create a positive image of Russia and Russians in the social perception of Slovaks, and in the meantime build new contact points that may later be useful in the continuation of the geopolitical game for zones of influence in this part of Europe. As a result, Slovakia may indirectly be a soft interaction theatre in the form of various information (partly intelligence) operations, but it should not be expected that it will become a target of hard influences, both of economic and military character.

Section III:
The assessment of the Russian influence potential on the Slovak decision-making process

Tomasz R. Waśniewski

Chapter 31: The use of quantitative methods in the assessment effectiveness of the Russian influence on Slovakia

This chapter is devoted to the presentation of the results of the research carried out with the use of quantitative methods to illustrate, in computable data, the measurement of the effectiveness of the Russian influence on Slovakia. The data was obtained from academic and specialized studies (Hess and Renner, 2019; Sanders and Sanders, 2019; Ventura-Cots et al., 2019; Chapman, 2020; Jenkins et al., 2020; Lavelanet, Johnson and Ganatra, 2020) treating the sources as verified and reliable materials of knowledge. In addition, a comparison with network sources was made, and finally, the countable results, based on these materials, were presented together with independent analyzes. For this purpose, the author presents the outcomes in a graphic form, which description pertains to the issues discussed in this chapter.

Slovakia's policy towards the Russian Federation has not changed for many years. After the 2019 elections, Zuzana Čaputova, who came from the 'Progressive Slovakia' party, became the president. She maintains the criticism expressed by her predecessor, Andrej Kiska, about the way the government's relations with Russia are structured. Čaputová recognizes the legitimacy of the sanctions imposed on Russia and, during the presidential campaign in Slovakia, classified the actions of the Russian authorities as "the greatest threat to world security". During her visit to Warsaw in July this year Madame President emphasized the need to maintain NATO's unity in action towards Russia. Its position is different from that of the government, which continues the policy of détente with respect to Russia. In June 2019, the Prime Minister of Slovakia, Petra Pellegrini, visited Moscow and Saint Petersburg in order to start obtaining gas from Nord Stream 2 and TurkStream. So far, Slovakia has opposed this project. This type of Slovakia's behavior may lead to a split in the Visegrad Group, which means a deepening of the split in the perception of Russia (Ogrodnik, 2019).

The government's policy towards Russia is the product of the approach of the three coalition parties: the social democratic Smer-SD, the Slovak National Party (SNS) and the Hungarian minority group Most-Híd. The SNS is considered to be the most favorable to the cooperation with Russia. Its leader Andrej Danko, as the chairman of the Slovak parliament, took part in both editions of the International Forum for the Development of Parliamentarism, a conference initiated by the Russian State Duma. He also questions the purposefulness of the economic sanctions imposed on Russia by the EU. This position is also shared by the largest coalition party, Smer-SD, and Prime Minister Pellegrini – just like her predecessor, and now chairman of the party, Robert Fico. The party of the Hungarian minority, Most-Híd, is the most critical of Russia.

The cooperation with Russia enjoys public support in Slovakia. According to a 2017 study by the US International Republican Institute (IRI), 75% of Slovak respondents expressed a positive opinion on closer cooperation with Russia in the field of security. Thus, they represent the most pro-Russian attitude among the Visegrad Group countries (although supporters of such a cooperation also prevail in the Czech Republic – 62%, and in Hungary – 54%). This approach is confirmed by a Eurostat survey from the same year, according to which 50% of Slovaks have a positive perception of Russia (the majority in the EU after Bulgarians, Cypriots and Greeks).

The Russian Federation is the fourteenth largest export economy in the world and is the 27th most complex economy according to the Economic Complexity Index (ECI). In 2017, Russia exported US $ 341 billion and imported US $ 221 billion, giving it a positive trade balance of US $ 120 billion. In 2017, Russia's GDP amounted to USD 158 000, and GDP per capita USD 25 500

Russia's largest exports are crude oil (USD 96.6 billion), refined crude oil (USD 58.4 billion), crude oil (USD 19.8 billion) hard coal briquettes (USD 16.1 billion) and wheat (USD 7,93 billion). The largest imported products are packaged medicines (USD 8.23 billion), cars (USD 7.69 billion), vehicle parts (USD 7.44 billion), broadcasting equipment (USD 7.04 billion), planes, helicopters, and / or spaceships (USD 6.33 billion).

The main trade partners to which Russia exports its goods are China (USD 39.1 billion), the Netherlands (USD 27.7 billion), Germany (USD 19.9 billion), Belarus (USD 18.5 billion) and the United States (15 USD 4 billion). The most important import directions are China (USD 43.8 billion), Germany (USD 27.2 billion), Belarus (USD 12.5 billion), the United States (USD 10.9 billion) and Italy (USD 9.2 billion).

In contrast, Slovakia is the 39th largest export economy in the world and the 16th most complex economy according to the economic complexity index (ECI). In 2017, Slovakia exported USD 77.5 billion and imported USD 78 billion, which gave a negative trade balance of USD 527 million. In 2017, Slovakia's GDP was USD 95.8 billion, and GDP per capita was USD 31 600.

Slovakia specializes in car exports (USD 15.7 billion), car parts (USD 5.51 billion), video displays (USD 4.99 billion), broadcasting equipment (USD 2.77 billion) and refined petroleum (1, USD 92 billion). The largest imports belong to electronics (USD 7.38 billion), broadcasting equipment (USD 4.77 billion), cars ($ 2.79 billion), petroleum gas (USD 2.27 billion) and crude oil (USD 2.06 billion).

Taking into account the share of Russian oil in the total domestic imports of raw material in a given country, the largest share of supplies from Russia is recorded (according to data for 2013) by Central European countries (Slovakia – 100%; Poland – 96.3%, Hungary – 94, 1%, the Czech Republic – 63.14%); Southern European countries (Bulgaria – 86.21%, Croatia – 70.41%, Greece – 48.8%) and Lithuania (99.25%). It is also worth noting that in 2014 most EU oil importers from Russia reduced the share of Russian oil in total domestic imports, including to the greatest extent Greece, the Netherlands and Belgium. During this period, Slovakia reduced gas supplies.

Crude oil and gas supplies from Russia for Slovakia are presented below (Figure 1).

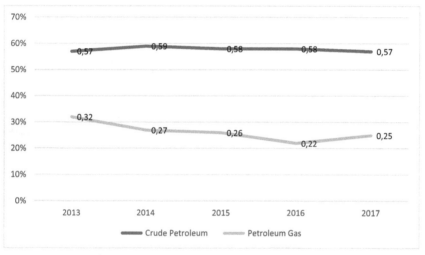

Figure 1. Oil and gas exports from the Russian Federation to Slovakia (Observatory of Economic Complexity).

Russians mainly import cars, chassis and car parts from Slovakia. This is Slovakia's largest share of imports to Russia. The figure below (Figure 2) displays how the import of products from Slovakia developed.

The figure below (Figure 3) shows all products exported by Slovakia to Russia in 2017.

As in the case of other countries of the Visegrad Group, Slovak-Russian trade has been reviving since 2017. Its reduction was driven by the EU sanctions from 2014, falling commodity prices and the weakening of the ruble. In 2018, Slovakia's trade with Russia amounted to approximately EUR 5.6 billion. Although it recovered from its lowest registration after the introduction of sanctions (EUR 4.07

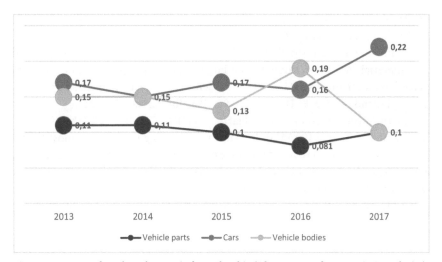

Figure 2. Imports of products by Russia from Slovakia (Observatory of Economic Complexity).

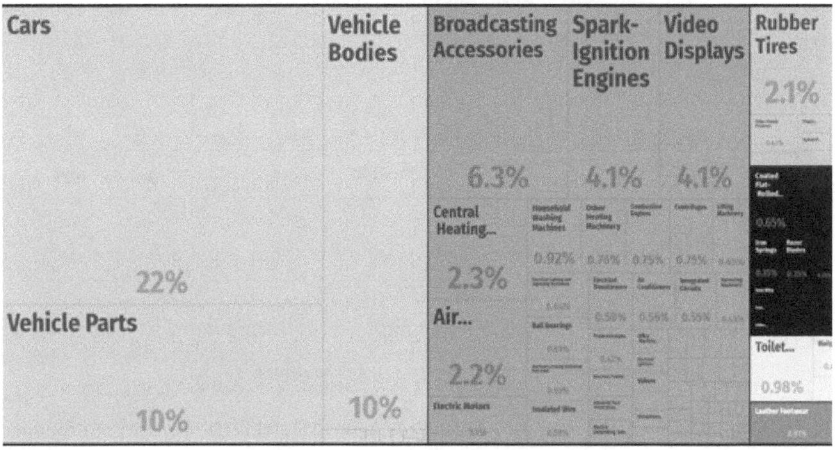

Figure 3. 2017 Import to Russia from Slovakia (Observatory of Economic Complexity).

billion in 2016), it is still more than twice lower than in 2013 (EUR 8.67 billion) (Figure 4). The work of the Slovak-Russian intergovernmental commission is an expression of support for a closer economic cooperation.

Slovakia and Russia carry on their energy cooperation. The Prime Minister Pellegrini's visit to Moscow resulted in the signing of two agreements in this area. The first was concluded by the Slovak Ministry of Economy with the Russian company Rosatom, and the second – the Rosatom company TVEL with the Slovak company Slovenské Elektrárne. They have extended the supply of nuclear

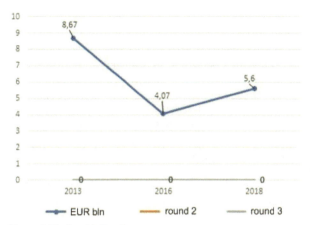

Figure 4. Trade with Russia.

fuel to the Bohunice and Mochovce nuclear power plants for the years 2022–025, with the possibility of extending them until 2030.

Slovakia is committed to maintaining the status of a transit country for Russian gas. This resulted in the opposition of the Slovak government to the creation of NS2. However, Pellegrini's cabinet is withdrawing from its current position as the scenario of the creation of this gas pipeline has turned out to be more probable. In addition, it has offered Russia the possibility of storing its gas. In turn, the Russian government assured Slovak partners about the facility of gas supplies after January 1, 2020. At the same time, Pellegrini's cabinet is striving to increase gas transmission along the North-South corridor. Its importance was emphasized in the government's program for 2016–2020. However, in addition to the efforts to diversify energy sources (last year, the construction of a gas interconnector with Poland was inaugurated, which would ultimately supply gas, e. g. from the gas terminal in Świnoujście), Pellegrini expressed the interest in gas from the Russian TurkStream gas pipeline. TurkStream is a project that will transport Russian gas via a pipeline under the Black Sea, bypassing Ukraine through Bulgaria, Serbia and Hungary. The investment will consist of two lines. One, with a capacity of 15.75 billion cubic meters, will serve Turkey. The second one will supply Europe with blue fuel. The project is the world's largest offshore gas pipeline at a depth of 2,200 meters.

In 2008, an agreement was initially concluded for the construction of a broadband trunk line from Košice via Bratislava to Vienna, concluded by Russia, Ukraine, Slovakia and Austria. The Slovak prime minister assured Medvedev that Slovakia would try to implement the project to extend the broad-gauge line from Košice to Vienna. He emphasized that he wanted to cooperate with Poland and Hungary.

References

Chapman B. (2020). 'Congressional Committee Resources on Space Policy During the 115th Congress (2017-2018): Providing Context and Insight Into US Government Space Policy', Space Policy, 51, p. 101359. doi: https://doi.org/10.1016/j.spacepol.2019.101359.

Hess D.J. and Renner M., (2019). 'Conservative political parties and energy transitions in Europe: Opposition to climate mitigation policies', Renewable and Sustainable Energy Reviews, 104, pp. 419-428. doi: https://doi.org/10.1016/j.rser.2019.01.019.

Jenkins K.E.H. et al., (2020). 'Politicising the Just Transition: Linking global climate policy, Nationally Determined Contributions and targeted research agendas', Geoforum. doi: https://doi.org/10.1016/j.geoforum.2020.05.012.

Lavelanet A.F., Johnson B.R. and Ganatra B., (2020). 'Global Abortion Policies Database: A descriptive analysis of the regulatory and policy environment related to abortion', Best Practice & Research Clinical Obstetrics & Gynaecology, 62, pp. 25-35. doi: https://doi.org/10.1016/j.bpobgyn.2019.06.002.

Ogrodnik Ł. (2019). Slovak striving for better relations with Russia, Bulletin of the Polish Institute of International Affairs No. 131, https://www.pism.pl/publikacje?kind=5fd04ea9-9d11-4e5c-b196-029f960f8bf4.

Observatory of Economic Complexity, https://oec.world/ Sanders M.C. and Sanders C.E., (2019). 'A world's dilemma "upon which the sun never sets": The nuclear waste management strategy (part II): Russia, Asia and the Southern Hemisphere', Progress in Nuclear Energy, 110, pp. 148-169. doi: https://doi.org/10.1016/j.pnucene.2018.09.009.

Ventura-Cots M. et al., (2019). 'Public health policies and alcohol-related liver disease', JHEP Reports, 1 (5), pp. 403-413. doi: https://doi.org/10.1016/j.jhepr.2019.07.009.

Tomasz R. Waśniewski

Chapter 32: The use of qualitative methods in the assessment effectiveness of the Russian influence on Slovakia

Quality is now a socio-economic problem in every country and in every area of human life. So we can talk about the quality of services, product quality and quality of life, quality of work or quality of processes. Hence, the generally understood quality should be the focus of every country, regardless of whether it is an importer or an exporter. It is commonly believed that the evaluation of quality consequently leads to various kinds of positive economic effects, and thus to the improvement of the welfare of the whole society. Therefore, it seems that the assessment and improvement of the quality level in all spheres of the economy is a general social and national interest.

In business practice, it often happens that the applied methods of measuring quality do not later find any reflection in improving activities or raising the quality level of the provided services.

To quote the statement made by Peters and Waterman, "Quality is not everything, but everything becomes nothing without quality" is of particular importance today in relation to each sector. On the one hand, you cannot focus only on quality, forgetting or ignoring other functional areas in analyzes, planning or controlling. However, on the other hand, it is important to remember that quality is what all the rest of the business has in common.

The purpose of the chapter is to analyze the effectiveness of the Russian influence on Slovakia. Theoretical research methods were adopted for scientific considerations – an analysis of contemporary literature on the subject (Hess and Renner, 2019; Sanders and Sanders, 2019; Ventura-Cots et al., 2019; Brumercikova and Bukova, 2020; Chapman, 2020; Frajkova et al., 2020; Heglasová et al., 2020; Kratochvíl and Mišík, 2020; Lavelanet, Johnson and Ganatra, 2020) as well as deduction and generalization.

Each country strives to be a superpower, being a superpower is determined by the size of its army, economic potential, road infrastructure, etc. Slovakia is a country with a rather specific location in Central Europe and covers an area of 49,034 km². It has always served as a bridge between the East and the West of Europe. The terrain is mostly mountainous, which makes up more than half of

the area. Slovakia is adjacent to Poland, Ukraine, Hungary, Austria and the Czech Republic. The Slovak government is not interested in defense policy as a strategic priority. The possibility of threats and the loss of sovereignty are taken into account only in strategic documents, but do not occupy a special place. The potential and equipment of the Slovak army has much to be desired and it is not able to fulfill the basic defense tasks on its own. The basic principles of Slovakia's security policy are:
a) protection of sovereignty,
b) compliance with the norms of international law,
c) ensuring universal, civic defense of the state,
d) maintaining the Armed Forces adequate to the defense needs of the country,
e) keeping the balance between the state's defense requirements and its economic and social potential.

In 2001, Slovakia had almost 27,000 of troops, which was equipped with, among others 272 T-72 tanks, over 700 armored personnel carriers (including over 400 BWP-1 and BWP-2), approx. 300 guns (including 136 Dana gun howitzers). The Air Force was equipped with 24 MiG-29 and 16 MiG-21 and approx. 60 helicopters (approx. 20 Mi-24). In Central and Eastern Europe, in 2002–2003, the defense system of the former Warsaw Pact countries was under constant reconstruction. The main purpose was:
a) securing the systematic building and modernization of the Armed Forces
b) preparing the territory of the state for defense in times of peace,
c) creating conditions ensuring the continuity of the management of the state's defense.

There is a conviction among Slovak experts that Slovakia should specialize in a specific field and decide to deploy combat units or develop, for example, engineering troops, and anti-chemical or sapper units. The last two types of troops have recently become a Slovak specialty.

2002 was the first year in the implementation of the long-term development plan of the Armed Forces. The implementation of the revised model of the army began, and the focus was on personnel changes and management. The changes concerned, among others the reduction of compulsory military service to six months and a major reduction in military personnel. However, in September 2003, the crisis triggered by the resignation of Ivan Szimka, a popular minister in NATO circles, called into question some plans of transformation of the Slovak Armed Forces. The implementation of the plans was to be secured, however, by financing defense needs at the level of 1.89% of GDP over the next six years. Yet, not everything has been implemented as planned and the Slovak army is still in a huge financial crisis. Table 1 compares the combat-able Slovak and Russian armies.

Table 1. Comparison of the Slovak and Russian armies

	Slovakia	Russia
Size of army	14 678	789 500
Defence budget ($)	1 025 000 000	44 600 000 000
Air Forces	71	3 794
Tanks	30	20 216
Armoured vehicles	530	31 298
Self-propelled artillery	16	5 972
Rocket (missle) launchers	17	3 793

Data in the table above (Table 1) shows the disproportions between the Slovak and Russian armies. There are 54 Russian soldiers per one Slovak soldier. The budget displays that $ 1 spent by the Slovak Government equals to $ 44 spent by Russia. The biggest disproportion is between tanks, self-propelled artillery and rocket (missile) launchers. Of course, the topography, which is mostly mountainous, allows us to believe that these disproportions in the number of tanks are not significant for the Slovak side.

In 2016, the Ministry of National Defense of Slovakia developed the so-called "White Paper", which contained the command organization, armament requirements and the principles of operation of the Armed Forces of the Slovak Republic. The document was written after Russia's annexation of Crimea, the change in the economic and political situation in Europe, and the imbalance of the European Union's energy security. These events made the Slovak government be aware of the need to accelerate the modernization of the army and reevaluate the conducted defense policy. In addition to accelerating modernization, it is necessary to rebuild the structures of the Land Forces, Air Forces and Special Forces by 2030. Moreover, it is planned to increase the number of professional soldiers from the current level of approximately 14,500 to over 21,000 by around year 2030.

The Ministry of National Defense of Slovakia plans to allocate approximately EUR 6.5 billion to the modernization of the Armed Forces by 2030. Reaching the 2% GDP ceiling for defense is a hard task for a NATO member. The government plans to meet the requirements of the North Atlantic Pact by 2024. In 2017 the budget of the Ministry of National Defense of Slovakia amounted to approx. EUR 972 million, which accounted for 1.18% of GDP, in the plans for 2020, GDP will be at the level of 1.6% to reach 2% in 2024.

May 29, 2018 at the Lieskovec research center, belonging to the Ministry of National Defense of the Slovak Republic, 21 combat vehicles, thoroughly modernized by the Slovak defense industry, were handed over to the Armed Forces of the Slovak Republic in two variants, belonging to the BVP-1 and 2 families.

Until 2024, all T-72 s will be modernized, and after 2025, it is planned to start the process of acquiring the next generation tank. In the years 2018–2021, 25 modified Zuzana 2 howitzers will be delivered (the potential contract value is EUR 175 million). The new howitzer weighs 26,500 kg and a gun with a barrel length of 52 calibers.

Rocket artillery launchers are 26 sets RM70 / 85 MODULAR and 4 RM-70. Relatively poor and outdated is the anti-tank component, which includes 90 self-propelled launchers 9P135, 6 9P148 and 15 9S428 (not counting anti-tank guided missiles mounted on infantry fighting vehicles). There are plans to acquire modern anti-tank systems and a fully interpretable communication and data transmission system, compliant with the one in force in most NATO member states.

The Russian armed forces are recreating large units, including army and division headquarters, which may prove useful in high-intensity operations. It is worth taking a closer look at it, the more so because a large part of these formations is located in the west of the country.

Such large groups of vessels require modern equipment. In 2018, the Russian Army achieved 61% of the level of equipment with modern equipment and ranks second after the United States of America. Russia's expenditure on armaments puts it in fifth place.

The Russians are planning a degree of modernization of the army to the level of 70% by the end of 2020. A worse level of modern equipment was achieved in the Russian land forces, which in 2018 reached 48.3% (i.e. 2.3% more than assumed). In 2018, more than 2.2 thousand new and modernized weapon systems were introduced there. The air and space forces received 126 modern helicopters and airplanes, 120 pieces of military air defense technology (e.g. radar stations) and nine space objects. In the air force alone, the level of modern equipment is 64%, and in the entire air-space force it is as much as 74%. The degree of modernization in the navy reached 62.3%. It was enriched with fourteen ships and cutters, eleven security ships and four coastal missile batteries "Bał" and "Bastion".

It is planned to equip the land forces with 719 combat vehicles, one "Iskander-M" missile brigade, and two "S-300W4" and "Buk-M3" anti-aircraft missile brigades. The pace at which Slovakia is modernizing the Armed Forces does not guarantee security in this region. Equipment which is outdated on the modern battlefield is modernized and its profitability is expensive. Slovakia should invest in new solutions that have proved successful in the Polish army. Russia, on the other hand, focused on modern solutions in the equipment of its troops. The Russian army retrofits all types of troops. Actions of this type may pose a threat to the European Union states that originated from the former Warsaw Pact. In 2014, Russia annexed Crimea, then Donbass was severed from Ukraine. These types of actions are due to better equipment and training of the Russian army. We do not know what the future may bring, Russia's imperialist aspirations may lead to the elimination of EU countries that have a poor military infrastructure and do not invest in the development and training of the Armed Forces.

References

Brumercikova E. and Bukova B. (2020). "The Regression and Correlation Analysis of Carried Persons by Means of Public Passenger Transport of the Slovak Republic", *Transportation Research Procedia*, 44, pp. 61–68. doi: https://doi.org/10.1016/j.trpro.2020.02.010.

Chapman B., (2020). "Congressional Committee Resources on Space Policy During the 115th Congress (2017–2018): Providing Context and Insight Into US Government Space Policy", *Space Policy*, 51, p. 101359. doi: https://doi.org/10.1016/j.spacepol.2019.101359.

Frajkova Z. et al., (2020). "Translation, Cross-Cultural Validation of the Voice Handicap Index (VHI-30) in Slovak Language", *Journal of Voice*. doi: https://doi.org/10.1016/j.jvoice.2020.04.003.

Heglasová I. et al. (2020) "Ticks, fleas and rodent-hosts analyzed for the presence of Borrelia miyamotoi in Slovakia: the first record of Borrelia miyamotoi in a Haemaphysalis inermis tick", *Ticks and Tick-borne Diseases*, 11(5), p. 101456. doi: https://doi.org/10.1016/j.ttbdis.2020.101456.

Hess D.J. and Renner M., (2019). "Conservative political parties and energy transitions in Europe: Opposition to climate mitigation policies", *Renewable and Sustainable Energy Reviews*, 104, pp. 419–428. doi: https://doi.org/10.1016/j.rser.2019.01.019.

Kratochvíl P. and Mišík M., (2020). "Bad external actors and good nuclear energy: Media discourse on energy supplies in the Czech Republic and Slovakia", *Energy Policy*, 136, p. 111058. doi: https://doi.org/10.1016/j.enpol.2019.111058.

Lavelanet A.F., Johnson B.R. and Ganatra B., (2020). "Global Abortion Policies Database: A descriptive analysis of the regulatory and policy environment related to abortion", *Best Practice & Research Clinical Obstetrics & Gynaecology*, 62, pp. 25–35. doi: https://doi.org/10.1016/j.bpobgyn.2019.06.002.

Sanders M.C. and Sanders C.E., (2019). "A world's dilemma 'upon which the sun never sets': The nuclear waste management strategy (part II): Russia, Asia and the Southern Hemisphere", *Progress in Nuclear Energy*, 110, pp. 148–169. doi: https://doi.org/10.1016/j.pnucene.2018.09.009.

Ventura-Cots M. et al., (2019). "Public health policies and alcohol-related liver disease", *JHEP Reports*, 1(5), pp. 403–413. doi: https://doi.org/10.1016/j.jhepr.2019.07.009.

Tomasz R. Waśniewski / Marcin Górnikiewicz

Chapter 33: Summary and conclusions: The perspective of the development of the Russian influence on the Slovakian internal and external policy

When assessing Moscow's ability to influence through the use of quantitative and qualitative methods of measuring the potential opportunities resulting from Russia's influence on Slovakia's internal and external policy, it is worth paying attention to the dependencies listed below.

The Slovak economy is largely based on industry, which generates one third of Slovak GDP. Despite its small size, the country ranks 32nd in the ranking of steel producers. On the one hand, this means that the economic stability of Slovakia depends on the stability of the supply of raw materials, and therefore on those countries that are able to provide these raw materials in the required quantities and prices.

The functioning of the industry, on the other hand, is based on a continuous energy supply, and therefore on efficiently operating power plants, of which two nuclear provide nearly half of the country's energy demand, one third is provided by gas and coal power plants and approx. 16% by hydropower plants. Obsolete infrastructure of nuclear power plants has resulted in shutting down some of the production and dependence on external energy supplies. In addition, the raw material needed to generate nuclear energy also has to be imported from other countries, which places the Slovak government in a difficult situation with the need to ensure continuous energy supplies to meet the constantly growing needs in this area.

Although Russia is not one of Bratislava's largest trading partners, it is Moscow that provides the largest supplies of fuels and natural resources, so necessary for the proper functioning of the Slovak economy. This means that any disruptions in supplies from Russia can very quickly trigger an economic crisis, as already happened in 2009 during the dispute between Russia and Ukraine, which resulted in a temporary suspension of gas supplies.

Under the previous regime, Slovakia also had a well-developed arms industry, which resulted in the industrial development focused on steel production. Currently, due to the poor condition of the armaments sector and the constantly maintained favorable conditions in the field of vehicle production, as well as access to relatively cheap labor, Slovakia has become an attractive location for the automotive industry, which resulted in the creation of production plants in this country by such global brands as: Volkswagen (a plant in Bratislava), Peugeot (production in Trnava), Kia Motors (Žilina) Jaguar Land Rover (Nitra) and large electronic companies, including Samsung Electronics (Galanta), Sony (Trnava and Nitra), as well as household appliances – Whirlpool (Poprad). Paradoxically, also for this reason, the possibility of influencing the decision-making process in Slovakia is highly appreciated in Moscow. This situation enables the creation of multi-level scenarios, including an impact on the position of the aforementioned corporations. This in turn influences the economic stability of Slovakia or directly the political and economic decision-making process. On the other hand, Slovakia has virtually no tools of economic influence on the situation in Russia, which means that Moscow has all the trump cards in achieving its goals in this country – not only economic, but also political.

Therefore, one cannot be surprised by the attitude of the Slovak authorities, which strive to maintain proper relations with Russia, which are additionally based on the personal and institutional ties that have been built for decades, similarly to the neighboring Czech Republic. The difference is that Russia's economic influence over the Czech Republic is much more limited than that of Slovakia.

A complement to the undertaken political and economic efforts is also institutional cooperation within the framework of various forms of international cooperation, e.g. within the Council of Europe or the OSCE. Criticism of the effectiveness of EU sanctions and good relations between politicians at the highest level were also visible in the previous years in Slovak-Russian relations. The declaration of joining the Russian energy projects Nord Stream 2 and TurkStream is therefore the next stage of rapprochement with Russia, which was supported by the progress of work on Nord Stream 2, the approach of the Slovak government and the policy of its neighbors, Austria and Hungary, towards Russia.

In conclusion, Slovakia is currently under a strong influence of Moscow, which has secured itself in this area all instruments of economic and resource impact, as well as personnel at various levels of national and local government authorities. This situation could only be changed by providing the Slovak authorities with an alternative in terms of supplies of raw materials necessary for the development of the Slovak economy and gradual independence from Moscow's economic influence. Otherwise, it cannot be expected that the Slovak authorities will stand firm against Russia's actions, both within the EU and within the Visegrad Group.

Section IV:
The forecast of the evolution of the Russian-Slovak relations in the context of the Slovak armed forces transformation

Anna Pęzioł / Anna Borucka

Chapter 34: The assessment of the changes in the armed forces in terms of selected factors

The size of the army undoubtedly proves the country's potential and its power. In relation to Russia, Slovakia is a very small state, inhabited by approximately 5.45 million people, which is a modest result compared to Russia of a multi-million population (144.5 million citizens). Slovakia's foreign policy, dominated by considerable caution, is also well-balanced. The military traditions of Slovakia are also not rich, which translates into defense policy and the functioning of the Slovak army. It is not large, and additionally it is one of the least equipped armies in the world. It has: 65 planes and helicopters, 30 tanks and 530 armored personnel carriers, and a budget of just over USD 1 billion (Kożulewska and Bartnicki, 2017; https://vvzs.mil.sk/). The size of the Slovak army is also many times smaller than Russia's potential, which is perfectly illustrated by Figure 1.

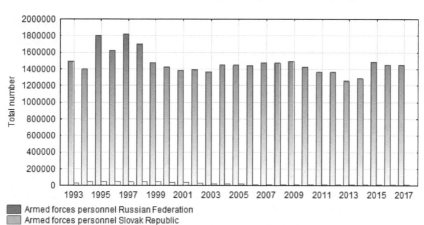

Figure 1. Comparison of the size of the armed forces of the Russian Federation and the Slovak Republic.

Apart from the number of people, the dynamics of changes is also an important element. The purpose of its presentation, the figure below (Figure 2) displays a comparison of how the potential of two armies changed, assigning each of them an independent number line. The staff turnover in the Russian army is clearly visible, which is constantly subject to sharp falls and increases.

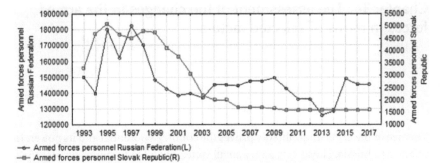

Figure 2. Dynamics of changes in the size of the Russian and Slovak armies.

After the collapse of the USSR, the Armed Forces of the Russian Federation were based on unchanged structures for several years and the conscription army was their basis. They were not subject to direct reform due to the difficult economic and geopolitical situation (Morozowa and Troshina, 2016). The distance of some NATO members from the aspirations of the former Warsaw Pact countries to Western international security structures meant that Russia saw in nuclear weapons the basis for maintaining the state's superpower and unwavering position on the international arena (Affek, 2014). So far, the army focused on global conflict has faced completely different challenges. In the times commonly known as the "Yeltsin sadness", the country struggled with the great returns of soldiers from the former Soviet republics. Therefore maintaining the current character of the army and its size posed a threat to the operational capabilities of the army, which was confirmed by the course of the Chechen war in 1994–1996 (Grabowski, 2011), and the upcoming NATO enlargement with new states was a change in the existing geopolitical balance of power.

The announcement of the new "Concept of state policy regarding military modernization by 2005" was also supposed to mean a change in the approach to the existing personnel policy in the army, by reducing the size of the army to approx. 1.4 million in 1999, which in relation to 1997 was 80 percent. After Boris Yeltsin's resignation from the presidency in 1999, a further reform of the army took place by adopting new plans, including The Development Plan of the Armed Forces of the Russian Federation for 2001–2005, and since 2008, a comprehensive reform of the Russian Armed Forces has been implemented (Spivak and Pridemore, 2004).

In the following years, despite personnel changes in the Ministry of Defense[1], the number of contracted soldiers was increased and conscription was maintained, taking into account internal conditions related to the need to ensure security in a significant area, still constituted the basis of the armed forces, however, the upward trend was to be stopped and maintained at an optimal level until 2025 (Grabowski, 2011).

The current model of the Armed Forces of the Russian Federation is based mainly on conscription service, but it is kept at a constant level, the number of contracted soldiers has been increased, and the number of officer positions should remain unchanged. The quality of changes in the armed forces is evidenced not only by their power, but also by their openness to changes and adaptation to the standards of a modern army. One of them is an increasing number of women.

The functioning model of military service of the Russian Federation, the basis of which is conscription, is not conducive to the increasing number of women in the army [0]. Women perform military service mostly on the basis of contracts. According to unofficial data presented in the media, the average women's military service in the Armed Forces of the Russian Federation amounted as follows: in the year 2012–40,000, in 2013–29,000, in 2015–35,000, in 2016–45,000, and in 2017–45,000 (https://www.rbth.com/defence). In recent years, more and more often the views that access to military service for women should be increased, e.g. by expanding the list of posts that can be filled by women have been present. Government circles indicate that more and more women have access to military education, and deputy defense minister Tatjana Shevtsova in 2015 indicated that over 1,000 women studied at military academies, over 2,600 were present in the officer corps – 72 of them in command positions, and approx. 19,000 in positions within the contracted service, mainly non-commissioned officers (https://www.rbth.com/defence).

The tendency to extend the possibilities of service by women in the Armed Forces of the Russian Federation was reflected in the further activities of the Ministry of Defense of the Russian Federation, in line with the human resources policy. Its main goal is to improve the qualifications and education of soldiers. According to the information of Minister Sergei Shojgu, released in the media in 2018, women serve mainly in positions in logistic units and military schools https://www.rbth.com/defence, while since 2018 they are allowed to perform their duties in the Russian Navy for scuba divers and undergo training at an air force school for pilotage of transport planes and combat helicopters (https://www.rbth.com/defence). Women account for approximately 10% of the personnel of the Armed Forces of the Russian Federation, including P-time posi-

---

1 On November 6, 2012, Sergei Shoygu replaced Anatoly Serdyukov as the Minister of Defense.

tions (Smirov, 2002). Every year the number of graduates of military academies will increase this number, supporting the officer corps. Considering the published data from the lists taking into account all NATO member states, which indicate average values of over 11% of the participation of women in the armed forces, it can be assumed that Russia will also indicate the increasing share of women in the service of the Russian army. On the other hand, the discussion in the media regarding the participation of women in the armed forces of the Russian Federation does not indicate a change in the current policy towards women's military service, referred to as the "no combat rule" (https://www.rbth.com/defence). Taking into account the announcements made by the Ministry of Defense of the Russian Federation to maintain the conscription system at the current level, it can be assumed that the structure of women's military service will only be changed in terms of contracted positions and in the officer corps.

The military service of females has been an integral part of the Slovak Armed Forces since its erection and issues of the women's service have been included over the years in all documents affecting the shape of military service. Since Slovakia joined NATO, females can attend training courses for NCO service, and after entering fully professional service, women are present in all military corps (Wratislaviensia et. All). The document adopted in 2005 indicating the observance of the provisions of the Constitution regarding the equality of all citizens in the Slovak Armed Forces, led to the provision of optimal conditions of service for both women and men (www.nato.int; Čukan, 2002). Another military reform, with the 2010 outlook, increased the participation of women in military service to 10% and included the United Nations' Resolution No. 1325 (2000) on women, peace and security guidelines on women's rights in military service. Access to all types of armed forces and positions also illustrates the participation of females in individual corps of the Armed Forces of the Slovak Republic. It is a continuing trend resulting from the nature of military service. In this relatively young army, the majority of women serve in the NCO and privates, about 70%, in the officer corps the average is slightly over 30% (www.nato.int). The presence of the Slovak Republic in NATO and UN international organizations and compliance with the provisions of the Constitution of the Slovak Republic regarding equality of all citizens regardless of gender, are the most important factors that shaped the military service of women in the Slovak armed forces (Martinská, 2018). Fulfilling allied obligations and bearing responsibility for ensuring security in the region also translates into the increasing number of women in the Slovak army. The females' military service in Slovakia is also a reflection of the personnel policy implemented among the army of the Visegrad Group countries, aimed at increasing the number of women in the armed forces. This model of service in the V4 armies has been designed since the changes after the collapse of the Warsaw Pact and as the consequence means unlimited access to military positions, depending on meeting the conditions and requirements for service regardless of gender. A further increase in the share of the military service of women in the armed forces of Slovakia is in line with the current direction of the personnel policy in the army among all Visegrad Group countries, as indicated by the percentage data from individual V4 countries. In 2017, the number of women was respectively: Slovakia 10.8%, Poland 5%, Hungary 19.3% and the Czech Republic 12.7%. The personnel policy of the Armed Forces of the Slovak Republic, maintaining over 11% of women in the army, is in line with the current NATO trend to increase the number of women serving in the armed forces and it can be assumed that this tendency will increase. The lack of precise information on the number of women in the Russian army prevents a thorough analysis of the dynamics of these changes. Only publications relating to the Slovak army allow such a study.

Due to the unstable number of troops (changing each year), the percentage share of women in the total number of soldiers was considered the best indicator in this respect. The sample collected in this area is presented in the figure below (Figure 3).

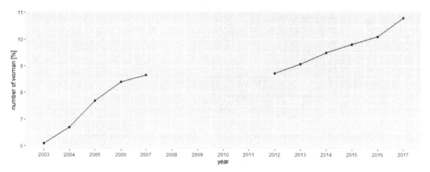

Figure 3. The number of women in the Slovak army.

Incomplete data – lack of information from 2007–2011 – meant that only observations from 2012–2017 were included in the study. Both their form and a small number determined the use of the linear regression model. The dependent variable is the number of women in particular years, while the independent variable is the calendar year. The results of its estimation are presented in the table (Table 1).

Table 1. Estimation results of the linear regression model

n=6	$R = 0.99$, $R^2 = 0.98$, $corrected.R^2 = 0.98$, $F(1,4) = 202.95$			
	b	Standard error from b	t(4)	p
Intercept	-782,32	55,59	-14,07	0,00
year	0,34	0,028	14,24	0,00

The resulting linear regression model is:

$$y = 0,34*year - 782,32 + \varepsilon_t$$

The calculated slope is statistically significant (p-value = 0.00) and means that each year the number of women in the army grows by 0.34%. The intercept (p-value = 0.000) is also statistically significant. The high value of the corrected coefficient of determination ($R^2 = 0.98$) proves that the model was well adjusted to empirical data. The diagnosis of the residue distribution is also satisfactory. The Shapiro-Wilk test statistic SW = 0.9715 and p-value = 0.9026 indicates that the distribution is normal. The figure below shows the histogram of the residual distribution (Figure 4).

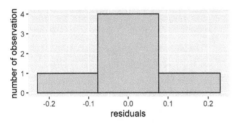

Figure 4. Histogram of the residual distribution of the linear regression model.

The developed model also allowed for the forecast for the coming years. The figure (Figure 5) presents a chart of empirical observations and the forecast for the next 6 years.

Research shows that the trend in the Slovak army is good and the number of women varies every year. According to the forecast, in 2023 the percentage of women will exceed 13% of the total army size. Compared to other countries, Slovakia looks favorably – Table 2.

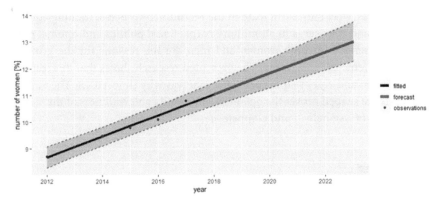

Figure 5. Graph of the fitted regression function and the forecast for future years.

Table 2. The number of women in the selected countries and NATO (www.nato.int; www.rbth.com)

Country/years	Percentage of women in military service			
	2014	2015	2016	2017
NATO	10,3	10,8	10,9	11.1
Slovakia	9,5	9,8	10,1	10,8
Hungary	14,6	20,2	20	19,3
Czechia	13,8	13,1	12,6	12,7
Poland	3,7	4,3	5	5
Russia	app.10	app.10	app.10	app.10

The percentage share of women in the armed forces is a sign of modernity and changes taking place in the army. For many years the military was a hermetic domain of men, therefore the emergence of women was a huge challenge for the armed forces, not only in the organizational sphere, but also in the mental one, related to the existing stereotypes. The stereotypes, apart from formal and legal issues, most often pose a barrier preventing women from joining the ranks of soldiers.

The assessment of the armed forces of the Russian Federation and the Slovak Republic in this respect presented in this chapter shows completely different faces. The Russian model of military service, based on conscription, is not conducive to increasing the number of women in the army. Contracted service of females makes up a small percentage of the adopted method of recruitment and limits the possibilities of its growth. The expected changes may take place at most within the framework of contracted positions and in the officer corps.

Slovakia's policy is open and focused on increasing the number of women in the army. They are taken into account in legislative matters concerning the shape of military service, they participate in the recruitment process, training equally with men, and they serve in all military corps. Equal politics and optimal conditions of service for both women and men are the reasons for the growing number of females in the army. The presented research shows that this trend is almost linear and every year the percentage increases by almost 0.4%. The way the forecasts are shaped proves the openness, modernity and readiness of the Slovak army for professionalism and competence.

References

Affek J., (2014). Reformy i modernizacja Sił Zbrojnych Federacji Rosyjskiej, *Zeszyty Naukowe WSOWL* Nr 1 (171).
Čukan K., (2003). Development of Views of the Slovak Public on the Armed Forces and NATO membership. *Public Image of Security*, 112.
Grabowski T.W., (2011). Rosyjska siła. Siły Zbrojne i główne problemy polityki obronnej Federacji Rosyjskiej w latach 1991–2010, Częstochowa.
https://vvzs.mil.sk/.
https://www.rbth.com.
https://www.rt.com/russia/397675-russian-ombudsman-advocates-conscription-service/, dostęp 18.02.2020.
Kużelewska E. and Bartnicki A.R., (2017). Grupa Wyszehradzka–nowe wyzwania bezpieczeństwa i perspektywy współpracy. *Rocznik Integracji Europejskiej*, (11), pp. 103–118.
Martinská M., (2018). Quality of Cooperation between Men and Women in the Armed Forces of the Slovak Republic: Gender-Integrated Organization. *Security Dimensions. International and National Studies*, (27), pp. 88–108.
Morozova O.M. and Troshina T.I., (2016). Woman's View at Men's Work: The Revolution and the Civil War through the Eyes of Women and Through Their Fates.
Smirnov A.I., (2002). Women in the Russian army. *Sociological research*, 41(1), pp. 78–88.
Spivak A.L. and Pridemore W.A., (2004). Conscription and reform in the Russian army. *Problems of Post-communism*, 51(6), pp. 33–43.
Ustinovich Y.S., (2003). Women and the Army: Recruitment problems. *Military Thought*, 12(3), pp. 109–114.
Wratislaviensia A., Wratislaviensia C., et Communicativa C.A., Wratislaviensia G., Góry L., Kultura K.J. and Slavogermanica O., Názory kadetiek Akadémie ozbrojených síl na regrutáciu a kariéru v profesionálnej armáde Slovenskej republiky.
www.nato.int.

Anna Borucka / Anna Pęzioł

Chapter 35: Mathematical model for the assessment of national defense expenditure of the Slovak Republic in relation to the Russian Federation

Slovakia's geostrategic situation in relation to the Russian Federation should be assessed taking into account many different areas. One of them is spending on national defense. However, the disproportion between these expenses (expressed in million USD) in Russia and Slovakia is very large (Figure 1) (https://www.defence24.pl).

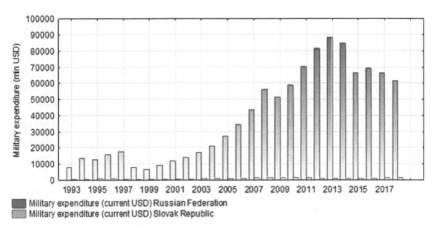

Figure 1. Defense expenditure in 1993–2018 of the Russian Federation and the Slovak Republic.

This outcome stems from the fact that the demographic, economic and military potentials are different. The analysis covers countries which, because of their history, geographic location, access to mineral resources, and the political system, are incomparable. Therefore a better indicator, defining the main trends, would be defense expenditure expressed in% of GDP, as presented in the figure below (Figure 2).

As it can be seen, the dynamics of changes over the analyzed period differs significantly for individual countries. This is due to many factors. Russia's policy is marked by aggressive actions of a hybrid war against smaller neighboring countries, and in some cases these are typically military actions. After the col-

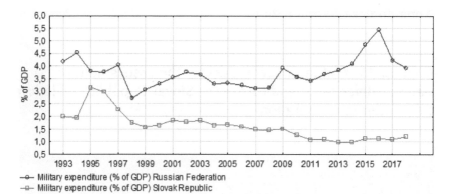

Figure 2. Defense expenditure as% GDP in the Russian Federation and the Slovak Republic (https://www.defence24.pl).

lapse of the Warsaw Pact in July 1991, the Union of Soviet Socialist Republics collapsed only a few months later. In August 1991, the Moscow coup took place, which became a catalyst for the independence of the Soviet republics, because all of them, by the end of October 1991, announced a declaration of independence, and in December this year, the USSR became an issue of the past. In the aftermath of the collapse of the USSR, new states were established and Russia turned into its legal successor. The 1990s in this region meant a deep collapse and a crisis in all sectors of the economy. In May 2000, the former prime minister, Vladimir Putin, was elected the president of the Russian Federation, who aimed to realize the vision of Russia as a great and internationally significant power (Security Strategy of the Slovak Republic, 2005). Expenditure on the army and its modernization began to increase, and in 2011 the implementation of the ten-year armaments program (Russian: GPW 2020) was launched, which envisaged that in 2011–2020 the Russian Federation would spend around 700 billion dollars on equipment and armaments, in order to reach 70% of replacement of equipment and weapons in the entire army (Kustrova, 2012; Petrufová and Nagyová 2019). At the same time, research related to defense spending should highlight the specificity of Russia's hidden, covert expenditure in the amount of around 30%.

Defense policy of Slovakia

An important element of Slovakia's international policy was the establishment of the Visegrad Group, taking into account the common history, experience and efforts to enhance the position of the countries of the region in the international arena (Cabada and Waisová, 2018; Cooper, 2016). The last decade of the 20th century meant for the countries of Central and Eastern Europe to function in a new geopolitical reality in which international relations in the field of security had been defined from the very beginning. The Slovak Republic based its security on the pillars of international cooperation – it is a member of the European Union, the North Atlantic Treaty Organization, the Organization for Security and Cooperation in Europe, the Council of Europe and regional cooperation as the part of the initiative of the Visegrad Group and the Central European Defense Cooperation Initiative, taking into account its economic capabilities and striving to maintain territorial integrity and sovereignty (Ambler and Neubauer, 2017). Slovakia, not directly bordering the Russian Federation, has a small military potential, mainly based on post-Soviet equipment, along with the armed forces of around 13,000 of professional troops, may consider its military commitment only in a possible auxiliary task of securing the NATO flank, de-escalating or deterring NATO's involvement in the conflict (Pajtinka 2018; Sandler and George 2016). The analysis of Slovakia's defense spending indicates that the issues of building military potential were not a priority of Slovakia's security policy in the new geopolitical system, and a direct conflict with Russia is considered unlikely (Usiak 2018). Political aspirations to remain neutral under the so-called Slovak pragmatism (Ambler and Neubauer, 2017). The geographic location of Slovakia means that, as in the case of other Central and Eastern European countries, the threat from Russia should be considered in terms of regional interests, and initiatives aimed at strengthening cooperation constitute the basis for a broader process of building stability and predictability in the field of state security and defense, and also enhancing the existing military potential.

After the collapse of Czechoslovakia, the direction of creating the Armed Forces of the Slovak Republic was defined, including the territorial consolidation of Slovak soldiers (after the collapse of the USSR) and the reduction of the number of troops and equipment.

The provisions of the first Defense Doctrine of the Slovak Republic, adopted in 1994, indicated the North Atlantic Treaty Organization as the main pillar of ensuring the security of Slovakia, and the direction of development of the defense system in the new geopolitical conditions also meant the necessity to adjust the armed forces to NATO standards.

The result of defining the foundations of Slovakia's international security was the adoption in 1996 of the Slovak army development plans by 2010 (Nadtochey, 2018), which primarily meant plans to change the management of the army, abandon the current model of conscription for full professionalisation and increase of defense expenditure to 1.89% of GDP.

The turn of the years 2003 and 2004 was significant for Slovak defense and security, as it began the process of transformation towards the complete professionalisation of the army. The Partnership for Peace program ended with success and on March 29, 2004, Slovakia was declared as a member of the North

Atlantic Treaty Organization. The adoption of the new Security Strategy (Defense Strategy of the Slovak Republic, 2005) and the Defense Strategy in 2005 confirmed Slovakia's position as a member of international and regional security structures (Toma, 2017). Since 2006, the armed forces of Slovakia have been fully modern, and the process of professionalisation itself has led to an increase in defense spending during this period, including modification of the existing infrastructure, changes in the allocation of financial resources, adaptation of the army to new operating conditions.

Later, the deepening economic crisis, the replacement of the Slovak koruna with the currency of the European Union and the change in the approach to the transatlantic partnership contributed to the reduction of military expenditure in the Slovak budget (https://data.worldbank.org).

Only the change in the geopolitical situation related to the crisis in Ukraine, as well as Russia's activity in the area of conventional and hybrid operations, resulted in the tightening of cooperation between the group of V4 countries, the increased importance of cooperation and strengthening the military potential in the region. In view of the above, in 2015, Slovakia began the process of increasing military spending, which at that time fluctuated at the level of 1.1% of GDP. The declaration related to defense expenditure was underlined during the visit to Slovakia of NATO Secretary General Jens Stoltenberg by Slovakia's Defense Minister Martin Glváč, who announced an increase in defense spending to 1.6% of GDP in 2020. This statement, taking into account other economic indicators in view of the current level of defense spending, meant a spectacular increase by approx. 50% (Biała Księga 2016).

Another impulse influencing the increase in defense spending was the NATO summit in Warsaw in 2016. The decisions of that event emphasized the need to change the approach to Russia's policy, and to increase commitment to enhancing security in the region of Central and Eastern Europe. Following the path set by NATO, Slovakia prepared a White Paper, a document in the spirit of the provisions of the NATO summit in Warsaw. The paper presented the assumptions of the long-term defense policy of the Slovak Republic in the perspective of 2024 based on the new challenges of the 21st century, pointing to the need to gradually increase defense spending (Defense Strategy of the Republic Słowacka, 2005). The goal of surging military expenditure set out in the White Paper since 2016 has been consistently implemented and amounted to approximately USD 1,003 million in 2016, USD 1,049 million in 2017 and USD 1,280 million in 2018 (https: // www.defence24.pl).

The upward trend in state defense spending means that Slovakia takes active steps to build security based on regional cooperation of the Visegrad Group countries and strives to deepen the financial commitment related to NATO membership (Persson, 2016). The necessary modernization of the Slovak army, replacing post-Soviet equipment with modern weapons, specialization of the army in selected directions in the face of changing geopolitical and regional challenges, taking into account the economic possibilities of the state, lead to a systematic increase in defense spending. Russia's aggressive policy in the international and regional arena, the consistent implementation of the army modernization plan, investment in defense research, implementation of hybrid operations and increased investment in new technologies make Slovakia incur an effort on military expenditure. Thus, it also implements the political tendencies in NATO concerning the mutual balance of the security level by obliging the member states to increase the financial commitment to defense in solidarity.

Taking into account the benefits of activities ensuring collective international security and the importance of regional cooperation within the Visegrad Group as strengthening the voice of the Central and Eastern Europe region, Slovakia has implemented a policy of increasing defense spending in order to maintain state security at a level that guarantees its position as an equal partner in talks on state security in the international arena (Gotkowska and Osica, 2012). The aim of the article is to assess the dynamics of changes in defense spending in Slovakia and to do the foresight for the future. The existing trend is clearly visible on the line chart (Figure 3) showing only Slovakia's spending.

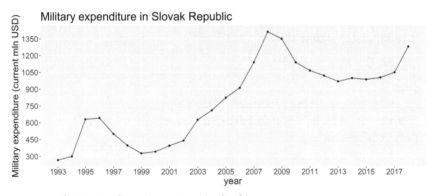

Figure 3. Military expenditure in 1993–2018 in Slovakia.

A moving average model was used to identify the development trend of the time series and to calculate the forecast. It is a simple forecasting method that smooths out the variables with their mean. Moving averages are arithmetic averages, calculated on the basis of a fixed number of consecutive observations of the series. The value of the calculated moving average should be assigned to the middle observation among those included in the calculation. Such an observation exists only for moving averages calculated on the basis of an odd number of observations, as represented by the formula:

$$y_{t(k)} = \frac{1}{k}(y_{t-k} + \ldots + y_{t-1} + y_t + y_{t+1} + \ldots + y_{t+k}) \qquad (1)$$

where: t - time variable,

k - the number of periods of the moving average,

y_t - implementations of the time series.

For an even number of words, the center of the moving average is between the middle observations. In this case, centering is used to perform the calculations $(k-1)$ of the whole observations and a half of the previous observation and a half of the next observation after $(k-1)$. In this way, the $(k+1)$ observations are used for calculations, which is an odd number and allows to unambiguously assign the value of the moving average to the value of the series, which is presented by the formula:

$$y_{t(k)} = \frac{1}{k}(\frac{1}{2}y_{t-k} + \ldots y_{t-1} + y_t + y_{t+1} + \ldots + \frac{1}{2}y_{t+k}) \qquad (2)$$

The Holt model is also used for forecasting based on the time series in which a trend and random fluctuations are present. The following equations are used to describe it:

– time series at time t:

$$F_t = \alpha\, y_t + (1-\alpha)(F_{t-1} + S_{t-1}) \qquad (3)$$

– trend increase at time t:

$$S_t = \beta(F_t - F_{t-1}) + (1-\beta)S_{t-1} \qquad (4)$$

where:

α and β are smoothing parameters in the range $[0,1]$

Parameters are selected on the basis of the criterion of the lowest average error of expired forecasts s^*, i.e.:

$$s^* = \sqrt{\frac{1}{n}\sum_{t=1}^{n} y_t - y*_t(\alpha, \beta)^{\,2}} \qquad (5)$$

When calculating an expired forecast, the following equation is used:

$$y^*_{t+1} = F_t + S_t \qquad (6)$$

The forecast for future periods is determined by the formula:

$$y^*_t = F_n + (T-n)S_n \qquad (7)$$

Several moving average models for different periods have been suggested for the researched series. A moving average of A 2, 3 and a period average of 4 were selected. The results are presented in Figure 4.

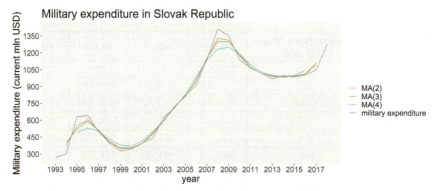

Figure 4. Graph of the tested variable and moving average models.

Then the parameters of the Holt model were determined. For the tested time series, they take the form:

$$\alpha = 0.9999 \quad \beta = 0.0001$$

The values of smoothed series for the moving average 2, 3 and the period average 4 as well as for the Holt method are presented in Table 1.

Table 1. Values of moving average models and Holt's model

Year	Defense expenditure (USD mln)	MA 2	MA 3	MA 4	HOLT
1993	267				287,174
1994	300	374,127	398,838		307,461
1995	630	550,200	523,725	488,598	340,540
1996	642	603,068	590,237	529,876	669,988
1997	500	509,553	512,894	504,269	682,231
1998	398	405,471	408,097	429,058	540,282
1999	327	348,563	355,695	378,462	438,248
2000	342	351,453	354,496	370,579	367,749
2001	394	392,594	392,126	413,054	382,806
2002	440	474,656	486,188	496,343	434,448
2003	625	600,092	591,953	596,128	480,519
2004	711	717,601	719,704	708,707	664,887
2005	823	817,322	815,325	831,956	751,785
2006	911	946,312	957,960	983,845	863,812
2007	1139	1150,367	1154,092	1137,270	951,912
2008	1412	1328,227	1300,400	1231,431	1179,671
2009	1350	1312,495	1299,895	1250,426	1452,234

Table 1 *(Continued)*

Year	Defense expenditure (USD mln)	MA 2	MA 3	MA 4	HOLT
2010	1138	1172,625	1184,273	1192,191	1391,112
2011	1065	1071,887	1074,234	1095,453	1178,548
2012	1020	1018,281	1017,649	1030,160	1105,525
2013	968	988,433	995,269	1002,797	1060,800
2014	998	987,312	983,847	990,789	1008,514
2015	986	993,146	995,556	998,792	1038,208
2016	1003	1010,272	1012,679	1044,303	1026,440
2017	1049	1095,460	1110,922		1043,534
2018	1281				1089,534

Forecast errors (MAPE – mean absolute percentage error, MAE – mean absolute error, ME – mean error), were then calculated for each of the models. The obtained results are presented in Table 2.

Table 2. Forecast errors

	MA 2	MA 3	MA 4	Holt's model
MAPE	0,04	0,05	0,07	0,15
MAE	25,72	34,29	46,82	102,19
ME	2,07	2,76	-5,30	4,59

The smallest error was obtained for the two-period moving average model, which makes it the best one. The graph of the time series, smoothed series and forecast are presented in Figure 5.

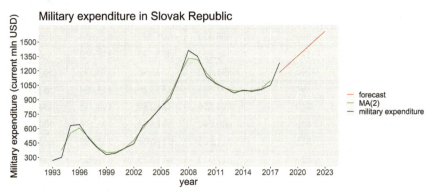

Figure 5. Prognosis of Slovakia's defense spending.

There are many factors that make Slovakia's defense spending tend to increase. The active attitude of this state towards building security, expressed by cooperation within the Visegrad Group and the North Atlantic Alliance, is reflected in the being implemented budget. Moreover, the developed mathematical model shows that this direction should be maintained. This is due to the need for continuous modernization of the Slovak army, and the improvement and specialization of soldiers, emphasized in the article, especially in the face of the challenges of the modern battlefield. Another stimulating factor is Russia's aggressive policy, its military modernization plan, the high scale of investment in defense research and the latest technologies in this area. The results obtained also reflect Slovakia's efforts to achieve the security level of NATO member states.

Anna Borucka / Anna Pęzioł

Chapter 36: Summary and conclusions: The forecast of potential forms of military and non-military influence of Moscow towards Slovakia

The forecast for the development of the Slovak armed forces, taking into account the differentiation of human resources (including gender) determined by accession to NATO, does not correspond to the large restrictions on the functioning of the thriving Slovak defense industry in the past. As a result, the Slovak armed forces operate on the border of two systems: the post-Soviet and Euro-Atlantic systems, which also does not have a positive effect on the potential of the armed forces which are also so limited in terms of numbers and technology. On the other hand, many factors contribute to the fact that Slovakia's defense expenditure is showing an upward trend despite difficulties. Evidence of the active attitude of this state towards building security, expressed by cooperation within the Visegrad Group and the North Atlantic Alliance, is the implemented budget, which secures funds for defense development appropriate to the possibilities. The process of modernizing defense capabilities focuses not only on technical modernization, but also on personnel training – especially in the face of challenges, opportunities and threats arising from the future battlefield. In conclusion, despite the undertaken efforts to modernize defense capabilities, the main axis of the strategic defense against possible aggression is active membership in the above-mentioned forms of institutionalized international cooperation, especially in NATO and, secondly, in the EU.

At the same time, the prospect of possible aggression from the Russian side against the probability of using the means of economic dependence is not very realistic. Russia will not risk a conflict with a country that is a member of NATO and the EU, but at the same time it will be able to achieve its own geopolitical goals using non-military means.

In the light of the quantitative and qualitative research carried out, it can therefore be assumed that Russia will continue the trend of economic dependence on Slovakia, especially by using all available political, economic and informational means to maintain the organization of the energy sector at the level requiring the supply of raw materials from Russia, as well as making it dependent on supplies proper functioning of the industrial sector. Any attempt to diversify the sources of supply of the necessary raw materials will surely meet Moscow's multidimensional actions aimed at paralyzing such initiatives. It will also be important to use the personal ties of key persons who have or may have an impact on the political decision-making process in Slovakia. In this respect, too, Russia will make efforts to maintain its defense potential on the border of the post-Soviet and Euro-Atlantic systems, thus ensuring for itself at least a limited influence on this sector of Slovakia's functioning. In the geopolitical game, Slovakia will be still used to implementation of Russia's strategic goals on the forum of the Visegrad Group, NATO and the EU.

Part IV: Hungary

Section 1:
Geopolitical and geostrategic conditions of Russian activity towards Hungary in the 21st century

Sławomir Byleń

Chapter 37: The Russian vision of geopolitical order in Central and Eastern Europe in relation to Hungary

Nowadays, geopolitical issues are the subject of both theoretical and practical considerations, especially in the context of mutual relations between centers of power, in the context of the implementation of international policy, economic and military security in global, regional and national dimensions. The subject of contemporary geopolitics is the determinants of the functioning of individual centers of power and the interactions that take place between them in all the most important spheres of a state activity. Geopolitics studies, among others factors that make up the total geopolitical potential (power) of the centers of power and those aspects that shape the power of geopolitical entities (Power, German Weltmacht). The subdisciplines of geopolitics deal with the study of detailed geopolitical issues. The most important of them are: geostrategy, geoeconomics, geohistory, astropolitics, astrostrategy, geoculture, geoecology. oreover, specialists also point to other areas of geopolitics, which do not have the status of a sub-discipline, but are important research instruments. They include: powernomics, powermetrics, didactics of geopolitics and geopolitical mapping.

Taking into account the theoretical foundations describing the meaning of the term geopolitics and the subject of research, it should be assumed that the aim of the study is to present, verify and assess the geopolitical situation of Hungary in relation to the current assumptions, concepts and geopolitical views of the Russian Federation. In order to achieve such a specific goal, this chapter attempts to solve two fundamental research problems. The first was formulated as the question: What geopolitical potential do Hungary and the Russian Federation have? The second research problem is: Can the geopolitical potential of the Russian Federation influence the functioning of Hungary as an independent state and to what extent? In an attempt to solve the research problems defined above, the research used empirical research methods: firstly, a critical analysis of the literature on the subject of research, and secondly, an analysis of source documents concerning the geopolitical situation of Hungary in comparison with the Russian Federation. The theoretical methods used here were: the method of synthesis and the inference methods, which are the final product of previously conducted analyzes.

The definition of medium-sized countries is often made on the basis of four analytical approaches (analysis models). The first (position approach) focuses on the country's positioning in the international hierarchy in terms of territory size, population, demographic, economic and military potential. The middle states are positioned at the "half of the rate", between the great powers and the small states. Many authors question this approach due to the immeasurability of all the factors determining the strength and power of the state. The supporters of the second approach – the geographical one – point to the location of middle states between the great powers. The normative approach, in turn, focuses on the responsibility and credibility of medium-sized states, which they benefit from the extensive use of diplomatic means and methods and commitment to maintaining global order. In the behavioral model of defining middle-ranking countries, the emphasis is placed on the characteristic behavior of these countries, including: reliance on multilateral cooperation in solving international problems, striving for a compromise or adopting the attitude of a "good citizen of the international community" (Włodkowska-Bogdan, 2015, p. 295).

Hungary are counted to the group of medium-sized states belonging to many international organizations, including: from 1955 the United Nations, from 1999 the North Atlantic Treaty and from 2004 the European Union. At the same time, Hungary has belonged to the Visegrad Group since 1991, called (after the collapse of Czechoslovakia) the V4 Group for short, which brings together four countries of the former Eastern bloc (Hungary, Poland, the Czech Republic and Slovakia). For this reason, in the author's opinion, it is worth looking at the geopolitical situation of Hungary compared to other V4 countries in relation to Russia, with particular emphasis on checking, verifying and assessing the connections and dependencies in the existing relations between Hungary and the Russian Federation.

Hungary is a landlocked country with a lowland landscape and a warm, temperate climate. The second-longest river in Europe, the Danube, flows through Hungary. The country is sparsely forested. Hungary's natural environment has been greatly transformed by human participation in the 20th century. Hungary is located almost entirely in the lowland and flat Pannonian Basin. The exceptions are the North Hungarian Highlands, i.e. the range of medium mountains belonging to the Carpathians (Börzsöny, Gödöllő, Czerhat, Mátra with the highest peak of Hungary, Kékes, Bukowe Mountains, Tokajsko-Slańskie Mountains) in the north-east of the country and the Hungarian Alps (Sopronskie and Kőszeg Mountains) on the western border. The largest rivers in Hungary are the Danube, Tisza and Drava. The largest lake in Central Europe – Balaton has also been built in Hungary.

Hungary covers an area of 93,032 km2, which corresponds to approx. 0.5% of the area of Russia and approx. 30% of the area of Poland. Hungary has a population of less than 10 million people (9 825 thousand), which gives an average population of 108 people per square kilometer. These three figures position Hungary respectively in place: 108 (in terms of area) and 93 (in terms of population potential) among all countries in the world (Table 1).

Table 1. Area and population density compared to the selected countries (EUROSTAT)

Country	As of 2018		
	Area (km^2)	Population density (person/km^2)	Population (citizens)
Hungary	93 032	108	9 825 704
Poland	312 685	124	38 420 687
Slovakia	48 845	111	5 445 040
Czechia	78 866	130	10 686 269
Russia	17 075 200	8,5	142 122 776

For Hungary, the presented table, especially in relation to Russia, cannot stand for a binding comparison in terms of the population potential and the area of the country. Hence, Hungary's strategic decisions to join the economic and political (EU) and military (NATO) alliances in order to improve the existing inequalities in its military and economic potential. Despite the fact that the presented comparisons are not very favorable, Hungary ranks much higher in economic and political rankings.

One of the indicators for assessing the geostrategic situation is the length of the state border, the number of neighbors, relations with them and their membership in specific international organizations (political, military and economic blocs). Hungary has a border of 2,171 km. It borders with seven countries, including: Austria (366 km), Croatia (329 km), Romania (443 km), Serbia (151 km), Slovakia (677 km), Slovenia (102 km) and Ukraine (103 km). In the case of Hungary, most of its neighbors belong to the same international blocs and alliances, with the exception of Serbia and Ukraine, which greatly facilitates shaping political, economic and military contacts.

Another positive factor is the fact that both Serbia and Ukraine participate in the PfP (Partnership for Peace) program and Austria remains a neutral country. The program defines a specific type of relationship between NATO member states and aspiring countries in order to ensure international order, security, and stabilization in Europe. The situation regarding the membership of these countries in the European Union is similar. Serbia has been officially a candidate country for EU membership since 2012, and Ukraine is one of the associated countries.

Population potential of Hungary, as the source of economic position in Europe is one of the crucial determinants of the industrial development of a country. The key conditions for the prospective development of the state should not take into account the potential and proper population development. The starting element, however, is the dynamics of changes in the number of people, assessed in relation to other countries. However, the demographic, social and professional structure of the population also determines the developmental characteristics of the population. Such an assessment of the demographic situation is of most importance as the European Union strives for a sustainable development based on knowledge, technological progress, innovation and better use of the achievements of modern science and civilization changes. It is also meant to be a development that will reduce social inequalities and exclusion in various dimensions of the social order, reducing poverty and improving the living conditions of the population (Table 2).

Table 2. Demographical situation of Hungary and Russia compared to the selected countries (Lach and Wendt, 2019, p. 760)

Country	2006	2011	2018	Position in the world
Hungary	9 981 334	9 976 062	9 825 704	93
Poland	38 536 869	38 533 299	38 420 687	37
Slovakia	5 439 448	5 477 038	5 445 040	118
Czechia	10 235 455	10 190 213	10 686 269	85
Russia	142 893 540	138 739 892	145 734 776	9

The research results presented in the table mean that in the twenty-first century, a population decline by 1.5% was recorded in Hungary. On the other hand, among the remaining countries of the Visegrad Group (V4), a noticeable population growth was found only in the Czech Republic (4.0). In contrast, Russia has recorded a population increase of 1.9%. This means that after joining the European Union, the population development of Hungary is slower compared to Russia. This relatively weakens Hungary's position on the population map, although experts say that the dynamics of population change itself is not the most important, as the structural characteristics of the population also count, which in the long run may limit or slow down the country's social and economic development.

Another indicator of the population potential is the percentage of married people. Hungary and Russia, among others, are the countries where less than half of the population (aged 20 and over) are legally married. However, the highest percentage (over 60%) was recorded in Poland, Cyprus, Malta, Greece and Romania.

Next parameter of state power is the average life expectancy of the population. In Western Europe and the Scandinavian countries, life expectancy is several years longer than in the countries of Central Europe. Men in Europe have the shortest life in Russia (average 63.4 years), and women a little over 75 years. It is significant that in Russia, where the life expectancy is relatively low, the difference between men and women is exceptionally large (a span of 11.8 years. Moreover, Hungary has a very unfavorable age structure of the deceased, which is the result of premature mortality. In 2014, in Hungary, those who died under the age of 65 accounted for 25%, and in Poland, for example, this percentage accounted for as much as 28% of all the deceased (Eurostat, 2019).

The presented properties of the current and future demographic development of Hungary indicate that in terms of the dynamics of population development and changes in the population structure by age, the population potential will not be strengthened. Hungary's demographic future is characterized by the following weaknesses (EUROSTAT, 2019):
- the lowest dynamics of population growth and decrease in population,
- the eduction of the working age population (potential labor resources),
- one of the lowest generation replacement rates,
- one of the highest mortality rates,
- one of the fastest population aging processes.

These demographic trends and the features of the demographic development of Hungary are therefore an important challenge for the state and should therefore be taken into account when designing and implementing a security and sustainable development strategy for the coming decades.

The contemporary political system in Hungary was shaped as a result of the process of socio-political transformations at the turn of the 1980s and 1990s. From the formal and legal point of view, the constitution of August 1949 is in force in Hungary, while due to the scope of the changes made in October 1989, it is de facto a new constitution. By the act of October 18, 1989, the number of chapters was increased from the previous 10 to 15, and of the previous 78 articles, only 8 remained unamended. Later, the constitution was amended several times (1990, 1993, twice in 1994, 1997, 2000 and 2001). The changes concerned, among others, the rights of national minorities, the composition of the Constitutional Tribunal and the use of armed forces in the country and in foreign operations.

The Hungarian constitution consists of 78 articles, divided into 15 chapters, which lists the basic goals of the amendments being introduced: a multi-party system, parliamentary democracy and social market economy. According to the constitution, Hungary is an independent, democratic state ruled by law, where all power belongs to the people (art. 2). An important element enabling the nation to exercise direct power is a referendum, for which a decision of the National Assembly is required, adopted by a majority of 2/3 votes of all deputies (Art. 28 / B). The Constitution retained the republican form of the state (Art. 1). It emphasizes the inviolability of fundamental human rights (Article 8), and the offices of the Parliamentary Ombudsman and Parliamentary Ombudsman for National and Ethnic Minorities (Article 32 / B) were established for their protection. The constitution guarantees the classic separation of powers into legislative, executive and judicial. An analysis of the dependencies between the most important authorities allows us to state that Hungary has developed a parliamentary-cabinet system with a very strong position of the prime minister.

In 2010, after Fidesz party won the elections, Viktor Orban took power in the country mired in crisis. At that time, the government's priority in foreign policy was the so-called opening to the east. These actions sparked serious controversy abroad, especially among Hungary's main partners in the west. This has led to a cooling off of relations with Hungary's western allies. According to its assumptions, in the face of the economic crisis among traditional partners in the West and the growing position of eastern countries, Hungary should open up to cooperation with emerging economic powers. Initially, the policy of "opening to the east" covered only the countries of Central Asia, the Persian Gulf and the Far East, led by China, but over time, Russia was included in this group of countries. The policy of "opening to the east" quickly showed its limitations. First, countries such as China and Saudi Arabia were not interested in financing the debt of foreign countries without seeing a clear political interest in it. Secondly, the announcements of the Hungarian government about the quick effects of "opening to the east" have not come true. Although it may bring beneficial effects in the long term in the form of diversification of Hungarian exports, European markets will remain the main direction for a long time, where 76% of exports are currently directed (only 6% to Asian countries) (Eurostat, 2019).

In the past, the right wing was dominated by a skeptical attitude towards Russia, resulting also from the important role played in Fidesz's political identity by the fight against communism and the memory of the anti-Soviet uprising of 1956. During Orban's first government in 1998–2002, relations with Moscow were almost frozen. When there was a rapprochement with Russia in the next eight years during the rule of the left, it was heavily criticized by Fidesz, and Orbán described Hungary's consent to the participation of the South Stream project as an attack against the Hungarian people. After the right wing came to power, however, the Hungarian-Russian rapprochement continued. Budapest sustained its involvement in Gazprom's flagship project, and in October 2012 a final investment decision was issued to build a section of the South Stream gas pipeline through Hungary.

Hungary under the rule of Viktor Orbán enhanced energy cooperation with Russia, one of the manifestations of which was the concluded intergovernmental agreement on cooperation in the field of nuclear energy, confirming the decision to expand the Hungarian nuclear power plant in Paks in cooperation with the Russians. The power plant produces approximately 52% of Hungary's electricity. The investment is to cost EUR 10–12.5 billion and will last until 2026; 80% will be financed by the Russian company "Rosatom". The expansion of Hungary's only nuclear power plant in Paks is not the only example of Hungary's cooperation with Russia. In addition to energy cooperation, political relations have also intensified, and recently Hungary has begun to call for unfrozen cooperation between the European Union and Russia.

The aim of Hungary's current economic strategy, striving to its opening to the east, is to reduce the dependence of the Hungarian economy on trade with the West. When Viktor Orbán won the parliamentary elections again in May 2018, he declared that he would like to stay in power until at least 2030. By then, Hungary would become one of the top five countries in the European Union. Despite these declarations, the Hungarian government realizes that Hungary is doomed to economic cooperation primarily with the countries of the European Union of which it is a member. At the same time, Orban offered an intensive cooperation to the Pannonian Basin countries, intending to make this region "the safest, fastest-growing, unified economic, trade and transport area" (Obucina, 2020).

Hungary is an emerging market with a free market economy which, like other countries in the former Eastern bloc, underwent a transformation in the 1990s from a centrally planned economy to a free market economy. The Hungarian economy is currently ranked 56th in terms of GDP and 58th in the world in terms of GDP measured in purchasing power parity (Table 3).

Table 3. Gross GDP of Hungary and Russia compared to other countries in the region (International Monetary Fund (A), 2019)

Country	GDP [USD mln]			
	2000	2010	2018	Position in the world
Hungary	47 311	130 923	161 182	56
Poland	171 276	479 161	585 816	22
Slovakia	20 691	89 662	106 573	61
Czechia	61 645	207 478	245 226	45
Russia	278 498	1 635 717	1 657 290	12

Table 3 displays a significant difference in gross domestic product between Hungary and Russia, which in the case of Hungary accounts for approximately 10% of Russia's GDP. The substantial disproportion is also evidenced by the position taken by both countries in the global perspective (Hungary 56, Russia 12). An even greater disproportion occurs in the case of GDP according to the purchasing power parity of GDP, where Russia is placed 6th and Hungary is 58th. Here is the graphical representation of the presented indicators (Figure 1).

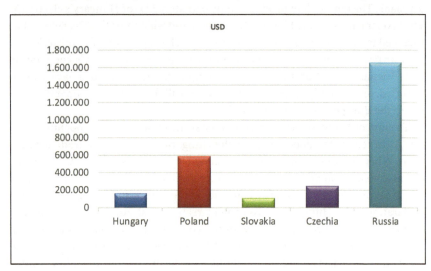

Figure 1. Gross GDP of Hungary and Russia compared to the other countries of the region.

A significant indicator of the state's potential (strength) is defined by gross domestic product per capita (Table 4).

Table 4. Gross GDP per capita of Hungary and Russia compared to other countries in the region (International Monetary Fund (B), 2019)

Country	GDP per capita (in USD)			
	2000	2010	2018	Position in the world
Hungary	4 628	13 074	16 484	51
Poland	4 476	12 602	15 426	56
Slovakia	3 833	16 634	19 579	42
Czechia	5 998	19 831	23 113	40
Russia	1 904	11 447	11 289	62

In 2018, countries with a high level of economic development included those countries, where the value of GNI per capita was USD 12 376 and more (Statistical Yearbook, p. 736). Table 4 shows quite different conclusions than in the case of the total GDP of the country. The analysis of the contents shows that in this case the relationship is opposite and the value of GDP per capita in Hungary is at a level 46% higher than that of a Russian citizen. This is also evidenced by the comparison of the positions taken by both countries in the global perspective (Hungary 51, Russia 62). The situation is similar in the case of comparing GDP according to the purchasing power parity of GDP per capita, where Russia is ranked 51st and Hungary is 46th. The presentation of GDP per capita is of a bar chart (Figure 2).

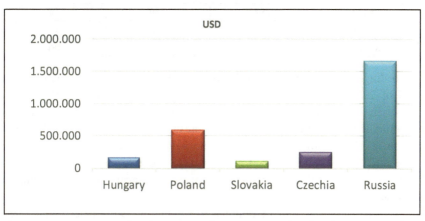

Figure 2. Gross GDP per capita of Hungary and Russia compared to the other countries of the region.

Another indicator of state power concerns the volume of foreign trade turnover, which includes the volume of imports and exports in individual countries of the region (Table 5).

Table 5. Foreign trade turnover of Hungary and Russia compared to other countries in the region in 2018 (Lach and Wendt, 2019, p. 564)

Country	Turnover in 2018 (PLN mln)		
	Import	Export	Saldo
Hungary	15724,0	25355,7	+9631,7
Poland	97083,1	95132,4	−19507,0
Slovakia	17507,9	24643,4	+7135,5
Czechia	33422,7	60653,0	+27230,3
Russia	692906,0	28796,6	−40494,0

The compilation displays that the volume of Russian imports is approximately 4.4 times higher than that of Hungary, and the volume of exports is similar. Yet another indicator of state power determines the remuneration of citizens (Table 6).

Table 6. Net monthly salary per person in Hungary and Russia compared to other countries in the region (EUROSTAT, 2019)

Country	Monthly salary in 2018 (in Euro)		
	Average	Minimum	Position in Europe
Hungary	726	445	25
Poland	846	503	22
Slovakia	894	480	19
Czechia	948	478	17
Russia	450	125	bd

According to the Russian Statistical Office, the average salary in Russia in the first half of 2019 was PLN 42,000. rubles (the equivalent of PLN 2.5 thousand). However, the spread of earnings between large urban centers and the province is gigantic. If in Moscow the average salary at that time was almost 80,000 rubles (about PLN 4.8 thousand), in Kabardino-Balkaria or Dagestan it is only 25 thousand. rubles (about PLN 1.5 thousand) (Rzeczpospolita). The presented comparison shows that the average net salary in Hungary is over 60% than in Russia.

In conclusion, one may be tempted to say that a medium size country, including Hungary, does not have to be weak. It may turn out to be an important and even a strong economic player in a global perspective in various areas. When assessing the potential of Hungary, taking into account the basic parameters such as population and size of the territory, it turns out that it is a country belonging to the group of middle-class countries. Compared to the Russian Federation, it is difficult to find a common denominator. Russia is the largest country in the world in terms of area, and one of the largest in terms of population (6th place). However, it is important to understand that the power of the state depends not only on the above-mentioned parameters, but also other indicators are assessed, taking into account such components as the manner of conducting domestic and foreign policy (Sułek, 2011, p. 13; Lach, 2014, p. 19).

The quality of this policy is a derivative of a number of different factors, such as the real economic potential, geographic location, type and stability of the political system, existing and internationally perceived state institutions and the way internal society is organized. An example of such an understanding of state power can be an attempt to compare countries with similar demographic potential, such as Hungary and the Czech Republic. The conducted research shows that the potential of Hungary does not differ much from that of the Czech Republic. Belonging to the same group in terms of area and population, they also have similar indicators in terms of potential. This allows us to conclude that unfavorable geographic parameters cause Hungary to be a middle-class country, but its position measured by real power (Sułek, 2015, pp. 27–28) causes Hungary to be perceived as a country playing a significant role internationally.

The geographic location of Hungary somehow forces us to look at its position in relation to the powerful state that is undoubtedly the Russian Federation. When attempting to assess the geopolitical situation of the Russian Federation in relation to Hungary, it is justified to define the parameters on which it should be conducted. These can be, for example, measurable parameters indicating the amount of resources or economic possibilities.

When analyzing and assessing the figures for Hungary and the Russian Federation, no unequivocal conclusions should be drawn. Firstly, Hungary, as a single state, is not an economic or military competitor to Russia. The awareness of this fact is present among Hungarian politicians and hence their activities aimed at strengthening political and military ties with the widely understood West, materialized in the form of the European Union and NATO. These two basic conclusions, in a way, direct the geopolitics of the Russian Federation towards Hungary. As a consequence of this situation, various political, economic and, in a sense military, activities aimed at, among others, Hungary are carried out by the authorities of the Russian Federation.

Secondly, it should be recognized that all activities of the Russian Federation have one major strategic goal in the geopolitical area. It is the rebuilding of the world empire. To achieve this goal, it is necessary to neutralize the United States, inter alia, by displacing its military and economic influence from Europe. After this stage is completed, the ultimate goal of the activities of the Russian Federation is to build three geopolitical axes: Moscow – Berlin, Moscow – Tehran and Moscow – Tokyo (Sykulski 2013, pp. 353–356; Sykulski, 2019, p. 31).

Thirdly, the Russian Federation uses the entire range of available instruments subordinated to the state administration, as well as nominally independent or private enterprises that are practically under the influence of state authorities, to achieve its strategic geopolitical goal. This applies in the first place to the intelligence and security services, diplomacy, the Armed Forces of the Russian Federation, state and private enterprises, as well as other scientific and economic organizations operating in the Russian Federation (Sułek, 2011; Kobryński, 2015).

Fourthly, the very close business relations between Orban's Hungary and Russia result from the conditions Orban found when taking power in 2010. From high-profile cases, they were, among others negotiations on the purchase of shares of the Russian "Surgutneftegaz" in the Hungarian state-owned energy company "Mol". The negotiations on increasing the purchase of (cheaper) gas from the West at the expense of that purchased from Gazprom had a similar political background. In both of these cases, Moscow has put political goals ahead of business goals. Orban and the Hungarians who sympathize with him remain alone in the construction of the Hungarian "national democracy", despite the fact that referring to national and Christian roots is not uncommon today. However, it seems that the government in Budapest has assumed that this "loneliness" is the price of independence. Therefore, not necessarily being "Moscow's agent" may push Hungary to destructive moves, but putting freedom of movement above all else in relations with other countries (Grajczyński 2018).

Fifthly, Russia has been the most important goal of the policy of opening to the East for Hungary for ten years. According to the Hungarian minister of foreign affairs, Hungary lost $ 8 billion by imposing sanctions on Russia in export. In 2018, he stressed that prior to the imposition of sanctions in 2014, annual trade with Russia amounted to $ 10 billion, and last year it was $ 6.7 billion. Both countries with a complex history of each other are trading partners once again, but Russia is more interested in having Hungary on its side in terms of sanctions and, more importantly, in terms of the Russian energy sector. Among other things, in 2020, the construction of the South TurkStream pipeline will be completed. Although only 15 kilometers will pass through Hungary, energy cooperation with Russia is a priority for them, as Russia provides about 60 percent of the total Hungarian demand for crude oil and 50 percent for natural gas (Obućina, 2020).

Taking into account the political, military and, above all, economic conditions, the Russian Federation uses its full potential to achieve its geopolitical goals. This is about intelligence, military and diplomatic potential (Sykulski, 2019). The Armed Forces of the Russian Federation, state and private enterprises, and all scientific and research institutions and even universities all of them, regardless of formal ownership or subordination, are dependent on the central authority and implement its policy. In turn, the existing global conditions characteristic of the first half of the 21st century require the Russian Federation to conduct geopolitics in relation to the European Union and the North Atlantic Alliance, including Hungary, in a veiled manner. It is based on the fact that all kinds of information policy tools are used, including internet portals, TV stations and other electronic media. They are co-created and financed by the power structures of the Russian Federation, and their task is to disseminate content that shapes the image of reality in line with the Kremlin's policy goals.

The activities of intelligence services, propaganda agencies, diplomatic missions and economic organizations are aimed at creating in some countries, including Hungary, an economic and political situation in line with the interests of the Russian Federation. In practice, this can take place, for example, by interfering with the election process. Such a situation, although not fully confirmed, took place during the last presidential ballot in the United States. In addition, the activities of the above-mentioned services strive to build a business infrastructure operating in accordance with the interests of the Russian Federation.

The Security Service of the Russian Federation, in consultation with the intelligence services, also deals with the manipulation and disinformation of public opinion, as well as with intelligence penetration of key opinion-forming centers and state authorities. There are also activities that inspire and escalate social conflicts and tensions in international relations.

Each time the selection of specific measures, methods and areas of influence depends on the specificity of a given state, with particular emphasis on its role and importance in the implementation of the strategic goals of the Russian Federation. In view of the above, the activities of the Russian Federation in the area of geopolitics, aimed at Hungary, are each time adequate to the goal that is to be achieved. As an almost certainty, it should be assumed that some instruments are universal and apply not only to Hungary, but also to other member states of the European Union and NATO. This may consist in creating confusion and destabilizing the social and political situation in individual countries. In relation to Hungary, it is symptomatic that the long-standing historical disputes between Slovakia and Hungary are heated.

In the 21st century, Central Europe and the Western Balkans remain the priority area of geopolitical activity of the Russian Federation. This area is considered a kind of strategic foreground of the Russian Empire. As a result, the above-mentioned methods and techniques of influence are used in this region in a long-term perspective, as they exert a significant influence on key political processes that determine the geopolitical situation in the region. In the long term, they are intended to allow them to take control of these countries, including Hungary, and drag them into the sphere of influence of the Russian Federation.

One of the traditional tools in shaping geopolitics by the Russian Federation has been and is the use of tensions between national minorities and individual ethnic groups. Russia is also involved in creating geopolitics and controlling religious conflicts. This is done by making up specific events and skillfully fueling them. This is evident, for example, in Hungary, where disputes are fanned with the Slovak minority in Hungary and vice versa with the Hungarian minority in Slovakia. It is no coincidence that the intelligence expansion of the Russian Federation in recent years has coincided with the revival and intensification of hostile attitudes of Hungarians towards the Slovak minority, and thus the deterioration of relations between these countries, although both countries are neighbors, members of the Visegrad Group, belong to common blocs political and military. In the recent past, in 2008, it even happened that the Hungarian Prime Minister Ferenc Gyurcsány canceled his visit to Slovakia in response to the insult of the Hungarian King Stephen I Saint. In the European Union, this is an almost unprecedented occurrence (Pawlicki, 2008).

References

(2019) EUROSTAT, Urząd Statystyczny Unii Europejskiej, Wydawnictwo Eurostat.

(2019) Hungarian Central Statistical Office (KSH).

(2019) Międzynarodowy Fundusz Walutowy (A), Gross domestic product, World Economic Outlook Database.

(2019) Międzynarodowy Fundusz Walutowy (B), Gross domestic product per capita, World Economic Outlook Database.

Balazs K., Faulkner W. and Schimank U., (1995). Transformation of the Research Systems of Post-Communist Central and Eastern Europe in: "Social Studies of Science", 25(4), Ed. SAGE Publications.

Grajczyński Ł., (2018). Czy Węgry rozsadzą Trójmorze? Uwagi na marginesie relacji węgiersko-ukraińskich, Wyd. Portal społeczno-polityczny "Jagiellonia.org".

Lach Z., Wendt J., (eds.), (2019). Geopolityka. Elementy teorii, wybrane metody i badania. Wyd. GUS, Rocznik statystyczny Rzeczypospolitej Polskiej, Warszawa: Wydawnictwo GUS.

Obućina V., (2020). Węgry coraz bardziej otwarte na wschód, https://forsal.pl/artykuly/1 450300,wegry-coraz-bardziej-otwarte-na-wschod-cel-zmniejszyc-zaleznosc-od-zachod u.html.

Pawlicki J., O co kłócą się Węgrzy i Słowacy, https://wyborcza.pl/1,75399,5227818, O_co _kloca_sie_Wegrzy_i_Slowacy.html.

Rzeczpospolita, https://www.rp.pl/Spoleczenstwo/306249923-Rosjanie-nie-chca-krocej-pr acowac-Boja-sie-utraty-zarobkow.html.

Skiba L., Rapkiewicz M. and Kędzierski M., (eds.), (2014). Węgry Orbana – wzór czy przestroga, Warszawa: Instytut Sobieskiego.

Sułek M., (2011). Metodyka analizy geopolitycznej (na przykładzie potęgometrii) "Przegląd Geopolityczny" tom 3, Polskie Towarzystwo Geopolityczne.

Sułek M., Kobryński R., (2015). Potęga 2015: międzynarodowy układ sił w procesie zmian: raport potęgometryczny Warszawa: Polskie Towarzystwo Geopolityczne.

Sykulski L., (2013). Integracja polityczna Eurazji we współczesnej rosyjskiej myśli geopolitycznej, in: P. Eberhardt (eds.), Studia nad geopolityką XX wieku, "Prace Geograficzne" nr 242.

Sykulski L., (2019). Rosyjska geopolityka a wojna informacyjna, Warszawa: PWN.

Włodkowska-Bagan A., (2015). Środki i metody polityki zagranicznej państw średniej rangi. (in:) J. Zając, A. Włodkowska-Bagan, M. Kaczmarski (eds.), Bezpieczeństwo międzynarodowe. Polska–Europa–Świat. Warszawa: Wydawnictwo UW.

Sławomir Byłeń

Chapter 38: The geostrategic position of Hungary in the Kremlin's foreign vital influence

The subdisciplines of geopolitics, which include geostrategy, geoeconomics, geohistory, astropolitics; astrostrategy; geoculture and geoecology deal with the study of detailed geopolitical issues. Today, geostrategic issues are the subject of both theoretical and practical considerations, especially in the context of the implementation of international policy and external security in global, regional and national dimensions.

Terminology encompassing geostrategic issues is often combined with geopolitics, and sometimes the interdependencies between these terms are shown. An example may be the recognition of geostrategy as a sub-discipline of geopolitics (Sykulski, 2013, p. 35) or the treatment of geopolitics and geostrategy as two equal subjects in political science (Baczwarow and Suliborski, 2002, pp. 44–54). On the other hand, some specialists believe that geostrategy is superior to geopolitics (Dybczyński, 2013, pp. 77–81). Considering the content promoted by various authors, it can be concluded that geostrategy is nowadays perceived as geopolitics related to wartime or through the prism of military potential.

This understanding of geostrategy is commonly used nowadays, although it should be noted that today's geostrategy has not only a military dimension, but is also ubiquitous in considering economic issues (Ištok et al., 2016 pp. 109-119). There are also views indicating that geostrategy should be seen as a part of geopolitics that focuses on issues related to competition or rivalry between the two sides in terms of both peace and war. Taking into account the above content, it seems legitimate to assume that geostrategy primarily relates to issues directly or indirectly concerning military aspects.

The subject of geostrategic analyzes in relation to Hungary should therefore be the current geopolitical conditions related to security issues. These analyzes will be necessary to assess the demographic, economic and military potential in relation to other countries, including the Russian Federation. The results of the conducted assessments seem necessary to specify economic strategies, military doctrines and to outline national interests, the fulfillment of which is necessary for the functioning of the state in the first decades of the 21st century. Therefore, it can be assumed that geostrategy in relation to Hungary should be the basis for defining assumptions for conducting foreign policy, taking into account the geopolitical environment in which the country exists and functions. Hungary, as well as other countries of Central and Eastern Europe, are obliged to adopt a geostrategic policy that takes into account the existing contemporary geopolitical conditions.

Bearing in mind the theoretical foundations describing the meaning of the term geostrategy and the subject of research, one should presume that the aim of the study is to present, verify and assess the geostrategic situation of Hungary in relation to the current assumptions, concepts and geostrategic views of the Russian Federation. In order to achieve such a specific goal, this chapter attempts to solve two fundamental research problems. The first was formulated in the form of a question: What military and economic potential do Hungary and the Russian Federation have to shape the national geostrategy? The second research problem is checking: Can the military potential of the Russian Federation affect the functioning of Hungary as an independent state and to what extent?

In an attempt to solve the research problems defined above, the research used empirical research methods: firstly, a critical analysis of the literature on the subject of the research, and secondly, an analysis of source documents concerning the geostrategic situation of Hungary in comparison with the Russian Federation. The method of synthesis and inference methods, which are the final product of previously conducted analyzes, were applied here.

Geostrategic factors are nothing more than a system of interrelated and mutually conditioned premises, the inclusion of which results in a specific, concrete effect, in line with the expectations of the authorities. However, it should be remembered that geostrategy is an extremely complex issue, as it must take into account a number of various factors that affect foreign policy, encompassing the real international environment. In theoretical studies one can find that these factors could be classified into two groups. One is causative factors and the other is determinant ones. Both of them contain various environmental variables, the occurrence of which may be favorable or difficult to achieve political and geostrategic goals (Zięba, 2004, p. 17).

The geostrategic situation of a given country, bloc, coalition or military alliances should be assessed consulting many different factors, criteria and parameters. According to the views of experts in the field of military security, the criteria presented in Table 1 are most often adopted to assess the situation.

Table 1. The assessment criteria of a geostrategic situation of a country

No.	Criterion	Indicator	Remarks
1	Territory size	Area / countrty	km^2
2	Population	Number/ country	persons
3	Average employment	Number	persons/km^2
4	Volume of GDP	GDP	Bn $ gross
5	Volume of GDP per capita	GDP per capita	USD/person gross
6	Defence expenditure	Number	USD bn
7	Defence expenditure per capita	Number	USD/person
8	Size of the armed forces	Number of soldiers	In mln
9	Number of soldiers per 1000 inhabitans	Number of soldiers	Per 1000 inhabitants
10	Number of soldiers per 100 km^2	Area	Soldiers km^2
11	Number of tanks	Number	Items
12	Number of armoured personnel carrier	Number	Items
13	Number of aircrafts	Number	Items

In theoretical studies, one can also come across the view that an important factor determining the foreign policy of a given country is the understanding of the international environment by its own society, the ruling elite and its attitude towards other countries. These determinants are a derivative of the level of political culture, education, perceived value system, religious beliefs and the views of a society. One should also not forget about the importance of historical experiences, which play an important role in relation to the functioning of the state (Łoś, 2007, p. 15).

It is also positive that both Serbia and Ukraine participate in the PfP (Partnership for Peace) program and Austria remains a neutral country. The program defines a special type of relationship between NATO member states and aspiring countries in order to ensure international order and security as well as stabilization in Europe. The situation regarding the membership of these countries in the European Union is similar. Serbia has been officially a candidate for EU membership since 2012, and Ukraine is one of the associated countries.

Another parameter to be assessed concerns the population potential, which is the source of both the economic and military position of the state, including Hungary. The determinants of the country's military security should therefore not ignore the population potential. The starting element, however, is the dynamics of changes in the number of people, assessed in the comparison to other countries.

Another indicator of the state's power concerns the volume of foreign trade turnover, which includes the volume of imports and exports in individual countries of the region. The military potential of Hungary and other countries in the region should be analyzed on several levels:
- in terms of its own military power – Hungary, like any other country in the Central and Eastern Europe region, does not belong to the group of superpowers or strong supra-regional players. Only Poland, at the time of admission to NATO (1999) and the EU (2004), could be considered a country capable of a limited repulsion of an attack on its territory from its eastern neighbor, as well as a significant participation in international missions;
- in terms of replenishing the potential of the EU and NATO – the countries of this region, including Hungary, were above all recipients of security than its co-authors (Stolarczyk, 1995, pp. 32–64). However, even a relatively strong country (such as Poland) needed supplies of modern equipment; the modernization and adaptation of the armed forces to NATO standards had to be spread not even over years – but over decades. On the other hand, weaker countries, such as the Baltic States demanded providing them with international military aid and embracing them with foreign support (e.g. the "Air Policing" mission);
- in terms of the geographic location of the countries belonging to the former Eastern bloc, the advantages seem obvious. The admission of Hungary and other Central European countries enlarged NATO's area and removed the borders beyond which the alliance could be attacked, which was of great importance to the "old members" of NATO. While the admission of eastern Germany (1990) shifted the NATO border from the Elbe to the Oder and the shifting of the border from the Oder to the Bug (1999), the subsequent accession to NATO reduced the threat from Russia (Baltic republics) and reduced instability in the Balkans (Slovenia, Croatia, Montenegro, North Macedonia).

At the time of the democratic changes in 1989, the Hungarian armed forces numbered 120,000 soldiers with quite modern weapons. From then on, the condition of the military equipment deteriorated. Successive governments refused to buy armament because the purchases themselves were considered too expensive, and the tenders were complicated and difficult to implement in a transparent manner. Currently, the Hungarian armed forces have about 30,000 soldiers, of which only 23,000 are on active service, and only about 4,000 are ready to participate in military missions in the country or abroad. The weakness of the army was especially revealed during the construction of the controversial wall on the southern border of the country in 2015, when it turned out that the army was unable to cope with this task and therefore prisoners were brought in for the construction of it (Hypś, 2019).

In 1999, Hungary, along with Poland and the Czech Republic, joined NATO and, as agreed by the alliance, should spend at least 2% of GDP on defense. However, in the following years, it fell to just 1.1% of GDP in 2017. Moreover, Hungary was not the only country that did not meet this criterion. Upon assuming the office of the President of the United States, Donald Tramp began to systematically call on European countries, including Hungary, to increase defense spending, threatening to make possible US military assistance dependent on it in the event of a threat. It has become clear that reform of the Hungarian military system is essential and requires a swift action.

In order to counteract this situation, in 2017 the Hungarian government initiated a program of modernization of the armed forces called "Zrínyi 2026". The plan assumes an annual increase in the defense budget by 0.1% of GDP, so as to achieve the desired 2% of GDP for defense in 2026. The second goal of the reform is to increase the number of active service soldiers to 37,650 in 2026 (Hypś, 2019). In addition, to increase the number of personnel, the program primarily provides for the modernization and technical modernization of weapons. One of the assumptions of the "Zrínyi 2026" plan is also to restart some of the arms production in Hungary. The first steps have already been made by purchasing licenses for the production of BREN 2 carbines, Scorpion Evo 3 submachine guns and P-07 and P-09 semi-automatic pistols from Česka Zbrojovka. At the start of the modernization program, fourteen JAS 39 Gripen fighters, leased from Sweden, were the basis of Hungarian combat aviation. In the first half of 2018, the aviation plant in Saint Petersburg renovated and modernized the Mi-24W and Mi-24P attack helicopters owned by Hungary. The total cost was $ 36 million and will keep the helicopters in service until 2024. In addition, in 2018 Hungary ordered twenty Airbus145M multi-role helicopters and sixteen French Caracals.

In addition to the technical modernization of the air force, the purchase of modern weapons also included armored weapons, including tanks and self-propelled howitzers. Until now, the basis of the Hungarian armored forces were T-72M tanks, which do not meet the requirements of the modern battlefield. Among others, in 2018, Hungary signed a contract for the purchase of the Leopard 2 main battle tanks and the PzH 2000 self-propelled gun howitzers and six Bergepanzer 3 technical support vehicles (Hypś, 2019). Under the agreement, Hungary will receive forty-four Leopard 2A7 + tanks and twenty-four 155-millimeter PzH 2000 self-propelled howitzers. Additionally, Germany will deliver twelve used Leopard 2A4s from the manufacturer's inventory, which will be engaged to train crews and mechanics (Hypś 2019).

When comparing the potential of both countries, the author accepted data published by the GlobalFirepower.com website as reliable, which is considered a company that publishes prestigious rankings of militarily important countries. It is characteristic that the list is not only based on strictly military data. The Global Firepower website explains that it examines fifty-five very different factors for ranking purposes, including: the country's geographic conditions and population, financial capacity, industry, transportation infrastructure (roads, airports, ports) and oil resources.

On the other hand, the published "State Power Index" also takes into account other indicators, such as diplomatic, cultural or financial activity. The state power index is a report that is created on the basis of data collected from knowledge repositories, including World Bank, the "International Peace Research Institute" (SIPRI), and the magazine "Forbes". The power of states analyzed in the report takes into account the sum of economic capital, military potential, diplomatic strength, area, human resources, popularity of culture, natural resources and energy security of a given country. The State Power Index ranges from 0 to 100 points.

The above-cited rankings have been selected for their versatility. Based on the reports presented in the "Globalfire power" (GFP) and "State Power Index" (IMP) reports, it can be indicated that the countries of Central Europe, including Hungary (except Poland) occupy distant places in the rankings of military power and potential (Table 2).

Table 2. Comparison of the military potential of Hungary and Russia against the background of selected countries of the world (http://www.globalfirepower.com)

Comparison of military potential				
No.	Global Fire Power (GFP) (127 countries)	Position in the world	State Power Index (SPI) (168 countries)	Position in the world
1.	USA	1	USA	1
2.	Russia	2	China	2
3.	China	3	Russia	3
4.	India	4	India	4
5.	France	5	Germany	5
6.	Great Britain	6	Great Britain	6
7.	Germany	9	France	7
8.	Poland	18	Poland	27
9.	Czechia	31	Czechia	68
10.	Hungary	63	Hungary	81
11.	Slovakia	74	Slovakia	96

Comparing the military potentials of Hungary and the Russian Federation, the following conclusions emerge from both rankings (Radwan, Arak and Lewicki, 2020):
- Hungary is unable to conduct an independent security policy on its own;
- Poland, as the only state in the Central European region, may try, without prejudging its effectiveness, to pursue an independent, active security policy. The other countries in the region are far too weak for that;
- Central Europe as a region can only attempt to act together and if it can jointly articulate its own interests, both on the European scale and in the supra-regional dimension, it can build its own subjectivity;
- Hungary, in comparison with Russia, the USA, China and India, is difficult to be compared to the rank of major countries of medium size in terms of ensuring military security.

Firstly, the relative military weakness of Hungary and other Central European states is demonstrated by the problem of technical modernization of its own armed forces. Apart from Poland, these countries possess modest defense budgets. Secondly, these states have not developed a method of purchasing modern equipment jointly, despite the fact that its standardization would reduce both the purchase costs and the subsequent operation or servicing. Thirdly, these countries do not cooperate with each other even in the repairs of older types of equipment, inherited from the membership in the Warsaw Pact, where the basic technical solutions would be common, the fear of revealing some secrets would be negligible, and the benefits of cooperation would be measurable (Table 3).

Table 3. Defense expenditure of Hungary and Russia compared to the countries of the former Eastern Bloc as of 2015 (in USD million) (https://www.sipri.org; www.globalfirepower.com)[1]

Country	1999	2004	2009	2013	2016	2017	Wzrost
Bulgaria	779	894	839	740	756	700	0,89
Czechia	2433	2687	2298	1669	1923	2220	0,91
Estonia	134	268	398	398	494	335	2,50
Lithuania	200	344	352	294	634	430	2,15
Latvia	97	311	309	239	406	280	2,88
Poland	5334	5897	7265	7709	9791	9360	1,80

---

1 Military expenditure of the states is calculated in million USD at fixed prices and exchange rates of 2015, except for the last column which is expressed in million USD at prices and exchange rates of 2016. For Russia, SIPRI estimates are provided.

Table 3 (Continued)

Country	1999	2004	2009	2013	2016	2017	Wzrost
Romania	1902	2095	2052	2047	2816	2190	1,15
Slovakia	930	1087	1183	805	1036	1025	1,10
Hungary	1261	1668	1249	1021	1258	1040	0,82
Russia	15548	27536	43458	57500	70345	69245	4,45

The Final Global Firepower Ranking below uses more than 50 individual factors to determine a country's PowerIndex Score ("PwrIndx") in terms ranging from military power and finance to logistics capability and geography. According to this ranking, for 2020, Poland is in 21st place out of 138 countries included in the annual GFP review. It has a PwrIndx of 0.3397, where 0.0000 is considered "ideal"; Hungary PwrIndx: 0.8215 (54th), Russia PwrIndx: 2nd 0.0681, the Czech Republic PwrIndx: 0.5531 (34 m), Slovakia 58th, Index PwrInd 0, 8466) (www.-globalfirepower.com).

When reviewing the geostrategic situation in terms of Hungary's military potential compared with that of the Russian Federation, one fundamental conclusion emerges. Individual figures, including defense spending (Figure 1) shows the overwhelming advantage of the military potential of the Russian Federation over Hungary.

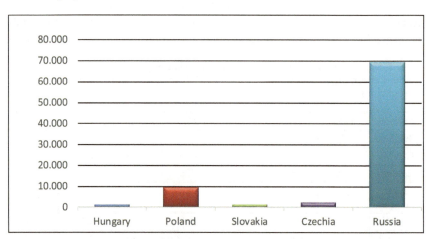

Figure 1. Spending of Hungary and Russia compared to other countries in the region.

It is clear that Russia's potential is many times greater than the Hungarian one and is able to dominate a country like Hungary. Such a statement results, inter alia, from the recent actions of the Russian Federation, e.g. in Ukraine or in the Caucasus region (e.g. Georgia), which proves that the Russian Federation is deliberately engaged in a geostrategic dimension, allowing the Russian Federation to exert influence on security in every selected region of Europe. Table 4 presents a comparison of the military potential of both countries in terms of the basic indicators for assessing the geostrategic situation.

Table 4. Comparison of the military potential of Hungary and the Russian Federation (Hypś, 2019; Armed Forces Personnel, www.globalfirepower.com)

No.	Specification	Hungary	Russian Federation	Ratio
1	National defence expenditure ($ bn)	1, 040	69,245	1:66
2	National defence expenditure per capita ($)	105	476	1:4,53
3	Size of the armed forces (soldiers)	25 000	1 454 000	1:58
4	Number of soldiers per 1000 inhabitants	2,5	9,9	1:3,96
5	Number of solider per 100 km2 of an area	0,26	0,11	1:0,42
6	Number of tanks	32	2200	1:68
7	Number of armoured personel carrier	1123	6700	1:6
8	Artillery means	300	6500	1:22
9	Aircrafts	35	3600	1:103
10	Helicopters	12	1633	1:136

The comparison of the military potential of both countries in the system of ratio forces in terms of the main means of combat; presented in the figure (Figure 2).

The land forces of Hungary numbers 10,900 soldiers and approx. 30,000 reservists, the air force 5,600 soldiers, while the command and auxiliary forces are about 8,500 men. The armed forces, which have been professionally active since 2004, are supported by approx. 5,000 Territorial Defense volunteers, of whom there will be 20,000 in 2026. In 2015, the Hungarian Armed Forces were equipped with: 32 tanks, 1,123 armored personnel carriers, 300 towed artillery units and 65 multi-purpose rocket launchers. The Hungarian armed forces also had 12 helicopters and 35 aircrafts. Hungarians are trying to replace post-Soviet equipment with Western ones, so they borrowed 12 SAAB JAS 39 Gripen fighters from Sweden (until 2026). However, the rest of the combat aircraft are Soviet MiG-29s, and the transport aircraft are An-26. Recently, the Hungarian Ministry of National Defense bought 4 modernized MiGs from the Russians.

Defense spending in 2018 was set at USD 1.7 billion, which is 0.95%. GDP. While 30 percent of this amount was allocated to the supply and modernization

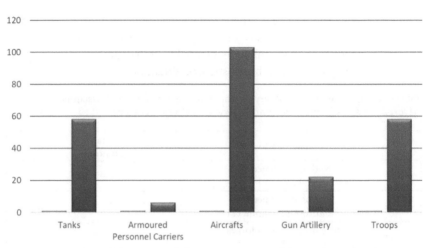

Figure 2. Comparison of the power ratio between Hungary and the Russian Federation.

of the armed forces. Hungarians are slowly increasing their defense budget: in 2017 it amounted to $ 1.21 billion, or 0.94%. GDP, and in 2022 it is expected to reach 1.4 percent. GDP. The level of defense spending proposed by the Alliance at 2% of GDP Hungary is planning to achieve in 2026 (Potocki, 2018).

Considering the above, there may be concerns about the geostrategic situation of Hungary in relation to the current foreign policy of the Russian Federation. In the event of a real threat, it is difficult to imagine a situation in which Hungary could be an opponent of the Russian Federation. It is enough to make a quantitative comparison of only some of the military parameters included in Table 4. The conducted research shows an unfavorable ratio for Hungary in all the compared indicators, ranging from 1 to 4.5 (national defense expenditure per capita) to 1 to 136, in the case of helicopters.

The presented figures do not reflect the full situation in terms of comparing the military potential of Hungary and the Russian Federation. On the part of the Russian Federation, it would be necessary to add elements of military potential that Hungary does not have. This includes: 2,038 nuclear warheads, 367 active warhead carriers, 130 tactical missile systems, 57 submarines and 191 surface watercraft, including 1 air cruiser, 4 cruisers, 15 destroyers, 4 frigates, and 78 corvettes.

Summing up, it can be said with full responsibility that the comparison of the geostrategic potential of Hungary and the Russian Federation is definitely to the disadvantage of the former. When making a kind of such a summary, it should be assessed that the differences in potential in every respect speak in favor of Russia. The situation changed dramatically with the accession of Hungary to the North Atlantic Treaty and the European Union. As a result, there is a military and economic power behind Hungary, which results in a relative sense of security, and military parameters no longer play a decisive role in considering Hungary's geostrategic situation in the context of its relations with the Russian Federation.

Answering the question "How is the comparison and assessment of the geostrategic situation of Hungary in relation to the Russian Federation shaped in the first decades of the 21st century?" one could state that it cannot be taken literally, taking into account only hard indicators. When assessing Hungary's geostrategic situation, one should also bear in mind other geopolitical conditions, including the membership in NATO and the EU. Only after encompassing these parameters it will be possible to unequivocally assess the geostrategic situation of Hungary

Experts and politicians agree that the Hungarian armed forces have been in a very bad condition for many years, and the situation is even worse compared to neighbors investing in modernization and other countries in the region. After the end of the Cold War, Hungarian politicians, as in other countries, were eager to believe that peace in Europe was achieved once and for all and that it was possible to take advantage of the peace dividend and use the saved money for other social purposes. The more so as Hungary lies in the middle of the continent – apart from weak Ukraine and a peaceful, neutral Austria, it is surrounded by NATO countries. The Russian illegal annexation of Crimea, the migration crisis, and the threat of classical and cyber terrorism have shown, however, that an efficient and ready for action armed forces are still needed.

Summing up the geostrategic situation of Hungary, it should be pointed out that Hungary is too insignificant country in terms of military, political and economic importance to establish an important front in the struggle for influence for the regional powers i.e. Germany, France and Russia. For Russia, Poland and Ukraine remain the key countries, for which Russia devotes the greatest resources and time. For these very reasons, it was easier for Viktor Orban to sever his ties with the EU and gain a lot of independence. This is evidenced by the example of the migration crisis in 2015.

References

(2019) Hungarian Central Statistical Office.
(2019) Międzynarodowy Fundusz Walutowy (A), *Gross domestic product*, World Economic Outlook Database.
(2019) Międzynarodowy Fundusz Walutowy (B), *Gross domestic product per capita*, World Economic Outlook Database.
(2019) *Rocznik statystyczny Rzeczypospolitej Polskiej*, Łódź: Główny Urząd Statystyczny. Armed Forces Personnel, https://data.worldbank.org/indicator/MS.MIL.TOTAL.P?locations=RU-SA.

Baczwarow M. and Suliborski A., (2002). *Kompendium wiedzy o geografii geopolitycznej i geopolityce. Terminologia.*Warszawa: PWN.

Dybczyński A., (2013). *Geopolityka*, Warszawa: Poltext.

EUROSTAT, *Urząd Statystyczny Unii Europejskiej*, https://ec.europa.eu/info/departments/eurostat-european-statistics_pl.

http://index.ineuropa.pl.

http://www.globalfirepower.com/countries-listing.asp.

https://www.sipri.org/sites/default/files/ Milex-constant-2015-USD.

Hypś M., (2019). *Węgierska modernizacja pod sztandarem Zrinskiego,* "Technika wojskowa", https://www.konflikty.pl/technika-wojskowa/na-ladzie/zrinyi-2026-wegierska-modernizacja.

Ištok R., Plavčanová D. and Wilczyński P.L., (2016). *Sytuacja geopolityczna Słowacji*, "Przegląd Geopolityczny".

Łoś R., (2007). *Polityka zagraniczna Słowacji*, Łódź: Wydawnictwo Uniwersytetu Łódzkiego.

Potocki J., (2018). *Węgry – bratanek i sojusznik,* "Polska Zbrojna", http://polska-zbrojna.pl/home/articleshow/25489?t=Wegry-bratanek-i-sojusznik.

Radwan A., Arak P. and Lewicki G., (2017). *Inicjatywa in.Europa*, http://index.ineuropa.pl.

Stolarczyk M., (1995). *Główne modele bezpieczeństwa europejskiego a państwa Grupy Wyszehradzkiej (1990–1994)*, in: J. Przewłocki, B. Osadnik (eds.), *Bezpieczeństwo państw Grupy Wyszehradzkiej. Nadzieje i realia*, Katowice.

Zięba R., (eds.), (2004). *Uwarunkowania polityki zagranicznej państwa, Wstęp do teorii polityki zagranicznej państwa*, Toruń: Adam Marszałek.

Sławomir Byłeń / Marcin Górnikiewicz / Radosław Bielawski

Chapter 39: Summary and conclusions: Hungary's geopolitical and geostrategic position as a key element of Russian influence in Central and Eastern Europe

Hungary is one of the largest countries in Central and Eastern Europe, but it does not play a greater role in the Kremlin's geopolitical plans. The importance of Hungary lies mainly in its presence in the European Union, and the potential benefits of making use of this country are stemming from the combined influence on the Czech Republic and Slovakia. This is possible through the so-called Visegrad formula which enables to achieve geostrategic goals of gradual disruption of the European Union's political stability. In these categories, the role of Hungary plays an important role in the Kremlin's plans, while Hungary alone can be of importance only in relation to the transport routes running through this country from the south to the north. On the other hand, the possibility of affecting the economic condition of Poland and the Baltic States may be very relevant in the geostrategic game. At the same time, Moscow is fully satisfied with its influence in the Czech Republic and Slovakia, which has been developed over the decades. The impact on the countries of Southern Europe, i.e. mainly the Balkan countries and Greece, can be carried out without Hungary. For the above reasons, Hungary is important in the Kremlin's geopolitics as long as it can be used for short-term or long-term disruptions to intra-EU stability.

In the experts' opinion, whose views were analyzed and synthesized in the previous two chapters, there is a belief that the perception of the role of the state only through the prism of the size of the territory or population is not correct. It is important to take into account, on the one hand, the comprehensively perceived power of the state and its location in a broader geopolitical and geostrategic context. Hungary, having a favorable geographic location and standardized relations with its neighbors, willingly undertakes a multi-vector game in which Russia plays a very important role (Balazs, Faulkner, Schimank 1995, pp. 613–632).

This is one of the reasons why Moscow has been striving for energy dependence for decades and supports various activities aimed at weakening the geostrategic position of Budapest, for example in relation to the structures of the

European Union and even Washington. Hungary's political and partly economic isolation is an excellent example of this.

To sum up, Hungary alone does not have a sufficient potential to stand in the near term as a significant front in the struggle for influence between the regional powers, i.e. Germany, France and Russia. For the latter, Poland and Ukraine are currently the key theaters of geopolitical combats carried out by various means (military or non-military). That is why Russia, by taking long-term and seemingly imperceptible actions to destabilize the structures of the European Union, concentrates significant resources, among others in Poland, the territory of which, from the perspective of Moscow, represents an ideal transcontinental corridor towards the heart of Europe. In Moscow's game, Hungary plays the role of an ad hoc destabilizer of the eastern-southern and central-eastern parts of the EU structures. At the moment of weakening of the EU structures, and thus also the benefits of Hungary's positioning in those structures, the chances of Russia's offensive economic activities aimed at subjugating Hungarian decision-making circles will increase. The existing interdependencies establish the foundation for the future infrastructure of such a negative, economic impact.

References

Balazs K., Faulkner W. and Schimank U., (1995). Transformation of the Research Systems of Post-Communist Central and Eastern Europe in: "Social Studies of Science", 25(4), Ed. SAGE Publications.

Section II:
Russian activity in relation to Hungary:
The mechanism of using "hard power" and "soft power"

Sławomir Byleń

Chapter 40: Russian "hard power" towards Hungary: The current state of play and its effects

The foreign policy pursued by the Russian Federation in the first half of the 21st century is multifaceted and ambiguous with regard to other states and alliances on the international arena. It can be light and even friendly towards some countries. At the same time, it is also noticed that a tough, even brutal policy is being pursued, for example in relations with Ukraine. Recognizing the ambiguous behavior of the Russian Federation in the international arena, it is advisable to present its relations with one of the smaller countries in Europe, Hungary, in more detail.

The European Union, including Hungary, is one of the main directions of foreign policy pursued by the Russian Federation in the 21st century. An important factor in this approach is the fact that the most relevant economic partners of the Russian Federation are located in Europe. This primarily applies to the recipients of Russian gas and crude oil. An additional characteristic feature of the countries in Europe is the pursuit of broad integration, which has an economic (EU), a political and military (NATO) dimension. The existence of strong international institutions, including Hungary, has an impact on the Russian Federation's approach to foreign policy. This forces Russia to make choices in terms of the methods of influencing individual states. It is worth trying to act hard with one country and not with another. One state will not succumb to pressure, another will stiffen its own position, and yet another will be forced to interact with a stronger partner or opponent (Potulski, 2011, pp. 353–371; Potulski, 2010).

The subject of the research, presented in this chapter, are the methods of the Russian Federation's hard influence on the geostrategic situation of Hungary, which in turn directly affects the state of national security. Taking into account the theoretical foundations describing the meaning of the term "hard power" and the subject of the research, it was assumed that the aim of the study is to present, verify and assess the impact of the hard influence of the Russian Federation as an element of shaping the geostrategic situation that affects the state of Hungarian national security. In order to achieve such a specific goal, the chapter attempts to solve three basic research problems. The first was formulated in the form of a question: What methods of "hard influence" can the Russian Federation destabilize the geostrategic situation of Hungary? The second research problem is checking: How can, and to what extent, the methods of "hard influence" undertaken by the Russian Federation affect the state of national security of Hungary? The third problem can be summarized in the question: Does Russia use hard methods of influencing Hungary and what goals can it pursue?

In an attempt to solve the research problems defined above, the study used empirical research methods, including a critical analysis of the literature on the subject of research, the analysis of documents and source studies related to the ways of shaping the geostrategic situation with the use of methods of hard influence of one country on the state of national security of another one. The method of synthesis and inference methods, which are the final product of previously conducted analyzes, were applied here.

One of the sources of geopolitical conflicts is the uneven development of geopolitical centers, which leads to the emergence of a potential difference and expansion of a center with a greater potential into a center with a smaller capacity (Potulski, 2008, p. 186). Such an understanding of geopolitics and geopolitical conflicts is, however, related to the pre-modern and modern world, dominated by nation states and territorial conflicts between them. Moreover, it is related to a realistic approach, adopting a simplified vision of the world in which it is assumed that the basis of international relations is human nature, and people care about their own interests, strive for power, which easily leads to conflicts and aggression between states

Traditionally, in international relations it was concluded that gaining control over a given territory and its resources increased power and possibilities of action, and a greater power allowed for extending control over the area. In the history of international relations, stronger states tried, directly or indirectly, to take control over state territories. In many cases, force allowed for direct, formal political sovereignty over a selected area. However, due to the gradual relativization of the spatial factor, understood as the basic source of strength, conflicts were limited, the main source of which was the desire to seize a specific area. As it is indicated, the conflicts and territorial wars ended in the post-Cold War world. This is because today taking over any territory is neither tantamount to victory, nor ensuring a safe tomorrow, because "fluid" postmodernity has led to the relativization of the spatial and geographical factor (Bauman, 2006, p. 107).

However, in the analyzes of the postmodern international environment, attention is often paid to the loss of importance of the territorial factor, as well as to a fundamental change in the nature of the ongoing international conflicts. The American scientist Samuel Huntington was one of the first people to pay attention to this fact. He put forward the thesis that after the end of the Cold War, geopolitical conflicts would not be reduced, but that they would take other forms. Instead of the East-West rivalry, there would be a conflict between civilizations. Huntington, also pointed out that the main and most dangerous dimension of the emerging post-Cold War global politics would be the conflict among groups belonging to different civilizations. Huntington, reflecting on the nature of the new geopolitical structure of the world, wrote that the first years after the end of the Cold War were marked by dramatic changes in the identities of different peoples and symbols of these identities, and global politics began to be reorganized along with the lines of cultural divisions (Huntington, 2003, p. 13).

With reference to the above-mentioned aspects, it is currently assessed that military power is gradually losing its importance and no longer plays a dominant role in ensuring state security, continuously giving way to economic, scientific, technical and cultural factors. The conducted research shows that at the present stage of development of international relations, the position of the state in the structure of global connections is more and more often determined not by military power (hardpower) but by cultural and ideological attractiveness (softpower) (Nye, 2007, pp. 77–88; Nye, 2009) which means that a soft interaction brings better results. The American scientist Nye also admits that only a skillful strategy that combines hard and soft interaction and building alliances and networks responsible for the global information age can bring the best results. Other scientists formulate similar theses that neither hard nor soft power alone deliver the desired effects.

On the other hand, the Russian geopolitician Irina Wsilenko points out that the change in the rules of the game in the international environment means that the world has entered the era of post-modern geopolitics. According to her, until recently geopoliticians were interested in the cartography of physical and geographical area, today the main subject of research is the "cartography of the human soul", and the main means of implementing geopolitical goals is shaping the "world map" of entire nations (Wasilienko, 2006, p. 5–8).

The energy sector is the basis of Hungarian-Russian economic relations. Hungary's tightening of political relations with Russia after 2010 was not associated with a significant increase in bilateral trade and investment, or with an increase in Russian influence outside the energy sector. The EU economic sanctions imposed on Russia and the introduction of counter-sanctions by it in 2014 resulted in a significant decline in Hungarian exports to Russia. However, this did not bring significant losses to the Hungarian economy.

The most important area of Russia's hard influence on Hungary is the energy sector, which is a key economic sector for both sides. In 2013, in order to negotiate prices directly at the highest political level, the state-owned Hungarian company MVM bought all shares of the subsidiary of the German concern E.ON on the Hungarian gas market. This was connected with taking over the obligations resulting from the gas supply contract with Russian Gazprom. Hungary covers 80% of its gas needs from Russian imports. Cheap gas and electricity are essential for the Hungarian government to ensure low utility bills. The retail price of gas and electricity in Hungary is one of the lowest in the EU, taking into account the purchasing power, which contributed to Fidesz's success in the parliamentary elections in 2014 and 2018.

The project that will make the Hungarian economy dependent on Russia for decades is the construction by the Russian company Rosatom of two new reactors at the Paks nuclear power plant. The Russian loan granted for its implementation amounts to EUR 10 billion and accounts for approximately 10% of Hungarian GDP. The details of the contract for the extension of the Paks power plant are not known. It was concluded in January 2014, two months before Russia's annexation of Crimea, and initiated the basis for further narrowing the relations with an EU member state in times of serious tensions with the European Union.

The enhancement of economic relations in the field of energy and thus in politics by the government of Viktor Orbán with Russia, is possible due to the positive attitude of the Hungarian society towards this country. The 2018 research shows a specific paradox. Among other things, the fact that the vast majority of Hungarians, who enjoy the benefits of membership in NATO and the EU, overestimate Russia's military and economic potential. The conducted research shows that 43% of the respondents thought that only the USA spends more of it on defense. Even its aggression towards Ukraine has not negatively affected Hungarians' sympathy for Russia. Among the supporters of individual political parties, the level of understanding for Russia is the highest among Fidesz voters (59%). They would choose Russia as Hungary's closest ally (51%), and only 39% would choose the United States (Jóźwiak, 2019).

In 2013, Russia was Hungary's third largest trading partner, i.e. before the EU introduced sanctions on Russia and imposed counter-sanctions on agri-food products from the EU. On the other hand, already in 2016, the decrease in the volume of trade with Hungary moved it to the 14th place. The declining importance of Russia for Hungarian foreign trade resulted primarily from the fall in the price of crude oil, and consequently the fall in the value of Russian imports, which consisted almost exclusively of energy resources. At the same time, in 2013 Russia was the 13th largest outlet for Hungary, in 2016 it was on the 16th place and in 2018 on the 19th place. With a share of 2.9% (2013), 1.5% (2016) and 1.4% (2019), respectively, in total exports. The value of Hungarian sales to Russia in 2013–2016 decreased significantly, i.e. by approx. 40%, despite the fact that in the same period the value of total exports increased by 13% (Jóźwiak, 2019).

The structure of Hungarian exports to Russia is still dominated by industrial products (including pharmaceuticals), machinery, mechanical and transport equipment. Agri-food products accounted for approx. 11% in 2013, and approx. 14% of exports to Russia in 2017 (EUR 265 million and EUR 247 million, respectively). This shows the relatively small impact of the Russian embargo on food products on Hungarian exports. The reasons for the decline in the value of Hungarian exports, independent of the counter-sanctions, are evidenced by the fact that the negative trend started even before their introduction in the first half of 2014, in all industries important for trade. Experts estimate that one of the reasons for the visible trend may be the generally poor condition of the Russian economy (Table 1).

Table 1. Hungary's trade with Russia

Trade flow	Trade balance (EURO bn)					
	2013	2014	2015	2016	2017	2018
Export	2,40	2,12	1,54	1,43	1,71	1,54
Import	6,15	5,42	3,28	2,37	3,19	3,89
Balance	-3,25	-3,30	-1,74	-0,94	-1,48	-2,35

Nevertheless, the Hungarian government attributes the reduction in the volume of bilateral trade only to sanctions. According to its calculations, the losses in the estimated profit from exports to Russia after 2014 total around EUR 7 billion (Jóźwiak, 2019). On the other hand, experts claim that these calculations are overestimated, because based on the data from 2013 and assuming that the value of exports would not change in the following years, it can be determined that the losses for the period 2014–2018 are totally of 3.6 billion euro. Meanwhile, the government's estimates suggest that without the sanctions, the value of Hungarian exports to Russia after 2013 would grow at a rate of around 10% year on year. This hypothesis is not confirmed by the trends in bilateral trade in 2008–2013, when the average increase was 2.44% per year (Jóźwiak, 2019).

Another area of Russia's hard influence concerns the volume of Russian investments in the Hungarian economy. The presence of Russian capital in Hungary is not significant either for Hungary or for Russia. The accumulated value of Russian foreign direct investments (FDI) in Hungary in 2017 amounted to EUR 65 million, which was only 0.08% of the value of FDI in this country. According to Russian data, in 2016 Hungary was ranked 11th among the recipients of Russia's direct investments in Central and Eastern Europe, with a share of 0.06% in the cumulative value of all Russian foreign investments. In turn, significant investments in Russia include, among others, Hungarian oil company MOL, Hungarian retail bank OTP and pharmaceutical concern Gedeon Richter. According to Hungarian statistics, the cumulative value of Hungarian FDI in

Russia in 2017 amounted to EUR 653 million (2.6%) of all Hungarian FDI (Jóźwiak, 2019).

Next examples of Russia's hard impact on the Hungarian economy, apart from the energy sector, include several other significant investments. One of them is the Russian Sberbank, owned by the Russian state treasury. In turn, the Rachimkułow family owns 7.4% of the Hungarian OTP. In addition, in 2019, the Russian government-controlled International Investment Bank, which was the development bank of the Comecon countries until 1990, moved its headquarters from Moscow to Budapest. Hungary again became a shareholder of this institution in 2018. The Hungarian authorities granted it its seat, and the Russian employees received diplomatic privileges and immunities. Since 2010, Russian investors and the state-owned Vnesheconombank, which is subject to US sanctions, have been the majority shareholders in the Dunaferr metallurgical plant previously owned by the Ukrainian steel group ISD. Both the Hungarian government and its private investors have tried repeatedly and unsuccessfully to negotiate the buyback of a controlling stake in a non-profit making company. Russia is refusing the transaction because it probably wants to maintain the possibility of using the steelworks as a supplier for the construction of new reactors at the Paks nuclear power plant (Jóźwiak, 2019).

Economic entities operating in various countries are a separate object put under pressure by the Russian Federation. By applying various economic stimuli, the Russian Federation leads to a situation where certain economic entities interested in cooperation with the Russian Federation put pressure on their state authorities to accept the attitude and policy of the Russian Federation. This activity becomes quite effective in some circles. Some anti-Russian political centers unknowingly take actions aiming at pursuing Russian plans. In diplomatic circles, the term "useful Kremlin idiots" is sometimes used, pointing to people and entire political groups which, by promoting the national interest, contribute to the implementation of the policy of the Russian Federation (Tchaikovsky, 2017, p. 132).

The methodology of Russia's hard influence on Hungary does not find fertile ground in this case, because the common interests of Hungary and Russia, which converge on many issues, stand in the way. For example on Ukraine. Both countries want it to be unstable, although the Russian Federation would change their mind if it regained power in Kiev. Both countries have territorial claims towards Ukraine, and moreover, there are both Hungarian and Russian national minorities in Ukraine. Moreover, if Kiev turned to Russia, Hungary could also win something for itself.

In the modern world, real independence is guaranteed by oil and gas. Countries that do not have these resources, including Hungary, cannot count on such autonomy. They rely on Russian suppliers and tedious fairs where prices are more determined by politics than by economy. In the opinion of the Hungarian authorities, relations with the Russian Federation, after several years of regression, caused by international sanctions against Russia, have gained new impetus. The Hungarian authorities argue that Western European countries, despite the prolongation of sanctions, still conclude much larger transactions with Russia than with Hungary. Hence, in line with the Hungarian national interest, the Hungarians are forced to dynamically develop Hungarian-Russian contacts.

When attempting to summarize the research carried out, one should first address the answers to the questions to the problems posed under this study.

When assessing the geopolitical situation in Hungary on the basis of tough methods of influence by Russia, the answer cannot be unequivocal. When responding to the first research question, the answer should be yes. Russia uses a wide range of "hard influence" methods, which may destabilize the situation not only in Hungary and in the region of Central and Eastern Europe, but may also indirectly affect the political situation throughout the European Union. After the research, the answer to the second studied question is not so clear-cut, on the one hand the examples presented in the chapter show that Russia can influence Hungary's national security, especially in the energy sector, by means of "hard power", and on the other hand, the EU membership as a political and economic alliance, limits these threats.

In the near term, the Hungarian-Russian rapprochement has a negative effect on relations within the EU, and this is in Russia's interest. In the longer term, after breaking up the European community by using hard and soft methods of influencing selected EU countries with which Russia, especially Hungary, maintains friendly relations, it wishes to break up the EU, and then reactivate the former sphere of influence by extending it on the countries of Central and Eastern Europe. It follows that the long-term geopolitical goals of the Russian Federation are rooted at a time when the Soviet Union was one of the world's two superpowers.

The second issue concerns the answer to the question whether the way of conducting a hard foreign policy by the Russian Federation towards Hungary brings positive results and here the answer is unequivocal. It is Hungary that is vulnerable to the influence of the Russian Federation. They are one of the few countries belonging to the European Union that is a staunch ally of the Russian Federation. It is Hungary, through the Russian Federation's tough influence on the EU that has become its camouflaged ally, which, at key moments, shows reliability and understanding for Russia's foreign policy. It is difficult to predict unequivocally what future actions in the area of Hungary's foreign and internal policy may be like. It seems, however, that in the near future the course on

European integration with simultaneous cooperation, especially economic, with the Russian Federation will be continued.

To sum up, the only thing that is certain in the policy of the Russian Federation are the geostrategic goals of foreign rule, which invariably include the reconstruction of the sphere of influence before the collapse of the Soviet Union, which means regaining the position of a superpower in the international arena. To achieve this goal, the Russian Federation is ready to pursue its policy by various methods, not only from the position of force or accomplished facts, but more and more often through methods of soft influence on states where it delivers specific benefits.

References

Bauman, (2006) *Społeczeństwo w stanie oblężenia*, Warszawa: PWN.
Czajkowski M., (2017) *Aktualna polityka zagraniczna Federacji Rosyjskiej a Unia Europejska – podstawowe zagadnienia*, Krakowskie Studia Międzynarodowe XIV nr 2, Kraków.
Huntington S., (2003) *Zderzenie cywilizacji*, Warszawa: Wydawnictwo Zysk i S-ka.
Jóźwiak V, *Węgiersko-rosyjskie stosunki gospodarcze*, Wyd. Polski Instytut Spraw Międzynarodowych, nr 105 / (1853).
Nye J.S, (2007) *Soft-power. Jak osiągnąć sukces w polityce światowej*, Warszawa: Wydawnictwo Akademickie i Profesjonalne.
Nye jr. J.S., (2009) *Konflikty międzynarodowe. Wprowadzenie do teorii i historii*, tłumaczenie M. Madej, Warszawa: Wydawnictwo Akademickie i Profesjonalne.
Potulski J., (2011) *Geopolityka w świecie ponowoczesnym*, Częstochowa: Wydawnictwo Instytut Geopolityki.
Potulski J., (2008) *Społeczno-kulturowy kontekst aktywności międzynarodowej Federacji Rosyjskiej*, Gdańsk: Wydawnictwo Uniwersytetu Gdańskiego.
Potulski J., (2010) *Współczesne kierunki rosyjskiej myśli geopolitycznej*, Gdańsk: Wydawnictwo Uniwersytetu Gdańskiego.
Wasilienko I.A., (2006) *Geopolitika sowriemiennowo mira*, Moskwa.

Sławomir Byleń

Chapter 41: Russian "soft power" as an example of rapprochement between Moscow and Budapest

The methodology of soft influence as a part of conducting foreign policy in the 21st century is broadening further and further and it is a tool that does not cause armed conflicts, and at the same time leads to the achievement of the assumed goals. It is used by almost all countries, but its scope and effectiveness vary. This is due to the fact that the goals of the external policy of each country in the world may be different, as well as the potential of soft influence used towards selected countries. The geopolitical and geostrategic conditions in which soft influence in foreign policy are also important.

The subject of the research presented in this chapter are the methods of the Russian Federation's soft influence on the geostrategic situation of Hungary, which in turn directly affects the state of national security. The results of the research can be used to specify the geostrategic situation and to outline national interests, the fulfillment of which is necessary to ensure security in the functioning of the state in the first decades of the 21st century.

Taking into account the theoretical foundations describing the meaning of the concept of "soft power" and the subject of research, it was concluded that the aim of the study is to present, verify and assess the impact of the soft influence of the Russian Federation on the national security of Hungary as an element of shaping the geostrategic situation. In order to achieve such a specific goal, the chapter attempts to solve three basic research problems. The first was formulated in the form of a question: What methods of "soft influence" can the Russian Federation destabilize the geostrategic situation of Hungary? The second research problem is checking: How can, and to what extent, the "soft impact" methods undertaken by the Russian Federation affect the state of national security in Hungary? The third problem can be summarized in the question: To what extent can the Hungarian state authorities be conducive to soft influence of the Russian state?

In an attempt to solve the research problems defined above, the study used empirical research methods, including a critical analysis of the literature on the subject of research, the analysis of documents and source studies related to the ways of shaping the geostrategic situation with the use of methods of hard influence of one country on the state of national security of another one. The method of synthesis and inference methods, which are the final product of previously conducted analyzes, were applied here.

The changes that have taken place in the contemporary international environment related to the way out of the Cold War confrontation, the increase in interdependence on a global scale and the development of information technology have resulted in the fact that an increasing role and importance in international competition, gaining allies and implementing foreign policy goals is attributed to intellectual resources, information, communication opportunities, the standard of living and education of the society, scientific and technological resources, as well as concentration of financial capital.

It is believed that military power gradually loses its importance and no longer plays a dominant role in ensuring state security, gradually giving way to economic, scientific, technical and cultural factors. Particular concern is attached in particular to the cultural factor. The conducted research shows that at the present stage of development of international relations, the position of the state in the structure of global relations is more and more often determined not by military power (hardpower) but by cultural and ideological attractiveness (softpower). Cultural factors in the contemporary world, which are an extremely strong element of impact on the external environment, often determine the attractiveness and might of a given country. Cultural attractiveness, representing a kind of softpower, means the ability of a given country to gain allies and legitimize its foreign policy thanks to the attractiveness of culture, political ideals and politics (Nye, 2007, pp. 77–88).

The concept of softpower was popularized in the late 1980s by the American scientist Joseph Nye, in which he emphasized the need to depart from conventional ways of understanding state power in favor of a new look at other activities in the world. During this period, traditional analyzes of power research ignored the ability to attract other entities in international relations and thus increase the probability that they would act in accordance with our expectations and interests. Nye defined this ability as soft-power and defined it as "the ability to get what one wants, due to the attractiveness of a country's culture and its political ideals, rather than by coercion or payment" (Nye, 2007, p. 25).

In discussions around soft-power, the question of the ways of realizing domination in the world by means of "soft power", that is, understanding how and with what instruments the contemporary competition for international domination takes place, plays a vital role. Experts believe that in the modern world, the most crucial element in subordinating other countries to their decisions is controlling the symbolic sphere, thanks to which one can influence how people think and what they demand. By dominating the symbolic sphere, one can impose a particular way of seeing the world and thus exercising power by shaping knowledge about the world around, in accordance with intentions and ideas, thus influencing the taken actions (Potulski, 2011, p. 19).

Contemporary analyzes of the international environment emphasize the growing importance of "symbolic strength" and "symbolic power", recognizing that rivalry in the 21st century is primarily an ideological competition between states, and conflicts in the modern world are primarily "informational" and their goal is to contain the symbolic realm. The extremely fast development of information and communication technologies is also noteworthy. The development of television networks, the Internet and the World Wide Web has produced a new transnational space, called cyberspace, or the infosphere, in which information flows and images are transferred, and the way to gain world domination is to control the circulation of information and images through telecommunications networks (Potulski, 2011, p. 144). Such an approach to analyzes of international reality is particularly clearly visible in the publications of contemporary Russian geopoliticians, such as, for example, Irina Vasilenko, Igor Panarin, or Alexander Panarin, for whom the struggle for world hegemony takes place today in the sphere of cultural values. According to them, the combat of the Western world with Russia is taking place not by military means but by cultural instruments. In order to defend their independence and position in the world, the Russians must first of all answer the question about their own identity and defend Russian values against external influences and reject the assumption of the universality of Western patterns, which is only an expression of the "new imperialism" of culture, the aim of which is to subjugate all the world's communities (Castells, 2008, p. 473).

The second type of contemporary geopolitical analyzes, devoted to the increasing role of information and the infosphere for international relations, focuses primarily on the "cultural" impact of information and the ability of tele-information messages to create a particular image of the world and is definitely closer to the idea of soft-power. The inclusion of such elements as the problems of shaping "geopolitical perceptions" through the mass transfer of information and products of popular culture into geopolitical analyzes makes geopolitics an interdisciplinary and multidimensional analysis tool, striving to combine various research perspectives and ways of thinking about the relationship between geography and politics (Potulski , 2011, p. 149).

This multidimensionality of geopolitics was forced by the fact that traditional elements of geostrategic analysis, such as territory, geographic location, climate, natural resources, population (its number and structure), and the specificity of borders, would not allow for the construction of valuable political analyzes. Therefore, greater importance is attached to the human factor and such phenomena as religion, ideology, public opinion, mass media, culture, language, communication, trade, economy, psychology, social structure, morality, etc.

Besides, new concepts were introduced into the geopolitical debate: Soft-power, infosphere, or cyberspace, which are increasingly replacing classical concepts and analyzes.

Contemporary investigations emphasize that the information revolution has brought a completely new quality to the sphere of geopolitics and has reevaluated all the regularities and norms of geopolitical conflicts. The Russian geopolitician Irina Wsilenko pointed out that in the emerging global information society, competition for space will take place mainly in the infosphere. As a result, all regularities and norms of geopolitical competition are subject to far-reaching transformations. Changing the rules of the game in the international environment means that the world has entered the era of post-modern geopolitics, in which the greatest role is assigned to spiritual and cultural-civilization elements. According to the Russian scientist, until recently geopolitics were interested in the cartography of physical and geographical space, today the main subject of research is "the cartography of the human soul", the symbolic capital of culture, and the virtual world of symbols. The core means of realizing geopolitical goals is control over an individual, its ideas, and shaping the "world map" of entire nations (Wasilienko, 2006, pp. 5-8).

To sum up, in the contemporary development of geopolitics, the elements establishing the basis of the development of the "new geopolitics" have been linked with traditional areas of geopolitical research, thus obtaining a richer picture of the world.

In official documents, the Russian Federation provides a number of rather detailed foreign policy objectives (Fiszer, 2016). By analyzing their content and referring them to the European area, it can be stated that the objectives of the foreign policy of the Russian Federation towards the countries of the European Union, and thus towards Hungary, are activities aimed at: – maintaining good economic relations, which will allow to maintain a high level and continue the economic development of the Russian Federation;
- reconstruction of the sphere of influence among the countries of the former communist bloc;
- ensuring global military security;
- ensuring the position of a global power with the ability to influence global economic and military policy.

The presented foreign policy objectives of the Russian Federation are, in real action, each time refined and adapted to the object, state or region they relate to at a given moment. It is publicly said that the strategic dimension of the Russian Federation's policy in the Euro-Atlantic region is oriented towards shaping peace, security and stability. It is also considered necessary to respect the principles of mutual trust, security and equal cooperation. From the declarative point of view, the presented content can be seen as an ideal approach to conducting foreign policy. Practice, however, shows completely different behavior.

Hungary's relations with Russia are one of the issues that divides the countries of the Visegrad Group (V4) to the greatest extent. The divisions between its individual members also transfer into their susceptibility to Russian influence. Among all the V4 countries, Hungary, along with Slovakia, are the most vulnerable to Russia's subversive influence in areas such as political leadership, civil society, public views, and state countermeasures.

The situation in Hungary seems extremely paradoxical. Despite the pro-Western attitudes of the citizens themselves and the Orban government's compliance with the obligations arising from membership in the EU and NATO structures, the policy of "opening to the East" promoted by the current government, assuming close cooperation with the Kremlin on political and energy at the same time, creates at the same time the possibility of corruption. There are three main layers of the aforementioned source of influence: the main political stream (previous and present), representatives of the extreme right, and radical extremists mainly representing the right wing of the political scene, due to the very poor condition of the Hungarian left (Lóránt and Krekó, 2017).

An example of a soft influence of the Russian Federation on the situation in Hungary was the official statement of the Russian Ministry of Foreign Affairs, published on August 15, 2014. The statement accused the Hungarian government, which after Orban took power in 2010, became the most important ally in Central and Eastern Europe, about illegal sale of T-72 tanks to Ukraine. This was to lead to an escalation of the armed conflict that broke out in eastern Ukraine shortly after the occupation of Crimea (20/02–26/03/2014). The accusation was, moreover, well in line with the Russian strategy of putting the blame on the enemy for Russia's wrongdoing. Of course, in this context, the enemy was not directly Hungary, but the European Union, which, according to the Russian narrative, is only a puppet in the hands of the United States. In the content of the statement, for example, one can read that "The supplies of arms by EU Member States (…) breach legal obligations, i.e. the Arms Trade Treaty (ATA)" (Lóránt and Krekó, 2017).

There is also an interesting fact that, at least in Hungary, has seen the light of day. This is about taking specific actions unlimitedly, in this aspect of foreign policy. The Russian Ministry of Foreign Affairs responded to an article posted by the far-right Hungarian portal Hídfő.net, i.e. "Bridgehead", which stands in opposition to the traditional media. Fake photos of tanks appeared in it and it was further alleged that "the US asked" NATO members with Soviet-era heavy weapons to hand them over to Ukraine (Lóránt and Krekó, 2017). This hitherto unknown Russian propaganda tube was created by a neo-Nazi Hungarian parliamentary faction called the Hungarian National Front (MNA) in late 2012.

Nevertheless, it was quite quickly transformed into the Kremlin's geopolitical platform, serving as a "Russian intelligence information board", as evidenced by the form and content of the articles posted there (Attila et al., 2015). In order to dispel any doubts as to its true source and purpose, the website was moved to a Russian server just after it was used by the Russian Ministry of Foreign Affairs. Currently, it operates under the name Hídfő.ru.

The aforementioned provocation with the T-72 tanks is one of the classic examples of the use of dormant disinformation cells (i.e. Hídfő.net) and the political party MNA, which most likely infiltrated Russian agencies in 2012 long before the Crimean crisis. Two years later, on October 26, 2016, István Győrkös, the chairman of the MNA, the founding organization of the aforementioned internet portal, fatally shot a policeman in the head. The incident occurred during a police raid on Győrkös' house in search of illegal weapons and ammunition. From information later revealed by investigative journalists, it turned out that the MNA had participated in the airsoft exercises along with Russian "diplomats" who, in fact, turned out to be members of the Military Intelligence Unit (GRU).

The increasingly stronger relationship between the neo-Nazi MNA, its media and representatives of the Kremlin is a part of Russia's disinformation strategy implemented in Central and Eastern Europe and increasingly decentralized after the events in Crimea. This scenario uses the local platforms of the new pro-Russian media, bringing together both far-right and far-left ideologies. It is estimated that in this part of Europe there are several hundred of them, while in Hungary alone their number may be as high as 100 (Bátorfy and Szánthó,). Some of these Facebook sites, blogs and pages on Facebook have recently appeared and others, such as the aforementioned Hídfő, have simply been taken over. It is said that the more radical and less known the site, the easier it is to control it from the outside.

This story not only shows the striking primitiveness of Russian secret intelligence operations in Hungary, which use the radical right, but also the role of the mainstream media. And although this tragic event was followed by a series of arrests, as well as an investigation, law enforcement agencies as well as government politicians focused solely on the radical thread of the whole matter and seemed to completely ignore any links with Russia. Meanwhile, Hídfő.ru still exists and is doing well. The website continues to spread Russian propaganda through social media dealing with conspiracy theories and publishing nationalist content.

Another example of Russia's soft influence on Hungarian politics is the return to power in 2010 o Viktor Orbán. One of his main goals, which he did not hide, was to establish "friendly" relations with Moscow, which seemed quite obvious, especially in the light of the economic policy pursued, assuming that Hungary was dependent on supplies of Russian gas, oil and nuclear fuel, even after the 1989. Although the Kremlin developed strong and institutionalized ties with the post-communist Hungarian Socialist Party (MSZP) and enjoyed profits while the socialists were in power (2002–2010), the geopolitical turn of pro-Russian right-wing elites after 2010 provided the Kremlin with further access to the mainstream Hungarian political system on energy exports, anti-liberal values and disinformation.

According to the 2017 data from Globsec Trends on Hungary, prepared by the Political Capital Institute, this has led to a seemingly paradoxical situation. The mainstream media, largely controlled by the ruling Fidesz-KDNP coalition, is an overt pro-Russian geopolitical platform, despite the fact that the electorate of both parties consists largely of EU and NATO supporters. On the basis of the conducted surveys, it can be observed that 39% of Hungarians believe that their country should belong to the group of Western countries, and only 5% were in favor of Hungary being part of the Eastern countries. At the same time, more than half of Hungarians (53%) believe that in both geopolitical and cultural terms they are somewhere between the East and the West (GLOBSEC, 2017).

The example of Hungary shows that it is not the nation that is trying to replace the elites who sympathize with the West, but rather it is the pro-Russian elites that are trying to take the place of citizens who have a positive attitude towards Western states. In order to be able to achieve this, the Hungarian government has not only taken a pro-Kremlin stance, but also aims to change the attitude of Hungarians, mainly through Russian propaganda. To this end, pro-Russian content is disseminated in the media which are more or less controlled by the authorities.

The pro-Russian media activity of the most important Hungarian political parties seems to be extremely important, because the mass media in the hands of Russians do not affect Hungarian citizens with a similar force. Anyway, there are no Russian stations on the Hungarian media market, especially since the closedown of the Hungarian version of the radio "Voice of Russia" and its transformation into the Sputnik channel in December 2014. In addition, due to the lack of knowledge of the language, Hungarians do not have access to Russian media on the Internet or via satellite links. Moreover, there is no significant Russian diaspora or Orthodox community in Hungary either.

After assuming power in 2010, the ruling Fidesz party announced a plan to "open to the East". A visible manifestation of this policy was the bilateral agreement between Russia and Hungary concluded in January 2014 on the Paks II nuclear power plant. Cooperation between the two governments has gained momentum to such an extent that, beginning since 2013, Hungarian Prime Minister Viktor Orbán and the President Vladimir Putin hold annual bilateral meetings, a rarity among European leaders, especially after the Russian invasion of Crimea. In addition, the government-controlled media that presented the government's stance on the 2016 refugee referendum for around 95% of its airtime (Media, 2017), along with the censorship of public television news (PBS) programs, led to a situation in which the pro-Russian foreign policy of Fidesz-KDNP and other anti-Western, pro-Kremlin content could be freely disseminated in Hungarian public discourse.

There are several examples that accurately reflect the level of pro-Russian propaganda in public and pro-government media. For example, at the beginning of the Maidan conflict (21/11/2013–22/02/2014), the Hungarian media, echoing the Kremlin, openly called the protesters "terrorists" (Lóránt and Krekó, 2017). Moreover, broadcasting the Russian news program, despite the fact that there are only a few thousand Russians in Hungary and the vast majority of them are fluent in Hungarian, was the tribute to Moscow by Hungarian state media.

However, the true power of Russian disinformation in Hungarian mainstream media is largely manifested by pro-Kremlin conspiracy theories spread by the government's media. For example, the Maidan revolution was the result of a coup by the US and NATO (Lóránt and Krekó, 2017). For instance the crash of a plane belonging to Malaysia Airlines (MH 17) was to be "prepared" by the secret services even before its take-off (Gyula Máté, 2015) or that Boris Nemtsov was murdered by Western intelligence agencies to throw suspicion on Putin, using for this purpose the "Russian Kennedy double" capable of mobilizing opposition groups. Rather, these theories arise from the Kremlin's geopolitical needs, and their importance for Hungary's internal affairs is indirect. Instead, they underline the dependence of the Orbán government on Moscow.

The Hungarian government also takes an example from Russia's anti-liberal legal and political regime. On June 13, 2017, the parliamentary Fidesz-KDNP coalition adopted the Hungarian version of the law on "foreign agents", thereby obliging non-governmental organizations to declare that they are financed from foreign sources if they receive from such entities, including EU funds, amounts above 7.2 million forints (approximately EUR 23,000) (Lóránt and Krekó, 2017). At the same time, the Hungarian prosecutor General Péter Polt met his Russian counterpart in January 2017 to discuss the terms of cooperation in the fight against corruption and money laundering. Cultural issues were also dealt with. Among other things, the Hungarian government announced the renovation of several old churches, and for this reason, the Patriarch of Moscow Cyril was invited to Budapest, who took part in the opening ceremony in 2017.

In light of the above reports, it is not surprising that Prime Minister Orbán openly praises the success of the Putin regime, as he did in January 2017 when he said, "Here is Russia, which, let's be honest, has endured Western attempts to isolate it and overthrow the government, low oil prices, sanctions and the internal activity of independent, impartial and non-governmental organizations, allegedly operating without any outside interference. Russia has survived all this and that is why it still exists today and for this reason, although we should not, especially in Europe, ignore the might and possibilities of this country" (Lóránt and Krekó, 2017).

The farther to the right or left, the stronger Russian influence becomes. The far-right Jobbik party, founded in 2003, made almost no secret of its pro-Russian direction, especially when Béla Kovács joined it in 2005, called by his party colleagues as KGBéla due to pro-Russian sympathies (Attila et al. ., 2015). Shortly after joining the party, he became the head of the Ministry of Foreign Affairs, immediately directing it towards Russia. Kovács, who was also the main sponsor of Jobbik at the beginning of its existence, started organizing summit meetings with Russian politicians and supporters of Gábor Vona, the party leader. This was largely possible thanks to the contacts he had made during his time in Russia. The pro-Russian position of the party seemed strange to say the least, especially in the world of traditional values and anti-communist attitudes common among Hungarian right-wing parties (Kovács 2019).

Since the obvious pro-Russian shift in 2007–2008, Jobbik has supported and legitimized Russian interests at all levels, both domestically and internationally. Already in the party's 2009 program, the construction of the Paks II nuclear reactor was announced, and four years later, Jobbik himself organized a joint energy conference with Gazprom. In the same year, at the invitation of Alexander Dugin, Gábor Vona and Béla Kovács gave a lecture at Moscow's Lomonosov University on "traditional values" and presented the European Union as a "traitor to Europe". Vona then praised the advantages of the Eurasian Economic Union: "For me, Eurasianism means that one day Hungary may become a bridge between Europe and Asia. (…) The advantage of the Eurasian Union is the fact that, contrary to European integration, it allows the independence of the countries cooperating within the continental community to be maintained" (Lóránt and Krekó, 2017).

In addition, Kovács participated in the illegal referendum in Crimea as an "independent observer". Jobbik has also made efforts to disintegrate Ukraine territorially by asking Russian Duma deputies for help in establishing a Hungarian-Russian autonomy in the Transcarpathian region in western Ukraine. After the Hungarian government accused Kovács of spying against the Union for Russia, he was replaced by Márton Gyöngyösi, vice-chairman of the Foreign Affairs Committee of the National Assembly and vice-leader of the Jobbik parliamentary group. In 2014, he watched the illegal referendum in the Donetsk People's Republic, and a year later, he also watched the "parliamentary elections" in Russia. In an open letter to the people of Ukraine, he emphasized the essence of "nation's self-determination" and at the same time accused the government of this country of crimes against humanity, which allegedly took place after the seizure of power as a result of a bloody coup d'état financed by the United States (Lóránt and Krekó, 2017).

Moreover, Jobbik for a long time agreed with the false information disseminated by Russia, for example treating the territorial integrity of Ukraine as an "illusion", so Hungary, in order to remain "neutral" in this matter, should suspend all aid to Kiev. The situation is different in the case of the Syrian conflict. The media sympathy to Jobbik supported the Russian military intervention carried out jointly with Bashar al-Assad, as well as the entire anti-terrorist narrative. Moreover, the documents of the Belarusian activist Alexander Usovsky show that Jobbik and one of the Hungarian paramilitary organizations, the Sixty-Four Committees Youth Movement (HVIM), have probably been actively involved in disinformation for years. It is also said that the Russians could have paid them for organizing anti-Ukrainian protests (Lóránt and Krekó, 2017).

Analyzes conducted by the "Political Capital Institute" showed that the Kremlin was in constant contact with extremist and paramilitary far-right organizations in Hungary and Central and Eastern Europe, the importance of which increased significantly after Russia took over Crimea. The Kremlin preaches a narrative that states that historical conflicts between the countries of the region can be renewed, and their borders can be changed based on "old claims" from before the First and Second World Wars. This would take place after the territorial collapse of Ukraine or its transformation into a kind of community of nations. The Kremlin expects such radical organizations to fulfill three basic functions, which are:
- destabilization of the EU, its member states and the most vulnerable regions and transatlantic relations;
- the legitimacy of the Russian regime and its policy;
- collecting information and disseminating false content.

Such actions are nothing new. For example, the Hungarian National Alliance for Prosperity (MNSZ), led by the charismatic right-wing radical Albert Szabó, in all his public appearances after 1994, called for campaigning against Hungary's accession to NATO and the EU, promoting the Eurasian alliance. Even then, there were serious suspicions that he had relations with Russian intelligence. They intensified a few years ago, when Szabó joined a group of pro-Russian propagandists organizing a welcome march for Vladimir Putin during his visit to Hungary in 2015 (Lóránt and Krekó, 2017). He then stated: "At such moments we see that it is impossible to precisely define Nazism. The skinheads, who are currently fighting on the side of Ukraine, from an ideological point of view, may oppose Russian aggression, but at the same time they sacrifice their own lives for the increasingly serious geopolitical goals of the USA (...) On the other side of the barricade there are Russian rebels, under the old flag of the USSR, who fiercely combat the geopolitical goals of the Zionists and the US. Their relationship with the principles of the National Socialists is symbiotic, as these directions and activities were their greatest enemy from the beginning."

Official measures to prevent false information being spread by the Kremlin in Hungary are practically non-existent. Mainly due to the pro-Russian attitude of Viktor Orbán's government and the role it plays in Russian propaganda activities. Official documents, including both the regulation 1035/2012 on the Hungarian National Security Strategy (Government Decision, 2013) and the regulation 1139/2013 on the state Cyberspace Security Strategy (Government Decision, 2013), mention the threat to the security of Hungary, which creates information warfare. Nevertheless, no measures have been taken to avert this danger, nor has Russia been identified as the main harmful factor in this case. In 2017, the government expelled several pro-Russian right-wing extremists from Hungary without giving any reason; the incident was likely a result of pressure exerted by NATO allies (Lóránt and Krekó, 2017).

The scandal with MNA proves that there is no political will to be able to fight Russian actions that threaten Hungarian national security. While the National Security Committee of the Hungarian parliament had promised to look into the MNA's ties to the Russian intelligence services (GRU), the Hungarian police closed an investigation in this matter, not to mention any interference by foreign intelligence. The case of Béla Kovács has also not been clarified so far, and Hungarian law enforcement agencies are surprisingly slow in examining all the evidence gathered so far. Kovács was not arrested, and despite the accusations in 2014, he is still active in Brussels and Hungary, despite the fact that the European Parliament lifted his immunity, and despite his obvious ties to Russia. The case was spiced up by the fact that not only MNA had contacts with the GRU, but Kovács himself and his wife, Swietłana, of Russian origin, were on friendly terms with the family of the leader of the group (Lóránt and Krekó, 2017). When attempting to summarize the presented content, one should first address the questions posing the problems under study. What methods of "soft influence" can the Russian Federation destabilize the geostrategic situation of Hungary? The second research problem is checking: How can, and to what extent, the "soft impact" methods undertaken by the Russian Federation affect the state of national security in Hungary ? The third problem can be summarized in the question: To what extent can the Hungarian state authorities be conducive to soft influence of the Russian state ?

When analyzing and assessing the content contained in the surveyed articles, websites and other source materials, the answer cannot be unequivocal. When answering the first research question, taking into account the examples presented, it should be responded in the affirmative that Russia uses a wide range of "soft impact" methods that destabilize the situation not only in Hungary and the region of Central and Eastern Europe, but the indirectly used methods may also affect the political situation of the European Union. After the conducted research, the answer to the second research question is not so clear-cut, on the one hand the examples presented in the chapter show that Russia can influence the state of Hungary's national security by means of "soft power", and on the other hand, it is a member of the military and political and economic alliance limits these risks. The biggest surprise is the answer to the third question, as one gets the impression that the Hungarian authorities are not only encouraging, but even inspiring, Russia's soft influence.

The only thing that is certain about the foreign policy of the Russian Federation are the geostrategic goals of foreign policy, which are invariably the reconstruction of the sphere of influence before the collapse of the Soviet Union, which means regaining the position of a superpower in the international arena. To achieve this goal, the Russian Federation is ready to pursue its policy by various methods, not only from the position of force and accomplished facts, but more and more often through methods of soft influence on states where it delivers specific benefits.

References

(2013) *Government Decision No. 1139/2013 (21 March) on the National Cyber Security Strategy of Hungary*, The European Union Agency for Network and Information Security, March 21, https://www.enisa.europa.eu/topics/national-cyber-security-strategies/ncss-map/HU_NCSS.pdf.

(2016) *Media Bias in Hungary During the Referendum, Campaign on EU Refugee Quotas*, Mertek Media Monitor, October 4, http://mertek.eu/en/2016/10/04/dri-mertek-study-media-bias-hungary-durning-referendu-campaign-eu-refugee-quotas/.

(2017) *GLOBSEC Trends 2017: Mixed Messages and Signs of Hope from Central and Eastern Europe*, GLOBSEC, August 1, 2017, https://www.globsec.org/publications/globsec-trends-2017-mixed-messages-signs-hope-central-eastern-europe-2/.

Attila J., Lóránt G., Krekó P., Dezső A., (2015). *I Am Eurasian The Kremlin Connections of the Hungarian Far-Right*, "Political Capital".

Bátorfy A., Szánthó Z., (2016). *Bivalybasznádi Álhírvállalkozók És Oroszország Magyar Hangjai*, VS, April 7, 2016, https://vs.hu/kozelet/osszes/bivalybasznadi-alhirvallalkozok-es-oroszorszag-magyar-hangjai-0407.

Castells M., (2008). *Społeczeństwo sieci*, Warszawa: Wydawnictwo PWN.

Fiszer J. M., (2016). *Zadania i cele polityki zagranicznej Władimira Putina*, Myśl Ekonomiczna i Polityczna nr 1 /52/, Warszawa: Oficyna Wydawnicza Uczelni Łazarskiego.

Gyula Máté T., (2015). *Moszkvai Jalta*, Magyar Hírlap, February 6, http://magyarhirlap.hu/cikk/16617/Moszkvai_Jalta.

Kovács B., (2009) *Jobbik*, May 13, https://jobbik.hu/rovatok/ep-lista/7_kovacs_bela.

Lorant G., Kreko P., (2017). *Russian disinformation and extremism in Hungary*, Ed. The Warsaw: Institute Review.
Nye J.S, (2007). *Soft-power. Jak osiągnąć sukces w polityce światowej*, Warszawa: Wydawnictwo Akademickie i Profesjonalne.
Nye jr. J.S., (2009). *Konflikty międzynarodowe. Wprowadzenie do teorii i historii*, tłumaczenie M. Madej, Warszawa: Wydawnictwo Akademickie i Profesjonalne.
Potulski J., (2010). *Współczesne kierunki rosyjskiej myśli geopolitycznej*, Gdańsk: Wydawnictwo Uniwersytetu Gdańskiego.
Potulski J., (2011). *Geopolityka w świecie ponowoczesnym*, Częstochowa: Instytut Geopolityki.
Wasilienko I.A., (2006). *Geopolitika sowriemiennowo mira*, Moskwa.

Sławomir Byleń / Marcin Górnikiewicz / Radosław Bielawski

Chapter 42: Summary and conclusions: The Russian mechanism of influencing the policy of Budapest with the system of "hard power" and "soft power"

As a part of the tough influence of the Russian Federation on Hungary and other European countries, there is a perceived desire to weaken or even completely eliminate European structures [Sykulski 2013, 354–355]. This is now the main goal of foreign policy, which in the language of diplomacy is called a geopolitical game. Its essence and sense are especially noticed in the second decade of the 21st century, when Great Britain leaves the European Union, and at the same time the crisis of European institutions is noticed. The authorities of the Russian Federation are taking advantage of the political turmoil in individual countries, thus seeking to weaken European integration. These activities are carried out on many levels, although sometimes they have negative economic effects for the Russian Federation.

Through the methods of hard interaction, the fear of the Russian Federation is growing in Europe, which is the breeding ground for the so-called "Building small homelands". As a result, the existing strong ties are impoverished, which is the main goal of the political activity of the Russian Federation. The striving of Russian politicians and decision-makers to weaken or even abandon the "soft power" policy by the European Union. Such a sequence of events could lead to the formation of a new European order, in which the Russian Federation may play a significant role. Using the divided continent and its geopolitical position, Russia will create politics in the countries of the former Eastern bloc, including, of course, Hungary.

For Moscow, Budapest is a smaller partner with whom it does not have a common border, but it can be used to shape relations within the EU. That is why the Hungarians do not feel threatened by the Kremlin. On the contrary. If the Russians conquered Ukraine and began to put pressure on, for example, Romania, then the Hungarians could start thinking about revising the provisions of the Trianon treaty. And regaining not only Transcarpathia, lost after World War II to Ukraine and Russia, but also Romanian Transylvania. This is why Viktor Orban started putting pressure on Kiev.

The incidents in Transcarpathia, increasing tensions between Hungary and Ukraine, are also certainly the result of the activities of the Russian agency, which is playing against Kiev and its neighbors. On the one hand, Viktor Orban adheres to the rules of the game imposed by the Union, opposing only within the framework of the applicable regulations, which Brussels itself ignores, and on the other hand, it plays a partnership game with Russia as far as the EU allows it. It should be recalled at this point that the sanctions imposed on Russia are still in force. Brussels had to agree to the expansion of the nuclear power plant in Hungary, which it did under certain conditions. On the one hand, the Hungarians do not allow themselves to be imposed on Germany's political will, for example, by loudly supporting Poland, they are against migration, and on the other hand, they are interested in Russian economic projects and investments in Hungary.

Budapest is taking advantage of the internal economic rivalry in the EU. The Hungarians are also interested in the construction of the North-South Via Carpatia motorway with Poland and the construction of the Nord Stream II gas pipeline with Germany. They are signing agreements with Russia on energy issues, and at the same time trying to convince the Chinese to follow the spur of the Belt and Road Initiative ("New Silk Road") running through Budapest, which is competitive for the Russian line. On the one hand, it is dangerous for such a small country, and on the other hand, it shows the independence of Hungary in relation to the mainstream in the EU.

With regard to Hungary as a small European state, in the opinion of the decision-makers in Moscow, there is no need for direct, hard political, military or economic influence. It is certain, however, that a hard influence on the European Union will result in a ricochet hitting Hungary as a full member of NATO and the EU. In the longer term, after the break-up of the European community, the Russian Federation will strive to reactivate its sphere of influence by extending it to the countries of Central and Eastern Europe, including Hungary. It follows that the long-term geopolitical goals of the Russian Federation are rooted in the times when the Soviet Union was one of the world's two superpowers.

Russia does not have a strong economic base in Hungary, other than the energy sector. Neither before the introduction of the sanctions nor at present, is one of the most important recipients of Hungarian goods, and its investments in Hungary are insignificant. The statistical data do not confirm the thesis that the EU sanctions against Russia will bring significant losses to the Hungarian economy. Hungary refers to this thesis, signaling the need to lift the sanctions imposed on Russia. On the one hand, it is therefore a message of a political nature, one of the numerous gestures made by the Hungarian government towards the Russian authorities. In return, it counts on low commodity prices, which can be used to ensure internal political stability.

On the other hand, the Hungarian authorities may be convinced of the profitability of developing economic relations with Russia. As a part of the East-to-East program, the government aims to increase the share of non-EU countries in Hungarian exports to one-third. Openness to political and economic contacts with Russia was facilitated by the positive attitude of the Hungarian society towards this country, and the pursuit of such a policy was characteristic of all Hungarian governments after 2002, regardless of the political option currently in power.

At the same time, Russia's importance for the Hungarian economy goes far beyond the value of trade and investment. The country is building its long-term presence in Hungary through energy contracts, including in particular the expansion of the power plant in Paks. With the scale of this undertaking, it gains influence on Hungary's domestic policy and may extend its economic interests to other sectors. Another rapprochement is likely to take place during the negotiations of the next long-term gas contract, ensuring supplies to Hungary for the period after 2021.

Finally, referring to the effectiveness of Russian soft power in relation to Hungary, it is worth paying attention to its noticeable and positive impact for Moscow. Hungary appears to be significantly vulnerable to the influence of the Russian Federation. They are one of the few countries belonging to the European Union that shows a very friendly attitude towards the Kremlin's policy, including situations where the Hungarian authorities' approval of Russian actions is in complete contradiction with the attitudes adopted by other EU and NATO member states. In fact, one can get the impression that Hungary, through the soft influence of the Russian Federation, has become its camouflaged ally, which at key moments shows compassion and understanding for the often offensive Russian foreign policy. It is currently difficult to indicate how Budapest's foreign and domestic policy may evolve in the light of the conflicting spheres of influence: the American, the EU and the Russian. It seems, however, that in the near future the course on European integration with the Russian Federation simultaneous cooperation, especially economic one, will be continued in the coming years. Therefore, it cannot be ruled out that this cooperation may also be developed with regard to the armaments industry, which in the case of Hungary has required extensive modernization and thus enormous funding for years.

Section III:
The Russian potential and the Hungarian potential: interaction and implications for regional safety

Małgorzata Grzelak

Chapter 43: The effectiveness measurement of the quantitative methods of the Russian impact in Hungary

Efficiency, in line with the praxeological approach presented by Tadeusz Kotarbiński, should always be equated with purposefulness. Its assessment should be made on the basis of an analysis of the compliance relationship of the obtained result of the activities carried out in relation to the assumed goals (Kozłowski et al., 2013). Measuring the effectiveness of Russia's influence on Hungary can be viewed in terms of both "hard" and "soft" impact (Harris, 2020). Pursuant to the contemporary standards of international politics, particular emphasis is placed on the use of "soft impact" methods and tools, based on influencing others in order to obtain the expected benefits (Weiner, 2016).

The purpose of this chapter is to present the quantitative methods available in the literature for measuring the effectiveness of the Russian influence on Hungary. Bearing in mind this goal, the research problem was formulated in the form of a question: is there any research conducted that measures the effectiveness of Russia's influence on Hungary and what quantitative measurement methods are used? In order to solve such a specific research problem, the method of analyzing the literature and all available information concerning the ways in which Russia influences Hungary and the effectiveness of this impact will be mainly used. On this basis, the main quantitative methods applied to measure the impact will be presented in a synthetic form, as well as the conclusions and inferences drawn from the analyzes.

The research on measuring the effectiveness of Russia's impact on Hungary is conducted mainly in terms of "soft impact", most often in economic and social terms. For this purpose, from an economic perspective, comparative analyzes of economic indicators of both countries, statistical methods (presenting the average values of the compared factors), and studies of development trends in a time series, are widely used. On the other hand, in the social aspect, questionnaire studies are conducted, indicating the social mood and the trends existing in it.

The conducted literature review showed that in the economic area, the analyzes conducted mainly concern the indicators of exports of goods to Russia, imports of Russian products into the territory of Hungary (including energy raw materials) and the value of foreign direct investment (FDI). With regard to the level of exports of goods, the conducted research indicates a decline in the effectiveness of Russia's influence on Hungary. The above fact was leveraged by the political situation which made the Russian market less important for Hungarian foreign trade. Annual indicators of the percentage share of exports to Russia in relation to total exports of goods by Hungary are presented in Fig. 1. In 2013, Russia was on the 13th place among the largest sales markets in Hungary. The situation changed in 2014 (see line on the chart), when Russia annexed Crimea, as a result of which economic sanctions were imposed by the European Union member states, and as a consequence Russia imposed counter-sanctions on agri-food products from the EU. Therefore, in the following years, a decline in the share of the Russian sales market in Hungarian exports was recorded. In 2016, it was ranked 16th among the largest recipients (1.5% of total exports) and 19th in 2018 (1.4%). In 2013–2016, the value of Hungarian exports to Russia decreased by approx. 40%, with the overall increase in foreign sales by approx. 13% (Figure 1).

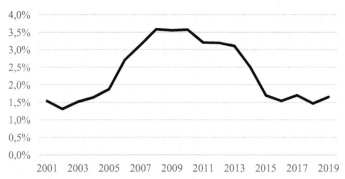

Figure 1. Percentage share of the value of exports of goods from Hungary to Russia (Data of the Hungarian Statistical Office).

The percentage structure of individual assortment groups of goods exported to Russia is presented in Figure 2.

In the structure of Hungarian exports to Russia, the dominant group of goods are industrial goods (including pharmaceuticals) as well as transport equipment and machinery. In 2018, agri-food products accounted for only 5% of the value of all goods exported to Russia. This indicates that the Russian embargo has had little impact on this sector of the Hungarian economy, and hence the low effectiveness of the Russian Federation's influence in this regard (Amon and Deák, 2015).

With regard to the import of goods from the Russian market on the territory of Hungary, the analysis of the main indicators related to trade between the above-mentioned countries shows that until 2013 Russia was one of Hungary's three

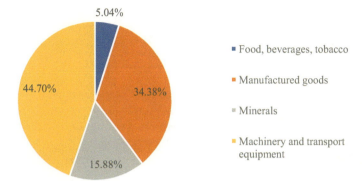

Figure 2. Percentage share of individual groups of goods for export to Russia in 2018 (Data of the Hungarian Stastical Office).

main trading partners (with a 8.6% share in the total value of imports). In the following years, a decline in the value of goods imported from Russia to Hungary was recorded (Figure 3). In 2016, the Russian market was ranked 14th among the main suppliers (with a 2.9% share in value).

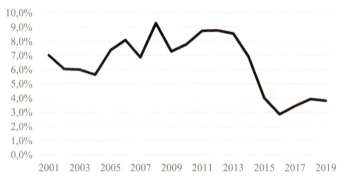

Figure 3. Percentage share of the value of goods imported from Russia to Hungary (Data of the Hungarian Statistical Office).

The structure of Hungarian imports of Russian goods, as displayed as groups of goods presented in Figure 4, shows that the largest percentage (87.48%) are fuels and energy. The share of the other assortment groups does not exceed 13% (including products manufactured in Hungary – 3.65%, chemicals – 6.95% and mechanical and transport equipment – 1.92%). The decrease in the value of imports of Russian goods is mainly due to the significant drop in oil prices, which reached the critical lowest level in 2016 (average prices per barrel were respectively $ 80 in 2010, $ 110 in 2013, $ 30 in 2016. and $ 70 in 2019). Currently, along with the increase in prices, there is an increase in the value of goods imported from Russia.

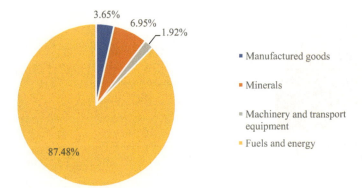

Figure 4. Percentage structure of individual groups of goods in imports from Russia in 2018 (Data of the Hungarian Statistical Office).

Despite the decline in the value of the share of imports from Russia in the total trade conducted by Hungary, it continues to be a key element of the country's economy. This is mainly due to the structure of imported products (87.48% are energy resources), but also the fact that Hungary covers over 80% of its energy demand from imports (Figure 5). This makes them very dependent on Russia in this respect, thus increasing the possibility of its effective influence.

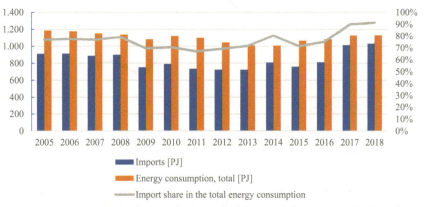

Figure 5. The division of energy raw materials imports in total energy consumption (Data of the Hungarian Statistical Office).

The comparative analyzes available in the literature indicate that in 2018 the consumption of natural gas in Hungary was 9.6 bcm. 8.8 billion m3 were imported to secure internal consumption, of which 7.6 billion m3 was supplied by the Russian company Gazprom. Russia's share in Hungarian natural gas imports was 86%. As regards crude oil, the research conducted shows that over 60% of

Hungarian demand for this raw material is covered by supplies of resources from Russia via the Druzhba oil pipeline, and the current agreement expires in 2025.

A similar phenomenon is observed in the case of supplying Hungary with electricity. Currently, energy supplies are secured by the nuclear power plant in Paks, the total capacity of which is 2 GW (representing 40% of the annual demand). However, analysts indicate that this facility was built during the USSR and operates solely on the basis of Russian technology. Additionally, another factor making the Hungarian economy dependent on Russia is the ten-year contract for the construction of two new nuclear reactors in Paks. The contract was concluded in 2014, and the main contractor for the project is the Russian company Rosatom. The Paks-2 complex will be based on Russian technology and fuel, enabling energy production at the level of 4.4 GW. For the implementation of the above project, Russia granted a loan to Hungary in the amount of EUR 10 billion (equivalent to approx. 10% of Hungarian GDP).

Table 1 presents the balance of trade between Russia and Hungary. There is a noticeable decline in the value of imports and exports after 2014, which is the result of the sanctions and counter-sanctions imposed between the EU countries and Russia. The analysis showed that apart from the energy sector, Russia does not have a strong economic base on the territory of Hungary and, additionally, is not one of the key recipients of Hungarian goods. It should also be noted that the presented balance is negative from the point of view of the Hungarian economy, which means that the value of exports is much lower than the value of imports (the smallest difference was in 2016 due to the low price of a barrel of crude oil).

Table 1. Balance of the trade value of Hungary and Russia (HUF million) (Data of the Hungarian Statistical Office)

	2005	2010	2013	2016	2017	2018	2019
EXPORTS	233.2	704.0	749.9	448.1	530.8	492.1	587.2
IMPORTS	970.4	1419.1	1895.0	740.7	987.4	1242.5	1292.3
BALANCE	-737.2	-715.1	-1145.2	-292.6	-456.6	-750.4	-705.2

Another economic indicator analyzed in the studies available in the literature is the value of Russian foreign direct investment (FDI) in Hungary (Jóźwiak, 2019). In 2017, their cumulative value amounted to EUR 65 million, representing 0.08% of the total FDI value in this country. On the other hand, the value of Hungarian FDI in Russia in 2017 amounted to EUR 653 million (representing 2.6% of all foreign investments). Additionally, in Hungary, apart from the energy sector, there are several significant Russian economic entities. One of them is the

Sberbank bank, which is owned by the Russian state treasury. Moreover, in the largest Hungarian bank, OTP, Russian capital accounts for 7.4% of the shares. In addition, Russian investors hold a majority stake in the ISD Dunaferr steel group, which, according to experts' forecasts, is to be used to secure supplies for the construction of the Paks power plant. However, the above indicators demonstrate that Russia (apart from the energy sector) does not have large capital in the territory of Hungary (Smyrgała, 2012).

Due to the presented aspects, the Russian influence and leverage on Hungary exceeds the value of trade and investments. The effectiveness of this influence is manifested through long-term energy contracts, including the construction of the Paks power plant, which makes it possible to influence Hungary's internal policy and to attempt to expand its interests to other economic sectors. Moreover, strengthening relations in the field of energy is expressed in the low prices of the raw materials on offer, which enables the Hungarian government to supply its citizens with gasoline and diesel oil at some of the lowest prices in Europe, as well as ensuring low gas and heating rates for the industry, thereby driving economy. The effectiveness of such influencing Hungary by the Russians is reflected in the surveys conducted, which indicate a high, positive attitude of the Hungarian society towards the Russian state.

The study carried out in 2016 by Globsec and Political Capital shows a marked increase in positive sentiment towards Russia. When asked which countries Hungary should maintain the closest relations with (indicate three countries), 16% of respondents pinpointed Russia, placing it in third place after Germany and Austria, followed by Great Britain, the USA and Poland (Table 2).

Table 2. With which countries do you think Hungary should maintain its closest relationship. Tick at least three countries (www.tarki.hu)

Ten most frequently mentioned countries	Ratio of mentions among first three countries (%)
Germany	44
Austria	28
Russia	16
United Kingdom	13
United States	13
Poland	13
Slovakia	8
France	8
Romania	6
Czech Republic	5

However, according to a 2018 study (Medián, 2018), Russia's 100-point rating increased to 48 points (with a score of 44 in 2014), while sympathy for the US in the same period fell from 64 points in 2014 to the level of 54 points in 2018. The results of the above-mentioned research also indicate that in 2014 only 25% of respondents believed that Hungary should maintain closer relations with Russia than with the USA, and in 2018 already 33% of respondents shared this view (Globsec, 2016).

Among the supporters of individual political parties, the highest level of sympathy for Russia is recorded among voters of the ruling Fidesz party – 59% (compared to 42% of supporters of the Jobbik party and 40% of sympathy of MSZP voters). Moreover, the majority of the Fidesz party electorate indicated Russia as Hungary's closest ally – 51%, while the USA was indicated by only 39% of respondents.

In conclusion, the literature analysis carried out showed that there are many studies available presenting quantitative methods for measuring the effectiveness of Russia's influence on Hungary. Most often, research is conducted in the aspect of the possibility of economic impact. Among the measurement methods, the most frequently used are statistical methods, comparative analysis or analogue research (e.g. trend study in relation to the relationship between countries). It should be noted that, in economic terms, the energy sector is a key factor in Russia's impact on Hungary. Through its tools and resources, such as crude oil or natural gas, it can effectively influence Hungary's domestic policy, making the country highly dependent on itself in this regard.

References

Ámon A. and Deák A., (2015). Hungary and Russia in economic terms-love, business, both or neither?.
Dane Węgierskiego Urzędu Statystycznego.
Globsec (2016). Central Europe under the fire of propaganda. https://www.globsec.org/wp-content/uploads/2018/04/GLOBSEC-Trends-2016.pdf.
Harris K., (2020). Russia's fifth column: The influence of the Night Wolves Motorcycle Club. Studies in Conflict & Terrorism, 43(4), pp. 259–273.
https://www.tarki.hu/sites/default/files/2019-02/358_371_Kreko.pdf.
Jóźwiak V., (2019). Węgiersko-rosyjskie stosunki gospodarcze. Biuletyn Polskiego Instytutu Spraw Międzynarodowych, Nr 105 (1853).
Kozłowski E. and Borucka A. and Świderski A., (2020). Application of the logistic regression for determining transition probability matrix of operating states in the transport systems. Eksploatacja i Niezawodnosc – Maintenance and Reliability 22(2) p.192–200, http://dx.doi.org/10.17531/ein.2020.2.2.

Medián, (2018). A fideszesek nagyon megszerették Putyint és Oroszországot [Fidesz voters have come to like Putin and Russia very much]. 444, https://444.hu/2018/03/14/a-fideszesek-nagyonmegszerettek-putyint-es-oroszorszagot.

Smyrgała D., (2012). Ukraiński kryzys gazowy 2009 a polityka energetyczna państw bałkańskich in: K. Taczyńska, A. Twardowska (eds.), Poznać Bałkany. Historia-Kultura-Polityka-Języki, Toruń.

Weiner C., (2016). New Forms of Russian Investments in Hungary. Contemporary Europe-Sovremennaya Evropa, (6), pp. 116–124.

Małgorzata Grzelak

Chapter 44: The effectiveness measurement of the qualitative methods of the Russian impact in Hungary

Hungary, like other countries of the Visegrad Group, has historically maintained strong political relations with Russia. In addition, the rule of the communist party meant that the country was considered a satellite state of the USSR. This situation changed at the turn of 1989/90, when the systemic transformation took place, as a result of which parliamentary democracy was introduced. The accession of Hungary to NATO in 1999 and to the European Union in 2004 resulted in even greater loosening of political relations with Russia. However, it should be remembered that there are still internal forces in Hungary seeking to curb the prevailing pro-Western sentiment, as well as those wishing to change the cultural and geopolitical orientation of the country. The above-mentioned internal activities are supported by the activity of foreign entities (mainly strongly connected with Russia), which are trying to increase discontent inside the country or create social divisions. Additionally, Russia is constantly carrying out diplomatic activities aimed at increasing its role in the Central European region through energy and economic policy, information warfare or support of Hungarian political forces (the mainstream and the marginalized one). All these activities are aimed at restoring influence in the region, weakening the position of the EU and NATO, and increasing their effectiveness (Milo and Klingova, 2017; Solodky, 2019).

The purpose of this chapter is to present the qualitative methods available in the literature for measuring the effectiveness of the Russian influence on Hungary. With this goal in mind, the following research problem was formulated: are there studies available that measure the effectiveness of Russia's influence on Hungary and what qualitative measurement methods are used? In order to solve such a research problem, the method of analyzing the literature and any available information on the qualitative methods, applied to study the ways of Russia's influence on Hungary, and the effectiveness of this impact will be used in the main part. Based on this, the main qualitative methods adopted to measure the impact, will be discussed in a synthetic form, as well as the conclusions and inferences drawn from the analyzes.

The application of qualitative methods in social research is aimed at obtaining an answer how and why a given phenomenon occurs, allowing for the identification of specific behaviors, patterns of thinking and behavior, as well as rules of operation. The use of qualitative methods to measure the effectiveness of Russia's influence on Hungary makes it possible to discover and analyze the underlying motives of the taken actions and to evaluate their effectiveness. Among the qualitative methods adopted to study the mutual impact of individual countries in international relations, the most frequently used are individual in-depth interview, focus group interview, experiment, observation and methods of analyzing the current condition, i.e. desk research.

There are many studies available in the literature aimed at examining the susceptibility of individual countries (including those belonging to the Visegrad Group) to subversive foreign influences (Schimpfössl and Yablokov, 2020, pp. 29-45; Surowiec and Štětka, 2020, pp. 1-4). 8). They are based mainly on quantitative evaluation methods, including primarily questionnaire surveys. The results of the above-mentioned studies were the basis for the development of a qualitative method for measuring the effectiveness of Russia's influence on Hungary based on the desk research technique and a focused group interview. The GLOBSEC Policy Institute (GLOBSEC, 2016) has developed a methodology that enables a comparative analysis of the results and analyzes of public opinion polls, based on a measurable set of social and political indicators, as well as the current political landscape, media structure and the state of society. The value of the indicator was estimated on the basis of an assessment of interviews with 38 experts from the four countries of the Visegrad Group. Thanks to the aggregation of data supported by analyzes and insights of experts from Central Europe, a ranking of individual weaknesses of the Central European region was created in terms of the possible influence of Russia. The developed index (Vulnerability Index of Central European), taking into account both quantitative and qualitative factors, illustrates the susceptibility of individual Central European countries to the external influence of other countries. Additionally, it provides information enabling understanding of the current dynamics of moods in the region and attitudes towards the US, EU, NATO and Russia. It also presents a comparative analysis of the measures that need to be implemented (per country) to ensure a higher level of security. The developed Vulnerability Index of Central European is measured on a scale from 0 to 100, where as it grows, the country's susceptibility to subversive influence of other countries increases.

Based on the analysis, it was found that Hungary, among all the countries of the Visegrad Group, is the country mostly exposed to hostile foreign influences. The above research was conducted in terms of social moods, the prevailing political landscape, the structure of the media, available tools and remedial measures minimizing the possibility of the influence of other countries, the structure and activities of "Third sector". Calculated on the basis of aggregation of the above criteria, the value of the vulnerability index was 57 units (on a 100-degree scale). This indicates a cooling down of relations between this country and Western Europe, the main source of which should be seen in the pro-Russian attitude of Hungarian political elites.

Among the countries of the Visegrad Group, in terms of criteria related to the political landscape, the structure of the media, as well as the available means and remedial apparatuses, Hungary ranks as the country most susceptible to Russia's influence. In terms of subversive activities of NGOs, they are in second place (after Poland). The situation looks best with regard to social sentiment, for which the conducted research indicates that Hungarian society is in third place in the Visegrad Group and is characterized by low susceptibility to the influence of other countries.

Research indicates that, politically, Hungary is the most vulnerable to foreign influence in the region. This is mainly due to the pro-Russian orientation of the Hungarian government, as well as the attitude of the opposition parties, i.e. the socialist MSZP (Magyar Szocialista Párt – Hungarian Socialist Party) which officially considers itself neutral (although the vast majority of the party's more experienced politicians declare pro-Russian views), and the far-right Jobbik is also pro-Kremlin. The above is compounded by the strong dependence of Hungary on Russia in the energy sector. In 2009, politicians from the Fidesz party were skeptical about Russian politics. After gaining a social mandate and coming to power, this approach has changed. The government announced the "Opening to the East" program, the foundation of which is a return to economic cooperation, among others with Russia. The result is the implementation of large public development projects with the participation of Russian capital, e.g. the Paks-2 project or a signed contract for the renovation of metro trains (Radi, 2016). Moreover, the Hungarian government is critical of the sanctions imposed by the EU on Russia, claiming that the value of Hungarian exports has dropped significantly as a result. Experts note that in addition to economic relations, there is also an ideological closeness between Hungarian and Russian politicians. The Hungarian government supports traditionalist, nativist, Christian and nationalist views that are close to Russian values. Moreover, they indicate the centralization of state structures by the government, as well as the employment of people with low professional experience, which negatively affects the state's ability to defend itself against foreign influences, increasing the effectiveness of Russia's influence (Pandi, 2016). Therefore, it is the political landscape and the manner of conducting Hungarian foreign policy that seem to be the highest risk factor and a possible area of Russia's effective influence (only a few minority parties have a pro-Western attitude).

Another factor which determines the effectiveness of Russian influence, indicated by experts, is the internal mechanisms and available remedies aimed at minimizing the possibility of its influence. The current security document in force in Hungary is the Hungarian National Security Strategy introduced by the government decree 1035/2012 in 2012. However, the above document does not contain any information on the possibility of protection against the effects of Russian influence. Currently, the document is being updated, however, based on the official positions of both the Hungarian prime minister and minister of foreign affairs, it is unlikely that it will identify any particular possibilities of counteracting the negative influence of Russia (Pandi, 2016; Tartalom, 2016). Both the results of public opinion polls in Hungary and the positions of many experts indicate that the greatest threat, and at the same time a chance for effective Russian influence, is the lack of a government policy or a plan to implement appropriate mechanisms to combat pro-Kremlin disinformation. Additionally, there is a noticeable lack of state experts who would support the government in developing and implementing the above-mentioned mechanisms or remedial measures, as well as in understanding and assessing Russian disinformation activities (Szablocs 2017). That is why the activities of Russian services that threaten Hungary's national security are not officially and effectively recognized by the means of the state apparatus. The situation is not improved by the fact that no de-communization has taken place in Hungary since the political transformation, and the list of Russian secret agents who are also members of the Hungarian Socialist Workers' Party has never been made public. This gives a lot of room for blackmail of the Russian community. Accordingly, the experts agree that the lack of state remedies is a large field for effective Russian influence over Hungary.

Experts' research indicates that the third factor enabling Russia to influence the countries of Central Europe is the condition and structure of the national media. This is done by carrying out activities aimed at undermining trust and creating a social worldview in independent media, regardless of the method of their financing (state or private capital). The media is a field for disseminating fabricated, emotional content and for the activities of the so-called "Troll farms" publishing content designed to sow fear, anger and distrust among citizens through the mainstream media. The comparative analysis of the results of questionnaire surveys and expert opinions carried out by the GLOBSEC Policy Institute shows that among the countries of the region, the Hungarian media is characterized by the least independence from state authorities (according to Special Eurobarometer 452, this fact is indicated by 37% of respondents of Hungarian origin) (Special Eurobarometer, 2016). Additionally, observers indicate that this country is the most susceptible to Russian influence in this respect. Most of the major Hungarian media are under the direct control of the government or pro-government oligarchs, disseminating information from unreliable foreign sources. As a result of the above, the Hungarian nation is deprived of reliable information, receiving mainly messages in line with the official position of the government, and many programs popularize the Russian point of view on the USA, NATO or the situation in Syria, and thus very susceptible to foreign manipulation. It should be noted, however, that there are, however, a few media that provide accurate current reports on everyday events, thus weakening the scope of Russian influence. The fourth factor of Russia's potential influence is the activity of non-governmental organizations, otherwise known as a "civil society" or a "third sector". On the basis of the research, it was indicated that the Hungarian state is on the second position of the risk of vulnerability to foreign influence among the countries of the Visegrad Group in this respect. In order to limit foreign influence, the Act on social organizations was adopted by the Hungarian parliament in June 2017. It introduces regulations that all associations and foundations that receive more than EUR 23,500 in capital from foreign sources each year, will have to register themselves as "foreign funded organizations". However, experts agree that both pro-Western, pro-government and pro-Russian organizations do not have a significant impact on a society, making this parameter insignificant in terms of the effectiveness of influence (the media play a much greater role in this regard).

The fifth factor on the basis of which the effectiveness of Russia's influence on other countries is measured, is the vulnerability of citizens to foreign impact. The studies available in the literature point out that the Hungarian nation ranks third among the citizens of the Visegrad Group, being one of the least susceptible to Russian influence. The bilateral history of these countries plays a major role in this attitude of the nation. The role of this country in suppressing the Hungarian revolution at the turn of 1848/1849 and in 1956, as well as suspicion of Russia's ambitions to dominate the region, had a particularly negative impact on the negative perception of Russia by the Hungarians. The 2016 GLOBSEC six-question multi-polarity index study on NATO, the US and Russia displays that Hungarian public opinion strongly supports the West. Nevertheless, the percentage of undecided respondents (36%) remains high, which indicates that the prevailing mood may be unstable and fluctuating under the influence of various international forces (including Russian). One should note that although the majority of the Hungarian society strongly supports the country's integration with the West, this support has deteriorated over the last few years. The migration crisis, which caused a slight drop in trust in the institutions of the European Union, played an important role, but did not change the public's views on membership in the treaty. Thus, in terms of the above factor, Hungary is characterized by a low susceptibility to Russia's influence. However, there is a large group of people who do not have a precise opinion about the geopolitical situation of the country, and thus becomes the main source of society's vulnerability to the influence of foreign forces.

Additionally, the literature review carried out indicated the existence of other qualitative methods for measuring the effectiveness of Russia's influence on Hungary. The most popular one is desk research or the Delphi method, presenting the results of considerations in the form of reports or expert opinions. Most often they contain an introduction to the geopolitical situation of both countries, they display the goals of Russia's foreign policy and the instruments used to exert the so-called "Soft impact". Moreover, they present good practices of combating Russia's excessive policies and recommendations on the methods of action and forms of counteracting Russian influence.

In conclusion, the literature analysis carried out showed that there are many studies available and presenting qualitative methods for measuring the effectiveness of Russia's influence on Hungary. Desk research studies are most often conducted to evaluate the existing situation, as well as based on expert interviews or Delphi analysis. They show that both the Hungarian political landscape and the implemented mechanisms and state remedies make the country particularly vulnerable to hostile foreign influences, mainly Russian. Experts unanimously highlight the strongly pro-Russian attitude of the Hungarian government, which is based mainly on the convergent ideological views and the common energy policy. A similar attitude is characteristic of the largest opposition party in Hungary, ie Jobbik, which is a pro-Russian, anti-European party. Such political moods result in the lack of or reluctance to introduce defense measures and mechanisms that could support the fight against pro-Russian propaganda.

References

(2012) Governmental decree 1035/2012, http://2010-2014.kormany.hu/download/f/49/70000/1035_2012_korm_hatarozat.pdf.
(2016) GLOBSEC Trends, Central Europe under the fire of propaganda: Public opinion poll analysis in the Czech Republic, Hungary and Slovakia. Globsec Policy Institute.
(2016) Special Eurobarometer 452 – October 2016 "Media pluralism and democracy" Summary, http://ec.europa.eu/information_society/newsroom/image/.
Milo D. and Klingova K., (2017). Subversive Russian Influence in Central Europe – Vulnerability Index. Globsec Policy Institute.
Pandi B., (2016). Orbán: Oroszország nem fenyegeti a biztonságunkat. http://index.hu/belfold/2016/10/20/orban_oroszorszag_nem_fenyegeti_a_biztonsagunkat.
Radi A., (2016). Oroszok a spájzban: Kik kavarnak a metrófelújítás környékén? https://atlatszo.hu/2016/02/10/oroszok-a-spajzban-kik-kavarnak-a-metrofelujitas-kornyeken/.
Schimpfössl E. and Yablokov I., (2020). Post-socialist self-censorship: Russia, Hungary and Latvia. *European Journal of Communication*, 35(1), pp. 29–45.

Solodky S., (2019). How to counteract Russian influence in Europe: Hungary's Experience. New Europe Center.
Surowiec P. and Štětka V., (2020). Introduction: media and illiberal democracy in Central and Eastern Europe. *East European Politics*, 36(1), pp. 1–8.
Szablocs P., (2017). Hungarian secret agent reveals in detail how serious the Russian threat is. http://index.hu/belfold/2017/03/21/hungarian_secret_agent_reveals_how.
Tartalom E., (2016). Szijjártó: Nem támadna meg Oroszország egy NATO-tagországot. http://www.portfolio.hu/gazdasag/szijjarto_nem_tamadna_meg_oroszorszag_egy_nato-tagorszagot.245250.html (dostęp 29.03.2020).

Małgorzata Grzelak

Chapter 45: Summary and conclusions: Implications resulting from the Russian potential to influence the Hungarian decision-making process

The quantitative research carried out has clearly demonstrated the possibility of Russia's influence through economic instruments consisting in the control of supplies of raw materials, mainly energy, which are necessary for the proper functioning of the Hungarian energy sector. The technological and numerical state of the Hungarian armed forces is not a defense potential that Russia would have to reckon with, so only membership of NATO and partly the EU is the only form of strategic deterrence that Budapest currently has in relation to Moscow. It can also be assumed that the level of penetration of political circles and those influencing the decision-making process of Budapest is also not as deep as in other smaller countries of Central and Eastern Europe. On the other hand, due to the political interest, the Hungarian government is pursuing a policy that is neutral or even friendly towards Moscow, which, combined with the possibility of economic influence, becomes a real field of Russia's current and future influence on Hungary.

Qualitative research, mainly conducted in the form of expert interviews and analysis of reliable source materials (e.g. official reports, scientific publications), shows the so-called "soft power" influences aimed at enhancing the positive perception of Russian culture and foreign policy by the Hungarian society. This in turn may lead to a creation of the basis for future intelligence activity targeted at the environment and people who could influence or even shape Hungary's internal and external policy. This scenario of operation has already been tested in several smaller countries of Central and Eastern Europe. Such an approach, as the research shows, delivers results of not only a positive attitude of politicians associated with the ruling option, but also of politicians connected with the opposition, such as Jobbik (a party with an anti-European and pro-Russian attitude). Therefore, there is no real will to oppose the pro-Russian propaganda, also spread through the Hungarian media, which opens the door to Moscow for further information activities aimed at shaping social and civic attitudes in line with Russia's expectations.

References

(2005) Strategia Bezpieczeństwa Republiki Słowackiej.
(2016) Biała Księga z 2016 roku, https://www.mosr.sk/data/WPDSR2016_HQ.pdf.
Ambler T. and Neubauer J. (2017). The nexus of military expenditure and economic growth in Visegrad Group countries. *Economic and Social Development: Book of Proceedings*, pp. 473–478.
Ambler T. and Neubauer J., (2017). Defense expenditure and economic growth in Visegrad group countries: a panel data analysis. In *35th International Conference Mathematical Methods in Economics, Hradec Králové*, pp. 6–11.
Cabada L. and Waisová Š., (2018). *Security, Foreign and European Policy of the Visegrad Group*. Prague: Metropolitan University.
Cooper J., (2016). The military dimension of a more Militant Russia. *Russian Journal of Economics*, 2(2), pp. 129–145.
Gotkowska J., Osica O. (edt.), (2012). *W regionie siła? Stan i perspektywy współpracy wojskowej wybranych państw od Morza Bałtyckiego do Morza Czarnego*, Warszawa: Ośrodek Studiów Wschodnich pp. 67–68.
https://data.worldbank.org/indicator/MS.MIL.XPND.GD.ZS.
https://www.defence24.pl/przebudzenie-panstw-wyszehradu-slowacja-zwieksza-wydatki-obronne-o-50.
Kustrova M., (2012). Trends in Slovak Republic's military spending, *Journal of Defence Resources Management*, Vol. 3, Issue 2 (5), pp. 51–56.
Nadtochey Y.I., (2018). Defence cooperation models at the northern and on the eastern flanks of the eu (Norden And Visegrad Group Experience). Comparative Politics Russia, 9(2), pp. 26–40.
Pajtinka E., (2018). European External Action Service As the European Union's Diplomatic Service and Representation of Individual Member States Within Its Staff. The Cases of Slovakia, Czechia, Hungary and Poland. *Politické vedy*, 21(2), pp. 26–55.
Persson G., (2016). Russian military capability in a ten-year perspective–2016. FOI, December.
Petrufová M. and Nagyová L., (2019). Globalization Trends in the Security Environment and Education of Military Professionals in the Slovak Armed Forces. In *International conference Knowledge-Based Organization*, Vol. 25, No. 2, pp. 305–315.
Sandler T. and George J., (2016). Military expenditure trends for 1960–2014 and what they reveal. *Global Policy*, 7(2), pp. 174–184.
Toma P., (2017). Creating Advance of the Armed Forces of the Slovak Republic. *Security Dimensions. International and National Studies*, (22), pp. 194–204.
Usiak J., (2018). Slovakia's perspective on NATO, *Communist and Post-Communist Studies*, 51, pp. 125–137.
www.nato.int/invitees-Slovakia.

Section IV:
The forecast of the evolution in the Russian-Hungarian interaction in the 3rd decade of the 21st century

Oliver Balogh / Jerzy Zalewski

Chapter 46: Qualitative methods of Hungary's national strategy forecasting

Qualitative forecasting related to the development of Hungary is related to the security function, for which ordinary and emergency situations assume the following identified and interpreted values: geopolitical location of the country, the nature of security challenges and threats, the state's protective and defense potential, and the international position of the alliance system. In the illustrated approach, the state security is as follows:

$F(x) = y$; where:
F – Hungary's security situation
x – security, jeopardy
y – values determining the level of security and jeopardy

Since 2012, the "Hungarian National Security Strategy" has been in force, defining the external and internal security environment of the state, the nature of challenges and threats as well as system solutions. Among the determinants of the security environment of Hungary, the greatest value is the development of cooperation for global and regional security and the shaping of the sensitivity of state institutions in identifying and analyzing civilization threats, in particular terrorism, violations of the principles of proliferation of mass destruction weapons, uncertainty and unpredictability from the side of failed states. The structure of challenges and threats to the country's security also includes demographic issues, the security of the Hungarian minority and various crises: economic, financial, climate, energy, refugee, migration and epidemiological (Kormánya, 2012).

Hungary does not recognize any state as an enemy, it declares an inalienable readiness to settle disputes with other entities according to the UN Charter, without the use of military force or aggressive measures (Kormánya, 2012). The National Security Strategy of Hungary takes into account the need to ensure the necessary conditions for the functioning of the Hungarian minority in the neighboring countries: Austria, Romania[1], Serbia[2], Slovakia[3] and Ukraine[4]. The new state ideology of Hungary was reflected in the program of the National Cultural Council (2019), emphasizing the need for active work for the nation's survival, prosperity and growth, and for shaping "Christian democracy".

The 100th anniversary of the Treaty of Trianon and Peace in Paris[5], which falls in 2020 (Romsics, 2018, p. 360), triggers patriotic revival among the Hungarians and revindication moods around the "Hungarian Holy Crown doctrine", a phenomenon symbolizing the continuity of Hungarian statehood and the "new order" – the national idea (Gerő, 2013). It is emphasized that over 10 million people declaring Hungarian identity and willingness to participate in the political life of Hungary live in "Carpathian Reservoir". Despite the passage of one hundred years, the territorial, national and demographic outcomes of the provisions of the Trianon Treaty remain a permanent element of the political consciousness of most Hungarians. Various emotional historical associations are articulated, including the context of the Russian-Ukrainian conflict that has been ongoing since 2014. The language and education policy in Ukraine restricting the emancipation of national minorities is causing concern (the Act on Language Law of 2019 and the Act on Education of 2017[6]). This led to a diplomatic conflict between Hungary and Ukraine, and Budapest blocked the decision in the North Atlantic Council on NATO-Ukraine and Ukraine cooperation in the European Union. Similarly, since 2008, unfavorable solutions of the language policy have affected the Hungarian minority in the Slovak Republic (Csernicskó and Szabómihály, 2010, p. 170). Significant ethnic tensions are also taking place over the background of the language policy in Romania. The North Transylvania region in some localities is 100% inhabited by the Hungarians. There is a growing problem of incompatibility of administrative solutions with regard to employing people of Hungarian origin with low qualifications and the lack of knowledge of the Romanian language. The factor negatively affecting the status quo of the Hungarian

---

1 According to the 2011 national census in Romania, about 1.2 million people belonged to the Hungarian ethnic minority, which means that it amounts to about 6% of the population. Most Hungarians in Romania lives in Transylvania, where the Hungarian minority amounts almost 20% of the population.
2 In Serbia, the Hungarian minority numbered 250,000 people in 2011 which was 3.5% of the population.
3 In Slovakia, the Hungarian minority numbered about 0.5 million people in 2011, almost 8.5% of the population.
4 In the Ukrainian Transcarpathia, among 1.25 million people in 2011, there were about 150 thousand Hungarians.
5 Hungary lost 2/3 of the territory of the former Kingdom of Hungary; about 4 million Hungarians found themselves abroad and the country lost the access to the sea.
6 The Ukrainian side does not allow dual citizenship. After adopting Hungarian citizenship, in many cases the authorities in Kiev revoked Ukrainian citizenship from the Hungarian minority

minority is the aging, emigration of young people and the process of assimilation with the local population (Csernicskó and Szabómihály, 2010, p. 173).

The idea of the spiritual and legal statehood of Hungary is based on the "Hungarian-Christian values" articulated in the Basic Law. The attention is drawn to the mythologization of the nation, its eschatological role in shaping regional security and the nature and scope of citizens' defense duties. The state's defense model is configured with the construction of "illiberal democracy" (delineation of new constituencies, vassalisation of state institutions, depreciating democratic opposition, limiting the role of independent media) and the pragmatics of multi-vector national security (agreements with the Russian Federation on energy fuel supplies and expansion of the Hungarian energy sector).

The national defense strategy of Hungary defined the goals, principles and tasks of the most important organs of the command and control system, as well as sectoral strategies, resulting from the act on the universal defense obligation. Since 1999, military security in Hungary has been based on allied and national potential (Tálas, 2015, p. 11). The events related to the annexation of Crimea, the conflict in eastern Ukraine as well as the refugee and migration crisis highlighted the need to improve the quality of the functioning of the army and police forces at the state border. Deficiencies in this respect were confirmed by the assessments of the participation of Hungarian contingents in missions in Afghanistan and Iraq (Szenes, 2017, p. 65).

It was not until 2016 that the governmental modernization program of the Hungarian Armed Forces was adopted, providing for an increase in expenditure on defense, the purchase of modern weapons and military equipment, intensified training and improvement of operational capabilities of the defense potential (Balogh, 2019a, pp. 197–212). Although the geopolitical location of Hungary is not attractive in terms of strategic military operations, it is gaining importance in the implementation of logistics tasks, including supporting the "eastern flank of NATO". Along with the needs of Hungary's national military potential, the National Assembly decided to increase the Hungarian Army from 29.7 to 36.75 thousand soldiers; purchases of equipment for the air and land forces, incl. Leopard 2 tanks (Balogh, 2019b, pp. 55–70). An expenditure rule was also adopted, assuming that in 2026 the defense budget will amount to 2% of GDP (Csíki, 2019, pp. 76–86).

According to IPSOS research from 2019 (for the needs of the Institute for Strategic and Defense Studies), the perception of threats to national security by Hungarians was focused mainly on concerns related to climate change and the extent of illegal migration. The threat index also included: international terrorism, conflicts in the Middle East, organized crime and dependence on hydrocarbon natural resources. Threats related to the military policy of the Russian

Federation or the announcements of reducing the US military presence in NATO were felt to a lesser extent. Threats to national security also include actions to limit the rights of the Hungarian minority abroad, pointing to the instability of the situation in Ukraine and the Balkans.

The public opinion polls conducted in February 2020 by the IDEA institute on Hungary's cooperation with selected countries (sample of 2,500 people) indicate that the most important partners are the European Union countries, then the Russian Federation and the USA in third place. People with primary and secondary education perceive the importance of Hungarian-Russian relations. On the other hand, those who emphasize support for the parliamentary and extra-parliamentary opposition distinguish the primacy of cooperation with EU countries. Among the respondents related to the ruling coalition there is a division of opinion, for 37% the role of the EU is the most important, for 25% the Russian Federation. The distribution of support indicates continued social support for the policy of the ruling Fidesz-KDNP coalition. The Hungarians have a diversified approach to US policy, the opposition-oriented circles emphasize the importance of this policy, while among Fidesz-KDNP voters the indications are divided into the Russian Federation – 22%), and the USA – 15%. Despite the launch of the policy of "opening the eastern gate" to the Far East countries, the Hungarians remain little interested in China. The research results indicate that the perception of the stability of development and security by the Hungarians is associated with the position of the European Union and the best possible relations with the Russian Federation (Magyar, no date). The issues of security threats are identified in the context of Hungary's foreign policy. The supporters of the political programs of the opposition parties notice that the intensity and scope of Hungarian-Russian relations generate a risk of lowering the level of state security. On the other hand, among the voters of the ruling party, the greatest threats are seen in the Middle Eastern policy of Israel (22%) and the European Union (24%). The dependence of Hungary's state of national security on the quality of relations with Russia and the United States was considered low. The chart below illustrates the distribution of public opinion depending on the declared support for the main political parties operating in Hungary.

Almost 54% of the Hungarian respondents on the perception of a threat to national security, indicate the lack of a common European army, whereas 32% are of the opposite opinion. For 65% of respondents, the entire European Union should strengthen its defense potential; the necessity to provide military support when one of the member states is attacked, is perceived by 64% of respondents (Etl, 2020, p. 8). In the research conducted by "Pew.Research.org", 33% of the Hungarians see the need to provide support to allied states in the event of aggression by the Russian Federation (Fagan and Poushter, 2020). The research reveals the lack of a sense of defense solidarity in over 1/3 of Hungarians, in the situation of functioning in a small country which, without external support, is not able to ensure its military security on its own. The occurrence of a specific defense anomy is associated with the assessment of only 35% of respondents convinced of the need to increase the state's defense budget (Etl, 2020, p. 8). The Hungarian society sees opportunities for strengthening national security in the good relations of the Visegrad Group countries (34%), at the same time noting the lack of a coherent policy of the Group towards military cooperation with the Russian Federation (Etl, 2020, p. 4.). Opinions on this issue are consistent with the results of the IDEA study, where people associated with the ruling coalition point to the benefits of the cooperation with the Russian Federation. Different opinions are formulated by people connected with the democratic opposition. Despite the declared interest in the Group by the Hungarians, their knowledge of the cooperation itself is low. Apart from distinguishing solidarity during the migration crisis, common positions presented on the EU forum and support in sealing borders, the respondents are not able to cite examples of cooperation in the fields of defense or socio-cultural matters. A diversified approach to defense duties is dominant among young Hungarians. In the 2015/2016 research related to the subject of the "basis of national defense", only 20% of respondents were interested in volunteer military service in reserves and 8% in volunteer military service (Jobbágy and Stummer, 2016, pp. 160–161). The challenge faced by the uniformed services in Hungary poses a serious challenge in terms of the increasing number of reservists and maintaining uniformed personnel.

References

Magyar A., Kettészakadt a közvélemény Magyarország szövetségeseivel kapcsolatban, https://hu.euronews.com.
Balogh O., (2019b). The Importance of the Zrínyi 2026 Defence and Military Development Program, in: *Czech Military Review*, Praga.
Balogh O., (2019a). Program modernizacyjny wojska węgierskiego na lata 2016–2018, (eds.) Śmiałek K., Śmiałek W., Ewolucja wojen wielość uwarunkowań, Warszawa.
Csernicskó L.G. and Szabómihály G., (2010). Hátrányból előnyt: a magyar nyelvpolitika és nyelvtervezés kihívásairól, in: Határon túli magyarság a 21. században., Budapest: Köztársasági Elnöki Hivatal.
Csíki Varga T., (2019). A magyar védelmi kiadások trendjei, 2004–2019, *"Nemzet és Biztonság"*, nr 1, http://www.nemzetesbiztonsag.hu.
Etl A., (2020). The perception of security in Hungary, Institute for Strategic and Defense Studies, ISDS Analyses, nr 3.
Fagan M., Poushter M., (2020). NATO Seen Favorably Across Member States, https://www.pewresearch.org.
Gerő A., (2013). Budapest: Nemzeti Történelemkönyv.

Jobbágy Z., Stummer J., (2016). *"Kihívások a Magyar Honvédség személyi állományának utánpótlásában. A katonai hivatás megítélése a fiatal generáció körében"*, Hadtudomány, rocznik, nr 26.

Magyarország Kormánya, (2012). Kormány határozata Magyarország Nemzeti Biztonsági Stratégiájáról, https://2010-2014.kormany.hu.

Romsics I., (2018). *Historia Węgier*, Poznań: Media Rodzina.

Szenes Z., (2017). Honvédelem – védelempolitika, Budapest: Dialóg Campus.

Tálas P., (2014). Negyedszázad magyar haderőreformkísérleteinek vizsgálódási keretei, (eds.) Tálas, P, Csíki T., Varga T., Magyar Biztonságpolitika, 1989–2014, Budapest: Stratégiai Védelmi Kutatóintézet.

Oliver Balogh / Adam Kołodziejczyk

Chapter 47: Quantitative methods of Hungary's internal and external policy forecasting

Since 2010, Hungary has been ruled by a coalition of the Young Democrats' Union – the Hungarian Civic Union (Fidesz – Magyar Polgári Szövetség) and the Christian Democratic People's Party (KDNP). The ruling coalition's program focuses on such elements of Hungary's national security as demography, education, employment, economy, defense and internal security. The purpose of this article is to use quantitative methods to evaluate and forecast changes in the above-mentioned areas of social life. The research method preferred by the authors of the article is the method of analyzing the available statistical data, also known as the desk research method or research studies[1]. In particular, the focus was on identifying trends that can be defined as favorable or unfavorable from the point of view of structural security and functionality of the Hungarian social system.

An important element of the security of any national community is demography (Cengiz and Tanık, 2019; Delmonico et al., 2019; 'Chapter Three: North America', 2020; Caamaño and Beato, 2020; Inci et al., 2020; Spijker, 2020). It is difficult to imagine the long-term functioning of any social system without the appropriate number and demographic structure of such a community. Demography is therefore an important component of the social policy of any country. In the analyzed case, which is Hungary, the statistical data provided by demography allows for a number of predictive conclusions. The analysis of demographic data from the past shows that in 1980, i.e. during the period of real socialism, in the population of 10.7 million citizens, the gender and age structure of this population was similar to a progressive pyramid with a marked tendency for the increasing population of the Hungarians. Moreover, the data from this period points out a favorable proportion of the number of children and adults. In

---

[1] Desk research is a research method that consists in analyzing, processing data and information from existing sources and formulating conclusions, including predictions related to the problem under study. Such research is also called secondary research, it uses primary research as a source of data for analysis, incl. reports of various institutions and organizations, statistical yearbooks, press releases, available databases.

2005, regressive tendencies appeared, as a result of which in 2019 the Hungarian population decreased to 9.78 million people. The general decline in the Hungarian population was accompanied by the negative trend observed by demographers in the demographic structure: the population over 40 increased by over 50% of the population. At the same time, the number of children decreased by 30% compared to 1980.

The current demographic situation in Hungary is influenced by various socioeconomic factors, including political decisions from the past, the tangible effects of the economic crisis (2008–2012) and cultural factors related to the change in the life model, in particular the postponement of the point of starting a family. Statistical data clearly shows that Hungarian society is aging, as in most European societies. For example, the fertility rate of women decreased from 1.9 in the 1990s to 1.53 in 2016 (Teljes termékenységi arány; KSH, 2016)[2]. The population growth rate is 4.2 per thousand people. There is a real risk that in 2030 the population of Hungary will decrease to 9.39 million people and in 2050 to 8 million people (Népesség és népmozgalom, 2020)

The national priority of Hungary's social and pro-family policy is to improve the demographic situation. The government package of pro-family policy includes, among others: tax breaks for large families, the lowest national pension for every mother with four or more children, increased maternity benefits, granting non-returnable financial assistance in buying or building houses and apartments, and even financial support for the family with many children when buying a car[3]. Despite the government's actions to introduce a pro-family policy package, the negative trends in the field of demography were slowed down only slightly. For the time being, the demographic structure of Hungary does not indicate that expanding the social package for young families would have a significant impact on increasing the birth rate. It should be noted, however, that the effects of demographic policy are postponed and may become visible in the long run (Figure 1).

Demography remains closely related to the health status of the population. In Hungary, diseases associated with cardiovascular failure, diabetes and respiratory failure are the greatest threats (A fenntartható fejlődés, 2018). Despite extensive information and preventive measures pointing to the harmfulness of smoking and alcohol abuse, the mortality rate remains high. A comparative analysis of the statistics shows that the average deaths per 100,000 people from smoking in the EU is 171, compared to 387 in Hungary (A fenntartható fejlődés: 2018). On the other hand, a positive trend is the decrease in alcohol consumption

---

[2] In developed countries, 2.1 children per family are considered to be the reproductive fertility rate.

[3] Hungary's pro-family policy package.

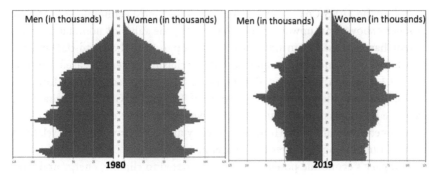

Figure 1. The structure of gender and age in 1980 and 2019 in Hungary (KSH, 2019).

since 2004 per statistical Hungarian from 11 liters of pure alcohol (96%) to 9.1 liters in 2017 (A fenntartható fejlődés, 2018).

Due to the health situation of the Hungarian society, the funds allocated to healthcare are far from sufficient. According to the Euro Health Consumer Index from 2018, Hungary was ranked far 32 (Poland out of 31) in the countries covered by the index research (Euro Health Consumer Index: 2018). The state of the health service in Hungary is one of the neglected sectors of social security. The World Health Organization (WHO) warns that the amount of GDP for healthcare in Hungary is systematically decreasing: from 8.1% in 2005 to 6.9% in 2017 (Health Expenditure Hungary, 2017).

In Hungary, since 2012, the reform of primary, secondary and higher education has been underway. In 2019–2020, 1.8 million people were covered by various forms of education, i.e. 20% of the population, including over 285,000. students (Elmúlt évek statisztikái). Raising the enrollment rate is related to the improvement of the economic potential of the state and flexible forms of professional activation of people with lower social competences. In Hungary, the economically inactive population decreased from 2.75 to 1.73 million in 2000–2019 (the retirement age for men and women is 65). Currently, the number of economically active people is almost 4.6 million (A 15–64 éves népesség, 2019). As shown in the chart below

Since 2016, a favorable employment rate of over 70% has been maintained in Hungary, reducing unemployment to an extremely low level of 3.5%. The reduction in the level of unemployment was caused, among others, by a new labor policy (Hungarian. közmunka), including a change in the rules for calculating benefits and a modification of the nature of work in the place of residence. The positive results of this policy were also expressed in the reduction of the poverty rate of Hungarian society. In 2018, 13% of Hungarians had an income below the national minimum wage of HUF 150,000 (A fenntartható fejlődés, 2018).

Before the SARS-CoV-2 coronavirus pandemic, most economic indicators in Hungary showed an upward trend. Since 1995, the value of nominal GDP per person has increased from 4.5 thousand USD up to 16.15 thousand USD in 2018, i.e. almost four times. In the same period, purchasing power increased threefold from 9.2 thousand USD up to 31.1 thousand USD per person (Az egy főre jutó, 2018). Under stable conditions, the value of Hungarian GDP per capita could increase by approx. one thousand USD. New prognostic economic indicators may appear only after the Hungarian society and economy return to relatively normal functioning, i.e. after the pandemic has passed.

Hungary's economic potential is closely related to climate, energy and environmental security. The implemented EU standards for the reduction of greenhouse gas emissions resulted in their reduction in the industrial sector by 1% annually. At the same time, CO_2 emissions in households increased by 1.8% (Magyarország, 2018). In 2017, Hungary issued 63.8 thousand kilotons of CO_2 equivalent, i.e. below the EU average by 87 thousand kilotons. Taking into account the new models of the EU climate, energy policy and the favorable growth trends in energy production from renewable sources (RES), greenhouse gas emissions in Hungary by 2030 will be further reduced by 1.5% in each annual emission cycle (Üvegházhatású gázok kibocsátása az EU-ban, 2018).

Hungary uses hydrocarbon, renewable and nuclear sources to generate electricity. Almost 50% of the total electricity demand is provided by the 2000 MW nuclear power plant in Paks. The remainder of the 665 MW demand comes from gas, coal, wind farms (330 MW) and solar batteries. The weakness of the Hungarian energy sector is the degree of technical wear of energy equipment, mostly from the 1980s, and a slow modernization process, with the risk of losing power by about 2,200 MW per year (A magyar villamosenergia, 2018). In 2016, the expansion of the Paks II nuclear power plant began, assuming the commissioning of two new 2400 MW VVER-1200 units (Hárfás, 2020, p. 52). It is worth noting that, according to the governmental program, by 2025 Hungary will no longer produce electricity from coal. As a result of the increase in expenditure on the production of energy from renewable sources – the total RES capacity in 2023 will be almost 2,500 MW and in 2033–4,500 MW. In turn, the total capacity of power units in nuclear power plants in 2033 will reach approximately 3,800 MW. However, should there be investment delays, the Hungarian authorities prepared alternative solutions, assuming immediate electricity imports from Germany, Slovakia and Ukraine at the level of 24–31% of demand.

One of the most important determinants of the state's military security is having the appropriate specialist human resources potential and the amount of budget funds dedicated to performing the necessary tasks. Hungary is one of the European countries and NATO members in which, from the beginning of the 1990s, the defense budget was systematically reduced over the next decades. In

2014, Hungary's defense budget approached the critical ceiling of 0.79% of GDP. In 2016, a ten-year governmental modernization program of the Hungarian Army – "Zrínyi 2026" was adopted, assuming the allocation of 2% of GDP to defense.

According to the Center for Strategic and Defense Studies in Budapest, adjusting the planning of the Hungarian military budget to the decisions of the NATO Summit in Wales, i. e. to 2% of GDP, will be spread over time. Assuming a stable economic situation in 2020–2024, the absence of crisis phenomena (e. g. pandemic crisis, natural disasters, migration crisis), Hungary may not reach the 2% ceiling until 2026. The implementation of this goal would involve the growth of the economy above 3% of GDP in 2020–2026. However, according to ad hoc estimates, the pandemic crisis will lead to a negative economic balance. In practice, this will make the Hungarian defense budget scenarios displayed at the beginning of 2018, unrealistic and will require far-reaching index and time adjustments.

Before the current epidemiological crisis in Hungary, the main topic of political narratives and media information was the issue of ensuring internal security in the context of the threats of the refugee and migration crisis. Particular attention was paid to the dangerous situation on the Turkish-Greek border. The Hungarian society has an extremely emotional approach to the migration issue, bearing in mind the 2015 migration crisis in Hungary. Then, due to the involvement of the army and the police, the situation was stabilized and the state border was sealed. Despite the fact that there is an over 200 km long fence[4] with wire entanglements in the border zone, the Hungarians feel threatened by a new wave of refugees. This sense of hazard is related to the more than threefold increase in border incidents caused by migrants, recorded since October 2019 (Hirek es informaciok hatarinfo illegalis migracio, 2019).

The mass migration crisis was introduced in Hungary in March 2016 with the possibility of its extension (tömeges bevándorlás okozta válsághelyzet). Due to the increasing incidents, the last extension of the crisis level was introduced on March 5, 2020 (Meghosszabbították: 2020). At present, there are no indications that the migratory pressure on Europe may decrease in the near future. Much data from the regions of natural disasters and armed conflicts indicate that the problem of migration to Europe will increase and that Hungary is on the main route of this highly possible new "migration of people". In this context, it should be noted that migration itself is not a problem, but the problem is the scale of migration, which affects all dimensions of European and national security at the same time.

---

4 178 km between Hungary and Serbia and 41 km between Hungary and Croatia.

References

"Chapter Three: North America" (2020). *The Military Balance*, 120(1), pp. 28–63. doi: 10.1080/04597222.2020.1707963.

(2019) A fenntartható fejlődés indikátorai Magyarországon 2018, KSH 2019, http://www.ksh.hu.

(2018) A magyar villamosenergia-rendszer közép-és hosszútávú forrásoldali kapacitásfejlesztése.

(1998) A 15–64 éves népesség gazdasági aktivitása nemenként (1998) https://www.ksh.hu/docs/hun/xstadat/xstadat_eves/i_qlf002.html.

(1995) Az egy főre jutó bruttó hazai termék (GDP) értéke (1995) https://www.ksh.hu/docs/hun/xstadat/xstadat_eves/i_qpt016.html.

(2018) Euro Health Consumer Index 2018, https://healthpowerhouse.com.pdf.

(2018) MAVIR, Budapest, http://mavir.hu.

Caamaño, D. S., Juliao and Beato, Alonso R. (2020) "Facial diplegia, a possible atypical variant of Guillain-Barré Syndrome as a rare neurological complication of SARS-CoV-2", *Journal of Clinical Neuroscience*, 77, pp. 230–232. doi: https://doi.org/10.1016/j.jocn.2020.05.016.

Cengiz G.F. and Tanık N., (2019). "Validity and reliability of the Turkish version of the Neurological Disorders Depression Inventory for Epilepsy (NDDI-E)", *Epilepsy & Behavior*, 99, p. 106471. doi: https://doi.org/10.1016/j.yebeh.2019.106471.

Csíki T., (2019). Explaining Hungarian Defence policy I. – Defense spending trends, Center of Strategic and Defence Studies.

Delmonico L. et al., (2019). "Mutation profiling in the PIK3CA, TP53, and CDKN2A genes in circulating free DNA and impalpable breast lesions", *Annals of Diagnostic Pathology*, 39, pp. 30–35. doi: https://doi.org/10.1016/j.anndiagpath.2018.12.008.

Elmúlt évek statisztikái: 2001–2019, https://www.felvi.hu/felveteli/ponthatarok_statisztikak/elmult_evek/!ElmultEvek/index.php/elmult_evek_statisztikai/osszesen.

Forrás munkaerö-felmérés, KSH, http://www.ksh.hu.

Hárfás Zs., (2020). Villamosenergia termelés a klímaváltozás árnyékában, Villanyszerelők Lapja, nr 1–2.

Health expenditure profile Hungary, http://apps.who.int/nha/database/country.

Hírek es információk határinfó illegális migráció, 2019, http://www.police.hu.

Hungary vows to help Greece amid rising migrant pressure, http://www.Abouthungary.hu.

Inci F. et al., (2020). "Treatment strategies of defect nonunion with vascular damaged by induced membrane technique: Is two-stage treatment sufficient?", *Injury*, 51(4), pp. 1103–1108. doi: https://doi.org/10.1016/j.injury.2020.02.082.

Magyarország 2018, KSH 2019, http://www.ksh.hu.

Népesség és népmozgalom http://www.ksh.hu/nepesseg-es-nepmozgalom.

Spijker J., (2020). "Los efectos de la Gran Recesión y las políticas de austeridad en la salud de la población Española", *Gaceta Sanitaria*, 34(3), pp. 220–222. doi: https://doi.org/10.1016/j.gaceta.2019.12.006.

Teljes termékenységi arányszám (1990–2016) https://www.ksh.hu/docs/hun/eurostat_tablak/tabl/tsdde220.html.

Üvegházhatású gázok kibocsátása az EU-ban (infografika), https://www.europarl.europa.eu.

Oliver Balogh / Adam Kołodziejczyk / Marcin Górnikiewicz / Radosław Bielawski

Chapter 48: Summary and conclusions: The forecast of potential implications for regional security resulting from the development of mutual Russian-Hungarian relations

The research carried out on the forecast of development and the impact of mutual Russian-Hungarian relations on regional security presents that Hungary will continue to pursue a policy of neutrality consisting in maintaining a friendly attitude towards Russia, at the same time taking into account the growing importance of China in Europe, and avoiding too sharp confrontation with the EU. This attitude of the Hungarian government suits Moscow, as it allows it to pursue many geopolitical goals that directly concern the European Union, as well as the growing competition for influence with the United States. The following trends emerged from the used quantitative methods:

1. The trends that have been marked in the demography of Hungarian society are not favorable, despite the introduction of a pro-family policy. Particularly unfavorable are the decline in the number of Hungarian population and the aging of the population. If this trend is not changed in the near future, it will have a negative impact on the entire social system of Hungary. This trend will not be used by Russia temporarily.
2. The reform of the Hungarian education system and its direct impact on the labor market and economy seem to bring positive results, providing Hungary with a sense of work and social security. Nevertheless, the situation of the coronavirus pandemic will certainly have a negative impact on economic growth, increased unemployment rates and lowering the sense of social security of the Hungarians. This situation may be exploited by Russia by using the energy supply chain, which will have a positive or negative impact on the condition of the Hungarian economy.
3. The developing Hungarian economy in recent years gave rise to optimism. All the characterized economic and energy indicators were favorable. At this stage of the pandemic's development, however, it is difficult to assess the extent of its impact on the entire Hungarian economy and its individual sectors. This situation may be used by the Russians for the same reasons as in point 2.
4. Until the pandemic, the Hungarian economy was developing dynamically and the economic development forecasts were optimistic. What the indicators of

economic development will currently be, depends on the duration of the pandemic. In overcoming the crisis, the experience of Hungarian society and state institutions in dealing with recent crises will be of importance. This situation may be used by the Russians for the same reasons as in point 2.
5. Hungary has been saving on defense for a long time, an indicator of which is the percentage share of Hungary's defense budget in GDP that differs significantly from 2% of GDP. According to the estimates, the pandemic crisis will result in far-reaching adjustments to the Hungarian defense budget scenarios adopted at the beginning of 2018. This situation can be exploited by strengthening the defense sector with Russian technologies, which would ultimately make the Hungarian armed forces dependent on supplies from Moscow.
6. The Hungarian society remembers the migration crisis that occurred in 2015. Then, due to the involvement of state institutions, the situation was stabilized and the state border was sealed. Despite the fact that an over 200-kilometer-long fence with barbed wire has been installed in the border strip, the Hungarians feel threatened by a new wave of refugees due to the increase in border incidents caused by migrants. This situation may be used by Russia as an important element of the information campaign showing the negative effects of ties with the Union, instead of remaining neutral and looking for mentally closer allies, i.e. the Russians.

The analysis of trends shows that the Hungarian authorities will continue to take steps to develop cooperation with Russia.

The qualitative research displays that the structure of the values of public life in Hungary corresponds to the axio-normative solutions of the political system and the practice of governing adopted in the Constitution. The process of decision-making and institutional centralization is accompanied by the growing importance of internal factors shaping foreign and economic policy, in particular energy. Since 2014, the political life of Hungarians has focused around:
- the protection of the rights of Hungarian minorities in neighboring countries,
- maneuvering between NATO and the European Union (including confusion over the functioning of the Central European University in Budapest – CEU),
- looking for alternatives in integration with the Visegrad Group and establishing closer ties with European non-liberal formations,
- defense against the influx of refugees and economic migrants (a categorical veto on the allocation expressed by 3.3 million Hungarians in the referendum in October 2016 – with a turnout close to 40%), arguing that the Hungarians are on the front line of the cultural war.

Experts' opinions show that the civilization and religious factor is the central value of shaping the national identity of Hungary, a small country exposed to the threats of returning to the "concert of powers" on the European continent, and imposing the will of several countries on other, smaller entities. This value is inscribed on their banners by Hungarian nationalist organizations, which recognize the nation as a supreme value for which European integration may or may not be a threat.

As a result, the Hungarian authorities, irrespective of the economic sanctions imposed by the West on the Russian Federation after the incorporation of Crimea in 2014, are developing intensive political and economic contacts with Moscow, declaring that Budapest intends to be one of the pillars of the renewed architecture of Russia-European Union relations.

In conclusion, the quantitative and qualitative research aimed at forecasting the development of Hungarian-Russian relations shows that these relations will continue to develop regardless of criticism from the European Union, and even more from Washington. At the same time, the Hungarian authorities are guided by hard pragmatism and profit and loss account in their actions, which suggests that Hungary could change its attitude towards Russia if it saw in such a move much more benefits than potential losses – not only political, but mainly economic ones.

Part V: Ukraine

Section I:
Geopolitical and geostrategic implications of the Russian policy with regard to Ukraine

Section II
Geopolitical and geostrategic frameworks of
the Russian policy with regard to Ukraine

Jan Figurski / Jerzy Niepsuj

Chapter 49: The geopolitical situation of Ukraine conditioned by the foreign policy of the Russian Federation

This chapter presents the main external and internal conditions aimed at improving the geopolitical situation in Ukraine. One of the key paths leading to this goal seems to be the taking, by the broadly understood international community, primarily the Euro-Atlantic community, decisive "disciplining" (e.g. various types of sanctions) and "softening" measures (e.g. a comprehensive policy of attracting international cooperation) towards the Russian Federation. The final effect of these actions should be the recognition by Russia of the right of the Ukrainian nation and state to national and state independence. However, for today, the basic condition for the improvement of the geopolitical situation in Ukraine seems to be the fundamental strengthening of the economic and military situation in that country by Ukrainians themselves. And such an enhancing will enable the Ukrainian state to meet the basic requirements making possible its accession to the European Union and the North Atlantic Treaty Organization (NATO).

Meeting these two fundamental determinants (external and internal) of improving the geopolitical situation of Ukraine requires decisive, synergistic actions both by the international community and the Ukrainian nation itself.

Without the aforementioned activities, the final result of which, on the one hand, will be results improving the functional processes of the Ukrainian state and, on the other hand, Russia's abandonment of the age-old idea of Russian imperialism aimed at subordinating the "space of the Great Limitrof" to itself, it seems impossible to improve the geopolitical situation of Ukraine.

Therefore, it is proposed and envisaged to appoint subject matter experts teams to initiate and coordinate, inter alia, processes improving, firstly: Ukraine's entry into the organizational structures of the European Union and NATO, and, secondly, improving the economic situation and national education (including primary, secondary and higher education) of the Ukrainian State. The functioning of individual teams is covered by an algorithm, the results of which will be transparent in the form of time and economic conditions. Algorithms will make it possible to control the results of the work of individual teams and, if necessary, to make personnel and time adjustments. The outcomes of the subject matter experts teams will allow for the presentation of conditions aimed at booming Ukraine's economic security in the planned time.

Ukraine is a country with wide development opportunities and ambitions aimed at increasing the living standard of citizens and the development of life that functions in Western European countries. Due to the existing functional conditions and the geopolitical situation, these plans require structural and economic improvement.

One of the functional plans of the state is to join the structures of the European Union. Operating in this structure would give Ukraine the opportunity to use the practical achievements existing in EU countries, especially in improving the area of agriculture, due to the "agricultural" financial subsidies in the European Union.

Another step that is important for Ukraine in terms of the geopolitical situation, is joining NATO's military structures.

Operating in the above-mentioned format will provide the Ukrainian state with a sense of greater security and the possibility of constantly advancing the level of training of its armed forces, e.g. by participating in allied military exercises.

To meet the above-mentioned conditions, it is necessary to undertake systematic work, understood as the improvement of basic subsystems that affect the functioning of the state. Specifying these subsystems is the responsibility of the state leadership. Each of the subsystems should also have clearly defined implementation tasks, including their completion dates.

In addition, in relation to the foreign policy of the Russian Federation, the need to strengthen the existence of the state, both domestically and internationally, has a fundamental impact on enhancing the geopolitical situation of Ukraine. In this process, it seems necessary to improve the functionality, for example:

1. A subsytem developing the conditions for the Ukraine's accession to the European Union,
2. A subsystem developing the conditions for Ukraine's joining NATO structures,
3. A subsystem developing the conditions improving the functionality of the industry, including the increase of exports,
4. A subsystem developing the conditions improving the functioning of the agricultural economy,
5. A subsystem developing the conditions improving the area of primary and higher education,
6. A subsystem developing the conditions improving the system of external and internal transport.

The operation of these subsystems will improve Ukraine's geopolitical situation and accelerate its entry into the functional structures of the European Union and NATO. Their activities should be controlled by state authorities and verified systematically on the implementation of the established tasks.

Within the proposed subsystems, the teams of experts should be employed, performing pre-determined partial tasks, the results of which should be included in the assessment efficiency of the functioning subsystems. The operation of the aforementioned specialized subsystems ought to be controlled by state authorities. Supervision and control is possible through the use of an IT system which will reflect the tasks of the functioning subsystems and teams within their effectiveness and functional failure. The assessment algorithm should work with the following points. Functioning of subsystems according to the structure presented in Figure 1.

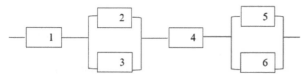

Figure 1. The structure of functioning of the subsystems (1–6 – subsystems' numbers).

The subsystems listed in Figure 1 should have precisely defined tasks and time of their performance. Such arrangements allow to control the function of feasibility of the tasks by the teams and the entire system. Determining the feasibility function requires the identification of the degree of impossibility over time, the variant of which is presented in Table 1.

Table 1. The values of the indexes

No.	Subsystem	n (t)		$In_g(t)$	$W_z(t)$
1	1	1	$1.1456 \ 10^{-5}$	0.8803	0.1197
2	2	3	$3.4247 \ 10^{-5}$	0.7408	0.2592
3	3	2	$2.2831 \ 10^{-5}$	0.8187	0.1813
4	4	2	$2.2831 \ 10^{-5}$	0.8187	0.1813
5	5	1	$1.1456 \ 10^{-5}$	0.8803	0.1197
6	6	4	$4.5662 \ 10^{-5}$	0.6703	0.3298

Where: n (t) – number of unperformed tasks by subsystems

(t) – intensity of unperformed tasks

$W_g(t)$ – task performance index

$W_z(t)$ – task unperformance index

The values mentioned in Table 1 were calculated according to the relationship:

$$\lambda(t) = \frac{n(t)}{T} = \frac{1}{87600} = 1.1456 \cdot 10^{-5}$$

T- operation time in hours

W_g (t) = exp (- > (t) • t) = exp (-1.1456•10⁻⁵ • 87600) = 0.8803

W_z (t) = 1 - W_g (t) = 1-0.8803 = 0.1197

Taking into account the functional structure of the subsystems shown in Figure 1 and the results of the calculations listed in Table 1, the functionality of the entire system W $_g$ (t) is determined by the relationship:

$$W_s(t) = W_1(t)(1 - W_{g2}(t)) \bullet W_4(t) \bullet (I - W_{g3}(t)) \tag{1}$$

Ultimately considering the computational results, it is obtained

$$W_g(t) = 0.88 \bullet (1 - 0.0468) \bullet 0.82(1 - 0.0396) = 0.66 \tag{2}$$

As it results from the dependence (2), the functionality of the system, including its subsystems, is assessed at the level of 0.66.

The management exercising supervision over the operating system may consider this result as satisfactory or unsatisfactory. In this case, functional improvement should be made, especially in subsystems No. 2 and 6. Increasing the functionality of these subsystems will definitely improve the efficiency of the entire system.

The operation of the advancing process of the geopolitical system of Ukraine should be supported by an IT system for managing the entire process. This system should have a modular structure, and each module should have separate executive tasks.

1. The recording module should collect information on the composition and performance of the tasks in individual functional subsystems. These tasks should be linked to time ranges and used in executive work.
2. In the planning module, execution plans should be prepared, appropriately assigned to individual subsystems. These plans should take into account the time schedules and projected implementation results, including the efficiency processes.
3. In the reporting module, executive reports are prepared, implemented by individual functional subsystems. These reports are the basis for assessing the results achieved by individual teams. The presented outcomes become the ground for making personnel and executive adjustments in individual subsystems and teams.

4. The functional assessment module collects information on the value of the function of the basic task performance and the assessesment of the degree of functioning of the entire management system.

The functioning of the IT system will ensure the day-to-day provision of information on the performance of work in individual subsystems. This will allow the management of the entire system to make decisions to improve system functionality. In the event of functional disruptions, it is possible to correct the activities on an ongoing basis, including the introduction of personnel or task-related conditions.

References

Figurski J. and Niepsuj J. M., (2015). Ekonomika logistyki, vol. 5, Warsaw: Military University of Technology, ISBN 978-83-7938-046-6.
Figurski J. and Niepsuj J. M., (2016). Assessment of the effectiveness of logistics operations in the aspect of the expected tasks related to migration processes, in: Material Management & Logistics, No. 5, pp. 194–203.
Figurski J. and Niepsuj J. M., (2017). Assessment of the reliability of the training of logistics specialists on the example of the "Homar" missile system, in: Gospodarka Materialowa & Logistyka, No. 5, pp. 150–159.
Figurski J. and Niepsuj J. M., (2018). Reliability assessment of logistics subsystems, in: Gospodarka Materialowa & Logistyka, vol. 70, No. 5 (CD), pp. 231–240.
Figurski J. and Niepsuj J. M., (2018). The cooperation of civil and military use of the possibility of mutual solutions and logistics technology in military and civilian logistics, in: Modeling systems and logistics processes in terms of dual-use technologies , Brzezinski M. H. (ed. p.), Warsaw: Military University of Technology, ISBN 978-83-7938-219-4, pp. 89–98.
Figurski J. and Ziemski B., (2019). Vehicle maintenance and repair processes Warsaw: Publishing House of the Military University of Technology.

Jan Figurski / Jerzy Niepsuj

Chapter 50: The geostrategic position of Ukraine in the strategic and operational plans of the Russian Federation

The essence of Russia's current foreign and security policy and its strategy towards Europe, in particular towards Central and Eastern Europe, are expressed, inter alia, by the term "finlandization". However, it is one of the many mutations and expressions of Russian imperialism over the past several hundred years aimed at subordinating the "space of the Great Limitrof" (Solozobov, 2009, p. 407; Lazari, 1993, pp. 49–56). This concept applies in a special way to Ukraine today (but not only). One could even risk a statement that it is the focal point of the foreign policy of the Russian Federation.

The subject of this chapter is an attempt to show the enormous influence of Russia's foreign policy on the geostrategic situation of Ukraine and its consequences for the security of Ukraine, Poland, Europe and the world. The paper begins with historiosophical antecedents, the presentation and understanding of which, according to the authors, is a *sine qua non condition for a* proper approach to and perception of the problem contained in its subject. Then, in the second point, an outline of the foreign policy of the Russian Federation is presented, including, in particular, its assumptions concerning world, European (Central European) security and relations between the Russian Federation and Ukraine. The third part of the chapter, against the background of the previous considerations, presents the impact of Russia's foreign policy on the geostrategic situation of Ukraine. The last, fourth part of the paper contains conclusions and recommendations resulting from the topic under consideration.

When undertaking scientific deliberations regarding the geostrategic situation of Ukraine in relation to the foreign policy of the Russian Federation, it should be clearly emphasized that the problem contained in the topic of the article, has already had quite a long origin in the history of human thought (Paweł II, 2007b, pp. 217–252; Paweł II, 2007a, pp. 273–296). Certainly, its roots do not lie only in the recent events in Eastern Europe (Ukraine) related to the collapse of the global, European and Polish thinking about security and defense, shaped after the end of the Cold War (Rotfeld, 2014; Asmus, 1997, pp. 385–424).). For a long time we have not shared the opinion of many noble, but at the same time, utopian thinkers – scientists – security theorists, politicians – security practitioners and military – security guards, who at least from the beginning of the 1990s authoritatively claimed that in the next 20–30 years Europe, the world, and Poland in particular, would not be threatened by a classic war with a range and effects comparable to the times known to us, for example in the 19th and 20th centuries[1].

As a part of the presented topic, we would like to draw your attention to its complexity, scope and interdisciplinarity at this point. The problem contained in the subject undertaken and presented by us, can be considered on the basis of many disciplines of knowledge. Today, representatives of all disciplines of science, including advocates of technical and social sciences, such as philosophy, ethics, law, economy, psychology, political science, pedagogy, axiology, history, logistics, etc., should air about state security and defense today. We will make an attempt to look at the undertaken problem and present it primarily from the point of view of philosophy, ethics, logic, history and political science.

Russia's aggression against Ukraine and Russia's annexation of Crimea is generally assessed as negative in the world, Europe and Poland. This assessment is correct. The taking by force of a part of the territory of another country is, in the modern world, treated as an unequivocally barbaric act, not fitting in with contemporary human thinking about international security (Brzoska, *et al.*, 2014).

At the same time, Russia's aggression against Ukraine dispelled many modern myths constituting human thinking about security, myths established mainly after World War II and especially after the end of the so-called cold war[2]. Exemplary, and at the same time beautiful in its content and expression, an example of such a myth is, for example, the *"European Security Strategy"* (2003) (Secure Europe in Better Word, 2003) or, in particular, the *"Paris Charter of New Europe"* adopted and announced in Paris on November 21, 1990. "(...) *The era of con-*

---

1 Such conclusions from the nature of the security environment of Poland, Europe and the world were drawn by, for example, distinguished authors (civil and military), including both Strategic Defense Reviews conducted at the Ministry of National Defense under the rule of Minister Jerzy Szmajdziński (2005) and Minister Bogdan Klich (2010) and the *White Book of National Security of the Republic of Poland*, prepared at the National Security Bureau of the Chancellery of the President of the Republic of Poland in 2013.

2 It was mainly politicians, intellectuals and Western ideologues of all sorts who contributed to the creation of these myths. They often ruthlessly opposed the views of those thinkers (including Polish) who put realism (and not, for example, Kantian idealism) at the basis of their perception of security. Jerzy Niepsuj, as a scholarship holder at the Institute for Peace Research and Security Policy at the University of Hamburg and at the Bundeswehr Command Academy in Hamburg, in the mid-nineties of the last century, encountered these myths, including during the discussion on the security model for the 21st century developed by IFSH scientists (Institut für Friedensforschung und Sicherheitspolitik an der Uniwersität Hamburg) (Die Europäische Sicherheitsgemeinschaft, 1995).

frontation and division of Europe has ended. (...) Europe is liberating itself from the legacy of the past. (...) Ours is a time for fulfilling the hopes and expectations our peoples have cherished for decades : steadfast commitment to democracy based on human rights and fundamental freedoms; prosperity through economic liberty and social justice; and equal security for all our countries. (...) With the ending of the division of Europe, we will strive for a new quality in our security relations while fully respecting each other's freedom of choice in that respect. Security is indivisible and the security of every participating State is inseparably linked to that of all the others. (...) Europe whole and free is calling for a new beginning. We invite our peoples to join in this great endeavour. (...) An abiding adherence to shared values and our common heritage are the ties which bind us together. (...) We recognize the essential contribution of our common European culture and our shared values in overcoming the division of the continent" (Paris Charter, 1990).

Russia by annexing Crimea and supporting the so-called pro-Russian separatists in eastern Ukraine, separatists who e.g. shot down a civil passenger plane (!!!), not only brutally canceled the hopes of the Europeans for the peaceful development of the continent and humanity, as enshrined in *the Paris Charter of New Europe*, but also burried human hopes for a permanent reevaluation of contemporary thinking about international security for a long time (Sadykiewicz, 1985)[3].

Suddenly it turned out that we Europeans feel not only crushed by the brutal, aggressive, imperial, etc. behavior of the Russians as a great European nation, but also amazed at the degree of our naive trust and attachment to the many myths that constitute our thinking about security. Suddenly, after Russia's forcible seizure of Crimea as a part of the territory of Ukraine, and following recent statements and actions by Russia's authorities and its society, as Europeans, we discover that our security has an extremely fragile foundation (Bujak, 1995, pp. 100–101)[4].

---

3 For Russian imperialism, thinking about security based on the canon of "the force of law" and the power of arguments has become unattractive and has no future prospects for Russia's preservation of the status of a world power. That is why Russia returned to thinking and acting in international relations based on the canon of the "law of force".
4 The author of the cited work mentions, inter alia, his conversation with a young boy he met by chance – a Russian, a Komsomol man. This young Russian, after the collapse of the USSR, on A. Bujak's statement that the Poles are finally a free nation, said: "If we want to follow you, a small gesture will suffice to grab you, and we will do it without the slightest stutter," if it is needed. These shocking words are as authoritative as in the mouth of a contemporary, or rather "historical Russian", typical of the Russian soul. The Russian does not consider his utterance "inappropriate" and offensive. On the other hand, he is offended and inclined by all statements of a Western man that say and treat Belarusians and Ukrainians as representatives of separate nations.

We, Poles and residents of other countries in Central Europe, discover it in a special way. Suddenly, we notice that the "ghosts of the past", forgotten by most, have always been an immanent feature of human thinking, including human thinking about war and peace, security and defense of the state[5] have become the content of our everyday life and the present day, violating our need (just need) to live in security[6].

Man as a rational being has numerous needs[7]. And among them, one of the first places is security. Also, various products of a human being, such as the state, also have specific needs, specific to them, and among them, security also occupies a prominent place (Trejnis, 2018, p. 45). The source of this human and state need lies, among others, in the unlimited nature of need as such.

Man, striving to satisfy his needs, has always resorted to various mechanisms. The oldest and simplest of these was and still is the mechanism of power. The most glaring and dramatic manifestation of man's use of the mechanism of power were wars (Allison, 2018, p. 69). As a result, some researchers of mankind history describe its history as the history of wars (History of Wars, 2004).

Man using the mechanism of power to satisfy his various needs, paradoxically, at the same time felt the need to live a secure life, i.e. life without various threats, challenges and risks lurking in the natural environment (natural and social)[8]. In a word, a human being felt the need for peace, a peaceful existence (Prayer of John Paul II, 2020). And although this need determined and still determines the life of successive human generations, paradoxically, it can be concluded here that in human culture and in the sphere of his civilizational achievements, the "war achievements" significantly exceed the "peace achievements". This is clearly evidenced by, for example, an attempt to compare his output with the number and cultural importance of works devoted to war and peace[9].

Among the recognized authors of polemological works (Huzarski, 2009, pp. 287–298) the leading position belongs undoubtedly for the loner of Königsberg, Immanuel Kant. He is the author of the tractate entitled *"To eternal*

---

5 Their special type of emphasis and juxtaposition can already be found, for example, in the classic Chinese tractate from 2,500 years ago by Sun Tzu, entitled The *Art of War* (Zi, 2011).
6 Z. Trejnis rightly emphasizes the often known fact that "security is a kind of community, a social bond based on mutual trust and relations without hostility and aggression" (Trejnis, 2018, p. 45).
7 Abraham Maslow claims that a need is a subjective feeling of lack, dissatisfaction or desire for certain conditions or things that a person considers necessary to keep him alive, enable him to develop, fulfill social roles, etc.;it is also a feeling of lack of satisfaction. The features of needs are individualism and subjectivism. The structure of human needs includes such needs as: 1) biological, 2) security, 3) social contacts, 4) recognition, 5) self-fulfillment (Maslow, 1970).
8 A very extensive definition of the concept of security can be found in Annex 2 of the document entitled White Paper of National Security, 2013.
9 However, there are works on peace in the history of human thought, they are usually side-reflections (Borgosz, 1989; Clausewitz, 1995; Grepon, 1994; Heisburg, 1998; Hobbes, 1954; Howard 1990; Kant, 1992; Kondziela, 1974; Kostecki, 1990; Xenophon, 1967; Tzu, 1994; Toffler 1997).

peace. A philosophical project" (Kant, 1995). In this work, as a researcher and an unquestionable expert on the subject, he also states categorically that "(...) The state of peace among people living next to each other is not a natural state (*status naturalis*), which is rather a state of war, i.e. if not a continuous eruption of hostile actions, it is, however, a constant threat. A state of peace should therefore be established, because the cessation of hostilities is not yet a guarantee and if the neighbors do not give each other such a guarantee (which can only be given in a legal state), then the one who demands it from the other may deal with it as with an enemy" (Kant, 1995).

This Kantian approach to the problem of war and peace – understanding their essence – is, in our opinion, of great importance for the proper presentation and understanding of the problem contained in the title of this study. Kant's view of the issue of war and peace is pessimistic as well as optimistic, and last but not least, universalistic for Western spirituality and thinking. Pessimistic is about understanding "war as a state of nature", while optimistic about understanding "peace as a masterful work of reason"[10]. Kant believes that only law – reliance the relations between states on law and morality – as a masterpiece of mind – is able to overcome determinism and pessimism resulting for human safety from the state of nature and from human relations with other people, and resulting from the RELATIONS of such human creations as the state and the relationship between them[11].

However, in order to present our problem "properly" (in a fuller light), it seems necessary to make complementary, though only a few, loose remarks, conclusions and antecedents on the "European East"[12]. It is all the more obvious and necessary because we Europeans – Westerners know so little about Europeans – Easterners. Anyway, Mikołaj Bierdyajev considered his text entitled *"The Truth of the Orthodox Church"* to begin with this astonishing and unbelievable statement that "The Christian world knows little about Orthodoxy" (Bierdyajev, 1952, pp. 4–10; Bierdiajew, 1993, p. 4). And if it already knows something, it can be in the form of, for example, "Letters from Russia", "Another world" or "On inhuman soil".

Since we Europeans – people of the West know so little about the spirituality of Europeans – people of the East, let us try to take a crumb of knowledge from

---

10 More on this in (Niepsuj, 2000, p. 68).
11 Thomas Hobbes argued that security was not guaranteed by the laws of nature. He also believed that "settlements, without a sword, are only words and have no power to keep a man safe" (Hobbes, 2009, p. 253).
12 How difficult this task is, let for example, the interesting observation of one of the experts on the subject, Józef Tymanowski testify to it. He in the 1990s posed the question about the limits of Europe. He asked: "How can the borders of Europe be defined today?" (Tymanowski, 1998, p. 73).

unquestionable experts on the subject, such as the Russian philosopher Mikołaj Bierdyaev, already mentioned by us[13]. This philosopher, trying to outline the features of Orthodox spirituality, stated, inter alia, that "(...) Orthodoxy is alien to rationalism and juridism, he is also alien to all normativism. The Orthodox Church cannot be defined in rational terms; its nature can only be understood by those who live in its womb and participate in its spiritual experience" (Berdyaev, 1952, pp. 6).

If so, we can easily see that already on the level of thinking there are fundamental differences between the culture of the people of the East and the culture of the people of the West. And this – according to Samuel P. Huntington, is the source and cause of the collision of civilizations and the shaping of a new world order. This is what he writes on this subject: "(...) Culture and cultural identity, broadly understood as the identity of civilization, shape patterns of cohesion, disintegration and conflict in the world that followed the Cold War (...) The competition of superpowers was replaced by the clash of civilization, and religion is the fundamental characteristic of civilization. [...] Common and different cultural features define interests, provoke antagonisms and influence the formation of state unions" (Huntington, 1997, pp. 14–22).

The above presented, although only selected, historiosophical antecedents will allow us – as we believe – to understand better the problem of establishing the subject of the thematic considerations.

In terms of the *Strategy for the Development of the National Security System of the Republic of Poland 2022* "(...) Foreign policy is one of the attributes of the state as a sovereign entity in international relations and is the accomplishment of its interests on the international arena" (Strategy for the development of the national security system, 2013, p. 31).; History of Polish diplomacy, 1995). Its main goals are, among others:
- "(...) protection of the sovereignty and independence as well as the territorial integrity of the state,
- ensuring the freedom and security of citizens,
- creating conditions for the permanent and sustainable civilization and economic development of the country on the international arena,
- protection of cultural heritage and national identity as well as the natural environment.

These goals are implemented in the sphere of external relations, on the bilateral and multilateral level" (Strategy for the development of the national security system, 2013, pp. 31–32; Kupiecki and Szczepanik, 1995).

---

13 On this scientist and philosophy of Mikołaj Bierdyajev in (Tatarkiewicz, 1983, p. 192).

The foreign policy of the Russian Federation after 1989, in particular after the self-dissolution of the USSR, i.e. after the end of the so-called Cold War, was aimed at preserving as much as possible the international legacy of the post-Soviet Union in the scope of the above-mentioned and other, not mentioned here, foreign policy goals. The eternal canons that created Russia's foreign policy were to serve this purpose. However, they were modified to such an extent that they corresponded to the current situation of Russia on the international arena.

It is crucial for our further considerations to recognize what has been the essence of Russian thinking about the world, European and its own security from, as we can say, the dawn of the Moscow State; and to explain the Russian strategy in this respect towards the world, Europe and in particular towards Central and Eastern Europe.

Russia's foreign policy has always been a function of the self – perception of Russians and Russia in the world, and thus of answering the question: what is Russia?[14] For the average Russian, Russia is a metaphor for the image of a man with his arms spread wide. It is this metaphor that is intended to signify (imagine) Russia in the fullest and at the same time in the least accurate way. According to a Russian man, his/her country is a special type of "artifact" with no beginning or end. And the political philosophy of the Russian foreign policy to this day is based on such a nebulous, metaphorical and unreal basis. This alone causes its internal contradiction and paradox.

Without feeling the need, due to the subject scope of our paper, to characterize the basic vectors of the foreign policy of the Russian Federation, we will limit ourselves only to the selection – in our opinion – to its three most important canons, i.e. imperialism, understanding of national and state security and freedom. In our opinion, understanding the content of these canons will allow us to understand the focal point of Russia's foreign policy towards Ukraine and its impact on the geostrategic situation of Ukraine as Russia's neighbor state and an important entity in the Eastern Europe region.

From the moment of the origin of the Moscow State, the basic canon of its foreign policy was the imperial idea – with time combined with the messianic idea – aimed at the conquest and dependence of neighboring (border) and more distant nations and states[15]. To this day, this idea has been the core of Moscow-Russia's foreign policy at various times in history and in various combination of words (Lazari, 1993, pp. 49–56). At first, this idea found its origin, foundation and

---

14 Russian explorer Adam Bujak asked this question to a young, accidentally encountered Russian in the mid-1990s. And, in response, he heard: "You want to know if it is Europe or Asia? It is simply Russia, which will not be understood by anyone who does not live here" (Bujak, 1995, p. 101). According to A. Bujak, the Russian soul cannot be decoded otherwise.

15 There was even such a conviction and statement among Russians that Russia may be an empire or it will not be at all.

sanction in the Orthodox religion[16] (Moscow as Third Rome), national ideology (nationalism), Pan-Slavic ideology (the concept of the Slavic nation) or class ideology (communism) (Lazari, 1993, pp. 49-56).

The canon of the nation's and state's security remained in a close, synergistic relationship with the imperial canon of Russian foreign policy[17]. Its understanding by the Russians for centuries has been tainted with some kind of internal contradiction, and even paradoxicality. This canon consisted in the permanent building and strengthening of Russia's security at the expense of the security of other nations, neighbors or the entire world community. This canon did not aim at the security symmetry of Russia and its neighbors, but the glaring asymmetry of Russia and others – other states. The implementation of this canon of the foreign policy of Russia and the Russian Federation was and still is based on the slogan of the fight for peace and security for all mankind (Niepsuj, 2004, pp. 369-391). So, striving to achieve goals such as imperialism, nationalism and national and state security mask them with the slogans of the fight for peace and international security. These slogans, being extremely noble in themselves and widely accepted by the international community, play a particularly mystifying role in the practice of Russia's foreign and domestic policy.

The situation is similar with another canon of Russia's foreign policy, namely the category of freedom. It did not and still does not prevent Russia and the Russian Federation from proclaiming that it is the epitome and bearer of freedom, the proverbial "Knight of Freedom"[18]. Almost every war that Russia has waged, it has been waged under the banner of the minister of freedom. This was the case with Poland and Poles with the annexation of the lands of the First Republic, suppression of Polish National Uprisings and the occupation of Eastern Poland between 1939-1941. This has also been the case in Chechnya, Georgia and Ukraine recently.

The Russian Federation, as the heir of the USSR and Russia of the tsars, as well as the Moscow State, in its foreign policy, depending on the historical period, is

---

[16] Mikołaj Berdjajew even stated that Orthodoxy is the Russian faith. Sergiusz Zenkowski, one of the Russian thinkers, wrote on this subject: "Orthodoxy – according to Mikołaj Bierdiajew – turned out to be the Russian faith. In the clergy's poems, Ruthenia is the Universe, the Russian Tsar is the Tsar of the Tsars, and Jerusalem is also Ruthenia. Ruthenia is where the truth of faith is. The Russian religious mission, unique of its kind, is linked to the strength and greatness of the Russian state, with the exceptional importance of the Russian Tsar. The imperialist temptation is combined with the messianic consciousness" (Zieńkowskij, 1970, p. 36).

[17] In the nineteenth century the idea of Moscow – the state, was replaced by the idea of Moscow – the nation (Lazari, 1993, p. 51).

[18] Adam Bujak describes this theme as follows: "(...) I once spoke to a singer from a patriarchal choir and this man proudly told me that his father fought for Poland's freedom. He wanted to show it to me. The Russians, as a nation, firmly believe that they brought us freedom, they freed us from fascism. Let us not delude ourselves that they will apologize to us for bringing us a new fascism..." (Bujak, 1995, p. 100).

still guided by the mentioned canons – ideas. They are timeless in its foreign policy. They create the content, some *explicitly* and some *implicitly*, of almost all the mottos of this paper, and thus they also express, in the fullest and most significant way, the fundamental vectors of the foreign policy of the Russian Federation towards Ukraine. So let's recall them again at this point in this block:
- "(...) The collapse of the Soviet Union was the greatest catastrophe of the century. It was a real drama for the Russian people"[19].
- "(...) the former Soviet Union cannot be seen as an area in which all CSCE orms are fully applied. The point is that this is a post-imperial area where Russia must defend its interests using all available means, including military and economic ones. We will strongly insist that the former republics of the Soviet Union join the new federation or confederation as soon as possible, and we will stand firm for this."[20].
- "(...) The conditions of freedom dictate the need for collective leadership of the world's major powers. It can be called the << concert of the powers of the 21st century >> (...). For this part of the world, which has been adopted as the Euro-Atlantic region, it would not harm to understand the three – the US, Russia and the European Union. (...) I agree that these "three" could "steer the world's boat into calmer waters""[21].
- "The maximum program for Russia [its strategy towards Europe – JMN] is the finlandization of the whole of Europe, but we must start with the re-organization of the Great Limitrof space" (Solozobov, 2009)[22].

---

19 This well-known statement of the Russian leader V. Putin is of course not shared in the world. No less known in the world is the diagnosis of the collapse of communism (USSR) made by the Pope John Paul II on the pages of the book *Cross the Threshold of Hope*. The Pope presents this problem as follows: "(...) Communism as a system collapsed by itself in a sense. It collapsed as a result of its own mistakes and abuse. It turned out to be "a medicine more dangerous than the disease itself". The system did not bring about real social reforms, although it became a powerful warning and a challenge for the whole world. But it *fell alone, because of its own immanent weakness*" (Paul II, 1994, pp. 108–109).
20 Excerpt from the statement of the Russian Minister of Foreign Affairs delivered on On December 14, 1992, during the ministerial meeting of the Conference on Security and Cooperation in Europe (CSCE) (Rotfeld, 2014, p. 393).
21 Russian Minister of Foreign Affairs Sergey Lavrov, Inaugural lecture at the beginning of the academic year at the Moscow State Institute of International Relations (forge of diplomatic cadres of the former USSR and present-day Russia), 3 September 2007 (www.gazetawyborcza.pl/1.86738, 4469179.html).
22 "Limitrof" – from Latin. *limitrophus* – borderline. According to the eminent expert on the subject – Adam Daniel Rotfeld, Yuri Solozobov, revealing the essence of Russia's strategy towards Europe and labeling it with the concept of "finlandization", meant such neighboring countries of Russia as Finland (the archetype and designation of the concept in question), Poland, and above all Ukraine (Rotfeld, 2014, p. 407).

Contemporary Greater Russians, reflecting in the spirit of the thesis that "Russia is not possible without the Empire" (Przebinda, 2001, p. 230) at the same time, most often add to the fact that "Russia as an Empire" is impossible without Ukraine[23]. In other words, the Russians consider Ukraine as "Russian canonical territories", a kind of "geographical space" waiting to be put in order by the "Russian hand." As in the case of Poland, the so-called The Great Russians believe that just as it is impossible for Poland and Russia to coexist independently, because, as they claim, the ideal of Poland is to replace Russia in the Slavic world, and in the case of Ukraine they deny Ukrainians a statehood separate from Russia, territorial self-existence and national distinctiveness (Przebinda, 2001, p. 230).

All this of "Russian thinking" means that in its foreign policy, Russia does everything possible to reduce modern Ukraine to the status and role of a failed state[24]. To this end, Russia is pursuing a policy of destabilizing Ukraine, one expression of which is actions aimed at its state fragmentation (Rotfeld, 2014, p. 385). An example of this type of policy was the annexation of Crimea, the so-called "Declarations of independence" of the so-called "Lugansk Republic" and the so-called "Donetsk Republic" as well as actions aimed at separating the so-called Novorossiya.

Russia does not respect any rights, from human rights to international law. This also applies, and perhaps in particular, to international treaties concerning Ukraine, of which Russia was not only a signatory but also a guarantor (Rotfeld, 2014, p. 386).

The most striking example – from the point of view of the subject of these considerations – of this type of attitude and behavior of Russia is its attitude to the norms of universal international law contained in the United Nations Charter (Article 2, points 1,2,3,4 and 5), the Final Act CSCE signed in Helsinki on August 1, 1975, or in particular to the commitments signed as a part of the CSCE Summit in Budapest on December 5, 1994, as well as to the earlier tripartite agreement – the commitment signed jointly with the US and Ukraine in Moscow on January 15, 1994.

Our special attention in the list of these documents deserves the so-called Budapest Memorandum. It concerned Ukraine's voluntary and unilateral withdrawal from the status of a nuclear state (from the post-Soviet nuclear weapons deployed on its territory) and Ukraine's accession to the Non-Proliferation Treaty (Rotfeld, 2014, p. 387).

---

23 AD Rotfeld rightly believes that "From the Russian perspective, Ukraine has the most important and greatest role to play in rebuilding Russia's imperial position" (Rotfeld, 2014, p. 385).

24 And thus posing a threat to regional, European and world security and requiring order by the "brotherly" Russian hand.

The signatories and guarantors of this memorandum were, next to Ukraine, the nuclear powers such as Russia, the USA and Great Britain. These powers undertook, inter alia, that:
- "will respect the independence and sovereignty as well as the existing borders of Ukraine";
- renounce "the use of force and the threats to use it against the territorial integrity and political independence of Ukraine";
- "their weapons will never be used against Ukraine";
- they will not "resort to economic pressures aimed at subordinating Ukraine to their own interests" (Rotfeld, 2014, p. 386).

All these guarantees of the Budapest Memorandum were ignored and violated by Russia in 2014 during the hybrid war directed against Ukraine.

Geostrategy according to Z. Trejnis "(...) determines how and where the state focuses its efforts on economic, military, diplomatic and other measures to optimize its development and improve position, even at the expense of other countries" (Trejnis, 2019, p. 53).

Ukraine's security conditions are the result of its geostrategic location at a specific strategic junction between the East and the West (on the eastern side of the western civilization's border). Samuel Huntington, drawing the boundary of civilization dividing Europe into Western civilization and Eastern civilization, left almost all of Ukraine, except its present western (former Borderlands of the Second Polish Republic) frontiers on the eastern border of Western civilization. So Agnieszka Legucka is right when she writes that "(...) From the point of view of geostrategy, Ukraine occupies a special place in Europe due to its location, demographic, political and economic potential" (Legucka, 2007, p. 143). The area of Ukraine is 603.7 km^2, which is almost twice as large as the area of Poland. As a state, it borders with such countries as Belarus, the Russian Federation, Poland, Slovakia, Hungary, Moldova and Romania. It has a population of about 50 million, 77.8% of which are Ukrainians and, which is extremely important from the point of view of the discussed considerations, 17.3% are Russians. Besides, this country is inhabited by national minorities of all neighboring countries, such as: Poles, Belarusians, Moldovans, Crimean Tatars, Hungarians, Bulgarians and others (Legucka, 2007, p. 143).

Since – according to Napoleon Bonaparte – Poland is the "keystone of the European vault", and therefore the element that determines the strength of its entire European structure (vault), in our opinion, from a geostrategic point of view, Ukraine is today its eastern basis. For this reason, Ukraine, from the very beginning of its history, had to solve the dilemma (curse?) of its geographical location; it was faced not only with the problem of how to defend itself against absorption by the West or by the East, but also against the threat of being absorbed by the Muslim South[25]. Although the over thousand-year history of Ruthania / Ukraine's struggle for its security seems to be a very interesting problem in itself from a cognitive and practical point of view, due to the fact that it goes beyond the scope of the topic we undertook, and in particular the framework of this work, we will not deal with it. Our focus and analysis will focus solely on the revived of Ukraine after the collapse of the Union of Soviet Socialist Republics. This state, at the time of its restoration in 1991, "rediscovered" that geography is its fate and thus the most fundamental and permanent factor of its foreign policy (Trejnis, 2019, p. 52) and, consequently, of its security. And no one is surprised[26]. After all, many contemporary researchers of national security, when analyzing the factors of power and weakness of the state, traditionally mention geographic among these factors in one of the first (if not the first) places, meaning: spatial location, size of the territory, topography, climate etc.[27].

According to, for example, Frederic H. Hartman, among the essential aspects of national security in the 21st century, besides the geographical one, there are also:
- demographic (population, structure and demographic trends);
- economic (raw material resources, needs and shortages, level of economic growth);
- historical-psychological-sociological (experiences, attitude to life, social cohesion);
- organizational and administrative (form of a government, society's attitude to power, effectiveness of its operation);
- military (organization and effectiveness of the Armed Forces, size in relation to the number of population in the recruiting age);
- information (media ownership structure, pluralism and freedom of speech)[28].

---

25 Gen. Charles de Gaulle claimed that "geography is fate and geopolitics is a choice" (Trejnis, 2019, p. 52).
26 Janusz Onyszkiewicz perceived this problem in the nineties of the last century: "(…) I thought that contacts with Ukraine should be started, because as long as Russia is with Ukraine, it is a superpower. If Ukraine separates from Moscow, Russia will only be a very large state (…) for Russia's democratic future it is better if it is not tied to Ukraine, because then its imperial temptations will be much weaker. In other words: Russia without Ukraine has a better chance of becoming a big, strong country. A state that respects a certain *status quo* that respects certain political mechanisms."
27 Robert Dawid Kaplan believes that although the development of new technologies has limited the influence of geography on the development of a given country (causing the phenomenon of globalization), modern countries (emerging powers) such as China, Russia, India, Iran or Turkey are returning to the geographical vision the world, seeking to restore their imperial tradition (Kaplan, 2019, p. 25).
28 Let us add, by the way, that contemporary Western experts on the subject believe that today, among the factors of national security mentioned, its economic and information aspects should be considered a priority. These researchers recall the words of the Chinese strategist Sun Tzu –

- the goal of Russian foreign policy towards Ukraine and the whole of Eastern Europe, from Estonia to Austria and Bulgaria, is to weaken all the above-mentioned factors that establish the strength of the national security of a given country. This is the new face of the Russian imperial tradition. And Ukraine is a model example of this tradition.

References

(1990) *Paris Charter of New Europe*, Paris, in "Collection of documents" no. 4.
(1995) *Die Europäische Sicherheitsgemeinschaft. Das Sicherheitsmodell für das 21. Jahrhundert*, Institut für Friedensforschung und Sicherheitspolitik an der Universität Hamburg (IFSH), Eine Welt. Texte der Stiftung Entwicklund und Frieden, Bonn.
(1995) *History of Polish diplomacy*, eds. G. Labuda, Warsaw: PWN.
(2003) *Secure Europe in Better Word, European Security Strategy*, Brussels, http://www.con silium.europa.eu/uedocs/cmsUpload/78367.pdf.
(2004) *History of wars. Illustrated history of world warfare from the times of ancient civilizations to the 21st century*, Warsaw: BELLONA Publishing House.
(2013) *White Book of National Security of the Republic of Poland*, Warsaw: National Security Bureau.
(2013) *Strategy for the development of the national security system of the Republic of Poland 2022*. Document adopted by the resolution of the Council of Ministers of April 9, 2013, Warsaw.
(2020) Prayer of John Paul II for peace in the world, in Calendar of the Polish Army Soldier 2020, Warsaw: Curia of the Military Ordinariate.
Allison G, (2018). *Condemned to war? Will America and China Avoid Thucydides' Trap?*, Bielsko Biała: Pascal, Bielsko Biała 2018.
Asmus RD, (1997). *FOR THIS. The concept of security in the 21st century*, Warsaw.
Bierdiajew M., (1993). *Prawda prawosławia*, in: ZNAK monthly, No. 453 (2), p. 4.
Berdyaev N., (1952). *Istina prawosławija*, "Messager de l'Exarchat du Patriarche Russe en Europe Occidentale", No. 11 (1952), pp. 4–10.
Borgosz J., (1989). *Dear and wilderness of a philosophy of peace. From Homer to John Paul II*, Warsaw.
Brzoska M., Ehrhart HG, Evers F., Neuneck G., (2014). *Fachgespräch "Die Ukraine als Herausforderung – Probleme und Perspektiven aus wissenschaftlicher Sicht"*, http://www.ifsh.de.
Bujak A., (1995). *Wandering through defiled Rus*, ZNAK Monthly, No. 480 (5), pp. 100–101.
Clausewitz C., (1995). *About the war*, Lublin.

---

the author of the work entitled "The art of war", which proclaimed that "war should be won without the use of an army – in the hearts and minds of opponents." Many countries, including Russia in particular, have long put into practice the teachings of this Chinese strategist. It is waging an information war, an asymmetric war and a hybrid war on new grounds, effectively fighting for the minds of people around the world in the so-called cyberspace. More about it in (Darczewska, 2014; Lelonek).

Darczewska J., (2014). *The anatomy of the Russian information warfare. Operation Crimea – case study*, Eastern Studies Marek Karpia, Warsaw.
Grepon P., (1994). *Religion and war*, Gdańsk.
Heisburg F., (1998). *Wars*, Warsaw.
Hobbes T., (1954). *Lewiatan*, Warsaw.
Hobbes T., (2009). *Leviathan or the matter, form and power of the Church and secular state*, Warsaw: Aletheia Foundation.
Howard M., (1990). *War in the history of Europe*, Wrocław.
Huntington S., (1997). *A clash of civilization and a new shape of the world order*, Warsaw: Warszawskie Wydawnictwo Literackie MUZA SA, pp. 14–22.
Huzarski M., (2009). *Polemology – "If you want peace, learn about war"*, Scientific Papers of AON, No. 2 (75), pp. 287–298.
Kant I., (1992). *About eternal peace. Philosophical Outline*, Wrocław.
Kant I., (1995). *A saying: This may be correct in theory, but is worth nothing in practice. To eternal peace. Philosophical project*, Critical study, introduction, comments, bibliography and index Heiner F. Klemme, Translation and foreword by Mirosław Żelazny, Toruń: COMER Publishing House.
Kaplan RD, (2019). *Revenge of geography*, "Forum" 2019, no. 26 (2633).
Kondziela J., (1974). *Peace Research – Theory and Its Application*, Warsaw.
Kostecki W., (1990). *Contemporary Research on Peace*, Warsaw.
Xenophon, (1967). *Socratic Letters*, Warsaw.
Kupiecki R. and Szczepanik K., (1995). *Polish foreign policy 1918–1994*, Warsaw: Scholar.
Lazari A., (1993). *Will Russia be the Third Rome*, ZNAK Monthly, No. 453, February (2), pp. 49–56.
Legucka A., (2007). *Institutionalization of Polish-Ukrainian cooperation in the field of security*, Scientific Papers of AON, No. 1 (66), p. 143.
Lelonek A., *Russian information warfare in Ukraine*, https://www.defence24.pl/rosyjska-wojna-informacyjna-na-ukrainie.
Maslow AH, (1970). *Motivation and Personality*, Second Edition. New York: Harper & Row, Publishers.
Niepsuj J., (2000). *The problem of security and peace in the Europe of Homelands*, in: *Europe of Homelands*. Materials from the seminar entitled *"The Role and Significance of Homelands in a United Europe"*, eds. Paweł Bromski, Warsaw: NAVO.
Niepsuj JM, (2004). *The idea of peace in relations between the state and the Catholic Church in Poland (Stalinist period)*, in: *The space of politics and religious affairs*. Essays dedicated to Professor Janusz Osuchowski the occasion of 75 – anniversary of the birth, eds. Beata Górowska, Warsaw.
Paul II J., (1994). *To Cross the Threshold of Hope*, Lublin: Editorial Staff of the Catholic University of Lublin, Lublin.
Paul II J., (2007). Encyclical *Slavorum Apostoli* of the Holy Father John Paul II addressed to bishops and priests to religious families to all believing Christians on the thousand-year anniversary of the work of evangelization of Saints Cyril and Methodius, in *Encyclical of the Holy Father John Paul II*, Krakow: ZNAK Publishing House, pp. 217–252.
Paul II J., (2007). Apostolic Letter *Euntes in mundum universum* on the occasion of the millennium of the baptism of Kievan Rus (January 25, 1988), in *Apostolic Letters of the Holy Father John Paul II*, Krakow: ZNAK Publishing House, pp. 273–296.

Przebinda G., (2001). *Greater Europe. The Pope towards Russia and Ukraine*, Kraków: ZNAK Publishing House.

Rotfeld AD, (2014). *Strategic Choice of Russia, in: The Road to Change*, Jubilee Book on the Sixtieth Birthday of President Aleksander Kwasniewski, eds. Danuta Waniek, Krzysztof Janik, Volume I, Warsaw-Krakow.

Sadykiewicz M., (1985) *Die sowietische Militärdoktrin und Strategie*, Koblenz: Bernard & Graefe Verlag.

Solozobow J., (2009). *Open on Polish wopros. In otnoszenijach mieżdu ROSSIJA and Polsza wozmożen stratiegiczeskij proryw*, "Politiczeskij Klass," 9.

Tatarkiewicz W., (1983). *History of philosophy*, Volume 3, Warsaw: PWN.

Toffler AH, (1997). *War and anti- war*, Warsaw: Muza.

Trejnis Z., (2018). *Political and military challenges and threats to the unity of the Euro-Atlantic community, in: Challenges and threats to the security and defense of the Republic of Poland in the 21st century in the political, military and economic dimensions*, eds. Zenon Trejnis, Warsaw: ASPRA-JR Publishing House.

Trejnis Z., (2019). *Geopolitical aspect of Poland's defense potential, in: Defense potential of the Republic of Poland*, eds. Konrad Stańczyk, Warsaw: PWN SA Scientific Publisher.

Tymanowski J., (1998). *Borders of Europe and NATO enlargement to the East, in: NATO and Eastern Europe. NATO Enlargement to the East – The Last European Challenge of the 20th Century*, eds. KA Wojtaszczyk, JM Niepsuj, Warsaw.

Tzu S., (1994). *The Art of War*, Warsaw.

www.gazetawyborcza.pl/1,86738,4469179.html.

Zi S., (2011). *The art of war. A Chinese Treatise on Effective Tactics and Strategies in Armed Struggle and in Life and Business*, eds. Robert Stiller, Krakow.

Zieńkowskij S., (1970). *Russkoje Old Believers. Duchownyje dwiżenija siemnadcatogo lid*, Munich.

Jan Figurski / Jerzy Niepsuj

Chapter 51: Summary and Conclusions: The Russian perspective on Ukraine's geopolitical and geostrategic position in Eastern Europe

According to eminent thinkers and philosophers, since wars originate in the minds of people, then one should also seek and build in their minds, the preliminaries of peace, including this eternal peace[1]. This truth also applies to Russian-Ukrainian, Russian-European (Euro-Atlantic) relations and Russia's relations with all other countries and regions of the world.

Since also, as we read in the *Charter of Paris for a New Europe*, "(...) [s]ecurity is indivisible and security of every participating State is inseparably linked to that of all the others" (Charter of Paris for a New Europe, 1990; Jacobsen and Souchon, 1993, pp. 181–182), we people defining ourselves as *homo sapiens* should reject the attributed "right" to own security at the expense of others (Manachinsky, 1998, pp. 152–158). Unfortunately, also in the modern world, these seemingly obvious matters are not heard by everyone (Manachinsky, 1998, pp. 152–158). And this happens due to the fact that among others the world still respects the age-old principle that the winner is not judged. We, Western Europeans know that, and Eastern Europeans know it too. At this point, the question arises whether, for example, the Russians feel any guilt for the past for genocide and enslaving other nations. So far, it is not visible in the theory and practice of the foreign policy of the Russian Federation. It is clear, however, that Russia is striving to revive in the form of the Empire.

Russia's aggression against Ukraine in 2014, preceded by Russia's aggression against Georgia in 2008 ended the period of peace in our part of Europe. According to many analysts, this change is from a strategic point of view relatively permanent. Russia has retreated in terms of cooperation with the West. For the second time, in its vision of the world and Russia itself, the Eastern option won over the Western one. This means Russia's confrontational course towards its

---

[1] The noble authors of the Preamble to the UNESCO Constitution also considered it appropriate to write down that since wars "(...) have their origin in the minds of people, then in the minds of people there must be a defense of peace" (*Collection of Statutes and Regulations of International Organizations*, 1966, p. 302).

environment. In this context, "(...) the *existence of a strong, democratic and independent Ukraine has a strategic dimension for Poland and is a significant factor contributing to its independence, just as the existence of an independent Poland has a strategic dimension for Ukraine*" (http://www.bbn.gov.pl).

After the end of the so-called Cold War, the fall of the so-called Iron Curtain, the bipolar system of world security, and the entry of a global society into the development phase referred to as the information society, many theorists and analysts of security science have formulated statements about the decline in the importance of such traditional and eternal security factors as e.g. the geographical factor or a military factor among the factors determining the security of individual states. It was also argued that information security and economic security should be regarded as the priority dimensions of national security in the present day. Other dimensions, such as geographic, military, cultural, social, demographic, historical – psychological – sociological, organizational – administrative and others do not have a determining influence on national security. Unfortunately, among these theorists there were also Polish researchers. Poland is a country in which the geographical factor as a priority for its security has been taken into account for centuries[2].

Russia, due to its aggression against Georgia and Ukraine, reactivated in practice the importance of the geographical factor as determining the policy of modern countries[3]. Since the collapse of the USSR and the simultaneous rebirth of the Ukrainian state, that is, since the beginning of the 1990s, the Ukrainian people have been making a historic effort to build a sovereign state. From the very beginning, the main challenge facing the Ukrainian nation on this path has been to ensure national security, understood as an existential need. Due to its geographical location, security of Ukraine is a fundamental value not only for itself, but also for Europe and the whole world. Because of the geostrategic location of Ukraine, the key location, above all, for European security, ensuring the national security of Ukraine is of great importance for the post-Cold War international order (world security). In conjunction with the creation of Ukraine's national security is not only a priority objective of Ukraine but also the international community, particularly the Europeans (and those of the West and East).

The historical experiences of Ukraine, especially those of western origin, prompted the Ukrainian nation to choose a western orientation on the way to

---

2 This was due to the lack of the ability of the Polish elite to think autonomously about Polish security (Figurski and Niepsuj, 2017, pp. 659–703; Marczak and Jakubczak, 2014).

3 "The policy of states is determined by geography" – this sentence was uttered by Napoleon (Marczak and Jakubczak, 2014, p. 49). Also prof. Zbigniew Brzeziński described the significant influence of geographic reflection on geostrategic thinking. He also noted that this influence is complemented by historical reflection. He stated on this subject as follows: "(...) The value of a map is enhanced by historical knowledge" (Kuźniar, 1994, p. 181).

protecting national security (the so-called Orange Revolution). However, this choice was and is not supported by the thinking of the entire Ukrainian nation. A large group of it, especially the Russian minority (the geographical east of Ukraine), is mentally still in the eastern and post-Soviet orientation. This mental split of the Ukrainian nation (along with other 'internal' and subjective factors of state security) allows Russia to pursue a policy towards Ukraine – from the beginning of its statehood – based on the old Roman principle of *divide et impera*.

After a short period of "trouble" in the 1990s, Russia returned to the imperial idea as the basic canon of its foreign and domestic policy.

An interpretation of this policy is Russia's desire to rebuild its state position as a world empire, i.e. a state which has global interests and which defines (or at least co-determines) the basic principles of world security. Most world analysts believe that Russia can not become an empire again without Ukraine. It does not have the appropriate potential on its own. That is why one of the priority goals of Russian foreign policy is to 'absorb' Ukraine again and thus recreate the geostrategic foundations of imperial Russia[4]. Knowing this, are the world and us, Western Europeans, able to convince Russia that the mark of the new Europe is, among others, the fact that the geographical location does not determine the fate of the peoples inhabiting it, "(...) because they can already build their future according to free choice"[5].

The essence of Ukraine's geopolitical situation, especially with regard to the foreign policy of the Russian Federation, is the systemic situation of its functioning, encompassing mainly internal procedures influencing external cooperation. In the functional process, it is important that internal activities in Ukraine should be focused on increasing the efficiency of the economic, industrial and other structural areas, aimed at improving the standard of living of citizens and strengthening the state's position on the international arena.

Obtaining the status of a wealthy state, recognized both internally and externally, will definitely improve the situation in terms of internal and external relations.

The following conclusions can be drawn from the above analysis:

---

[4] Since Russia's strategy is to "absorb" Ukraine as the foundation and buttress of neo-imperial Russia, as Sun Tzu teaches, the best way to counteract this is to win with Russia's strategy. The Chinese strategist stated on this subject as follows: "(...). Win strategy, the best strategy in a fight is to destroy the plans of enemies, the most important thing in a war is to destroy the enemy's strategy" (Tzu, The *Art of War*, 1994, pp. 35–38).

[5] NATO Secretary General Javier Solana expressed the above-mentioned words on March 16, 1999, during the hoisting ceremony of the state flags of Poland, the Czech Republic and Hungary in front of NATO Headquarters in Brussels.

1. In the process of enhancing Ukraine's geopolitical situation, activities are targeted at areas that have a major impact on functional efficiency. These areas include the problematic accession to the European Union and NATO and the advancement of the industrial, agricultural and educational sectors. To this end, one can forsee the establishment of functional teams, at the state level to, improve the above-mentioned areas.
2. In the execution process, it is expected that the functionality of the appointed subsystems will be organized according to a functional, serial-construction or repair structure. Such a functionality will allow to determine the feasability of the system and of the particular subsytems, as well as additional evaluation indicators. As a result, the designated functional values will make it possible to provide additional adjustments in the process of implementation of the tasks.
3. The inncentive for facilitating the functioning of the system improving internal and external processes of Ukraine is the implementation of supporting tasks through the IT management system. The presented IT modules will support the planning processes of individual and team executive activities. This support will enable the systemic operating to be monitored on an ongoing basis and to make supporting corrections.
4. An additional advantage of the functioning of the evaluation system is the possibility of identifying the functional effectiveness of individual subsystems in any period of their operation. This will allow to ensure about the corectness of the adopted solutions.

References

(1966) Collection of Statutes and Regulations of International Organizations, (eds.) Hubert S., vol.2, part 1, PISM, Warsaw: PISM.

(1990) *K arta Paris for a New Europe*, in: "The collection of documents" No. 4.

(1993) Declaration of the ministers of foreign affairs "On the principles of shaping Polish-Ukrainian partnership", http://www.bbn.gov.pl/?Strona=pl_pl-ukr_dek_min.

Figurski J. and Niepsuj J., (2017). On the need to restore the "order of thinking" in the Polish reflection on state security and defense, in: Polish defense in the 21st century, Leśniewski Z., Ostolski PR, Palczewska M., Warsaw: Akademia Sztuki Wojnej.

Jacobsen HA and Souchon L., (1993). *In the service of peace. Bundeswehr 1955–1993*, Warsaw: BELLONA Publishing House.

Kuźniar R. (eds.), (1994). *Between politics and strategy*, Warsaw.

Manachinsky A., (1998). Ukraine and NATO: Reality and problems, in: NATO and Eastern Europe. NATO Enlargement to the East – The Last European Challenge of the 20th Century, (eds.) Wojtaszczyk KA and Niepsuj JM, Warsaw: ELIPSA Publishing House.

Marczak J., Jakubczak R., (2014). Strategic report: The Polish Armed Forces in the second decade of the 21st century. Strategic Concept of the Territorial Defense of the Republic of Poland, Warsaw: National Defense Academy.

Tzu S., (1994). *War Art*, Warsaw.

Section II:
The Russian mechanism of interaction on the Ukrainian decision-making process with the use of the methodology of hard and soft impact

Arkadiusz Jóźwiak

Chapter 52: The methodology of Russian hard impact in Ukraine

The Ukrainian Republic was the largest republic of the USSR, and Kiev (the current capital of Ukraine) is the third largest city in the USSR with a population of approximately 2.8 million people. Since 1991, Ukraine also mattered enormously in the former USSR, as it was a republic where most of the Soviet heavy industry was concentrated (Jastrzębska, 2015, pp. 137–148). Ukraine has become a sovereign state. To this day, however, Ukraine remains under a strong Russian influence. These influences are achieved with the use of different methods of interaction on various grounds. In the world of dynamic globalization and breaking all communication barriers, military actions alone are not a sufficient means to achieve goals. Therefore it can be seen, that global powers with a particular impact on other countries, apply diverse methods to accomplish their objectives. Various criteria can be used to divide these methods, however, they can be generally grouped as the "hard and soft impact" methods.

The aim of the study is to describe the hard impact of the Russian Federation on Ukraine.

The originator of the concept of the division of state power into "the soft one and the hard one" is Joseph S. Nye. He assumed that the ability to "attract" other countries is the basic determinant of the position in the world today. He separated the state's military and economic potential (hard power) from such assortments as culture, values and foreign policy (soft power). It was presumed that it is the latter factors that make societies of other countries have a positive attitude towards a given country and are more willing to cooperate (Jędrowiak, 2019, pp. 4 3–56). One can assume that more and more "hard states" focus their attention on soft powers that complement the hard ones. On the other hand, when referring to the resources that make up the soft power, in literature one can find many angles expanding the perspective proposed by JS Nye.

The hard methods of interaction between states include, among others military, economic or financial activities. In turn, the soft impact is, among others politics, information, cultural and educational activities.

Ukraine has two types of borders with Russia: a land one (approx. 2,200 km) and a sea one (approx. 300 km). The border delimitation was introduced into force in 2004. It was not until 2010 that an international commission was established to carry out the demarcation. Unfortunately, to this day, for various reasons, this border is a flashpoint in Ukrainian-Russian relations. The recent years of Ukrainian politics have shown that this country cannot define unequivocal goals in its international policy. The relations between the states (Russia and Ukraine) have changed at the turn of these years. One of the main factors influencing these ties is the presidential election. Depending on what political option the president of Ukraine came from (whether he was a pro-Russian or a pro-European), these relations were clearly better or worse. Analysts compare Ukraine's foreign policy to a pendulum. They note that during the presidency of Leonid Kuchma (1994–2004), Kiev cared for a balance in relations between the West and Russia.

Russia is constantly trying to maintain its sphere of influence, and any other action by the Ukrainian authorities that is not in line with the Kremlin's line, is met with retaliatory actions by Russia on various levels. These areas include: diplomacy, politics, economy, military issues, social issues and media. For example, in the area of politics, when in July 2008 Dmitry Medvedev took over as the Russian president, the concepts of foreign policy of the Russian Federation were approved in 2009. It was recognized that the most crucial aspect is to ensure security and to strengthen sovereignty and territorial integrity. Therefore, the expansion of NATO for Ukraine and Georgia was found as one of the threats to Russia (Łos, 2017, pp. 565–579).

When analyzing Ukrainian-Russian relations, it is impossible to ignore the military themes between the countries that have taken place in their recent years. The Russian Federation has repeatedly and deliberately breached international water borders, especially the air zones. Actions of this type, perceived as "flexing muscles" are to show that the Russian army is ready for action here and now, and at the same time, exert various pressures on other countries.

The deployment of military units of the Russian Federation in the vicinity of the Ukrainian border and around the Sea of Azov is also no coincidence. Such deployment of military units is a certain way to control such an area. On the other hand, the Azov Sea is a strategic zone of this region for two countries. From the Russia's point of view, it was one of the routes used for providing the fighting separatists with the supplies. From the Ukraine's perspective, it is the main route for trade exchange and supplies delivery for ports and metallurgical plants on the coast.

The annexation of the Crimean peninsula by the Russian Federation in March 2014 was a milestone after the referendum that was held by the Russian side. At the same time, there were riots in the Donbass (Donetsk and Lugansk regions), where the fighting separatists were unofficially aided by the Russian side.

It is worth recalling that officially the Russian Federation does not conduct any military actions against Ukraine, but the so-called the *green men* armed and well-equipped soldiers in uniforms without any identification, shoulder patches and names, operating in the Crimea, Donbass then officially have nothing in common with Russia. The model of operation adopted in this way is nothing more than a hybrid war. This is conditioned by the complex of forces and means used by Russia. A hybrid threat is both external and internal, national and transnational, military and intelligence, which cannot be answered symmetrically. Hybrid operations are run both by states and non-state entities in secret and half-overt way, using legal and illegal methods. The operations are performed in both physical and informational-psychological capacities (Darczewska, no date, pp. 40–67).

When considering the issue of the presence of Russian armed forces in Ukraine and quantitative estimates, one should take into account the specificity of a hybrid war, i.e. the aspect of propaganda, disinformation and inspirational activities by the parties to the conflict, aimed at enhancing or minimizing their mutual participation. The image is intentionally distorted and, above all, highly fragmented. Moreover, the Russian side, for international reasons, has developed at least four variants of its own military presence, aimed at concealing such a fact and such a scale (Impact of the war with Ukraine, 2015):

- united divisions or subunits of the armed forces, the Ministry of the Interior, Federal Security Service of the Russian Federation (FSB), Main Intelligence Administration GRU, the Mimnistry of Emergency Situations are transferred to Ukraine temporarily and rotate in the conflict zone; they either wear their own uniforms and with Russian identification marks, or are characterized as separatist units, fighting under the symbolism of the People's Republic of Donetsk (DNR) and the People's Republic of Lugansk (ŁNR);
- groups of the so-called volunteers, i.e. professional cadres of soldiers and officers of the Russian armed forces delegated to the combat zone and pretended to be civilians or private "vacationers" from the armed forces;
- groups of mercenaries – citizens of the Russian Federation – who underwent military training and were secretly recruited to fight in Ukraine; from the available information it is known that recruitment is carried out in military groups and nationalist organizations, and even among criminal elements (penal colonies);
- groups recruited from paramilitary formations called "militia", such as the Cossack and Caucasian troops (Chechnya, Ossetia, Ingushetia), fighting in Ukraine in dense national and organizational formations.

The fact that uniformed and armed groups as well as supplies and armaments columns, including heavy equipment, were crossing the Russian-Ukrainian border, was confirmed by the US and NATO interviews and recorded by OSCE observers (Wpływ wojny z Ukrainą, 2015).

The situation is aggravated by the fact that, according to UN data, more than 1.4 million people have left Donbass since the beginning of the armed conflict in the east, mostly due to the pro-Ukrainian position. The journal "Зеркало недели" published the results of a large-scale survey conducted among residents of the uncontrolled territories of Donbas on how they see the future of Lugansk and Donetsk in the context of war. The survey found that only 5 percent wants the territory to be restored to Ukraine, and 65 percent believes that the territory of the unrecognized "republics" should become a part of Russia (www.new.org). The results of the survey also show how the narrative and the information message are conducted in this part of the country.

Other ocurrences between the countries of a military character include the shooting by Russian special forces and the subsequent seizure of three Ukrainian naval ships (two armored cutters and a tug) in the Kerch Strait that separates the Black Sea from the Sea of Azov. The parties accused each other of "an act of Russian aggression" and "an Ukrainian provocation".

The economy is a very complex subject that can be considered in many respects. The study was limited only to its main indicators. Despite the fact that Ukrainian policy (sometimes closer to the east – Russia, other times closer to the west – the EU) changes dynamically over time, it tries to approach nearer to the EU economically. One of the milestones is Ukraine's accession to the Eastern Partnership program in 2009 (a program defining the eastern dimension of the European Union's policy under the European Neighborhood Policy). Since 2014, it has been a country associated with the European Union, and since 2016 it has been a member of a free trade zone with the European Union. In opposition to these steps, the Russian Federation attempted to stop these measures by using the hard economic impact, including proposing Ukraine to participate in the so-called Eurasian Customs Union (EUC) in 2013. Such arrangements were to be made after the talks between the President Viktor Yanukovych (a pro-Russian politician) and the Russian President Vladimir Putin. One of the main assumptions of the EUC is the common foreign trade policy imposed by its largest member. It was supposed to bring Ukraine closer to Russia economically and, at the same time, move away from the EU. Nevertheless, after the change of the president of Ukraine in 2015 (a pro-European policy supporter), Ukraine decided to cooperate with the EU economically.

The territories of Ukraine are very diversified in terms of economy, from the least prosperous ones in the west of the country to the most flourishing ones in the east of the country. This translates into a disproportionate creation of Ukraine's GDP in relation to these regions.

The Russian Federation, with its activities involving, inter alia, the suport for the separists operating in the east of the country, cuts off Ukraine from its main economic areas. On the one hand, the conflict in the so-called The Donetsk Republic and the Lugansk Republic, on the other hand, the annexation of Crimea and the fact that the country is cut off from the south-east from the Sea of Azov, causes Ukraine to lose control over approx. 20% of GDP.

Energy policy and its sources are an important economic issue. Data shows that about 70% of the different fuels are imported from Russia and Belarus (https://www.energetyka24.com/dywerskuje-rynku-paliw-ukrainy-analiza). Belarus does not possess its own oil sources.

Fuel has been imported from Russia since 1999. Russia was also a major supplier of LPG to the Ukrainian market. For Russian and Belarusian producers, it is a natural area of growth because of the geographical proximity and profitability of exports. Since its inception, the Russian Federation has pursued an aggressive economic policy based on oil. It not only tries to make the biggest part of the fuel market dependent on itself, but it also reduces the potential of these countries. Numerous pipelines have been constructed through Ukraine's territory. Since 2000, oil transit through Ukraine has been declining.

Moreover, it is an element of economic policy that pushes Ukraine into the background. Furthermore, the constantly growing import of raw materials causes the neglect of own production and even stronger dependence on external suppliers. Since the beginning of the 21st century, fuel production in Ukraine has been declining, weakening the internal market, and fuel imports have been increasing, mainly from Russia. Other actions by the Russian side include imposing sanctions on the Ukrainian neighbor. In December 2018, Prime Minister Dmitry Medvedev expanded the list of people and companies subject to Russian sanctions, including the blockage of money, securities, and property of persons and companies in Russia. Another type of sanction imposed is the list of goods that cannot be imported from or exported to the Ukraine.

Arkadiusz Jóźwiak

Chapter 53: The methodology of Russian soft impact in Ukraine

The Russian-Ukrainian conflict and Russia's policy are a threat to Poland. This was emphasized in the newest National Security Strategy of the Republic of Poland, adopted in November 2014. The document highlights that the rebuilding of Russia's superpower status at the expense of its environment and the intensification of its confrontational policy, which is reflected in the conflict with Ukraine, including the annexation of Crimea, negatively affects the security situation in the region (Cybersecurity Doctrine, 2015).

Moving on to the most important theses of this study, it should be stated that Russia is destabilizing the European order and the international security system by its actions towards Ukraine. Actions against Georgia, and now Ukraine, have been the most serious security threat since the end of the Cold War (Czaja, 2015, pp. 27–42).

Aggression against Georgia, Syria or Ukraine (Pisciotta, 2020, pp. 87–106), a "brotherly nation", as it could be heard many times from the "mouth" of Kremlin propagandists, and the annexation of Crimea are events that will undoubtedly affect international security, and may also have a huge impact on the overall perception of Russia in the international arena, including the economic one, as an aggressive and unpredictable country (Czaja, 2015, pp. 27–42).

Countries with a broadly understood hard policy are beginning to see soft impact as another tool to achieve their goals. These changes are also noticed in the Russian doctrinal documents, which mention the soft impact. In the content of the 2013 Concept of the Foreign Policy of the Russian Federation, the concept of soft power is used twice:
- for the first time, the authors of the document included it in the part diagnosing the specifics of contemporary international relations (it was found that soft power is an integral part of international politics and has a comprehensive character; this complexity consists, while solving foreign policy tasks, taking into account a wide range of tools that are an alternative to classical diplomacy; especially in this context, the possibilities of influencing by: "civil society", "information and communication", "humanitarian" and stemming

from "other methods and technologies" were counted (Concept of foreign policy of the Russian Federation, 2013);
- the 2016 Russian foreign policy concept paper reiterated the importance of soft power in the structure of international policy instruments; however, it was the only place in the document where the name of Joseph Nye's concept was mentioned; this tool was also omitted when discussing Russia's foreign policy (Concept of the foreign policy of the Russian Federation, 2016);

However, the above-mentioned fragments of the concept documents of the Russian foreign policy provide a certain outline of the perception of the idea of soft power by the Kremlin authorities, and in this context, the following issues can be indicated (Jędrowiak, 2019, pp. 43–56):
- their meaning is noticed, although the notion itself is used incidentally in doctrinal documents;
- are considered as complex and comprehensive actions;
- soft power is not considered as a replacement tool for real policy instruments, but as a complement to them.

The weakness of the foreign policy of the Russian Federation was practically the inability to construct a new order and the system's ability to change its influences. It was important because the beginning of the 21st century surprised the Russian authorities with the so-called "Color revolutions" which shook its position in the CIS region (Commonwealth of Independent States). In particular, the Ukrainian revolution of 2004, and later Euro- Maidan, forced Russian decision-makers to introduce changes (Ł os, 2017, pp. 565–579).

According to the popular ranking The Soft Power 30 (https://softpower30.com/), Russia dropped to the 30th place in 2019, which is the worst result in the ranking since 2015. The Olympic Games in Sochi or the organization of the World Cup did not help Russia in 2018. These were good opportunities to transform and reset Russia's relations with other countries, but no such gains seem to have been achieved.

The Russian Federation successfully applies economic and military tools in its foreign policy, especially on the example of Ukraine. In terms of the use of armed forces, Russia often goes for them, even when it is possible to apply other tools of influence. Moscow, which has a considerable military power, can command respect, but is not able to gain the recognition of the international environment. In addition, the rulers in Russia were not able to calibrate the actions that were intended to raise its image in the world (Los, 2017, pp. 565–579).

By Russia's soft political impact, it should be understood that these are the attempts aiming at putting pressure, in various forms, for example on Ukraine's political decisions, election manipulations and other political and diplomatic activities. In the literature, there are described examples of the use of soft impact by Russia in order to undermine or influence Ukraine's decisions (Barrett, 2018, pp. 80–103).

An example of this type of action was the presidential election in 2004, in which the pro-Russian candidate Viktor Yanukovich (leader of the Party of Regions) won. As it turned out, the results were falsified, which led to the outbreak of the Orange Revolution. After the political crisis, a second round of elections was organized, in which the pro-European candidate Viktor Yushchenko won.

However, in the next elections in 2010, the pro-Russian candidate, Viktor Yanukovich won, and Ukraine chose a pro-Russian orientation, while excluding membership in NATO. At the same time, the attitude of Russians towards Ukrainian society is changing. In 2010, a positive posture towards Ukraine was declared by 52% of Russians, in 2011 as many as 72%. In 2009, when the pro-Western Viktor Yushchenko was the Ukrainian president, only 29% of respondents in Russia were positive about Ukraine. The number of Russians who notice their country's rapprochement with Ukraine is also increasing. In 2009, they accounted for 9%, and at the beginning of 2011–29% (www.money.pl). The presented results show how the Russian policy works, the way of conveying information and interpreting reality. The Russian Federation recognizes that public support in certain activities is one of the elements of achieving the goals, therefore uses various possible methods.

Viktor Yanukovich's presidential term is a continuation of pro-Russian policy through, inter alia, common celebration of state ceremonies, for example the 1025th anniversary of the baptism of Kievan Rus, where both presidents emphasized the common spirituality of the unity of both nations.

The Russian language is spoken in the world by approx. 270 million people, and more than half of it outside the Russian Federation. People who speak Russian are a particularly important element of the "Russian world" (Russian: Russkij Mir), and therefore a community of people who culturally identify themselves with "Russianess" (Jędrowiak, 2019, pp. 43–56). The key element of Russian soft power in the cultural dimension is the Russian-speaking minority. It is a kind of "broadcasting channel" of the above-mentioned values and elements of culture, and it is also the goal of impact in this regard (Jędrowiak, 2019, pp. 43–56). In the context of Ukraine, it is a very important argument and consent that, especially in the east of the country, more than half of the citizens speak Russian. It was one of the main reasons why Russia supports the people living in eastern Ukraine, as well as one of the arguments for the annexation of Crimea.

Another area of the soft impact is education and science that bolsters and shapes the future political, economic and military elites. According to UNESCO statistics from 2014, over 170,000 foreign students learnt in Russia, 30% of which were the students from the former USSR republics. The Moscow State University named after Lomonosov decided to open its faculties in Uzbekistan (Tashkent), Kazakhstan (Astana), Ukraine (Sevastopol), and since 2009 in Tajikistan (Dushanbe) and Baku (Azerbaijan). The opening of the branches of the University in countries "of a close proximity" supports to educate perspective staff and directly affects the image of Russia, especially among young people (Łos, 2017, pp. 565–579).

The most well-known example of attempts to exert economic pressure on Ukraine are the so-called gas wars. These are the efforts to put pressure on Ukraine by Russia in terms of prices and supplies of natural gas (Jastrzębska, 2015, pp. 137–148). When analyzing the literature in this area, it can be seen that energy has become an important political force and economic instrument in Russia, and at the same time it is not an integral part of the implementation of foreign and security policy goals (Horemuz, 2017, pp. 27–48).

Another element of Russian economic pressure on Ukraine is the problem of restructuring its debt. The scale of the country's foreign debt is now 109.8%. This is one of the most important obstacles to carry out structural reforms of the economy (Jastrzębska, 2015, pp. 137–148).

The economic coercive measures exerted by Russia on Ukraine show that geoeconomics and geopolitics are not opposing paradigms, on the contrary, they complement each other perfectly and benefit from each other. Often, the geopolitical goal is the basis for geoeconomic means of achieving it through its designation and the lack or inability to apply appropriate methods characteristic for geopolitics (e. g. territory annexation). States apply geoeconomic methods for a faster and more effective implementation of the plan (Jastrzębska, 2015, pp. 137–148).

Another action taken by Russia against Ukraine from the soft impact area, was the mass asylum granting to refugees from Donbas in 2014. According to the Federal Migration Service of the Russian Federation, approx. 130 000 Ukrainians requested for political asylum. At that time, there were no mass political persecutions in Ukraine, and the whole action was to weaken and slander the ruling camp in Ukraine. The granting of Russian citizenship to the former Ukrainian authorities (President Viktor Yanukovich and his closest associates) is also a kind of slap in the face of the Ukrainian nation, and at the same time, shows how much Russia appreciates for "loyalty and cooperation".

The annexation of Crimea in 2014 was a multifaceted and multi-stage event. The process was framing under the scope of the soft impact to convince the public that this fact was right. A study conducted by Russian public opinion research centers shows that more than half of Russians support the annexation of Crimea to Russia (Wpływ na wojnę z Ukrainą, 2015). From the Russian perspective, Russia has the right to protect its citizens living in Crimea, and in this case, it does so under international law. According to the research, most Russians believe there were no Russian soldiers in Crimea. It illustrates how information is interpreted and conveyed in the Russian media. Disinformation about Crimea and the conflict in Donbas are also factors of soft impact on Ukraine.

Religiousness and spirituality of the societies are of great importance in the culture of both countries. The Kremlin also used this road as a tool for cultural and ideological influence. However, in 2018, the Synod of the Constantinople Orthodox Church annulled the decree of 1686 in which the Constantinople subordinated Orthodoxy in Ukraine to the Moscow Patriarchate. Separation from the Moscow Church was seen as a step towards independence, but also as a detachment from the Kremlin's influence.

The crisis in Ukraine in 2014 resulted in greater coherence in Moscow's approach, which became more strategic and combining various elements in the pursuit of foreign policy goals. Russian soft power is a significant resource that should be considered a phenomenon in itself and distinguished more clearly from the direct implementation of the state's interests (Matveeva, 2018, pp. 711–737). It also indirectly influence the decisions of other states.

References

(2013) The concept of the foreign policy of the Russian Federation.
(2015) *Cybersecurity Doctrine of the Republic of Poland*, Warsaw: National Security Office.
(2015) *The impact of the war with Ukraine on the internal situation in Russia and its relations with the West*, Warsaw: Report of the Amics Europace Foundation.
(2016) Concept of the foreign policy of the Russian Federation.
Barrett R., (2018). *Reform in Ukraine and the influence of foreign actors after Euromaidan*, Center Independent Social Research, vol. 10 (2), Sankt-Peterburg, 2018, pp. 80–103.
Czaja J., (2015). *Some legal and political aspects of the Ukrainian crisis and its impact on international security*, Security Theory and Practice, No. 1, pp. 27–42.
Darczewska J., *Active measures as Russian hybrid aggression in retrospect. Selected problems*, Review of Internal Security 18/18, pp. 40–67.
Horemuz M., (2017). *The conflict in Ukraine and its impact on Russia's energy policy*, Belianum-Matej Bel Univ Press, Fac Political Science & Int Relations, vol. 20 (2), pp. 27–48.
http://dylewski.com.pl/ukraina/.
http://www.new.org.pl/6212-donbas-kruchy-pokoj.
https://softpower30.com/.
https://www.energetyka24.com/dywerskuje-rynku-paliw-ukrainy-analiza.
https://www.money.pl/archiwum/wiadomosci_agencyjne/pap/artykul/rosnie;sympatia;rosji;do;ukrainy,223,0,770783.html.
Jastrzębska O., (2015). *Geoeconomic Motives of Russia's Activity Towards Ukraine*, Ante Portas – Security Studies, No. 2 (5), Uniwersytet Wrocławski, pp. 137–148.

Jędrowiak P. and Baraniuk K., (2019). *The soft power of "hard states" – a comparison of Turkey and Russia,* Historia i Polityka, No. 29 (36), pp. 43–56.

Konończuk W., (201 7). *The endless collapse of the Ukrainian oil sector,* Warsaw: Report of the Center for Eastern Studies.

Łos R., (2017). *Soft power of Russia,* Strategic Review, No. 10, pp. 565–579.

Matveeva A., (2018). *Russia's Power Projection after the Ukraine Crisis,* Europe-Asia Studies, Routledge Journals, Taylor & Francis LTD, vol. 70 (5), pp. 711–737.

Pisciotta B., (2020). *Russian revisionism in the Putin era: an overview of post-communist military interventions in Georgia,* Ukraine, and Syria, Italian Political Science Review, vol. 50 (1), pp. 87–106.

Arkadiusz Jóźwiak / Marcin Górnikiewicz / Radosław Bielawski

Chapter 54: Summary and conclusions: Russian interactions of "hard power" and "soft power" as the elements of the mechanics of Russian influence on Ukraine

Since the collapse of the USSR, Ukraine has been an area of intense influence of the Kremlin, both with the use of hard and soft power. The goal was to keep Ukraine in the Russian sphere of influence, despite the formal and legal independence and neutrality of the Ukrainian society. The foundation for taken the actions was to secure Moscow's strategic interests by controlling Crimea, which is the base for the navy and the exit to the Black Sea, overseeing the heavy industry, including the armaments industry, which still produces the elements used in the post-Soviet weapons – not only in the Russian army, but also in the armies of countries friendly to Moscow. Ukraine also played the role of the so-called a buffer zone separating the states, and thus the forces of the North Atlantic Alliance, from the borders of Russia. Hard actions focused on bringing economic impact, and soft actions carried out as information operationism on shaping pro-Russian or pro-Soviet attitudes in the Ukrainian society. For these reasons, the resistance of the society after the outbreak of the war in eastern Ukraine was a big surprise for Russian social engineers, as the conducted and updated research clearly showed that only right-wing nationalist circles would be ready for active resistance. According to Russian research, the majority of society will either remain neutral or will more or less officially support the Russians, treating them almost as their "distant cousins". As it came out, the reaction of the vast majority of society was completely different and decidedly anti-Russian. This means that the social research carried out by the Russians in Ukraine turned out to be wrong, because a very important element within the mental cultural programming of the so-called "dormant codes". As a result, after the successful operation of incorporating Crimea into the Russian Federation, while maintaining the appearance of observing international law, a regular war broke out in eastern Ukraine, contrary to forecasts, and the "revolt" which was supposed to affect fourteen Ukrainian cities in the east of the country was limited to two of them. At that time, the Russians switched to a contingency plan, which was to maintain the conflict in such a way as to keep up the impression of a politically, economically and socially unstable Ukraine, which would prevent the country from being included in NATO structures. From the perspective of six years, it can be assumed that this goal has been achieved today, and the civil war in Donbass has been continually burning from the very beginning, but it is not gaining a momentum either. It is no secret that, without powerful support from Russia, the separatist republics would have collapsed at the very beginning of the conflict. As a result, through the conflict in the east of the country, Ukraine cannot become a NATO or EU member state, which fully coincides with Russia's strategic interest in this part of Europe.

Russia currently uses the hard power resource, both from economic means, and the military ones. In the case of industrial ones, there are mainly supplies of energy resources, which in turn has a direct impact on the condition of the entire economy, and thus indirectly on the social and political mood. When it comes to the military means, Moscow provides a continued support to separatist republics, heating up the conflict and preventing Ukraine from establishing permanent forms of international cooperation with other powers. Thus, military resources mostly serve to influence international opinion and as an element of pressure during talks with other powers over the future of this country. The economic resources affect the decision-making process of Ukrainian power circles.

At the same time, the Russians, since the beginning of the Ukrainian crisis, have intensified information operations aimed not only at the circles influencing the political decision-making process, but also at the entire socjety, divided into specific target groups (most often using the criterion within which religion is as important as political views). In this area, the only thing that can be achieved is to suppress world-view divisions within the Ukrainian society, influencing it to a limited extent (for example: the government and local government elections). On the other hand, strongly anti-Russian and thus anti-parliamentary attitudes still prevail in the Ukrainian society, and the EU is seen as the only reasonable way to develop international cooperation.

To sum up, hard power is definitely more effective than soft power in achieving Russian strategic goals, therefore Moscow, if it continues to conduct intensive information operations (social engineering) towards Ukrainian society, will achieve tangible strategic benefits due to the further conquest of the civil war. Moreover, Moscow will be gradually increasing economic pressure, striving to ensure greater influence on the internal decision-making process, and over time also on foreign policy.

Section III:
The assessment of the effectiveness of the Russian impact on Ukraine's internal and foreign policy with the use of the measurement of the Russian impact potential

Paweł Ślaski

Chapter 55: The effectiveness measurement of the quantitative methods of Russia's influence in Ukraine

The Russian Socialist Soviet Republic and the Ukrainian Socialist Soviet Republic were the part of the Soviet Unino until 1991. Its break-up created a number of challenges and threats for both countries and their neighbors. Due to their potential and location, Moscow and Kiev play a leading role in the post-Soviet area – therefore it was necessary to establish inter-state relations between them. Influences in Ukraine have become an important prerequisite for the great-power position of the Russian Federation in the international arena. The reintegration of Ukraine with Russia would increase the economic and demographic potential of the latter, broaden its access to the Black Sea, and finally bring it geographically closer to the EU. In practice, Ukraine rejects such a scenario, and since the collapse of the USSR, it has been a consistent critic of Russia's projects to reintegrate the post-Soviet area.

Bilateral relations between Russia and Ukraine also play an important and, at the same time, a very special role, from the perspective of both countries under discussion. The Russian Federation is interested in cooperation with Ukraine because of not only the historical and social ties that bind the two countries, but also of the geostrategic importance of Ukraine for Russian politics. The Ukrainian problem, however, does not only concern territorial or population issues, but the very identity of Russia in the new political and spatial conditions (Szeptycki, 2013).

The analysis of the quantitative dependence of Ukraine on Russia was carried out on the basis of source material and the literature on the subject. The book by Andrzej Szeptycki entitled: "Ukraine versus Russia. The study of dependence", Warsaw University Publishing House, Warsaw 2013 – the main source of theoretical analyzes, turned out to be helpful in developing the chapter. The Internet also came out to be a substantial source, which made it possible to obtain various types of statistics and summaries.

The complexity of the issues raised, required an appropriate research problem, in the form of the following question: *How to use the selected quantitative tools to measure the effectiveness of the Russian influence in Ukraine?*

The quantitative measurement of the relationship between Russia and Ukraine should be considered in six areas (systems):
- political system,
- economy,
- security and defense,
- society,
- culture and ideology,
- foreign policy.

However, due to the limitations of the use of quantitative tools, the attention has been focused on one (according to the author – a key), namely economic relationships.

The chapter consists of two parts. In the first – the literature on the studied area was reviewed. The second part presents a proprietary universal analytical tool for measuring the effectiveness of influences in a given sphere.

The following quantitative scientific methods and tools were used to solve the research problem:
- Statistical data analysis,
- The Pareto-Lorenz rule,
- Visual Basic for Application programming,
- Excel application.

Ukraine's quantitative dependence on Russia in the economic sphere is mainly related to the energy sphere and trade cooperation. The most recognized example of attempts to exert economic pressure on Ukraine are the so-called "Gas wars". These are attempts to put pressure on Ukraine by Russia in terms of prices and supplies of natural gas.

The Ukrainian economy is largely dependent on supplies of energy resources from Russia. This is due to its ineffectiveness (energy consumption) and the fact that the existing pipeline connections allow Ukraine to import energy resources (mainly gas) only from or through Russia. Over the past twenty years, Ukraine has not taken effective action to reduce dependence on Russia in the energy era. The markets of European countries are the main direction of Russian gas exports transported through gas pipelines – 85–90% of all exports, showing a significant 38% growth rate in recent years (from 146.6 billion m3 in 2014 to the record-breaking level of 201.7 billion m3 in 2018). However, this data is incomplete because it is related to the fact that Ukraine has ceased the purchase of Russian gas directly from Russia since 2015 and has switched the import of gas from the western direction, mainly from Hungary, Slovakia and Poland. The dynamic growth of exports resulted in the strengthening of Gazprom's position as a leading player on the European gas market, where its share increased from 34.7%

in 2017 to 36.7% in 2018. In deliveries directed to the west, 81% (163.4 bcm) falls to the countries of Western Europe, and 19% (38.4 bcm) to the countries of Central and Eastern Europe (Rutkowski).

The main route of Russian gas transport to European markets is the Ukrainian transit gas pipeline system. In the last 5 years, 42.4–48.1% of Russian gas received by European countries passed through Ukraine. Under a 10-year agreement in 2009, Gazprom undertook to transport 110 billion m3 of gas annually through the Ukrainian system. However, already in 2015 the company informed that it did not intend to extend it, and from the beginning of 2020, gas would be supplied to European consumers via new transport routes. These will be roads in the south through the previously forced South Stream gas pipeline, currently through the Turkish Potok gas pipeline, and in the north through Nord Stream 1 and 2. Forecasts formulated in Russia claim that the demand for gas in Europe will increase with a decrease in own production in the coming years by 70 billion m3, and half of this decline will be compensated by an increase in Russian gas supplies. Over time, in order to improve relations with European countries regarding the construction of Nord Stream 2, Russia has declared that it is ready to sign a new gas transit agreement with Ukraine for a short period, although in rather symbolic amounts of 10–15 billion m3 (compared to the actual 82–93.5 billion m3 transmitted in the last three years). If Russia had not increased its exports, due to the low level of readiness of alternative transmission infrastructure, in the coming years it would still have to send significant amounts of gas via Ukraine, including at least 70 bcm in 2020. The transport capacity of Ukrainian transit gas pipelines in the western direction is 144 bcm, of which 26 bcm is in the south-west direction (Romania, Bulgaria, Greece, Turkey, Macedonia). The highest value of Russian gas transit was in 1998–141.1 billion m3. In 2018, it was 86.8 billion m3–43% of all Russian gas exports to the west. Transit fees of approximately USD 3 billion are quite an important element of Ukraine's foreign exchange inflows, but the game is not only about these amounts. The essence of the Russian-Ukrainian disputes involving the EU side, concerns the functioning of the entire 37.6 thousand km, the largest Ukrainian gas transit system in the world. Annually, the system is able to accept 288 billion m3 of gas, while the amount of gas exported may reach almost 180 billion m3, including 144 billion m3 per year to the west. 240 million m3 of gas flows through Ukraine to Europe daily – before the launch of Nord Stream, it was as much as 390 million m3. The Ukrainian gas pipeline system also includes 72 compressor stations and 12 underground gas storage (UGS) with the largest capacity in Europe of almost 31 billion m3 (approx. 21% of European capacity), compared with 22.3 billion m3 in the case of Germany, 18.6 Italy, 12.7 France, 12.4 the Netherlands and 6.4 Austria. It is not without significance for the security and stability of the transit that the largest of the Ukrainian UGS Bilcze-Wołycko-Uherski, with a capacity of 17,050 million m3, is located close to the western border of Ukraine (Rutkowski).

Ukraine is formulating the terms of a new agreement with Russia, which would provide financial guarantees for the functioning of its transit system of gas pipelines. The basic ones include the guarantee of the volume of supplies at the level of 60 billion m3 per year for 10 years. At the same time, it guarantees the maintenance of transmission capacity at the level of 90 billion m3. The agreement should take into account the standards applicable on the European gas market, which would result in approx. 50% an increase in transit rates from the current $ 2.7 per 1000 m3 / 100 km to around $ 4. Ukraine expects that the financial guarantees of the operation of the transit as a new agreement, would provide grounds for attracting a strategic investor to this venture (Rutkowski).

Russia hoped that, in accordance with the schedule, from the beginning of 2020, new gas export routes to the European market would be launched, which would allow, with the expiry of the transit agreement at the end of 2019, to effectively reduce transit through Ukraine, new routes are primarily a 2 Nord Stream pipeline under the Baltic Sea from Russia to Germany with a capacity of 55 billion m3 (two lines, each of 27.5 billion m^3) and the Turkish Stream under the Black Sea from Russia to the European part of Turkey (two lines, each of 15.75 billion m^3). The first line of the TP gas pipeline, which is intended to handle all supplies for the needs of the Turkish market, has been put into operation and, from January 2020, may fully take over the supplies to Turkey carried out so far by the Balkan gas pipeline from Ukraine via Romania and Bulgaria (Rutkowski).

Trade cooperation is an important element of the relations between the Russian Federation and Ukraine. This situation results from at least three reasons. First, Russia is Ukraine's most important trading partner; only the EU can compete with it on this point. Secondly, over the past fifteen years, trade issues have repeatedly been the subject of Russian-Ukrainian disputes, both of which have an economic as well as a political background. Thirdly, the trade relations of the two countries are of significant importance in the context of Russia's attempts to reintegrate the post-Soviet area (CIS, CES, Customs Union) and the membership of Ukraine and Russia in the World Trade Organization.

Ukraine's commodity exchange with Russia in 2010 amounted to USD 35.6 billion, according to Ukrainian data. It accounted for 31.8% of Ukraine's foreign trade turnover and only 2–2.7% of Russia's foreign trade. The above asymmetry results from the differences in the economic potentials of both countries, as well as the fact that Ukraine is more dependent than Russia on foreign trade (Szeptycki, 2013).

The structure of Ukrainian-Russian trade is largely the legacy of the USSR. Ukraine exports to Russia mainly machinery, in particular motor vehicles, metallurgical products, agricultural and food products, and chemical products.

Some branches of Ukrainian industry are significantly dependent on the Russian market. This applies in particular to the machinery and electromechanical industries (58.4% of its exports went to Russia in 2009), wood and paper (37.9%), and in the past also to agri-food and chemical industries (Table 1).

Table 1. The structure of Ukrainian exports to Russia in 2009 (Szeptycki, 2013)

Group of commodities	Ukrainian exports to Russia (USD million)	Share in exports to russia (in %)	Share in the total exports of a given group of commodoties to Ukraine (in %)
Agri-food products	1384,1	11,6	14,5
Energy resources	557,3	4,7	26,2
Other mineral products	228,9	1,9	13
Chemical industry products	823,3	6,9	32,7
Wood, wood products, cellulose and paper products	559,4	4,7	37,9
Metals and metal products	1611,5	13,5	12,6
Machines, devices and means of transport	2926,5	24,5	58,4
Other commodities	404,1	3,3	9
Services	3452,2	28,9	36,3
Total	11947,3	100	-

The structure of Russian exports is relatively permanent. The most important role in it, is played by energy resources (56%) as well as machines and devices (30.1%) (Table 2).

Table 2. The structure of Ukrainian imports from Russia in 2009 (Szeptycki, 2013)

Group of commodities	Ukrainian exports to Russia (USD million)	Share in exports to russia (in %)	Share in the total exports of a given group of commodoties to Ukraine (in %)
Agri-food products	534,5	3,8	10,8
Energy resources	8191,9	59	56
Other mineral products	302,7	2,2	22,8

Table 2 *(Continued)*

Group of commodities	Ukrainian exports to Russia (USD million)	Share in exports to russia (in %)	Share in the total exports of a given group of commodoties to Ukraine (in %)
Chemical industry products	1394,3	10	26,2
Wood, wood products, cellulose and paper products	303,1	2,2	18,3
Metals and metal products	805	5,8	30,1
Machines, devices and means of transport	1412,3	10,2	22,6
Other commodities	292	2,1	0,7
Services	652	4,7	12,6
Total	13887,8	100	-

The asymmetrical ties linking Ukraine with Russia in the economic sphere deserve an ambiguous assessment. Cooperation with Russia, especially in the energy and trade spheres, allows the Ukrainian political and economic elite to derive economically unjustified financial benefits that prevent from economic reforms, which in turn, would contribute to the modernization of the country and reduce dependence on Russia. The Russian Federation uses the economic dependencies, existing between the two countries, as an instrument of pressure on Ukraine. According to Ukrainian data, at the end of 2010, Russian foreign direct investments were concentrated mainly in the financial sector (approx. 70% – in 2010) – Table 3.

Table 3. Russian direct investment in Ukraine by a type of activity (2010)

	Cumulative volume at the end of 2010	Share of Russian FDI in Ukraine (in %)
Financial sector	2334,3	69,41
Industry	255	7,58
Transport and communication	239,7	7,13
Construction industry	204,8	6,09
Trade, repair of cars, household and personal goods	143,2	4,26
Real estate turnover	120,5	3,58

Table 3 *(Continued)*

	Cumulative volume at the end of 2010	Share of Russian FDI in Ukraine (in %)
Other	65,8	1,96
Total	3363,3	100

When conducting research in social sciences, data collection methods are used that are characteristic for two types of analysis: quantitative and qualitative. Quantitative research is carried out in order to falsify, modify or accept existing theories. They are conducted by a researcher in a deductive way by deriving hypotheses from the adopted scientific theory, and then using the data collected during the research to test their truthfulness.

The Pareto rule and ABC static analysis were used to develop the analytical tool, therefore the elements were divided into three groups depending on the examined attribute (Balon et al., 2017):
- group A includes elements that are of approximately 20% of the total number of the set of heteregenious elements, but with a substantial contribution in the amount of the analyzed attribute, witth the range of 75–80%;
- group B includes elements that are of approximately 30% of the total number of assortment stocks and 15% of the amount of the attribute;
- group C includes mass elements with the largest contribution in the assortment quantity id est approximately 50% and a very low contribution in the amount of the attribute – approximately 5%.

This analysis allows for the reduction of the dimensionality of the issue, thus enabling the concentration of attention on sensitive items, determining the economic results of industrial activity. The tool – a computer application – was developed in an Excel spreadsheet with the use of VBA programming – Visual Basic for Application.

The application consists of six sequential stages, which finally define the appropriate classes (groups) of elements' classification depending on the type of an attribute. It ends with the so-called graph of the Pareto-Lorenz concentration curve.

The verification was based on the data on the structure of Ukrainian exports to Russia in 2009.

Table 4. ABC analysis of the value of Ukrainian exports of goods and services to Russia in 2019.

Group of commodities	The value of Ukrainian exports to Russia (USD mln)	Export share to Russia (in %)	Cumulative share in exports (in %)	Class
Services	3452,2	28,90%	28,90%	A
Machines, devices and means of transport	2926,5	24,50%	53,39%	A
Metals and metal products	1611,5	13,49%	66,88%	A
Agri-food products	1384,1	11,59%	78,46%	A
Chemical industry products	823,3	6,89%	85,35%	B
Wood, wood products, cellulose and paper products	559,4	4,68%	90,04%	B
Energy resources	557,3	4,66%	94,70%	B
Other commodities	404,1	3,38%	98,08%	C
Other mineral products	228,9	1,92%	100,00%	C

The analysis presented in the table (Table 4) shows that the key exports of Ukrainian goods should focus on services, machinery, metals and agri-food products (78.46%) – of the value of all exports to Russia.

References

(2011) The Military Balance 2011, International Institute for Strategic Studies, London: Routledge.

Balon P. and Buchtova J., (2017). *Use of the 80/20 Rule in Metallurgy, Conference: 26th International Conference on Metal lurgy and Materials* (METAL) Location: Brno, Czech Republic.

Cerdan J., Guerrero D. and Marin J., (2020). *Preconditioners for rank deficient least squares problems,* Journal of Computational and Applied Mathematics Volume: 372 Article Number: 112621.

Chokkalin gam B., Raja V., Anburaj J., Immanual R. and Dhineshkumar M., (2017). *Investigation of Shrinkage Defect in Castings by Quantitative Ishikawa Diagram,* Archives of Foundry Engineering.

Ciesla P., Nodzynska M., Baprowska A. *et. al.*, (2017). *Implementation of Ishikawa Diagram into project based education,* Conference: 15th Conference on Project-based Education in Science Education Location: Praha, Czech Republic.

Kaminski B. (eds.), (1996). *Economic Transition in Russia and the New States of Eurasia,* Armonk – London: ME Sharpe.

Motyl A., (1992). *Dilemmas of Independence: Ukraine after Totalitarianism,* New York: Council on Foreign Relations Press.

Motyl A., (2001). *Imperial Ends. The Decay, Collapse, and Revival of Empires,* New York: Columbia University Press.

Rutkowski J., *Obserwator finans.pl,* Ukraine is irreplaceable in gas transit from Russia.

Ślaski P., (2017). Inventory management in logistic systems, Warsaw: WAT.

Szeptycki A., (2013). Ukraine and Russia. Dependency Study, Warsaw: Publishing House of the University of Warsaw.

Liang W. and Yiming D., (2020). *Wavelet-based estimations of fractional Brownian sheet: Least squares versus maximum likelihood,* Volume: 371, Article Number: 112609.

Paweł Ślaski

Chapter 56: The effectiveness assessment of the Russian influence on the Ukrainian decision-making process with the use of qualitative methods

Since the collapse of the Soviet Union, the actions of the Russian Federation towards Ukraine are aimed at maintaining and strengthening the country's dependence on Moscow. Russia not only wants to influence the current policy of its Ukrainian neighbor, but also aims to transform the dependence existing between the two countries into a relationship of imperial domination. It wishes to impose certain patterns of the political system and methods of international reactions on Ukraine. Such a policy is not perceived properly as it is inconsistent with the basic norms of international relations established at the UN and CSCE / OSCE forum. The policy of the Ukrainian state towards Russia is inconsistent because Ukraine has not taken systematic actions aimed directly or indirectly at limiting its dependence on the Russian Federation. Such an attitude results both from the fact that dependence on Russia benefits Ukraine and the fear that attempts to change the existing state of affairs would have negative consequences on the internal arena (the need to undertake socially unpopular reforms) and internationally (criticism from Russia). The subjection linking Ukraine with Russia is not imposed, but is actually accepted by the majority of Ukrainian political elites and society (Szeptycki, 2013).

The analysis of the qualitative dependence of Kiev on Moscow was carried out on the basis of the source material and the literature on the subject. Andrzej Szeptycki's book entitled: "Ukraina wobec Rosji. Studium zależności", Warsaw University Publishing House, Warsaw 2013, proved to be helpful in the preparation of the chapter. The Internet turned out to be an important source of information, which made it possible to obtain various types of statistics and summaries.

The complexity of the issues raised here, required an appropriate research problem posed in the following question:

How to measure the effectiveness of the Russian influence in Ukraine through selected qualitative tools?

The qualitative measurement of the relationship between Russia and Ukraine should be considered in six areas (systems):

- political system,
- economy,
- security and defense,
- society,
- culture and ideology,
- foreign policy.

The chapter consists of two parts. In the first, the literature on the studied areas was reviewed. The second part presents universal analytical tools to measure the effectiveness of influences in a given sphere.

The following quantitative scientific methods and tools were used to solve the research problem:
- Analysis of statistical data,
- Trend analysis (the method of least squares),
- Cause and Effect Diagram (Ishikawa),
- Excel application.

Contemporary Ukrainian society was significantly shaped during the Soviet era. Therefore, it is characterized by a low level of involvement in political and social life – both at the national and local levels. The economic crisis in the 1990s contributed to the intensification of such phenomena as emigration and the related demographic decline (Table 1).

Table 1. Russia and Ukraine – basic social indicators (2009–2010) (Szeptycki, 2013)

	Russia	Ukraine
Population size (in mln)	142,9	46
Demographic decline in 1990–2010	4,8	5,9
Life expectancy at birth (men / women in years)	62/74	62/74
Human Development Index: value and place in the world	0,719 (65)	0,71(69)
Index of social inequality	40,1	26,4

Similar social problems exist in contemporary Russia, although some differences can be observed between the two countries. The Ukrainian society is less diversified in economic terms; Crime is also relatively less of a challenge. Moreover, the inhabitants of Ukraine are characterized by greater individualism than in the case of Russia and by lesser respect for the authority of the ruling power (Figure 1).

Most of the inhabitants of Ukraine are convinced of the need to cooperate with their Russian neighbor, and also feel a kind of inferiority towards Russia.

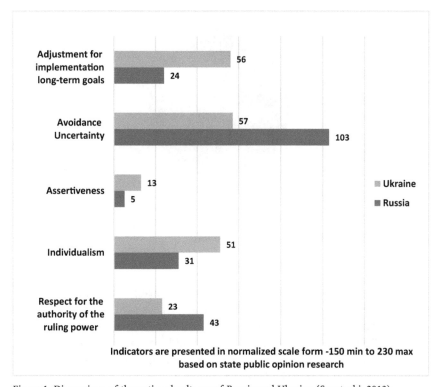

Figure 1. Dimensions of the national cultures of Russia and Ukraine (Szeptycki, 2013).

The Ukrainian Russians, the second largest ethnic group in Ukraine, and, more broadly, the inhabitants of the south-eastern part of the country, are supporters of the cooperation between the two states. Russia skillfully plays out the regional and existing divisions in Ukraine, striving to weaken and destabilize that country. Ukrainians living in Russia are also interested in the condition of bilateral relations, especially immigrants from Ukraine who do not possess Russian citizenship and work in the territory of the Russian Federation.

The people of Ukraine attach great importance to relations with the Russian Federation. In their opinion, Russia is a "brother country" (23.9%), a "friendly state" (18.9%), and a "strategic partner" (14.5%) – Figure 2.

The cultural and ideological dependencies between Ukraine and Russia are a consequence of the common history of both countries and the effect of its cultural, linguistic and religious ties.

The most important manifestations of the relationship linking Ukraine with Russia in the discussed area are the position of the Russian language in Ukraine, the popularity of the Soviet – close to Russian – historiography, the activity of the Russian Orthodox Church and its part of the Ukrainian Orthodox Church

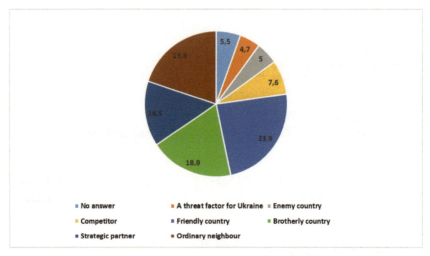

Figure 2. The importance of Russia for Ukraine in the social assessment (Szeptycki 2013).

(Moscow Patriarchate), and finally Russian influence in the Ukrainian media system. According to official data, Russian language is used as a mother tongue by nearly one third of the inhabitants of Ukraine. In practice, its position is stronger. The Ukrainian has become an official language in Ukraine for good, while the Russian plays a dominant role in mass literature. Ukraine is a religiously divided country. The largest religious communities are the Ukrainian Orthodox Church (Moscow Patriarchate), which is the part of the Russian Orthodox Church, and the Ukrainian Orthodox Church of the Kiev Patriarchate, considered by the Orthodox world to be non-canonical. The Moscow Patriarchate and the Ukrainian Orthodox Church (Moscow Patriarchate) are actively working to maintain the relationship between Ukraine and Russia.

Russian influence on the Ukrainian media system is manifested in two ways. Firstly, Russian newspapers, TV stations and internet portals are very popular in Ukraine. Secondly, the Ukrainian media are eager not to use the products of their Russian counterparts. In both cases, the existing situation results from the fact that the offer of Russian media is cheaper and more attractive to Ukrainian recipients than the domestic production. Cultural and deological dependencies are one of the instruments actively used by the Russian authorities to maintain Ukraine's dependence on Russia. The Russian Federation is in favor of strengthening the position of the Russian language in Ukraine and is critical of attempts to build a national historiography based on an anti-Russian discourse. The activities of the Russian Orthodox Church and the Russian media in Ukraine are also consistent with the interests of the Russian authorities. In the cultural dimension, such a policy is intended to control the presence of Russian culture in

Ukraine, and thus – the ties existing in this area between the two states and two societies.

The Ukraine's foreign policy, analyzed as a whole, is not unequivocally dependent on the Russian Federation. Ukraine wishes to be seen as a significant European state independent from Russia. However, the issue of dependence between the two countries appears in some areas which are important from the perspective of Ukraine and Russia. In this context, the most important role is played by a cooperation in the territory of the former USSR (primarily Russia's efforts to rebuild ties between post-Soviet states) and relations with Western countries, in particular Ukraine's cooperation with the EU and NATO (Szeptycki, 2013) – Table 2.

Table 2. Russia and Ukraine towards selected international institutions (as of 2012)

	Russia	Ukraine
United Nations	Founding Member Permanent Member of the Security Council (1945)	Founding Member (1945)
World Trade Organization	Member (2008)	Member (2012)
Organization of Security and Cooperation in Europe	Founding Member (1973)	Member (1992)
G8	Member (1997)	-
Council of Europe	Member (1996)	Member (1995)
Commonwealth of Independent States	Founding Member (1991)	Participating country -1991
Common Economic Space	Founding Member (2003)	Founding Member (2003)
Customs Union (Russia, Belarus, Kazakhstan)	Founding Member (2010)	-
Organization for Democracy and Economic Development (GUAM)	-	Founding Member (1997)
Organization of the Black Sea Economic Cooperation (BSEC)	Founding Member (1992)	Founding Member (1992)
European Union	Partnership and cooperation agreement (1994)	Partnership and cooperation agreement (1994)
NATO	Foundig Act on Mutual Relations, Cooperation and Security between NATO and the Russian Federation (1997)	Charter on a Distinctive Partnership between Ukraine and NATO – 1997

The contemporary political system of Ukraine, understood as all entities engaged in political activities and the rules governing their mutual relations, is largely dependent on Russia. This dependence is the result of the former affiliation of both countries to the Soviet Union, the specifics of the transformation process in Russia and Ukraine, and the position that the Russian Federation plays as a successor to the USSR in the post-Soviet area. The main manifestations of Ukraine's dependence on the Russian Federation in the discussed area, are the political similarities between the two countries, the conviction of most entities of the Ukrainian political system about the need to cooperate with Russia, and finally Russia's direct interference in Ukraine's political life.

Alexander Motyl presented in detail the significance of particular conditions that hinder the reform of the political system in Russia and Ukraine (Figure 3).

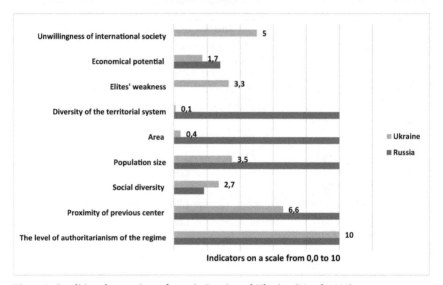

Figure 3. Conditions hampering reforms in Russia and Ukraine (Motyl, 1992).

Dependencies in the field of security and defense mainly result from:
- Asymmetry of military potentials of both countries.
- The future of the post-Soviet nuclear arsenals deployed in Ukraine.
- The Black Sea Fleet stationed on the Crimean Peninsula.
- The unregulated status of the Ukrainian-Russian border.
- Dependence on Russia in the area of the arms industry.
- Conflict in Transnistria.

Ukraine has a significantly smaller military potential than the Russian Federation (Table 3).

Table 3. Military potential of Russia and Ukraine (2010) (The Military Balance, 2011)

	Russia	Ukraine
Size of armed forces and paramilitary units (in thousands)	1495	215
military expenditure (in billions)	58,7	3,7
military expenditure in relation to GDP (w %)	4,3	2,9
nuclear weapon	Yes	No

The Russian Federation has used the position of the Ukrainian authorities on the post-Soviet arsenals to discredit this country in the international arena, publicizing the possible threats posed by Ukraine's policy. The declaration signed in January 1994 by presidents Bill Clinton, Boris Yeltsin and Leonid Kravchuk obliged Ukraine to hand over nuclear warheads to Russia as soon as possible and become a non-nuclear state. In return, it was to receive financial aid from the United States and low-enriched uranium for nuclear power plants from Russia. However, the Russian Federation enjoyed greater benefits. It achieved its main goal: thanks to the cooperation with Western countries, it regained the post-Soviet nuclear arsenals deployed in Ukraine. In this way, it confirmed its status as a great power and successor of the USSR. It made Ukraine more dependent on itself, prompting it to accept Russian and Western guarantees. The Black Sea Fleet (FC) plays a specific role in the Ukrainian-Russian relations – both due to its size and location (ethnically mostly Russian Crimea), and the existing legal and political conditions. Thanks to the maintenance of a part of the Black Sea Fleet, the Russian Federation thus achieved its main objective: to retain control over most of it and the infrastructure in Ukraine. This was possible thanks to Russia's consistent and decisive policy, which raised the issue of the future of FC to the rank of one of the important problems in Ukrainian-Russian relations and made progress in other areas dependent on its resolution (e. g. reducing Ukraine's debt or signing an inter-state treaty). Ukraine has the longest border with Russia. After the collapse of the USSR, the authorities of the Russian Federation delayed the confirmation, delimitation and subsequent demarcation of the border. In this way they wanted, among others to bolster the belief that the border is temporary in both countries, make the cooperation between Ukraine and the European Union more difficult (liberalization of the EU visa regime in relation to Ukraine requires an effective control of its borders by that state), and finally persuade the Ukrainian authorities to make concessions on other issues (division of the Black Sea Fleet). The links between the two paradises in the defense industry are a consequence of the centrally planned economic policy of the former USSR and the importance of the industrial and defense complex. Ukraine's dependence on the cooperation with Russia has negative consequences, as it hinders the development of partnership in the sphere of the arms industry with other partners, such as the North Atlantic Alliance. The Transnistrian Moldavian Republic is supported by the authorities of the Russian Federation. It is a challenge above all for Moldova, of which Transnistria is formally a part. However, it also affects Ukraine, with which it is directly adjacent. The conflict in Transnistria entails specific threats to Ukraine, such as the activities of organized crime groups or increased smuggling. It also makes it difficult for Ukraine to develop cooperation with the EU, especially in the field of visa liberalization. Nevertheless, Ukraine does not take systematic solutions to resolve the above-mentioned steuggle, de facto supporting the authorities of Transnistria. Such an attitude results both from the fact that the existence of an unrecognized republic brings certain financial benefits to Ukraine and from concern for relations with Russia.

As already mentioned in the previous chapter, the most important element of the bilateral economic cooperation is energy relations. The Ukrainian economy is largely dependent on supplies of energy resources from Russia, which is due not only to its ineffectiveness (energy consumption), but also to the fact that the existing pipeline connections allow Ukraine to import energy resources (mainly gas) exclusively from Russia or with its assitance. Russia is Ukraine's most important trade partner. Ukraine plays a relatively smaller role in Russia's foreign trade. This situation is the result of both the strong, asymmetric ties that were developed between the individual Soviet republics before 1991, as well as the low competitiveness of the independent Ukraine's economy and difficulties in finding new trade partners interested in Ukrainian exports. Due to the importance of the Russian market, Ukraine is striving to develop a bilateral or multilateral free trade agreement with Russia. The Russian Federation, however, is reluctant to such a solution, which comes up from its concern for the protection of its own market and the hope that it will be able to persuade the Ukrainian authorities to adopt a more advanced form of integration.

When conducting research in the social sciences, data collection methods that are characteristic for two types of analysis: quantitative and qualitative, are applied. In the qualitative research, the method of inductive analysis is used. By conducting qualitative research, researchers collect data, formulate hypotheses on their basis, then test hypotheses by analyzing the collected data, and finally try to build a scientific theory.

In this part of the chapter, the following proprietary tools for measuring the effectiveness of impacts in the studied sphere will be presented:
- trend analysis with the use of the method of least squares,
- Cause and effect diagram (Ishikawa).

The first of the developed tools uses the method of least squares o conduct a trend analysis of a selected research area. The least squares method is one of the most important computational methods in statistics. This mode is aimed at determining the regression line, a trend line for the collected data. It is used both to estimate a linear as well as a non-linear relationship. The purpose of this approach is to match the collected data to a pair of results of such a straight line (linear model) which is best suited to them.

From the mathematical point of view, to calculate the least squares regression coefficients (straight line) using the method of least squares, the appropriate parameters should be calculated in the data set (Cerdan, *et. Al.*, 2020; Wu Liang, 2020):

$$b = \frac{\sum(X \bullet Y) - N \bullet \bar{X} \bullet \bar{Y}}{\sum X^2 - N \bullet \bar{X}^2} \tag{1}$$

$$a = \bar{Y} - b \bullet \bar{X} \tag{2}$$

On the other hand, the trend line looks like:

$$Y = bx + a \tag{3}$$

A computer application, as a tool, was developed in an Excel spreadsheet using VBA programming – Visual Basic for Application. The analysis was based on data on trade in goods between Ukraine and Russia in the years 1993–2010 (Figure 4 and Figure 5).

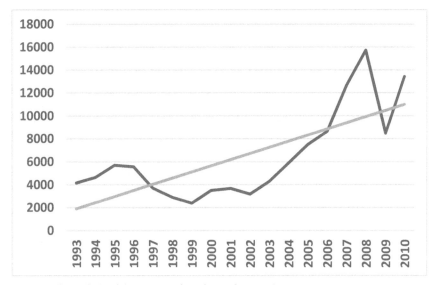

Figure 4. The analysis of the exports of goods trend to Russia.

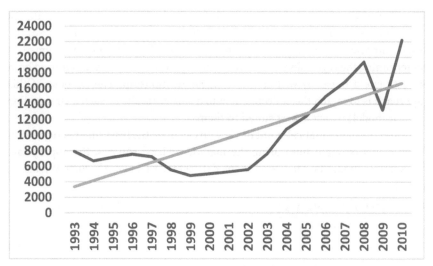

Figure 5. The analysis of the export goods trend in Ukraine.

The analyzes of trends show that both exports of goods to Ukraine and to Russia are growing in nature, and in the longer term it may lead to stabilization of this type of trade.

The cause and effect diagram (Ishikawa) is used to present and analyze a selected problem in many ways. Due to a clear and transparent structure, it is possible to illustrate the cause -and-effect relationships arising on many levels of the issue under consideration in a simple and understandable way. And so, when we apply a specific observed effect on the diagram, as a result of the analysis carried out, potential causes of its occurrence will be identified and systematized, emphasizing the mutual ties between them. Thus, the Ishikawa diagram helps to identify significant relationships occurring between various causes, and thus aids to identify the main sources of their formation. The purpose of the method, after improving the incorrectly conducted process, is also to choose the correct course of action in the future in order to avoid the found errors. Achieving the intended goal is possible thanks to such structural features of the diagram as: accuracy of the analysis, emphasis on localization or elimination of the causes of the problem. The Ishikawa diagram often becomes an important source of information for other methods and tools (Chokkalingam, *et al.*, 2017) – Figure 6.

Based on the methodology of constructing a diagram, the author of the chapter proposed a detailed analysis of the main problems (causes) that shapes Russia's negative influence on Ukraine.

Table 4. Exchange trade in goods between Ukraine and Russia in 1993–2010 (Ukrainian data) (Kaminski, 1996, p. 386)

	1993	1994	1995	1996	1997	1998	1999	2000	2001	2002	2003	2004	2005	2006	2007	2008	2009	2010
Trend Analysis	1	2	3	4	5	6	7	8	9	10	11	12	13	14	15	16	17	18
Export to Russia	4165	4659	5698	5577	3723	2906	2396	3516	3679	3189	4311	5889	7496	8651	12668	15736	8495	13432
Export to Ukraine	7901	6701	7149	7547	7240	5560	4792	5024	5282	5585	7598	10770	12403	14979	16837	19414	13236	22198
Abscissa export to Russia	1362	1362	1362	1362	1362	1362	1362	1362	1362	1362	1362	1362	1362	1362	1362	1362	1362	1362
Slope export to Russia	536	536	536	536	536	536	536	536	536	536	536	536	536	536	536	536	536	536
Trend export to Russia	1898	2435	2971	3507	4043	4579	5115	5651	6187	6723	7259	7795	8331	8867	9403	9939	10475	11011
Abscissa export to Ukraine	2579	2579	2579	2579	2579	2579	2579	2579	2579	2579	2579	2579	2579	2579	2579	2579	2579	2579
Slope export to Ukraine	782	782	782	782	782	782	782	782	782	782	782	782	782	782	782	782	782	782
Trend export to Ukraine	3361	4144	4926	5709	6491	7274	8056	8838	9621	10403	11186	11968	12751	13533	14315	15098	15880	16663

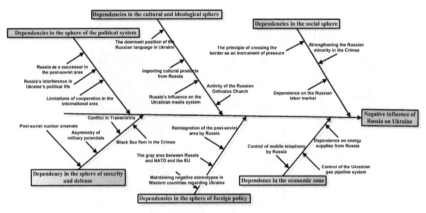

Figure 6. Cause and Effect Diagram (Ishikawa).

References

(2011) The Military Balance 2011, International Institute for Strategic Studies, London: Routledge.

Balon P. and Buchtova J., (2017). *Use of the 80/20 Rule in Metallurgy, Conference: 26th International Conference on Metallurgy and Materials* (METAL) Location: Brno, Czech Republic.

Cerdan J., Guerrero D. and Marin J., (2020). *Preconditioners for rank deficient least squares problems,* Journal of Computational and Applied Mathem atics Volume: 372 Article Number: 112621.

Chokkalingam B., Raja V., Anburaj J., Immanual R. and Dhineshkumar M., (2017). *Investigation of Shrinkage Defect in Castings by Quantitative Ishikawa Diagram,* Archives of Foundry Engineering.

Ciesla P., Nodzynska M., Baprowska A., *et. al.* (2017). *Implementation of Ishikawa Diagram into project based education,* Conference: 15th Conference on Project-based Education in Science Education Location: Praha, Czech Republic.

Kaminski B. (eds.), (1996). *Economic Transition in Russia and the New States of Eurasia,* Armonk – London: ME Sharpe.

Liang W. and Yiming D., (2020). *Wavelet-based estimations of fractional Brownian sheet: Least squares versus maximum likelihood,* Volume: 371, Article Number: 112609.

Butterfly A. (1992). *Dilemmas of Independence: Ukraine after Totalitarianism,* New York: Council on Foreign Relations Press.

Butterfly A. (2001). *Imperial Ends. The Decay, Collapse, and Revival of Empires,* New York: Columbia Univ ersity Press.

Rutkowski J., *Obserwator finans.pl,* Ukraine is irreplaceable in gas transit from Russia.

Ślaski P., (2017). Inventory management in logistic systems, Warsaw: WAT.

Szeptycki A., (2013). Ukraine towards Russia Dependency Study, Warsaw: Publishing House of the University of Warsaw.

Paweł Ślaski

Chapter 57: Summary and conclusions: Determinants and implications of the Russian influence on Ukraine

Social science requires knowledge of many methods and techniques. The presented considerations focus on indicating the possibilities of using quantitative methods in formulating, analyzing and solving research problems, with particular emphasis on the Pareto rule and computer programming. An even wider range of scientific issues, such as social sciences embrace, forces the search for more effective modes of solving them, and computer programming becomes more useful. It is therefore worth noting that quantitative methods play a significant role in basic and applied social sciences research.

The developed quantitative tool, in conjunction with the Visual Basic for Application computer programming, enables an initial classification of the available statistical data in each area of the country's functioning. The simplicity of the procedures used, makes the developed application an easy and effective quantitative tool.

The conducted qualitative research, supported by a methodological and quantitative workshop, shows that the main reasons that have a negative impact on Ukraine by Russia relate to dependence in the area of security and defense, as well as in the sphere of economy and culture – ideology. Therefore, the suggestions to improve the negative impact in the indicated areas are as follows:

1. Limiting Ukraine's dependence on Russia requires, first of all, undertaking a pro-development economic policy by Ukraine. In this context, limiting the budget deficit and balancing the balance of payments, finding alternatives for viable suppliers of strategic raw materials and outlets for domestic production, a stable exchange rate, attracting foreign investments and ensuring access to new technologies are of utmost importance.
2. Reducing the dependence in the area of security and defense would require a number of actions of both – a detailed nature, aimed at solving individual problems discussed in this chapter, as well as the general ones. The former include initiating a dialogue with Russia on the conditions for stationing the Black Sea Fleet and the possibility of renegotiating the date of its withdrawal from Crimea, completing the delimitation and demarcation process of the

common border, continuation of the conversion process of the Ukrainian arms industry and development of cooperation with other partners in this area. Finally to undertake, together with Moldova and the European Union, more determined efforts to regulate the situation on the border with Transnistria, which would hinder the functioning of this unrecognized republic.

A pro-development cultural policy, based on financial support for Ukrainian scientists, artists and the media, seems to be a prospective solution in the cultural and ideological sphere. It is also important that the aid from public funds is granted not on the basis of political criteria, but merit-based considerations. Such a policy would contribute to the development of Ukraine's cultural and scientific potential and, as a result, to reduce the asymmetric nature of its relations with Russia.

Section IV:
The forecast of the development of the situation in Ukraine: The Russian-Ukrainian relations in the third decade of the 21st century

Magdalena Rykała / Jarosław Zelkowski

Chapter 58: The situation in Ukraine in the 2nd and 3rd decade of the 21st Century: Qualitative Forecasting Methods

The example of Ukraine proves that the global community was not prepared for the geopolitical consequences of the Ukrainian attempt to build a democratic state, following the example of Western countries. The confrontation between the West and Moscow was in this case unexpected. Russia still sees Ukraine as a key issue in its policy. It aims to undermine the Ukrainian state and has consistently made it difficult to carry out the systemic transformation. The direction of this policy is still valid, as Russia is simply 'obsessed' with Ukraine and wants to 'absorb' its area, treating it as an undisputed part of its national identity. Ukraine, in turn, is desperate to flee from the influence of its eastern neighbor. In the absence of ideas on how to anchor the concept of Ukraine among its society, Russia put on direct hostility towards its "little brother", as many Russians historically understand Ukraine. Russia consciously chose the conflict with Ukraine because of the fear of a possible confrontation with the United States. This choice was also motivated by an attempt to distract its own citizens from their everyday problems, as a real test of patriotism and loyalty. The activities of the Russian media and the elite were aimed at constantly highlighting the conflict and fueling the (alleged) chaos that is taking place in Ukraine, which still occupies a special place in the Russian consciousness. This has many reasons, ranging from historical to economic, and ending with the power issues of Russia's ambitions. The elite has consistently denied Ukraine the right to independence, while Ukraine's independence would leave Russia deprived of Kievan Rus, which is the cradle of Russian Orthodoxy. Russia's patronage of the "little brother" has become the norm for the past twenty years. Putin conducted a couple of "gas conflicts" (in 2006, 2008 and 2009, among others) with his western neighbor. The intentions in this case were obvious: strengthening Russian control by temporarily cutting off or reducing the supply of gas. In turn, the year 2004 brought the so-called The "Orange Revolution" which ended in protests against electoral fraud in favor of the pro-Russian candidate Viktor Yanukovych. Another protest took place in the years 2011–2012 as a result of the fraudulent elections and the announcement of the increase of the Russian sanctions in domestic and foreign policy towards Ukraine. The Ukrainian Revolution in the period 2013–2014 foreshadowed the brutal response of the Russian state. Immediately after Yanukovych fled the country in February 2014, Russia annexed the Ukrainian Crimean peninsula. Moreover, it sent troops to Donbas in Ukraine, where some enclaves were under the control of pro-Russian separatists. Fighting continues in this area. To sum up, Ukraine has become a battlefield between Russia and the West and is also an excellent excuse for Moscow's hostile behavior during the war (Bartosiak et al., 2015; Bērziņš, 2014, pp. 2002–2014; Beyrer et al., 2011; Czaja, 2015, pp. 27–48; Götz, 2015, pp. 3–10; Hurak, no date; Larrabee, 2010, pp. 33–52; Wilson, 2014).

The aim of this paper is to present the qualitative dependencies of military activities on the society and national economy of Ukraine with the use of the scoring-point method.

The figure (Figure 1) shows the population in Ukraine, which includes all residents regardless of their legal status or citizenship. The chart shows a clear downward trend in 2008–2018 (in 2008 there were 46.2 6 million people, while in 2018 it was 1.64 million less).

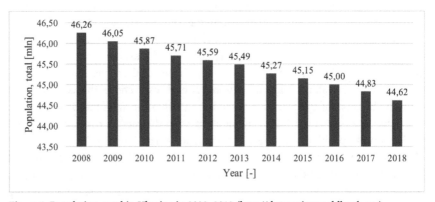

Figure 1. Population, total in Ukraine in 2008–2018 (http://datatopics.worldbank.org).

The figure (Figure 2) displays the relocation of the population that took place in the Crimea region and the non-governmental area in Donbas. The annexation of Crimea and military operations in Donbas have become the cause of forced internal migration in Ukraine. According to the data of the Interministerial Coordination Center for Social Security of Internally Displaced Persons (IDP), since July 2016, 1.029 million people have been displaced from non-governmental areas to other regions of Ukraine (1 007 112 people from Donetsk and Lugansk regions, 22 459 people from the Autonomous Republic of Crimea and the city of Sevastopol, including 170 581 children, 495 093 disabled and elderly people). Moreover, the presented data also show that the majority of internally displaced persons live near the regions of their previous residence, which may indicate their intention to return to previously abandoned homes.

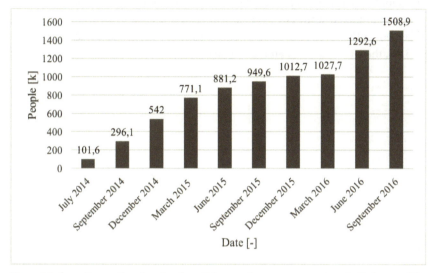

Figure 2. Information on the relocation from Crimea and non-government controlled areas of the Donbas to other regions, 2014–2016, thousand people (IOM, 2016).

Having gained independence, the cross-border mobility of Ukrainian citizens has increased, mainly due to the possibility of crossing the western border. In 2013, i.e. before the annexation of Crimea, the number of trips by the Ukrainian population to Poland exceeded the number of trips to Russia for the first time (Figure 3). Since the beginning of the conflict, there has been a significant decrease in the number of foreign trips, especially in the number of trips to Russia. In 2014, the Ukrainians traveled abroad by approx. 30% less than in 2013, while the number of trips to the European Union continued to increase (10.5 million in 2014 to 12.5 million in 2015).

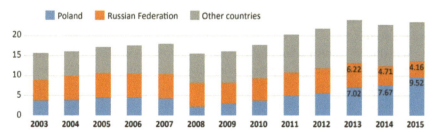

Figure 3. The number of state border crossings by Ukrainian citizens exiting Ukraine in 2003–2015, million times (IOM, 2016).

The figure (Figure 4) presents the age dependence rate of young people, defined as the ratio of dependent young people (people under 15) to the general working age population (people aged 15–64). In 2008, the discussed ratio was 20.13% and it was maintained until 2010. Then, from 2011, a clear growing trend can be observed to the level of 23.34% in 2018 (value for the world 39.48%, Poland – 22.32%, the USA – 28.57% and for Russia: 26.57%).

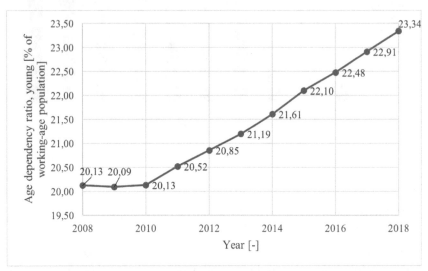

Figure 4. Age dependency ratio of young people (% working age population) – ang. Age dependency ratio, young (% of working-age population) (http://datatopics.worldbank.org).

On the other hand, unemployment in Ukraine (Figure 5) fluctuates between 6.36% – 9.38% in 2008–2018, recording a clear increase by about 2.1% during the period of the aforementioned conflict in the Donbas in 2013–2014. There are also human losses related to warfare (Figure 6). By 2018, the conflict had claimed a total of around 6,500 people.

The figure (Figure 7) presents the added value (a sector net result after summing up the results and subtracting indirect inputs) per employee depending on the sector:
- agriculture – forestry, hunting, fishing, plant growing and animal husbandry,
- industry – production, construction and public utilities (i.e. electricity, gas and water),
- services – wholesale and retail trade, restaurants and hotels, transport, warehousing, communication, financial, insurance, and business services, etc.

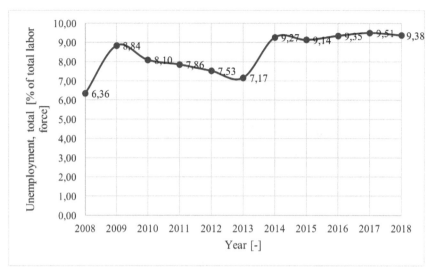

Figure 5. Total unemployment in Ukraine in 2008–2018 (% of total labor force) (modeled ILO estimate) (http://datatopics.worldbank.org).

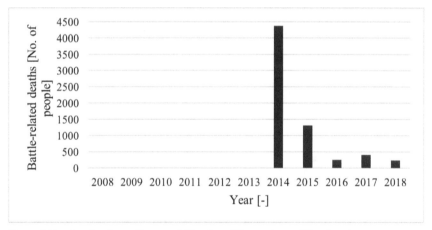

Figure 6. Deaths related to military activities (http://datatopics.worldbank.org).

The added value in 2008 per employee in agriculture was at a low level in relation to industry and services (it was only about 30%), however, we can observe that this value increased significantly in 2014 – almost twice.

Hossa of Gross Domestic Product (in short GDP) in Ukraine (Figure 8) in the period of 2009–2013 (117.11 billion US dollars in 2009, r., 183.31 billion in 2013 r.), was interrupted in the period of 2014–2015 due to military operations. Currently, Ukraine's GDP is slowly increasing to the level of 2010. In comparison to other countries, Ukraine's GDP is as follows:

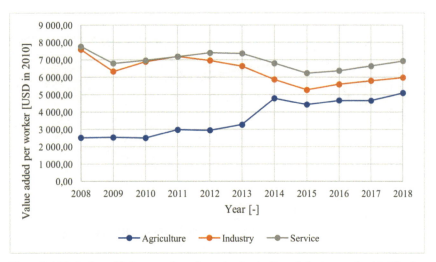

Figure 7. Added value added per employee by sector (agriculture, industry, services) in Ukraine in 2008–2018 (http://datatopics.worldbank.org).

- 2014: US $ 17,521.75 billion (USA), US $ 2,059.98 billion (Russia), US $ 545.39 billion (Poland),
- 2018: USD 20,544.34 billion (USA), USD 1,657.55 billion (Russia), USD 585.66 billion (Poland).

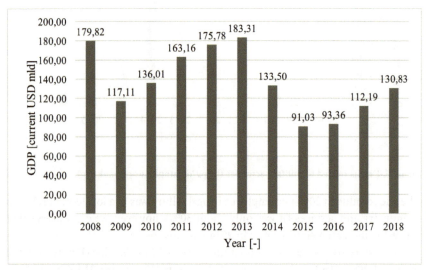

Figure 8. Ukraine's GDP in the years 2008–2018 in billion USD (http://datatopics.worldbank.org).

Another important aspect in the functioning of the national economy is the ratio of exports and imports to GDP (Figure 9). In the discussed case, the surplus of imports in relation to exports in the period 2008–2018 is noticeable. Moreover, in 2014 an approx. 6% leap in the surplus of exports in relation to the above-mentioned index in the previous year can be observed. Then, in the following years, exports gradually decrease (to 45.21% in 2018), while imports remain at around 54%.

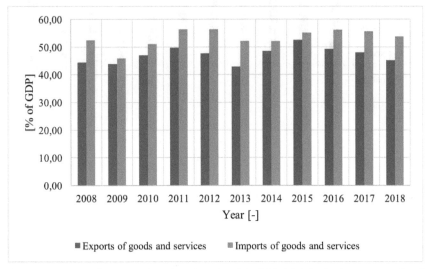

Figure 9. Exports and imports of goods and services (% of GDP) in Ukraine in 2008–2018 (% of GDP) (http://datatopics.worldbank.org).

The boom in Gross National Income (DNB in short) from 2009 to 2013 was interrupted in 2014 (Figure 10). Then, a gradual decline in the value of GNI to the level of USD 2,260 in 2017 is observed. In turn, 2018 brought an increase in the value of GNI to the level of approx. USD 2,660 and a further increase in the above-mentioned ratio is forecasted for the coming years.

The warfare of 2014 strongly weakened the exchange rate of hryvnia to the US dollar (Figure 11), in the period of 2014–2015 the currency decreased its value approx. three times and maintains approximately the above rate to the beginning of 2020. Similarly, the exchange rate of hryvnia has also been weakened to the Russian ruble (Figure 12), but in this case it lost its value about 1.5 times.

Foreign direct investments refer to the capital flows of direct investment and is the sum of equity, profit reinvestment and other capital. Foreign direct investment in the case of Ukraine in the period 2008–2018 recorded a significant, approx. 5 – fold decrease in the value (Figure 13) with a booming period in the years 2009–2012. The lowest value of the mentioned ratio falls in 2014 and is approximately 0.85 billion USD.

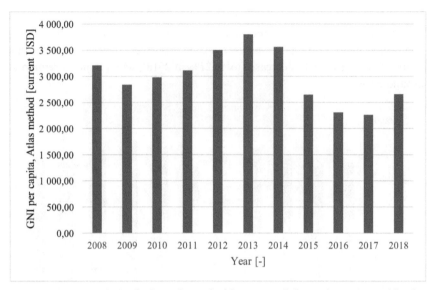

Figure 10. GNI per capita in Ukraine, Atlas method (current US $) (http://datatopics.worldbank.org).

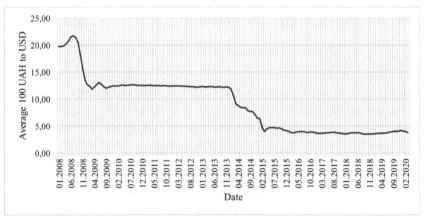

Figure 11. Average 100 Ukrainian hryvnia (UAH) to US dollars (USD) 2000–2020 history (https://stooq.pl/).

On the other hand, expenditure on research and development (Figure 14) in the years 2008–2013 remained constant at approx. 0.85% level, a decline of this indicator can be observed in the period of 2014–2017 until approx. 0.45% level. In contrast, the situation looks completely different in the case of military spending, which in the period 2013–2015 increased by approx. 1.7 – times to approx. 4%.

The increased military spending (Figure 15) implies an increase in the personnel of the armed forces (Figure 16). Figure 15 presents a constant level of the

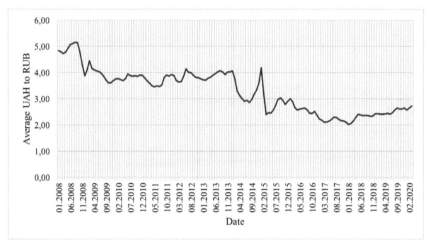

Figure 12. Average Ukrainian grivna (UAH) to Russian rubles (RUB) 2000–2014 history (https://stooq.pl/).

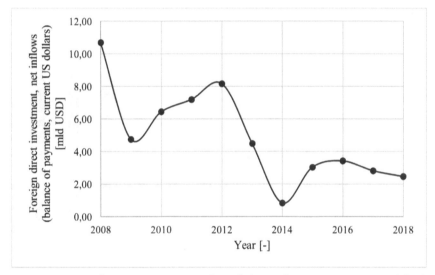

Figure 13. Foreign direct investment, net inflows (balance of payments, current US dollars) (http://datatopics.worldbank.org).

indicator in the years 2008–2012, a significant decrease to the level of 121 000 soldiers in 2013 (military operations) and a gradual increase in the personnel of the armed forces to the level of approx. 300 000 in 2017.

In the case of air transport (Figure 16) it can be seen clearly an upward trend in 2013–2018. The tense political situation in the period of 2011–2013 has con-

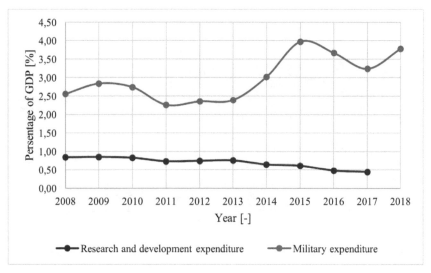

Figure 14. Military expenditure (% of GDP) Research and development expenditure (% of GDP) (http://datatopics.worldbank.org).

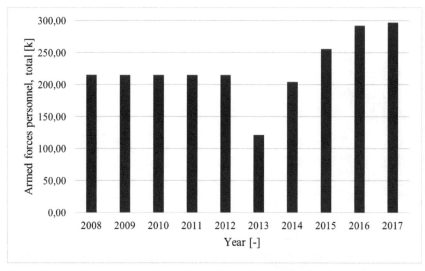

Figure 15. Armed forces personnel, total (http://datatopics.worldbank.org).

tributed to a drastic turn of approx. 4 – fold decline in air freight to approx. 14.38 million tonne – killometres.

In the case of traffic in the container port (Figure 17), a sharp drop in the flow of containers in 2013–2015 is noticeable, and an increase in the period 2015–2018. These data refer to coastal shipping and international travel.

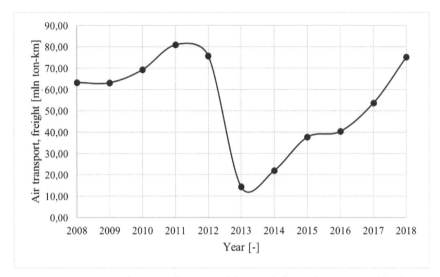

Figure 16. Air transport, freight (million tonne kilometers) (http://datatopics.worldbank.org).

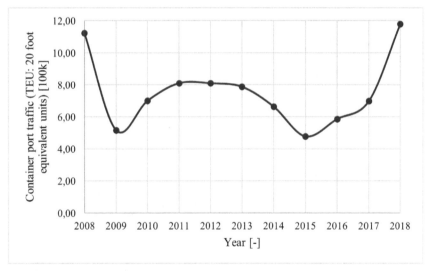

Figure 17. Container port traffic (TEU: 20 foot equivalent units) (http://datatopics.worldbank.org).

On the other hand, the data from international tourism displays an interesting picture (Figure 18): inflows and outflows were defined as percentages of total exports and imports, respectively. In the case of the period 2008–2013, the inflows exceeded the expenses, the breakdown of this trend is visible in 2014. This leads to a huge difference in the above-mentioned indicators, equal to approx. 8% in 2018.

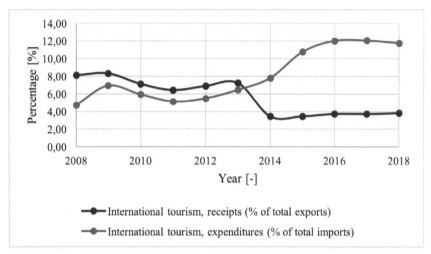

Figure 18. International tourism, receipts (% of total exports) and expenditures (% of total imports) (http://datatopics.worldbank.org).

The number of passengers transported by air (Figure 19) gradually increased in the period of 2008–2012, in turn, in the years 2012–2014, due to military operations, the number of passengers decreased by a total of approx. 2 million. Whereas, in the period of 2014–2018, a clear growing trend can be observed to the level of approx. 8 million in 2018.

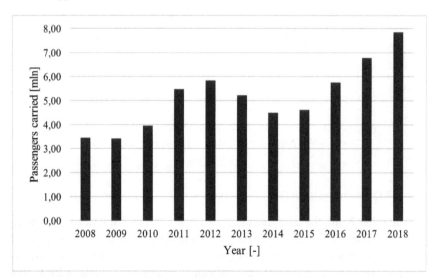

Figure 19. Air transport, carried passengers (http://datatopics.worldbank.org).

The situation in Ukraine: Qualitative Forecasting Methods   **483**

To assess the impact of the Russian Federation, the scoring-point method was used, which makes it possible to evaluate several or even a dozen of parameters. For specific qualitative features, the following points were adopted (Table 1). The scoring-point method was applied to assess the impact on various aspects of the Ukrainian economy.

Table 1. Scores accepted for the scoring

Quality feature	Rating
No impact	1
Slight impact	2
Medium impact	3
Huge impact	4
A very big impact	5

To assess the impact of military actions on the social life of Ukrainian citizens, the following parameters were selected (Figure 20), where:

A1 – Population,
A2 – Migration of the population,
A3 – Unemployment,
A4 – Deaths related to military activities (warfare),
A5 – Age dependence indicator,
A6 – Personnel of the armed forces,
A7 – Relocation.

Based on the analysis, one can conclude that the greatest impact was achieved by two parameters (A4 and A7), directly related to the conflict in the so-called The Donetsk Republic and the Lugansk Republic, as well as the annexation of Crimea. The next largest parameter is the migration of people – Ukrainian citizens, often losing their possessions overnight, migrated to EU countries for work – often leaving their home and families. According to the data of the Economic Analysis Department of the National Bank of Poland, the inflow of Ukrainian citizens to the Polish market in 2018 stabilized at the level of 800,000 people.

The impact of military operations on the various parameters of the Ukrainian economy is shown in Figure 21, where:

B1 – The exchange rate of the Ukrainian hryvnia against the US dollar (UAH – USD),
B2 – The exchange rate of the Ukrainian hryvnia against the Russian ruble (UAH – RUB),

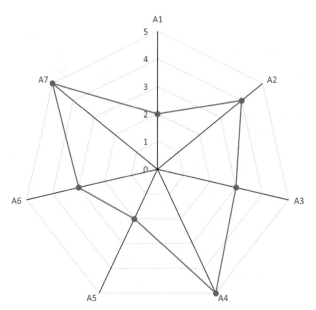

Figure 20. Radar chart of the influence of military actions on the social parameters of the lives of the Ukrainian people in Ukraine.

B3 – Exports of goods and services (% of GDP),
B4 – Imports of goods and services (% of GDP),
B5 – Gross domestic product GDP,
B6 – Foreign Direct Investments – net inflows,
B7 – Trade in goods (% of GDP),
B8 – Air transport – transported passengers,
B9 – Air transport – freight,
B10 – Traffic in a container port,
B11 – International tourism – receipts (% of total exports),
B12 – International tourism – expenses (% of total imports),
B13 – Military expenditure (% of GDP),
B14 – Research and development expenditure (% of GDP),
B15 – Gross national income per capita (GNI).

On the basis of the diagram, it can be observed that military operations have a very large impact on the parameters: B1, B6, B12 and B13. However, no changes (and thus no effect) were observed in parameters B4, B7 and B9.

The radar charts presented above release a high impact of military actions on the lives of Ukrainian citizens and on the national economy in qualitative terms.

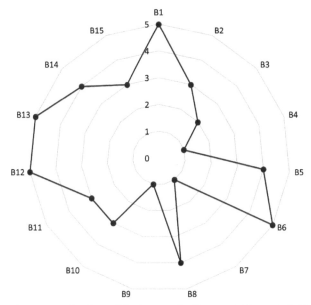

Figure 21. Radar chart of the impact of military activities on individual parameters (B1-B14) of the functioning of the Ukrainian economy.

Magdalena Rykała / Jarosław Zelkowski

Chapter 59: The situation in Ukraine in the 2nd and 3rd decade of the 21st century: Quantitative Forecasting Methods

The subject of a further analysis is the quantitative presentation of the effects of military operations (warfare) in 2014–2018. The choice of the above-mentioned period was dictated by the geopolitical importance for Ukraine and Europe.

The figure (Figure 1) shows the dynamics of changes in the Ukrainian population. On its basis, it can be observed that it has a downward trend. In 2014, compared to 2013, it amounted -0.48%. According to the forecast (Migration in Ukraine: Facts And Figures), if the number of births, life expectancy and migration rates remain unchanged, then in 2050 Ukraine's population will reach 32 million people. The share of people over 60 in the social structure, will increase by 50%.

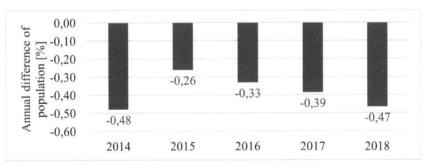

Figure 1. Changes in the population of Ukrainian citizens in 2014–2018.

The military effects had an impact not only on the population of the Ukrainian population, but also on an increase in unemployment among them. In 2014, the unemployment rate increased by 29.29% compared to 2013 (Figure 2). In 2018, it shapes at the level of 9.38% (which is a decrease by 1.36% compared to the previous year).

Changes in the value of the Gross Domestic Product had a downward trend in 2014–2015 (compared to 2013, it decreased by 27,17%, and in the following year

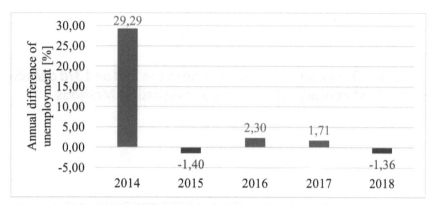

Figure 2. Dynamics of unemployment of Ukrainian citizens in 2014–2018.

by 31,81%). Since 2016, the nature of the trend has changed, with an increase of 2,55% compared to the previous year (Figure 3).

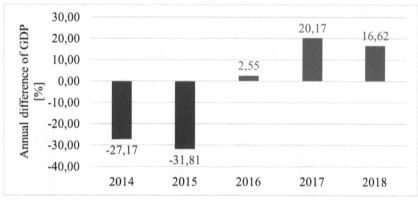

Figure 3. Change in Gross Domestic Product in 2014–2018.

A similar situation occurs in the case of the Ukrainian currency – the hryvnia, because the largest decrease was recorded in February 2015 (it amounted 2,86% in relation to the US dollar, and 24,65% in relation to the ruble) – Figure 4. Since September 2016, the difference in the currency exchange rate fluctuates within the limits of <-5%, + 5%>.

Since 2014, one can observe a decrease in expenditure on research and development, the lowest value was recorded in 2016 (21,3% compared to the previous year), with a simultaneous increase in military expenditure (in 2014, an increase by 26,25% compared to 2013, while in 2015 an increase by 31,52% compared to 2014). The years 2016 and 2017 are an exception, where a negative increase can be observed for this parameter (Figure 5).

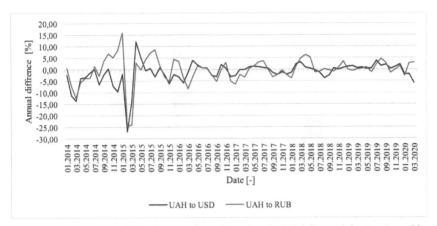

Figure 4. The difference of the Ukrainian hryvnia against the US dollar and the Russian ruble.

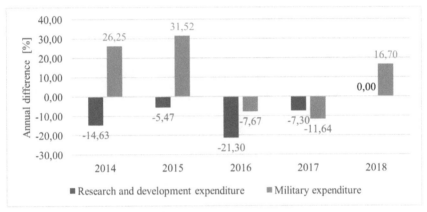

Figure 5. Annual difference between expenditures: research and development and military in 2014–2018.

In the first year of the conflict, there was a decrease in passenger transport by air (by 13,7%). Then, in the following years, a growing trend can be observed by an average of 15,21% per annum in the period of 2015–2018 (Figure 6).

Figure 7 shows the dynamics of changes in the transport of goods by air and sea. One can notice that the transport of goods by air in the period 2014–2018 reveals an upward trend, while the hostilities in 2014–2015 had a very negative impact on transport by sea (decreases respectively: 15,76% and 27,9%).

In 2014 and 2015, there was an increase in the importance of exports of goods in GDP (10,68% on average), then in the following years a downward trend can be observed (4,91% on average). However, in the case of imports, no repetitive trend is shown (oscillation of changes of approx. 6%) – Figure 8.

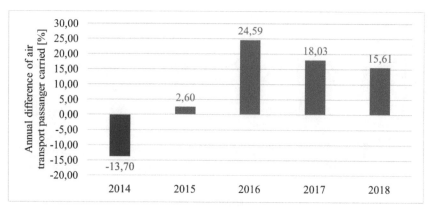

Figure 6. Dynamics of air transport – carried passengers.

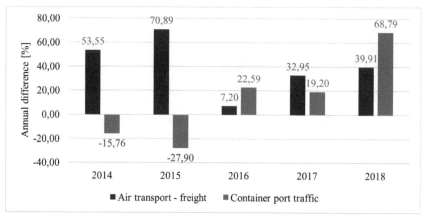

Figure 7. The dynamics of changes in the transport of goods by air and sea.

The hostilities significantly reduced the influence of international tourism in creating exports in Ukraine (in 2014 by 52,33% compared to the previous year). In the following years, the revenues from the tourism industry are positive (there is a slight increase – on average by 2,67% per year). In turn, international tourism expenditure shows an increase in the years 2014–2016, and then a slight downward trend in the remaining years (Figure 9).

Figure 10 presents the changes in direct foreign investments, where one can clearly notice a decrease in 2014 (by 81,22%), and then in the next year an increase by 260,09%. In subsequent years, this value fluctuates around 18%.

The armed conflict in Ukraine had a huge impact on the decline in Gross National Income in the period 2014–201, only 2018 was a breakthrough year, when Ukraine revealed an increase of this indicator by 17,7% compared to the previous year (Figure 11).

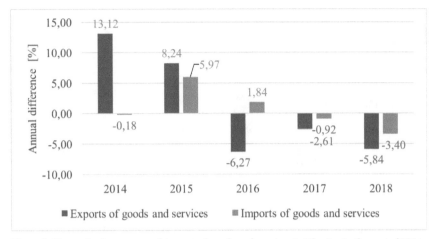

Figure 8. Change in the export and import of goods and services in Ukraine in the period 2014–2018.

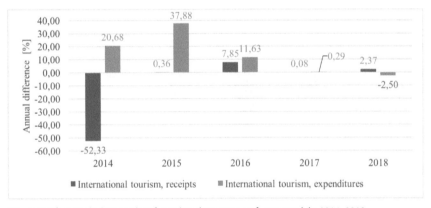

Figure 9. Changes in international tourism (revenues and expenses) in 2014–2018.

On the basis of the carried out analysis, one can notice that Ukraine was acutely affected by the consequences of the conflict with separatists (unofficially supported by the Russian Federation) and the effects of the annexation of Crimea. This can be observed not only in the society – through migrations within the country, but also through economic emigration caused by high unemployment. The ongoing conflict in Donbas does not improve the situation, as it divides Ukraine into the pro-Western and pro-Russian one state. Despite Kiev's declaration of readiness to end the conflict, the inhabitants of the towns located near the front lines often openly say that they are losing hope for a solution to it. The outcomes of the negative impact of warfare can be seen primarily through the analysis of data on the national economy of Ukraine, which was in a deep

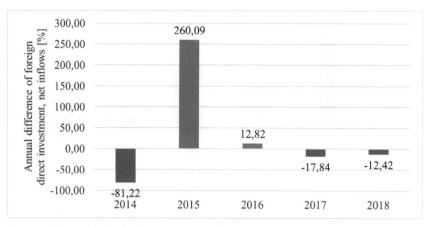

Figure 10. Changes in foreign direct investment (net receipts) in 2014–2018.

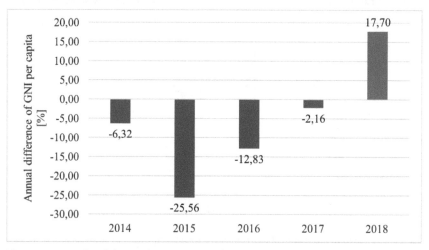

Figure 11. Dynamics of changes in Gross National Income per capita in 2014–2018.

recession in 2014–2015. Since 2015, the governments of Ukraine have been trying to improve the situation (the then president Petro Poroshenko) by announcing the "Strategy 2020". However, Ukraine did not meet the forecasts assumed in the report.

The next step in the reconstruction of Ukraine was the introduction in 2019 of the agenda of the govermental activites until 2024, which main goal is the rapid economic development of the state. The government's activities programme will include development plans for the next five years, including the 40% GDP growth, the creation of new jobs (around 1 million), an increase in foreign direct investment of USD 50 billion and the introduction of free trade in agricultural lands from October 2020. As a part of the suspension of the moratorium on the land trade, Ukrainian citizens who own a land, will have a greater scope for action. Until now, landowners could only lease them for a small price, which resulted in the slow development of the agricultural sector. As a part of the activities carried out, it is also intended to reduce the budget deficit to 1.5% and reduce the public debt from the current 59% to 40%. Increasing exports is another step in the Ukrainian government's agenda, as the plans assume doubling its value in the coming years. The government of Ukraine is also planning to curtail customs duties by 10% on key commodity items exported to key trade partners (https://www.Obserwatorfinansowy.pl/).

The Supreme Council adopted a number of bills to advance the transparency of public finances. The process related to privatization, public tenders and the lease of state property has been simplified. In order to limit the possibility of committing corruption in the process of examining applications, it is planned to introduce new or extend the existing online services for people and enterprises (https://www.Obserwatorfinansowy.pl/).

The intensions of the Ukrainian government also contain the rapid development of communication infrastructure, i. e. the improvement of the condition of roads (approx. 24,000 km), the development of railways, the construction of deep-water ports and 15 airports. The government's announcements regarding the citizens of Ukraine are that "everyone will be guaranteed a real minimum subsistence level", due to which the negative demographic growth will be overcome (higher number of births and returns to the country than deaths and emigration cases) (https://www.financialobserver.pl/).

When analyzing the above-mentioned data, it can be seen that these are undoubtedly ambitious plans, but the reality is different. According to Maria Repko from the Kiev Center for Economic Strategy, GDP growth is possible, but in reality it would require a miracle on the Dnieper. On the other hand, according to the macroeconomic forecast published by the government in October 2019, the GDP growth in the optimistic variant is 17.8% (in the pessimistic 12%). In recent years, Ukraine recorded the greatest increase in 2011 (when there was no war), which could have been related to investments preparing for Euro2012 (https://www.Obserwatorfinansowy.pl/).

Ukraine improved its position in the Doing Business ranking (up from 71 to 64) in terms of progress in areas such as protection of minority shareholders' rights, obtaining a building permit, connection to the electricity grid, international trade or property registration, while worsening its assessment of the tax system and enforcement by companies of receivables from debtors announced by the World Bank (Ukraine ranks 146th out of 190 countries included in the ranking) (https://www.Obserwatorfinansowy.pl/).

If, however, Ukraine succeeds in implementing its agenda, it will have to wrestle with the problem of settling debts for foreign entities (in 2015, the Ukrainian government concluded a debt restructuring agreement). On the basis of this agreement, the government of Ukraine decided to pay tchem one part of the GDP when the growth is 3-4% year on year - the amount of payments will be 15% of the surplus over 3%. For a growth greater than 4% annually, as much as 40% of the surplus. In the case of a smaller increase per year, the so-called "Development penalty" will not be enforced.

The unstable situation on the territory of Ukraine adversely affects the achievement of the assumed goals. A divided society and the lack of reaction from the West make the society fear for its future. In addition, Russia's continuous actions show its power (the concentration of almost 90,000 soldiers along the border with Ukraine, 1100 tanks, 2500 armored fighting vehicles, 1600 artillery and missile systems, 340 combat aircraft and other weapons and equipment). So far, 40,000 people have suffered the conflict in the area, 14,000 people have died, and 1.5 million people have run away as a result of forced internal migration. The occupied regions (Donetsk and Luhansk), occupying 7% of the territory of Ukraine, are the area where the citizens of Ukraine are directly exposed to hostilities on a daily basis.

References

(2016) International Organization for Migration (IOM) Mission in Ukraine. *Migration in Ukraine: Facts and figures* http://iom.org.ua/sites/default/files/ff_eng_10_10_press.pdf.

Bartosiak J., Cheda R. and Chodkowski K., (2015). *The impact of the war with Ukraine on the internal situation in Russia and its relations with the West,* eds. Kowalczyk, Warsaw.

Bērziņš J., (2014). *Russia's new generation warfare in Ukraine: Implications for Latvian Defense Policy.* Policy Paper, 2, pp. 2002-2014.

Beyrer C., Wirtz AL, Walker D., Johns B., Sifakis F. and Baral SD, (2011). Scenario 2 Country Studies: Russian Federation and Ukraine.

Czaja J. (2015). *Some legal and political aspects of the Ukrainian crisis and its impact on international security.* Security. Theory and Practice, 18 (1), pp. 27-42.

Götz E. (2015). *It's geopolitics, stupid: explaining Russia's Ukraine policy.* Global Affairs, 1 (1), pp. 3-10.

http://datatopics.worldbank.org/world-development-indicators/.

https://stooq.pl/.

https://www.Obserwatorfinansowy.pl/tematyka/makroekonomia/trendy-gospodarcze/ukraina-ambitne-plany-i-szara-rzeczywistosc/.

Hurak I., Political myths propagated by the Russian Federation in Ukraine.

Larrabee FS, (2010). *Russia, Ukraine, and Central Europe: the return of geopolitics.* Journal of international affairs, 63 (2), pp. 33-52.

Wilson A., (2014). *Ukraine crisis: What it means for the West.* Yale University Press.

Jarosław Zelkowski / Magdalena Rykała / Marcin Górnikiewicz / Radosław Bielawski

Chapter 60: Summary and conclusions: The forecast of the Russian Influence on Ukraine in the third decade of the 21st century

The geopolitical situation in Ukraine has been unstable for six years, the annexation of the Crimean peninsula and the loss of control over the Donetsk and Lugansk oblasts caused significant turmoil in the functioning of the national economy and the lives of Ukrainian citizens. The presented qualitative and quantitative analysis showed the influence of military actions on the parameters presented above. Based on the data, one can observe growth in certain sectors, e.g. GDP, GNI in 2018. However, the lack of a common position of the member states belonging to the European Union or even to NATO towards the conflict in eastern Ukraine provides Russia with an open way to provide separatists with powerful support, without which the conflict would have ended in a month or two. As a result, the Ukrainian economy is subject to fluctuations caused by economic and military activities, which effectively destabilize the functioning of the state in this area.

After the annexation, Crimea was quickly transformed into a fortified and heavily armed fortress with an exit to the Black Sea, which in fact allowed Russia to take control of the entire basin, and thus the entire maritime trade. Moscow restricted vessel traffic in the Kerch Gulf and blocked Ukrainian ships from using the port in Mariupol. This led to a situation in November 2018 where three Ukrainian navy units were taken over by the Russian border guard. Russia, despite receiving international sanctions for the annexation of Crimea, is still trying to maintain its position in the ongoing conflict.

Russia's original intention was probably to destabilize the whole of eastern Ukraine, but this plan failed largely due to the enormous resistance of society, which Russian analysts dealing with information warfare (social engineering) had not foreseen despite social research on ideological and political attitudes in Ukrainian society. In this surprising situation for the Kremlin, an emergency plan was implemented, which resulted in the outbreak of a regular civil war, which prevented Ukraine from joining NATO and the EU. Russia's strategic goal of maintaining an apparently neutral Ukraine as a buffer zone between Russia and NATO member states has been achieved. It can be assumed that Moscow could consider allowing Ukraine to join the European Union and thus increasing Russian influence on Brussels decision-making process, having a great potential to influence also several other countries belonging to the community. On the other hand, if Ukraine did become a member of the EU, then the risk of joining NATO would increase significantly, which is already in complete contradiction with Moscow's strategic vision of regional security architecture in this part of the world. Thus, both initiatives that arose from below were treated by the Russian authorities as a fundamental threat to the security of the Russian Federation. At that time, Moscow reached for the para-military variant, which ended in full success, i.e. taking over the complete control of Crimea – so important to the control of the Black Sea. The second step was unsuccessful, but made it possible to keep Ukraine outside the international structures to a limited extent, and the structures are treated in Moscow with a great distrust. Therefore, the strategic goals have been temporarily achieved, although the condition for sustaining them is to constantly support the civil war – it is therefore an expensive solution, but also necessary from Moscow's perspective.

To sum up, Russia will continue to maintain the conflict in eastern Ukraine, destabilize this country economically and conduct intensive information operations aimed at influencing both the political process and shaping general social attitudes in line with Moscow's intention. If these attitudes cannot be favorable to Russia, they will most likely be discredited, and perhaps with time aversion towards Euro-Atlantic structures. Then Moscow's strategic interest would be secured enough to end the conflict, which, in the event of the return of the threat, can always be refreshed. On the other hand, even if political power was taken over by Kremlin supporters in Kiev, it is doubtful in the face of enormous social resistance that they would be able to lead to a peace process and consent to the creation of an autonomous state separated from part of Ukrainian territory. As a result, the situation in Ukraine will not change in the coming years, and we may even expect an eruption of fighting in the east of the country, should the international situation, according to Moscow, require it. On the other hand, Ukraine is a country which, in the current balance of power, is definitely more favorable to NATO and the EU than many other countries that have acquired the status of a member state in the meantime, and therefore it is a country worth considering in the plans of the Alliance in this part of the world.

Summary and final conclusions

The prospect of the development of relations between the Russian Federation and each of the surveyed countries is original and therefore extremely absorbing. At the same time, each of the prepared forecasts contains a lot of common content, allowing for the formulation of comprehensive final conclusions for the security of the entire studied region. The forecast takes into account two scenarios:
– The US and the EU maintain their current strong position in Central and Eastern Europe
– the influence of the US and the EU is significantly weakening in individual countries of Central and Eastern Europe

In each of these situations, the prospect of the evolution of mutual relations between the Kremlin and the capitals of the studied countries will develop differently, which is also presented below. All the revealed conclusions are the result of applying the methods, techniques and tools belonging to the methodological workshop of security sciences, strategic sciences, political sciences, international relations, management sciences and economic sciences. This allowed for independent formulation of conclusions by individual scientists and experts, which in turn made it possible to compare them in order to identify common features and dissimilarities. Such an approach meant that the scientists retained full independence in the research process and the preparation of final conclusions and were not influenced by the research and results of other authors. An additional criterion allowing to maintain the research impartiality was to entrust individual authors only with fragments of research on a given country, and only after all the results had been submitted, the editorial team examined the entirety of these results, developing partial and final conclusions. Thus, thanks to the application of these two criteria favoring the objectivity of the scientists and experts involved, it can be assumed that the obtained results are not only unbiased, but also have a high level of credibility. After all, it is not possible for researchers representing various fields and sciences and applying their own research methodology to independently arrive at similar conclusions, if these conclusions do not correspond to the current state. Ultimately, it is the future that will precisely verify whether the forecasts made have been accurate.

In the Kremlin's geopolitical game, Poland occupies a special place as a country located at the junction of three spheres of influence: the American, the EU and the Russian. In this particular triangle of colliding geopolitical influences, the Americans have been the strongest since the end of the last century. This means that any actions aimed against the interests of Warsaw are perceived by Moscow as a parallel weakening of Washington's position in this part of Europe. At the same time, as long as Poland is discerned as the closest ally of the United States in Central and Eastern Europe, the Russians will not take too aggressive actions, limiting themselves to the so-called soft forms of influence, mainly occuring as information, propaganda and intelligence measures. In addition, due to the dynamic weakening of the possibility of exerting pressure with economic means, it should also be expected that in the coming decades Moscow will develop information impact through mass and social media using the methodology of the so-called social engineering. In parallel, special activities will be carried out aimed at developing an agency of influence and recruiting people to cooperate with the Russian special services. In this way, by shaping public opinion and using key people in politics, economy and social life, the Russians intend to pursue their goals aimed at internal conflict of states belonging to the European Union and decreasing Washington's very strong position. If the White House withdraws from the geopolitical game for influence in Central and Eastern Europe, it can be assumed with a high degree of probability that Moscow will significantly increase its influence on the Polish decision-making process, the aim of which will be to rebuild strong economic and, in the future, military ties between the two countries. It can be assumed that the attitude of Polish society to Moscow's policy will then be divided into two extreme camps: opponents and supporters of closer integration with the Russian Federation. At the same time, it should be emphasized with full awareness that such a scenario would only be justified in the event of a significant weakening of the position of the United States in this part of Europe, including Poland.

The Czech Republic is characterized by a convenient geostrategic location due to its key position at the intersection of trade routes running from the north to the south, as well as mountain ranges enabling effective blocking of these routes, if necessary, and facilitating defense against possible aggression from the north and west. The Russian Federation for decades has been mainly developing information activities aimed at enhancing and advancing meticulously a constructed impact of its agencies. Moreover, the Czech media favorable to Russia and the virtual space are increasingly involved in promoting the narrative favorable to Moscow, which is to shape pro-Russian public moods. Special activities related to building both the aforementioned agency of influence and recruiting collaborators in Prague's decision-making elites have positive effects on the shape of Czech foreign and domestic policy. Due to the successes achieved in this area, the Russians do not take negative actions towards the Czech Republic, which could adversely affect the effectiveness of the information activities described above. To sum up, the Czechs belong to one of the societies of Central and Eastern Europe more favorable to the Russians, which means that if the position of the EU and the US weakens, we can expect a closer Russian-Czech cooperation, which will gradually orient the Prague's decision-making process towards a pro-Russian one.

Slovakia's geopolitical and geostrategic position is no longer as favorable as it is in the case of the Czech Republic directly bordering Germany and Austria, but is significant due to the potential direct impact on the Czech Republic. Trade turnover is also not particularly important, the Russians for decades have been focusing their efforts on a similar mechanism of influence as they use in the neighboring Czech Republic: strengthening the agency of influence, developing recruitment operations aimed at influencing the Slovak decision-making process mainly in the area of foreign policy and using the media to shape public opinion – also with particular emphasis on virtual space. For a number of years, these activities have had positive effects, and thus the Slovak society is partially neutral and partially positive about Russian policy. Due to this particular geopolitical orientation of Bratislava, in the event of the diminishing of the EU and US structures, Slovakia, like the Czech Republic, would be very susceptible to Moscow's actions aimed at rebuilding the sphere of influence lost in this part of Europe in the 1990s.

Hungary is a country with a relatively large territory, but without much significance for the Kremlin's geopolitical and geostrategic plans. The only real advantage of this country lies in the membership in the EU, which Moscow, based on the specifically understood "neutrality" of Budapest, tries to play its own interests, the real goals of which are Poland, Germany and France. From the Kremlin's point of view, Hungary is a convenient geopolitical tool as a wedge driven into the unity of the old EU countries, where the interests and aspirations of other member states belonging to the Visegrad Group, including Poland, are used simultaneously in these games. On the one hand, in this particular game of influence, Poland is an opponent of Russian actions, which results from the strong alliance between Warsaw and Washington, but at the same time the EU's dislikes and Visegrad sympathies are used to weaken the Union as such. The decision-makers in Moscow know very well that the diminishing of the EU will not cause Poland to start orbiting towards the Kremlin, but that the fate will befall the other countries belonging to the Visegrad four. Then, it will ruthlessly weaken Poland's position in the region, and thus the ability to influence Warsaw's most powerful ally and Moscow's most dangerous competitor, not only in Europe, but all over the world. From this perspective, Hungary is an important element of the Russian game for influence in Central and Eastern Europe. The Russians are also aware that in the case of Hungarians, this would be a powerful economic incentive as real and long-term benefits. Then, should the EU diminish, Budapest could also follow the path set by Moscow. At present, the Kremlin has the possibility of economic influence in the energy sector, which, if the above-described scenario was to be fulfilled, it would become the basis for even stronger cooperation in this sector. According to the research carried out, the level of information operations conducted with regard to Hungary is much lower than in the case of the Czech Republic and Slovakia, and the only form of influence maintained at a high level is media influence aimed at shaping pro-Russian attitudes in the Hungarian society. The course of the elections in Hungary and the public opinion are generally friendly towards Russia, so this activity by the Kremlin brings positive results. Summing up, a strongly independent Budapest will continue to pursue a policy favorable to the Kremlin, trying to maintain a kind of neutrality, balancing between the interests of the Kremlin and the EU, and at the same time being guided by pragmatism and the profit and loss account, striving to achieve the highest possible benefits from this special situation.

From the perspective of Russian interests, Ukraine is a key element of Kremlin's national security, insuring Russia's south-eastern border. According to Russian optics, Ukraine's accession to NATO and the EU would mean a potential threat to a sensitive part of the Russian Federation. Decision makers in the Kremlin do not see such a situation as a threat at a given place and time, but as a possible threat even in the distant future. For this reason, such a scenario was completely unacceptable in Moscow and was associated with the launching of various activities gradually aimed at preventing Kiev's formalized alliance with the West in the form of EU / NATO. The information activities undertaken by Russia in Ukraine are characterized by surprisingly low effectiveness – both in the area of recruiting agents of influence and collaborators located in decision-making centers, and in influencing social attitudes in the media. In this situation, Moscow is left with only "hard power" tools, mainly economic and military, which are in constant use. Therefore, the forecast in the case of Ukraine is pessimistic, as it not only confirms the continuation of the current policy towards the east of Ukraine and Crimea, but even allows for the possibility of developing offensive actions and further "taking Ukraine into bits" under various pretexts. Undoubtedly, the current epidemiological situation and the crises caused by climate change and competition for resources will contribute to exacerbating the situation, which may even result in a regular military operation on a limited scale. On the one hand, it will consolidate Moscow's 'gains' to date, and on the other, it will prevent Ukraine from joining the EU / NATO for the next decades. Should the position of the EU and the US in this part of the world weaken, Moscow would most likely launch a large-scale offensive aimed at gaining control over the entire territory of Ukraine. Such a show of power would also make most Visegrad countries with a high degree of probability opt for pro-Russian rhetoric.

In order to summarize the research carried out, the following conclusions can be formulated regarding the forecast of the development of the situation in the area of regional security in Central and Eastern Europe

- Socio-economic stability and further economic development of the studied societies is closely related to the presence in the internally strong European Union, which is one of the pillars of the security of these countries against possible economic, para-military (hybrid-asymmetric) or armed aggression;
- The military and economic security of the surveyed countries is also directly correlated with the presence of the United States in this part of Europe, expressed both by the potential of American investments (private and public) and by an appropriately strongly manifested military presence. At the level of international structures, the formal and legal expression of this presence is membership in NATO, whose strength is mainly based on the potential offensive-defensive United States.
- The Czech, Slovak and Hungarian societies predominantly reveal bias, neutral or favorable towards Russian policy attitude, and therefore policy makers in the run of foreign policy, balance between the interests of the EU, their country, and the Russian, in such a way as to ensure their own countries to the highest possible benefit. This means that these societies identify themselves only partially with the presence in the EU, guarding their own presence in this structure primarily through the prism of economic benefits.
- Polish society is divided, some are neutral-positive, and some definitely negative towards Russian policy. Poland is perceived as the closest ally of the United States in this part of Europe and as such is not considered by the Kremlin as an object of stronger influence in the field of "hard power", especially since the possibilities of economic impact were almost completely eliminated in 2020/2021.
- The majority of the Ukrainian society is anti-Russian, and the Kremlin influences the country's decision-making process mainly with the use of "hard power" in the shape of economic and para-military (hybrid- asymmetric) measures.
- In the event of a crisis and weakening of the EU structures, some Visegrad countries would establish stronger alliances with Russia, changing the international view from pro-Western to pro-Russian.
- If the position of the US in the region is declined, Russia will move to strong and aggressive actions towards Poland and Ukraine.

The independence achieved with difficulty by the nations of Central and Eastern Europe is still strongly correlated with a sufficiently strong presence of the US in this part of Europe and the presence in the EU structures. These two pillars of the political, economic and social stability of the surveyed countries actually protect against aggression by the Russian Federation, which aims to rebuild the sphere of influence lost over thirty years ago. The further direction of evolution in the negative relations of the Russian Federation with the studied countries of Central and Eastern Europe strictly depends on the strength of mutual alliances with the US and the internal cohesion of the EU. This first alliance is mainly of a military and partly economic character, and its presence in the European community is of an economic and social nature. A weakening of any of them means that the decision-makers in the Kremlin will launch military, economic or information measures (socio-cultural and recruiting influence), as appropriate, in order to "fill" the resulting gap as quickly as possible and lead to further diminishing of the two security pillars in Central and Eastern Europe.